Complementarity

Anti-

Epistemology

after

Bohr and

Derrida

COMPLEMENTARITY

Arkady Plotnitsky

Duke University Press   Durham and London 1994

© 1994 Duke University Press
All rights reserved
Printed in the United States of America
on acid-free paper ∞
Typeset in Ehrhardt by Tseng Information Systems
Library of Congress Cataloging-in-Publication Data
appear on the last printed page of this book.

That this insecure and contradictory founda-

tion was sufficient to enable a man of Bohr's

unique instinct and tact to discover the major

laws of the spectral lines and of the electron

shells of the atom together with their sig-

nificance for chemistry appeared to me like

a miracle—and appears to me as a miracle

even today. This is the highest musicality in

the sphere of thought.—Albert Einstein

CONTENTS

Acknowledgments   ix
Introduction   1

**Part I. From General to
Complementary Economy**   15

1   General Economy 1: Bataille   17
2   General Economy 2: Derrida   37
3   From the Quantum Postulate to
     Anti-Epistemology to
     Complementarity   65

Part II. Quantum Anti-Epistemology   89

4   The Age of Quantum Mechanical
     Reproduction   91
5   Complementarities,
     Correspondences, Asyntheses   121
6   Locality and Causality   149

**Part III. Complementarity and
Deconstruction**   191

7   Undecidability and
     Complementarity   193
8   Closures   225
9   Transformations of Closure   261

Notes   271
Bibliography   297
Index   309

ACKNOWLEDGMENTS

I would like to thank many of my friends, students, and colleagues for their help and support during my work on the book. I am especially grateful to Barbara Herrnstein Smith. My thanks to Brian Rotman and Gregory Ulmer, who read the manuscript and helped to improve it. My thanks also to Claudia Brodsky, Stuart Curran, Vicki Mahaffey, Gerald Prince, Andrew Pickering, Jean Michel Rabaté, Frank Trommler, Gwen Wells, and Silke Weineck. I am grateful to Ken Wissoker for his help and advice, and to the Duke University Press for its support of the project. My thanks also to Cheryl Resetarits for her thoughtful copyediting, and to Jean Brady, Mary Mendell, and Marc Brodsky and others at the press who worked on the book. Paula Geyh, Jeanne Gurley, Patrick Hartigan, Sharon Anne Jaeger, Walda Metcalf, and Carola Sautter helped at various stages of my work on the project. Finally, my thanks to Nina and Marsha.

INTRODUCTION

This study is a joining of two ideas that have shaped the epistemological or, as it turned out, anti-epistemological revolutions of modern intellectual history—Niels Bohr's complementarity and Georges Bataille's general economy. By further coupling both ideas with Derrida's deconstructive anti-epistemology, this book provides a comprehensive theoretical framework within which it is possible to relate them and to explore and develop the implications of their conjunction.

Complementarity is drawn from Niels Bohr's interpretation of quantum physics, inaugurated by Max Planck's discovery of the quantum nature of radiation in 1900. The principle and then the framework of complementarity were developed by Bohr in order to account for the indeterminacy of quantum systems and to describe comprehensively, but without classical synthesis, their conflicting aspects. As a physics and *meta*-physics, Bohr's theory enacts a powerful critique or deconstruction of both classical physics and classical *metaphysics*—the classical philosophy of matter. Complementarity was the basis of Bohr's great confrontation with Einstein, and the radical—fundamental and far-reaching—anti-epistemological implications of quantum theory became apparent in the course of this debate.

General economy denotes a mode of theory that relates the configurations it considers to the loss of meaning—a loss it regards as ineluctable within any given system. The concept of general economy was introduced by Bataille and deployed by Derrida, although Nietzsche may be seen as the first practitioner of general economy and Bohr as the second. According to Bataille, "the *general economy* . . . makes apparent that *excesses of energy are produced, which, by definition, cannot be utilized. The excessive energy can only be lost without the slightest aim, consequently without any meaning."* The general economy is juxtaposed by Bataille to classical theories or *restricted economies*—such as, in particular, Hegel's philosophy or Marx's political economy. *Restricted economy,* however, defines classical theories across a broad spectrum of Western intellectual history: in philosophy, the social and human sciences, history, and other fields. Mathematics and the natural and exact sciences, too, can be seen as restricted economies, when their practice is governed by metaphysical epistemologico-ontological agendas, as they have often been even in the works of many revolutionary scientists, from Kepler to Einstein, and beyond. Restricted economies consider their objects and the relationships between those objects as always meaningful and claim that the systems they deal with can avoid the unproductive expenditure of energy and control multiplicity and indeterminacy within themselves. General economy exposes such claims as untenable.

While other contributions to anti-epistemology—such as those of Freud, Heidegger, Lacan, Deleuze, and Foucault, or Feyerabend and others working in science studies—have been important and will be addressed in the course of the analysis to follow, the present study is specifically concerned with anti-epistemological theories as general economies. I believe the general economic anti-epistemologies to be the most radical theories to date—the theories transforming most radically the spectrum of theoretical possibilities available to us, both in their critical or deconstructive and constructive or theory-building potential.

Nietzsche was the first practitioner of radical anti-epistemology and in many ways his contribution remains unsurpassed. He had a decisive influence upon both Bataille and Derrida, and, although often indirectly, on the whole modern and postmodern theoretical landscape. Bataille's contribution is indispensable as well—by virtue of his introduction of general economy, many of his anti-epistemological ideas, his proximity to Nietzsche, and his impact in Derrida and elsewhere. I shall consider both Nietzsche's and Bataille's ideas throughout this study. My main focus, however, will be on Bohr's and Derrida's theories. These theories may be seen as the culminations of general economic anti-epistemology in their respective fields, and through them the conjunction of complementarity and general economy can be most productively explored and developed.

The analogy between the key anti-epistemological ideas of quantum physics and Derrida's ideas easily invites itself; and this analogy has been made in commentaries on deconstruction, along with connections, overtly suggested by Derrida himself, between his ideas and Gödelian incompleteness and undecidability in mathematical logic. The goal of the present study, however, is to make the affinities in question specific, rigorous, and systematic, and also to show some crucial differences between deconstruction and complementarity by similarly exploring the conceptual and metaphorical affinities between Derridean and Gödelian theories. As shall be seen, Derrida himself sees his theoretical work expressly in terms of undecidability rather than, and in opposition to, indeterminacy. In this sense—and in the second sense of the word "after"—the anti-epistemology of this study is more *after* Bohr than after Derrida.

Insofar as it relies on the transcendental economy of truth, Gödel's own philosophy of mathematics is classical. Epistemologically, therefore, Gödelian metamathematical undecidability and Derridean metaphilosophical undecidability can be juxtaposed as a restricted and a general economy. From that perspective, Derrida's relation to Gödel can be seen as parallel to Bohr's relation to Einstein. For Einstein can be seen as, in Abraham Pais's words, the grandfather of complementarity, which he resisted all his life. The parallel can in fact be further grounded, historically as well as conceptually. Einstein and Gödel were coworkers in Princeton during the time of the Bohr-Einstein debate, and Gödel made a contribution to general relativity by finding a new solution to Einstein's equations. The Einstein-Podolsky-Rosen (EPR) argument concerning the question of the completeness of quantum mechanics (1935), which played a major role in the Bohr-Einstein debate, may have been influenced by Gödel's terms and ideas, although one must, naturally, keep in mind the differences between them. Bohr, too, on several occasions, specifically refers to the field of mathematical logic and metamathematics; and one cannot, I think, help thinking of Gödelian echos and parallels when the consistency and completeness of quantum mechanics are considered, as they are in the Bohr-Einstein debate. The modern examination of foundations of mathematics, in many ways culminating in Gödel's findings, can be seen as beginning with David Hilbert's *Gründlagen der Geometrie* [*Foundations of Geometry*], published in 1899, although preceding work by Gottlob Frege, Georg Cantor, and others has been crucial to this history. This examination thus, more or less, coincides with the genesis of quantum physics, which begins with Planck's law in 1900, although again preceded by some key experimental and theoretical findings, and culminates with the discovery of quantum mechanics and the development of the theoretically consistent interpretation of it around the time of Gödel's theorem. Both the latter and quantum mechanics may be seen as announcing the irreducible incompleteness of knowledge (as classically understood) in their respective fields.

The two sets of relationships themselves—between Derrida and Gödel, and Bohr and Einstein—are not strictly parallel, whether one considers them in historical, theoretical, or institutional (field-specific) terms. For one thing, in the case of the Bohr-Einstein confrontation one encounters a direct debate within a given field, while, in the case of Derrida and Gödel, at issue is a partial and qualified transfer of undecidability as a metaphorical model from one field to another. In addition, Gödel himself saw undecidability as compatible with his classical philosophy of mathematics, while Einstein saw quantum mechanical indeterminacy as incompatible with his philosophy of physics. John S. Bell's work, to be considered in chapter 6 of this study, would offer another example of that type. The metaphysics of quantum mechanics is of course possible, too. As a general economy, Bohr's matrix is not compatible with any form of, in Derrida's terms, the metaphysics of presence or onto-theology, or with their uncritical obverse, positivism, from which Bohr's anti-epistemology must equally be distinguished. Conversely, more anti-epistemological interpretations of Gödelian undecidability are possible, as are more anti-epistemologically suggestive metamathematical theories. As shall be seen, Thoralf Skolem's work on nonstandard models of arithmetics may offer interesting possibilities in this respect.

The relationships between complementarity and undecidability or Derrida's deconstruction thus entail both affinities and differences, or juxtapositions. They are multiply interactive or multiply complementary, in the extended sense of complementarity to be developed here. The task of this study is to foreground such interactions, specifically, the conceptual and metaphorical analogies between quantum physics and Gödelian mathematics, on the one hand, and Derrida's deconstruction and related anti-epistemologies, such as Nietzsche's and Bataille's, on the other. At stake are not so much the analogies themselves, although they are important and will be discussed, but first, the process itself of metaphoricity in theory formation that such analogies illustrate and second, the radical anti-epistemological implications of both this process and resulting models or paradigms. This task forces one to explore the acausal, nondialectical efficacy (the term I shall contrast to the conventionally more causal 'efficacy' here) of both the commonalities and differences—

or complementarities—of the fields involved without attempting to subject them to full, Hegelian synthesis. In order to do so an analysis must itself conform to, interactively, both general economy and complementarity. Such an analysis allows one not only to show the impact of modern scientific ideas and the metaphorical models which they generate in the humanities and social sciences, but also to suggest the possibilities that general economic theories offer for the understanding of modern mathematics and science—their epistemology and anti-epistemology and their functioning. This analysis allows one to introduce general economy into our theories of scientific knowledge and to show that in great measure Bohr has already done so—both by employing general economic thinking and modes of theorizing and by performing a deconstruction, at times quite Derridean, of classical theories in physics and philosophy alike. At the same time, however, Bohr's matrix and his practice suggest, closer to Nietzsche, a theoretical model or paradigm—complementarity—which is not strictly (Derrida's) deconstruction and which enables a critique of certain, possibly residually metaphysical, aspects of deconstruction.

To offer a preliminary outline, complementarity as developed by Bohr enables one to describe comprehensively and employ productively the conflictual aspects of quantum phenomena that cannot be accommodated by classical theories. In Bohr's interpretation such aspects become their *complementary* features—the features that are mutually exclusive but equally necessary for a comprehensive, *complete*, description and analysis of all quantum processes. Bohr speaks of "a new mode of description designated as *complementary* in the sense that any given application of classical concepts precludes the simultaneous use of other classical concepts which in a different connection are equally necessary for the elucidation of the phenomena." Due to Heisenberg's uncertainty relations, quantum mechanics introduces a certain irreducible—general economic— loss in representation and thus irreducible incompleteness of knowledge as classically understood. Quantum mechanics, however, and specifically complementarity form, as Bohr argues, a complete theory of its data—as complete as a theory can be under these conditions of irreducible incompleteness. Complementarity, thus, connotes both mutual exclusivity and completeness of description, as the word complementarity, which carries both these meanings, would suggest.

Two forms of complementarity are of particular significance in Bohr's framework—one combining that which is always dissociated in classical physics; the other, conversely, dissociating that which is always united there.

The first is the wave-particle complementarity, reflecting the duality of the behavior of quantum objects and relating the continuous and discontinuous representations of quantum processes. These two types of representation have always been unequivocally dissociated in classical physics. There are two types of objects that are always distinctly identifiable: the discontinuous, particle-type phenomena, such as atoms, or elementary particles, such as electrons; and the continuous, wave-type phenomena, such as light waves or other forms of radiation. In the quantum world, such unequivocal identification becomes impossible. Light, classically a wave phenomenon, acquires a double nature or, more precisely, requires two modes of representation: at times it must be represented as particles—photons—and at other times as waves, but never as both simultaneously. There have been classical corpuscular theories of light, such as Newton's. Prior to quantum mechanics, however, for light and matter alike, there was always either one form of representation or another, never a complementary combination of both. By contrast, in order to develop a coherent interpretation of its data, quantum physics Bohr argues, must employ both representations of light or matter. By the same token, however, one cannot do so in the form of classical synthesis, since one must engage classically incompatible systems of representation without resolving their incompatibility. Bohr's complementarity equally deconstructs both the classical, unequivocal unifications and classical, unequivocal dissociations of features through which physics constructs, describes, and interprets its objects.

The second complementarity is the complementarity of coordination, defining a position or a configuration of positions of a quantum object or system, and causality, classically determining the behavior of such an object or system. This complementarity dislocates the causal dynamics through which the behavior of classical systems is determined and which thus allows one to know with certainty the positions and motion of their elements, such as elementary particles. Or better, it suspends or deconstructs the *claim* of such causality, which claim defines all classical physics and, one might add, all classical metaphysics. Coordination and causality are always united in classical theories, and these theories are in fact defined by this unity. In quantum mechanics, however, in Bohr's defining formulation: "The very nature of the quantum theory . . . forces us to regard the space-time co-ordination and the claim of causality, the union of which characterizes the classical theories, as complementary but exclusive features of the description, symbolizing the idealization of observation and definition respectively." Bohr's word "idealization" is extremely important here. Both coordination and causality must be seen as *idealizations*, symbols, metaphors. This understanding is crucial in defining complementarity as a theoretical matrix and specifically in making it a general economy. In contrast to the classical theories, then, we cannot ultimately establish or calculate, or postulate, the causal dynamics—or, one might say, the history of a system—given the positions of its elements at a given point. The claim of the possibility of this connection may be seen as the postulate of causality, which defines all classical physics. This disjunction between the classically united observation of position and definition of causality leads to what may be seen as the anticausality or indeterminacy postulate of quantum theory. The latter is in fact a consequence of the so-called quantum postulate—the law of nature reflecting the discrete or particle character of light, or of the representation and idealization of light, which must be considered alongside the continuous or wave character, or representation and idealization, of light. A decisive feature of the quantum postulate, however, is that it also implies the acausal character of the quantum behavior of light, as against the causal character of the wave or continuous theory of light. Thus the quantum postulate leads to the anticausality and indeterminacy of quantum theory.

The complementarity of coordination and causality is directly connected to the complementarity of position and momentum, or the kinematic-dynamic complementarity as it is sometimes called, which precludes one from measuring or even meaningfully defining both variables—position and momentum—simultaneously at any given point. By virtue of this connection, the mathematical counterpart of the complementarity of coordination and causality becomes Werner Heisenberg's uncertainty relations. Uncertainty relations may be seen as inhibiting the possibility of obtaining information about some components of a given system, if one wants to increase information about or fully define other components. The term 'indeterminacy' may be preferable to 'uncertainty' in this interpretation, although both terms are used, and 'unknowability' has been suggested as well. Throughout this study I shall use 'indeterminacy' in order to designate a general concept referring to the situation just described. Following common usage, however, I shall retain 'uncertainty relations.' The determination of position, for example, precludes the simultaneous determination of momentum within the same system; and the same relations characterize other structurally paired or, as they are called, conjugate observables of quantum physics, such as time and energy. One may know one or the other, but not both at once; and, according to Bohr, one cannot even meaningfully consider both variables—position and momentum—as simultaneously applicable or their concepts as simultaneously well defined in the quantum mechanical situation. Bohr brilliantly grasped that this inhibition may be understood in very broad epistemological, or again anti-epistemological, terms as a mutual inhibition and then a complementarity between coordination and causality.

It can be said that uncertainty relations connote a radical, irreducible loss in representation affecting—in advance, always already—any quantum system and ultimately making all such representations idealizations. Bohr directly invokes the inevitable loss of knowledge on several occasions. In terms of the present study, this loss defines Bohr's complementarity as a general economy. This "loss" is so radical that, strictly speaking, it prohibits one from assuming that there is somewhere a complete or unified system, existing in itself or by itself, concerning which system some information is lost in the processes of observation, measurement, and interpretation. As Bohr stressed throughout his writing, the statistical character of quantum mechanics is radical—irreducible—insofar as, contrary to Einstein's hope, it does not imply some "hidden" large complete, unified, and causal system about which quantum mechanics provides partial, statistical information. Quantum-mechanical data is, it is true, mathematically treated in terms of probability or statistics and is sometimes interpreted in this way. As Bohr warns, however, in conceptual terms this language can be misleading. Quantum statistics appears to result from a radical—irreducible—multiplicity, which becomes particularly pronounced in modern quantum electrodynamics and field theory. But such a multiplicity cannot be conceived in classical terms, and it could be contrasted to classical multiplicities, including those of classical statistical physics. Whether in physics or meta-physics, or philosophy, an assumption of a complete large system would restore the classical, metaphysical appurtenance to the interpretive and theoretical framework based on it. One needs instead a very different and more complex economy of difference, exteriority, alterity—general economy. By the same token, the irreducible loss at issue leads to the irreducible fragmentation, the fracturing in advance of any quantum system. One thus is also prohibited from speaking of complete quantum systems, although within its limits quantum mechanics must, as I said, be seen as a complete theory—as complete as a theory can be under these conditions of irreducible incompleteness.

Resulting from the radical loss and fragmentation involved in quantum physics is, thus, not the impoverishment but the enrichment of the emergent configurations. This richness became apparent, beginning with Paul Dirac's pioneering work, in quantum electrodynamics—the theory connecting quantum mechanics and the electromagnetic nature of light and, thus, also Einstein's special relativity. Quantum electrodynamics or QED, as it is often referred to, is the theory most fully confirmed within the available limits of experimental precision. Quantum electrodynamics suggests that if "the very nature of quantum theory forces us" to renounce the claims of causality and the possibility of representation without loss, it also forces us to regard all quantum systems as fields defined by an irreducible, infinite multiplicity and incessant, unending transformations of their constitutive elements. This multiplicity equally redefines one-particle systems, or rather the systems classically defined as one-particle systems—one photon, one electron, and so forth—which are all transformed into irreducibly multiple fields. All quantum mechanical configurations are, thus, simultaneously both irreducibly incomplete and irreducibly rich.

The features just described allowed Bohr to develop complementarity into a comprehensive framework that encompasses both quantum physics and quantum meta-physics—the ontological-epistemological and, as it turned out, the anti-ontological and anti-epistemological dimensions of quantum theory. In this sense, Bohr's *meta*-physics is *anti-metaphysics*, as metaphysics has been developed from (or before) Plato and Aristotle, in their physics and metaphysics alike, to Heidegger, via Descartes, Leibniz, Spinoza, Kant, Hegel, Husserl, and most other major figures in the history of philosophy or intellectual history in general. Aristotle's works after his *Physics*—*ta meta ta physika*—the phrase apparently introduced by commentators on Aristotle to refer collectively to these works, were seen as dealing with things beyond nature or *physis*. These works, however, continued and reinforced the grounding structures defining philosophical discourse as developed before Aristotle, particularly in Parmenides and Plato. Throughout the present study, I shall mean by *metaphysics* this grounding theoretical economy as the metaphysics of presence or onto-theology in the post-Heideggerian, and specifically, Derridean sense, which is more or less equivalent to restricted economy, while the term *meta-physics* refers, generally, to extraphysical considerations, which may proceed by means of general economy.

Heisenberg reports the following remarks by Bohr on Philipp Frank's lecture in which Frank "used the term 'metaphysics' simply as a swear-word or, at best, as a euphemism for unscientific thought": I "began by pointing out that I could see no reason why the prefix 'meta' should be reserved for logic and mathematics—Frank had spoken of metalogic and metamathematics—and why it was anathema in physics. The prefix, after all, merely suggests that we are asking further questions, i.e., questions bearing on the fundamental concepts of a particular discipline, and why ever should we not be able to ask such questions in physics?" (*Physics and Beyond*, 210) In view of the history of the term 'metaphysics,' however, it may no longer be possible to use it outside its metaphysical-philosophical appurtenance to the metaphysics of presence. Bohr's meta-physics implies and in fact practices an anti-epistemological general economy of physics, rather than any form of metaphysics developed in the history of philosophy. As such, Bohr's meta-physics can be used to dislocate all classical or, in terms of the present study, restricted-economic metaphysics, the metaphysics of presence—all its ontology, epistemology, phenomenology, ontotheology, and so forth—and the philosophy of physics that such metaphysics has produced. This dislocation implies that one can neither fully separate physics and meta-physics nor fully unite them, for example, by encompassing physics within philosophy, as Hegel wanted to do. These relationships may instead be defined as complementary, even variably complementary, with shifting border lines between physics and meta-physics.

The *anti-epistemology* of my title refers, broadly, to the general possibility of a dislocation, or as we say now, deconstruction of classical or metaphysical theories—epistemologies, ontologies, phenomenologies, or, to return to Derrida's more encompassing terms, forms of ontotheology, logocentrism, and the metaphysics of presence. The theoretical base of this dislocation in Bohr's work is the general economic character of complementarity as a theoretical matrix. This character is, once again, codetermined by the irreducible loss—and thus indeterminacy—in the process of representation and by the equally irreducible heterogeneous multiplicity of all representations that such a matrix generates and employs.

I shall extend the term "complementary features" to various aspects of such multiple and heterogeneous representations, using the complementary features of quantum mechanics as the minimal model for such multiplicities. All general economies deal with arrangements (between and within the configurations they consider) that are complementary in the broad sense of being heterogeneous but interactive—heterogeneously interactive and interactively heterogeneous. The latter expression (also applicable to the complementary features of Bohr's matrix) may be understood to mean that, while they multiply interact, the elements or fields engaged in such relationships never allow for a complete synthesis, Hegelian or other.

As I shall argue throughout this study, most specifically in chapter 5, the general economy of asynthesis is a fundamental aspect of Bohr's complementarity, which makes it a profoundly anti-Hegelian, or a-Hegelian, theory. In both Bataille and Derrida, general economy is explicitly defined in relation to Hegel and Hegelianism. Derrida, in fact, uses the name "Hegel" to connote the culmination of the history of the philosophical understanding of interpretive, theoretical, historical, and political processes, the history defining what he calls the closure of the *epistēmē*—the closure of the metaphysics of presence—on which we might still depend even in our anti-epistemological projects and practices. The pervasiveness and power of this closure is one of the main reasons why one is compelled to see general economy as "anti-epistemology."

The dislocation created by a general economy is never a simple or uncritical dismissal of classical theories, but is instead their *rigorous suspension*—an analytical exposure of their limitations and a refiguring of classical concepts through a general economy. In quantum mechanics this relationship to the classical theories is rendered by what Bohr defines as the correspondence principle, "which expresses our endeavours to utilize all the classical concepts by giving them a suitable quantum theoretical re-interpretation." As shall be seen, an absolute abandonment of classical theories—or, for that matter, anything absolute—never amounts to a sufficiently radical transformation of the field, and in a great many cases such a transformation is not radical at all. Radical anti-epistemology and anti-Hegelianism may be defined by their anti-absolutism, whether a positive or a negative absolute is at issue. *Radical* suspensions of epistemology are possible, however. The degree of such a departure from classical theories, specifically philosophy, and the differences between the resulting general economies become interesting and important questions in their own right and are addressed by this study. Radical suspensions do appear to imply the introduction of complementary modes of description and analysis.

This study itself employs a mode of analysis that is both complementary and general economic. In fact, it must do so. The history of complementarity or of general economy, or jointly of both, is itself general economic and complementary, engaging the metaphoric and conceptual traffic between the theories of modern science and the ideas of Nietzsche,

Bataille, Derrida, and several other thinkers. Different fields of inquiry considered by the present analysis must, thus, themselves be seen as *complementary*—interactively heterogeneous and heterogeneously inter-active.

In the course of this complementary exploration, I will discuss several major developments of modern physics, which involve the idea and the metaphor of complementarity, and the Gödelian concepts of incompleteness and undecidability in the context of the relationships between complementarity and deconstruction. As a result, beyond exploring the extraordinary conceptual and metaphoric possibilities offered by Bohr's matrix, this study develops a new perspective on the epistemological and anti-epistemological aspects of Bohr's complementarity by interpreting it as a general economy.

At the same time, one must confront the complexity of the interactions between recent, and some no longer recent, epistemological and anti-epistemological developments in, on the one hand, the humanities—or the authors and fields, such as those considered here, more closely related to the humanities—and, on the other, the social sciences and historical studies, particularly recent developments in the history and sociology of science (although, it appears, not quite in the philosophy of science). The argument of this study suggests productive intersections with these latter developments. Such intersections, however, are not always easy given the complex economy of discourse differentiation between such fields, for example, in view of the fundamental relation between Derrida's texts and Continental philosophy. The argument to be offered here must, therefore, negotiate these differences and complexities, and it attempts to do so in part by utilizing them. This book is not written for an exclusively Derridean, or post-Derridean, or deconstructive audience. In many ways its aim is the opposite—to offer the deconstructive line of argument as part of a broader anti-epistemological configuration, which can be represented or, one might say, cross-represented to practitioners in different fields. The extensive treatment of Bohr takes into account the audience in critical theory that may be unfamiliar with Bohr. Conversely, the extended treatment of Bataille and Derrida may be useful to the interested audience in science and science studies. At the same time, however, this book is not an introduction to or a report on Derrida—or conversely on Bohr—but a critical, explorative reading of them and other relevant figures and a work of theory in its own right. Hence I proceed by mutually illustrating Bohr's and Derrida's major anti-epistemological ideas, or by similarly engaging other figures such as Nietzsche, Freud, Heidegger, and Bataille. The book's aim is to present these figures—and Bohr as a new figure in this landscape—as key anti-epistemological thinkers of modern or postmodern intellectual history and to explore their ideas and the implications of these ideas.

While, however, one must, in view of these considerations, relate the relevant concepts and metaphors in different fields as richly as possible, one also must respect the differences between fields, such as science studies or science itself, in the latter case specifically with regard to the mathematical formalism and experimental data on which modern science relies. My main goal here is to develop *in terms of the present study* an analytic framework suited to the requirements of the humanities and social sciences, rather than to those of the natural and exact sciences. In the latter fields, mathematical or technological results may be independent, or more independent of epistemological or anti-epistemological economies for interpreting them. Certain findings in mathematics and physics, however, would complicate the question; and more recent studies suggest the increasingly complex nature of these relationships, even insofar as their general interdependence is concerned. Certainly, as Bohr's case, or Einstein's—or most major figures considered here—would demonstrate, this independence of mathematico-technological determination does not translate into an analogous independence of the work of a given physicist. Nor does it translate into an independence of the functioning of physics or any other science as a field. Such interactions are much more complex, demanding at the very least a general economy and complementarity. These interactions are, thus, very much within the field of this study, the aim of which is to develop a historico-theoretical framework capable of accounting for—complementary—interactions of that type.

PART I

From General to

Complementary

Economy

The goal of Part I is to introduce the major topics and conceptual frameworks of this study—general economy and complementarity—and their interconnections.

Chapters 1 and 2 discuss the concept of general economy as developed, respectively, by Bataille and Derrida, and suggest the connections to quantum mechanics and the theories of Bohr, which will be developed in subsequent chapters. Chapter 2 also serves as an introduction to Derrida's deconstruction.

Chapter 3 considers, first, some of Bohr's key formulations concerning complementarity and the conditions necessitating its introduction in quantum mechanics and then introduces a broader concept of complementarity extending, jointly, both Bohr's ideas and the principles of general economy. The remainder of the chapter considers the relationships among the different theories and fields under discussion, their demarcations and the boundaries between them. The analysis of such relationships, I argue, be they historical or theoretical or interactively both, requires a complementary model and often a manifold of complementary models.

CHAPTER 1

General Economy 1:

Bataille

Genealogies

General economy is the theoretical mode developed by Bataille in response to the ideas and discoveries that both defy traditional thinking and define modern intellectual history. Beyond Bataille's own insights concerning the conditions demanding such a new—anti-epistemological—theoretical mode, these developments include the work of Nietzsche, with whom Bataille felt a particular affinity and who is the single most important presence in Bataille's writing; modernist literature and art, especially the works of Proust, Joyce, Blanchot, the surrealists, and the Cubists; the modern social sciences such as economics and anthropology; psychoanalysis; and modern mathematics and science. Bataille's ambition and ability to interrelate these diverse frameworks and fields enabled him to practice this discursive multiplicity in his writing and extend general economy into a very broadly conceived theory—anti-epistemology—of social, historical, and political, or politico-economic, processes. Responding to the conditions, including those of his own experience and writing, no longer accountable for in classical terms, Bataille conceived of and practiced a complex variety of discursive modes, styles, and genres. General economy is what, according to Bataille, theory could be under these conditions.

The genealogy of general economy is complex and multilinear. Hegel, Marx, Nietzsche, and modern anthropology, as developed by Emil Durkheim, Marcel Mauss and Claude Levi-Strauss, appear to be its most significant sources. One can argue, however, that Bataille's work on general economy was significantly influenced by modern science and, specifically, quantum physics, often directly invoked by Bataille himself. Consider-

able textual evidence is available to support this claim: the relevant references, ideas, and metaphors permeate Bataille's texts.[1] In historical terms,
Bataille developed and refined his theoretical ideas more or less simultaneously with Bohr's development of complementarity. There is, however,
a curious bit of historical evidence, by way of a footnote—an acknowl-
edgment (in either sense)—in *The Accursed Share:* "Here I must thank my
friend Georges Ambrosino, research director of the X-Ray Laboratory,
without whom I could not have constructed this book. Science is never
the work of one man; it requires an exchange of views, a joint effort. This
book is also in large part the work of Ambrosino. I personally regret that
the atomic research in which he participates has removed him, for a time,
from research in 'general economy.' I must express the hope that he will
resume in particular the study he has begun with me of the movements
of energy on the surface of the globe" (*The Accursed Share,* 191 n. 2; *La
Part maudite,* 54 n. 1).

Both historically and theoretically, then, one can ascertain not only the
general economic character of quantum mechanics, particularly Bohr's
complementarity, but also a kind of "quantum mechanical" and complementary character of general economy. Genealogies of both ideas overlap.
It is true that one can equally relate Bataille's conception to thermodynamic—entropic—theories. Insofar, however, as the interactions with,
and the metaphorical models based on, physics are concerned,the more
radical anti-epistemological implications of general economy connect it to
quantum theory.[2] For, as will be seen, general economy entails more radical statistics—a deeper stochasticity and something deeper than stochasticity—analogous to quantum physics, or to certain anti-epistemological
interpretations of this physics, such as Bohr's. As Deleuze has pointed
out in *Nietzsche and Philosophy,* the indeterminacy of Nietzschean play,
which is one of Bataille's key sources, is far more radical than the statistical dreams of chemistry or thermodynamics or, by implications, of any
classical model. More generally, the theories whose metaphorical models
are based on classical physics—whether Newton's mechanics, classical
statistical physics such as thermodynamics, special or general relativity,
(some versions of) chaos theory, or more classically conceived quantum
theories—appear to be restricted economies—*epistemologies* rather than
anti-epistemologies. More recent examples would include Foucault's,
Deleuze's (his own or with Guattari), and Michel Serres's economies,
many recent applications of chaos and complexity theories, and Adorno's
earlier metaphorical economy of force-field (Kraftfeld). Deleuze's analy-

sis in *Foucault* shows how classical geometry and physics function in Foucault's economy. It can be shown, however, that Foucault's geometry of force is still a restricted economy, as are "geometries" developed in Deleuze's own works, such as *A Thousand Plateaus* and *The Fold: Leibniz and the Baroque*, even though Deleuze uses complex mathematical models, such as Riemann spaces, which are also the basis of Einstein's general relativity. More classical, restricted-economic interpretations of quantum mechanics, or of Bohr's views, are also possible and have been advanced throughout the history of quantum physics. The argument of this study is for the general economic character of Bohr's complementarity and, conversely, the complementary character of general economy.

Bataille's ideas have had a major impact upon recent anti-epistemological developments and throughout modern intellectual history. One can trace his influence across poststructuralist theory—in the work of Lacan, Deleuze, Foucault, Lyotard, Baudrillard, Irigaray, Cixous, and many others, most of whom commented on Bataille's significance for their work and elaborated on Bataille's ideas directly. Deleuze and Guattari's analysis of capitalism and schizophrenia in *Anti-Oedipus* and *A Thousand Plateaus* may be seen as, among other things, a recasting or translation of Bataille's *The Accursed Share*, which may itself be seen as, among other things, an analogous recasting of Marx's *Capital*. The *Accursed Share* is invoked at the outset of *Anti-Oedipus* (4), and one can trace its significance throughout Deleuze and Guattari's work. Derrida's work, however, offers arguably the most radically anti-epistemological application of the principles of general economy.

Definitions

According to Bataille, the *general economy* is a "science"—a theoretical framework and a textual practice—by means of which one can relate to the production, material or intellectual, of excesses that cannot be utilized. As he writes:

> The science of relating the object of thought to sovereign moments, in fact is only a *general economy* which envisages the meaning of these objects in relation to each other and finally in relation to the loss of meaning. The question of this *general economy* is situated on the level of *political economy*, but the science designated by this name is only a restricted economy—restricted to commercial values. In question is the essential problem for the science dealing with the use of wealth.

> The *general economy*, in the first place, makes apparent that *excesses of energy are produced, which by definition cannot be utilized. The excessive energy can only be lost without the slightest aim, consequently without any meaning.* This useless, senseless loss *is* sovereignty. (*Méthode de Méditation; Oeuvres Complètes* 5, 215–16; emphasis added)[3]

Sovereignty can, thus, be defined in very general terms, although one also can and must, as Bataille does, consider it in relation to specific individual and social practices. By the same token, general economy cannot be confined to the analysis of the structural matter of loss of representation in a formal system. That it must relate to irreducible losses in representation and meaning in any interpretive or theoretical process remains, however, a decisive determination of any general economy. This determination introduces a fundamental *indeterminacy*, a kind of structural "vagueness" or "more-or-less-ness" within all (non)systems it considers.[4] This loss and indeterminacy—and the multiplicity that results from them—would characterize any general economy—in philosophy, the human or social sciences, literary or critical theory, or (in their theoretical aspects) literature or art itself, psychoanalysis, or the natural and exact sciences. Thus, the loss in the content of observation or measurement makes quantum mechanics a general economic theory, thereby also prohibiting the strict continuity and causality upon which the classical theories are based. The (sovereign) operation itself—the relation to loss—is thus formalizable, and it defines a potentially broad class of theories in various fields.

Although the significance of Marx's political economy is immediately apparent in Bataille's definition just cited and is pronounced throughout Bataille's work, Bataille's general economy is equally opposed to, or is an ambivalent displacement of, both Marx's political economy and Hegelian dialectic. Dialectic of master and slave in the *Phenomenology* is often directly engaged by Bataille, but general economy relates even more significantly to Hegel's dialectic as an overall (restricted) conceptual economy. The latter provides a kind of universal philosophical model of meaning, particularly conscious meaning, to which Hegel gave an historical and, therefore, also political character. At issue in Bataille is always a general economy (in either sense of the term) of meaning, interpretive or theoretical, extending to and extended by various fields of engagement, rather than only the politico-economic configuration suggested more directly by the definition just cited. Any restricted political economy, however, be it Adam Smith's, Hegel's, or Marx's, would still be predicated

Bataille 21

on the value of meaning, and particularly conscious meaning—meaningful investment, meaningful expenditure of labor and capital, meaningful production and conservation.

That the general economy of sovereignty in Bataille must be specifically juxtaposed to or is, again, a displacement of Hegel's restricted economy of mastery (Herrschaft) is apparent throughout Bataille's discourse on sovereignty and on Hegel, although Bataille himself sometimes claims a closer proximity to Hegel, especially via Kojève's interpretation. Derrida shows the significance of this displacement of Hegel in Bataille in his reading of Bataille in "From Restricted to General Economy: A Hegelianism without Reserve" (in *Writing and Difference*). This relationship to Hegel is equally, if not more, significant for Derrida himself. Hegel's claim, which defines the possibility of mastery (Herrschaft), is that at least at a certain level—the level of Spirit, *Geist,* and specifically Absolute Knowledge—it is possible to avoid the unproductive expenditure of intellectual, theoretical, or political energy. For Bataille, there is no level at which this can be achieved, in practice or in principle. For, if one maintains the possibility of avoiding unproductive losses only in principle, the resulting theory of this practice would remain fundamentally a restricted economy, even when the practice itself involves losses and expenditures. Bataille's sovereignty cannot be approached by such theories.

'General economy' designates, thus, a science—a rigorous theory—which accounts for or relates to the operation of sovereignty and analogous forms of loss and expenditure. One can also speak of the *economy* of sovereignty or expenditure, insofar as one uses the metaphor of economy to designate the interplay of energies and forces within a given process. The unequivocal separation between such economic operations and the theories inscribing and processing them is, in fact, impossible in general economy, and the interpenetrations between them may be as theoretically productive as they are inevitable. For one thing, our theoretical economies produce the economies or operations for which we want to account. In a general economy, however, there can be no absolute, Hegelian, fusion between accounts and processes that are accounted for. The difference between them can never be fully reduced in a general economy, whereas such a reduction is possible or necessary in some restricted economies, such as the Hegelian economy. The latter may well offer the most general philosophical calculus of that type. The relationships between different levels of economic interplay are thus not only metaphorically parallel but also metonymically connected. They are complementary—interactively heterogeneous and heterogeneously interactive. Thus, against Hegel, they cannot be fully unified within one system. For such a system would fully control its own operation, its own meaning, its "its-own-ness," which is impossible under the conditions of general economy.

Nor can there conversely be an absolute difference between an account and that which is being accounted for in a general economy. Once difference is absolute, it is not radical enough for a general economy. An absolute difference or exteriority of that type would always lead to a restricted economy, repressing the radical—but again never absolute—difference defined by and defining the field of general economy. This type of repression characterizes the Kantian economy of "things-in-themselves." The Kantian economy appears to provide a kind of general calculus of absolute difference or exteriority, just as the Hegelian economy offers a general calculus of overcoming it. Some key elements of either calculus are found, however, already in Plato's dialogues, particularly *Theaetetus* and *Parmenides,* or in the pre-Socratics.

Similarly, while Bohr sometimes speaks of the wholeness of and within experimental arrangements in quantum mechanics, the interactions, always irreducible, between the objects and the measuring instruments conform to an *interactive* (general) economy, which neither absolutely separates them in the Kantian fashion nor fully unifies them in the Hegelian fashion. As shall be seen, the border line—the 'cut'—between the object and the observing or measuring device is, in principle, arbitrary, although, in practice, it depends on the technologies of experimentation. These interactions between the inside and the outside (the terms preferable to 'subject' and 'object' under these conditions) entail a shifting complementarity between them, which is at the core of Bohr's economy of matter—or of mind. With this crucial qualification in *mind,* however, Bohr's complementarity and all general economic anti-epistemologies are materialist theories—general economies of *matter.*

One can, thus, neither fully identify sovereignty and general economy, nor unconditionally separate them. General economy is a theoretical—scientific—discourse. It takes account of sovereignty and related operations of that type introduced by Bataille, such as interior (or inner) experience, sacrifice, communication, or unknowledge. While it is rigorously theoretical, however, general economy cannot be seen as in any way *representing* (the structure of) sovereignty or "this useless, senseless loss" itself. General economy only makes *apparent* that unutilizable excesses of energy are produced and unrecuperable losses in representation take place, and it must relate its theoretical knowledge to such losses. This is why Bohr's complementarity can be seen as a general economy, and this is why I pursue the connections of both concepts in this study, which is concerned mainly with theoretical discourse. General economy defines the limits within which one can consider Bataille's sovereignty or analogous conceptions elsewhere in theoretical terms. As Derrida writes:

> Insofar as it is a scientific form of writing, general economy is certainly not sovereignty itself. Moreover, there is no sovereignty *itself.* Sovereignty dissolves the value of meaning, truth and a *grasp-of-the-thing-itself.* This is why the discourse that it opens above all is not true, truthful or "sincere." Sovereignty is the impossible, therefore it *is not,* it *is*—Bataille writes this word in italics—"this loss." The writing of sovereignty places discourse *in relation* to absolute non-discourse. Like general economy, it is not the loss of meaning, but, as we have just read, the "relation to this loss of meaning." It opens the question of meaning. It does not describe unknowledge, for this is impossible, but only the effects of unknowledge. "In sum, it would be impossible to speak of unknowledge, while we can speak of its effects" [*Conférences sur le non-savoir*].
>
> To this extent, we do not return to the usual order of knowledge-gathering science. The writing of sovereignty *is neither sovereignty in its operation nor current scientific discourse.* This latter has as its *meaning* (as its discursive content and direction) the relation oriented from the unknown to the known or knowable, to the always already known or to anticipated knowledge. Although general writing also has a meaning, *since it is only a relation* to nonmeaning this order is reversed within it. And the relation to the absolute possibility of knowledge is suspended within it. The known is related to the unknown, meaning to nonmeaning. "This knowledge, which might be called liberated (but which I prefer to call neutral), is the usage of a function detached (liberated) from the servitude from whence it springs: the function in question related the unknown to the known (the solid), while, dating from the moment it is detached, it relates the known to the unknown" (*Méthode [de la meditation]*). A movement that is only sketched, as we have seen, in the "poetic image." (*Writing and Difference*, 270–71; *L'écriture et la différence*, 397–98; translation modified)

This movement is actually described in great detail in and constitutes the textual movement of *Inner Experience* and its companions in *La somme athéologique*, and it is analyzed in a more theoretical (general-economic) mode in the third volume, "Sovereignty," of *The Accursed Share* and in other works. Exceeding the protocols of theory or science, even those of general economy (while utilizing them, whenever necessary), the more "poetic" writing of *La somme athéologique* may offer a closer approach to and a better communication of certain forms of sovereignty or interior experience than do more theoretical modalities of general economy. This distinction can only be made by keeping in mind the complex—heterogeneously interactive and interactively heterogeneous—interplay of multiple modalities and genres within and among Bataille's texts. Thus, Bataille's "interior experience" as considered in *La somme athéologique* is also a project, even a theoretical project—"no matter what"—or jointly a project and a counter-project, in contestation both with the classical, particularly Hegelian, philosophical project and with itself (*Inner Experience*, 22; *L'expérience intérieure*, 35). Bataille adds further qualifications to that effect in *Inner Experience* (174–79). Many other elaborations throughout *Inner Experience* and *La somme athéologique* can be cited. Conversely, while a general economy is not an "experience," any practice of general economy is experiential and some forms of this practice can contain elements of interior experience or sovereignty. Bataille pursues the explication of these interactions and the interactions themselves throughout his works. Their complexity does not exclude the possibility and at times necessity of the differentiation, along with the interaction, between general economy and other forms of writing of sovereignty, or between such writing and sovereignty itself. This is why one is compelled to speak of both interactiveness *and* heterogeneity or complementarity rather than synthesis.

Derrida's phrase "the writing of sovereignty [l'écriture de souveraineté]" can be read either as writing that concerns itself with or pursues sovereignty, or as writing produced by sovereignty in its operation; or, perhaps necessarily, as interactively both, rather than that of any given subject (individual or collective). Such would be the case even though, and indeed because, sovereignty itself cannot be written, cannot be *in itself*, and *is not*, to begin with. Even as "it" "writes" "itself," and quite possibly everything else, "sovereignty" produces losses in "its own" representation and makes all these terms, including sovereignty itself, and the classical—restricted—economy of signification inadequate. In part it does so by "placing discourse *in relation* to absolute non-discourse," as Derrida says. One cannot, however, attribute self-own-ness, and thus subjectivity, Hegelian or other, to sovereignty. Hence this writing "is not the loss of meaning [which loss itself is unavailable to any inscription] but a relation to the loss of meaning." An analogous dynamics is *inscribed* within Derrida's matrix, as *writing* (in Derrida's sense) is produced by *différance*, or more precisely is generated within the interplay of forces within Derridean economy of *différance*, trace, dissemination, (the process of) *writing* itself, and so forth. The writing of sovereignty can only convey, obliquely, the sense of confrontation with the unknowable and the radical difference it entails. This confrontation exceeds all theory, even general economy, which, to the degree available to theoretical knowledge, relates to and accounts for this unknowable and this difference.

Derrida is right to stress that "we do not return to the usual order of knowledge-gathering science." This proposition applies across the spectrum of Bataille's writing, whether in his more theoretical—general economic—mode as in *The Accursed Share* or in the more "poetic" modes of *La somme athéologique*. "The usual order" is an important qualification; for, at a certain level, general economy is a knowledge-gathering science. It must even deliver the best classical knowledge, and many "usual order[s] of knowledge gathering science" must be incorporated in the process. A movement from the known to the unknown or the unknowable does define all sovereign processes in Bataille and their difference from the classical processes of knowledge—from the unknown to the known or the knowable—culminating in Hegel's dialectic. Thus, it defines the difference between Bataille's sovereignty and Hegelian mastery or lordship (Herrschaft), here especially as scientific or philosophical, always conscious and self-conscious, mastery. In both cases, however, that of general economy and that of interior experience, such as Bataille's own as considered in *La somme athéologique*, this movement is not possible without passing, within a complex interactive process, through the best *knowledge* available at the moment. The radically unknowable at stake in Bataille could not be reached otherwise. In order to approach the best, the highest unknowable, one must pass through the highest knowable. Without this interplay of knowledge and unknowledge, the interior experience Bataille aims at or general economy cannot be achieved.

La somme athéologique combines both a (general economic) theoretical and literary project or anti-project and an "interior experience" of a *human* subject. The practice of sovereignty there becomes the economy of the interactions—heterogeneous interactions and interactive heterogeneities—between a human and a theoretical, or artistic, subject and between different fields of sovereign practice without subjecting these interactions to a Hegelian synthesis, in part by virtue of the unrecuperable losses defining all sovereign practice. General economy may, at certain levels, require the sovereign practice of theory, which practice (and by implication, at bottom, any theoretical practice) is never only theoretical, although, unlike interior experience, the theoretical—scientific—practice of general economy may not be a practice of sovereignty or the process designated as interior experience. To the extent that they can be (always imperfectly and obliquely) represented, in Bataille's own case both sovereignty and interior experience are represented by the text of *La somme athéologique*. To the extent that they can be approached theoretically, such an approach would require general economy; and, conversely, insofar as such experiences involve a theoretical component, this component must, by definition, be general economy. These considerations need not imply that a general economic analysis is bound to be concerned with itself, as would be largely (although by no means exclusively) the case in *Inner Experience, Guilty,* and *On Nietzsche.* Such a project may, and in Bataille does, consider sovereign practices elsewhere—in politico-economic fields, as in *The Accursed Share;* sexuality, as in *Erotism;* literature, as in *Literature and Evil;* philosophy, as in "Hegel, la mort, et le sacrifice"; or religion, as in *Theory of Religion*—although Bataille considers and combines such various practices in all these works.

Heterologies

Bataille's general economic ideas have many implications—historical, political, theoretical, aesthetic, and literary. Bataille develops general economy into a broad theory of—interactively—social, historical, political, and artistic processes. As we have seen, he himself employs plural or again complementary discursive, institutional, and political practices. *Inner Experience,* in particular, engages and, in terms of style and genre, combines (without synthesis), among others, Hegel's *Phenomenology of Spirit,* Nietzsche's *Gay Science,* Joyce's *Ulysses,* Proust's works, Aquinas, and religious mystics; and it also refers to a good deal of modern science. The textual field of the work becomes still more complex, once one takes into account the book's companions in *La somme athéologique: Guilty* and *On Nietzsche,* each in turn a complex, multi-layered text, and related writing, in particular *Literature and Evil* and *The Tears of Eros* or, in a more theoretical mode, *Theory of Religion,* which, along with *The Accursed Share, Erotism,* and related earlier essays, such as "The Notion of Expenditure"

(*Visions*), would serve as examples of Bataille's more overtly theoretical texts. These texts, however, are much more than theoretical while,
conversely, most of Bataille's texts, including his novels, contain crucial
theoretical dimensions. Added to, and in many ways responsible for, his
ideas, this complexity has defined Bataille's preeminence as a modernist
and postmodernist figure.[5] Equally significant is the plurality or complementarity among his various texts and theoretical, artistic, institutional,
and political practices.[6]

The connection to political economy already implies a broad historical,
social, and political field. Of course, many restricted theoretical economies, for example, and in particular, Hegel's, are also historical and
political economies. Marx understood the politico-economic aspect of
Hegelian philosophy beginning with his earliest encounters with Hegel.
He speaks of Hegel's standpoint as that of modern political economy.[7]
Hegel's economy is then refigured by Marx as a materialist political economy; and both Hegel and Marx have a common source in Adam Smith's
political economy. General economy, however, entails much richer and
more complex interactions between various fields—theoretical, historical, political, or still others. Such different fields, furthermore, cannot be
unequivocally separated, or conversely united, or their interaction controlled, as in the case, or according to the claims, of restricted economies.
General economy extends the fields it considers much further than any
restricted economy would allow. It does so in part by consistently relating the thematics of political economy to those forces and activities
which can only be theorized through unreserved expenditure—the unconscious, sexuality, sacrifice, literature, and so forth. Classical political
economies suspend such activities, or marginalize or uncritically subordinate them to the politico-economic base. In *The Accursed Share* and
other works, Bataille considers these practices across human history. He
explores both broad spectrum or collective practices—considered along
their anthropological, cultural, economic, social, political, and linguistic
dimensions—as well as the interpretive, theoretical, psychological, and
social practices of individual figures. Nietzsche is the most important
presence in *The Accursed Share*, around whom the concluding discussion
of the full, three volume, version of the work is centered. Throughout
the book, however, and in *La somme athéologique*, Bataille relates his discursive practices to Nietzsche's and claims a unique proximity between
Nietzsche and himself. The introduction of various forms of sovereignty
transforms politico-economic theory. One cannot say that irreducible

losses, unreserved expenditure, and other general economic processes or at least some of their aspects are never considered by classical theories. But when they do consider such processes, the analyses they offer always conform to restricted economies, for example, by placing these processes fully outside or defining them as absolutely exterior to a given classical field—a persistent and pervasive strategy.[8]

Bataille's radical treatment moves the understanding of the processes at issue, and by implication others, in truth all, processes from restricted economy—be it the classical political economy or the restricted economies defining classical anthropology, linguistics, sociology, and psychology—to general economy. The latter simultaneously redefines and enriches the relationships among such fields themselves. By doing so, general economy supplements the politico-economic field by the activities that restricted economies leave out of account, marginalize, or subordinate to the economy of consumption. In this sense, general economy enacts a deconstruction of classical philosophical or political economies, or classical theories in linguistics, anthropology, and certain forms of psychoanalysis. That which is left in the margins and claimed to be reducible or treated as contamination by classical theories—the unconscious, the meaningless, the improper, the distasteful, the impure, the wasteful, the perverse—is not only incapable of being marginalized or reduced, but is in fact *constitutive* of that which is unequivocally opposed to these contaminating forces and is supposed to be purified of them—the conscious, the meaningful, the proper, the tasteful, the pure, the normal.

General economy expands its field irreducibly; and if it "makes apparent that *excesses of energy are produced, which by definition cannot be utilized*," it equally makes apparent that excesses of homogeneity—or of a containable, controlled heterogeneity—are also produced and, by definition, cannot be contained or controlled. As Bataille writes in introducing the second volume of *The Accursed Share*, "The History of Eroticism": "My book might be seen as an apology for eroticism, whereas I only wanted to describe a set of reactions that are *incomparably* rich. But these reactions I have described are essentially contradictory" (*The Accursed Share* 2 and 3, 18). He could also have said "essentially complementary." Bataille's views here are also close to Blake's, to whom Bohr's complementarity is compared sometimes. *The Accursed Share* opens with the epigraph—"Exuberance is beauty"—taken from Blake's *The Marriage of Heaven and Hell*. Blake's notion of contrariety developed there is close to complementarity insofar as the latter entails the necessity of operating with conflicting modes of description—"contraries," as Blake calls them—without synthesis. Bataille's general economy contains both these Blakean dimensions: contradictoriness and richness—incomparable and exuberant richness.

General economy is always what Bataille calls *heterology*, the science of the heterogeneous, which is another major dimension of his theory explored and practiced throughout his writing.[9] By introducing, to use Derrida's terms, the uncontrollable dissemination—or *différance*-dissemination—and the irreducible remainder or remnant (réstance) of any form of containment or control of loss, indeterminacy, and heterogeneity, general economy makes its configurations fundamentally uncontainable and uncontrollable.[10] By the same token, it extends and pluralizes its own field, even though any given analysis remains subject to various constraints and limitations.

These de-formalizations and de-systematizations, which are also re-formalizations and re-systematizations, are in fact enacted or further enhanced by *connecting* the irreducible loss and incompleteness to the irreducible multiplicity or heterogeneity of a system or nonsystem that may be under consideration. From his earliest writing on, Bataille profoundly understood the relationships between expenditure and multiplicity or heterogeneity.

Intuitively, it seems apparent that expenditure leads to multiplicity and heterogeneity, in view of the inexhaustible remainder of any given interpretation and the fundamental iterability, in Derrida's sense, of any given sign or mark—trace—resulting from this loss. This point, as shall be seen presently, must be further qualified so that the resulting (general) economies do not presuppose a hidden totality, present to itself but unavailable to interpretation. The relationships between the irreducible loss and the irreducibly heterogeneous do, however, take different forms in different situations. In *The Accursed Share* and his other writings on the subject, Bataille shows the specific relationships between the multiple or the heterogeneous (and these are not always the same either) and various psychological (or biological), anthropological, social, political or politico-economic, and discursive practices based on expenditure. In the practice of postmodern literature, theory, or mass culture, such relationships between the loss in knowledge and heterogeneity demand a still different analysis. Many of Bataille's ideas, however, can and have been utilized in this analysis, along with those of such thinkers as Deleuze, Foucault, Derrida, and Lyotard.

In quantum mechanics, the relation between the loss in and indeterminacy of representation and multiplicity is equally important, since
one confronts there an irreducible, infinite multiplicity of all the systems
considered, including those that are classically defined as one-particle
systems. In quantum physics, particularly in quantum electrodynamics
and quantum field theory, one can no longer meaningfully consider the
interaction between single particles, but only between multiple complementary—and multiply complementary—ensembles. That nature itself
obeys this joint model was a major discovery of quantum physics. But
these relationships between loss and multiplicity also take their specific
shape there: in particular, quantum multiplicity does not imply a hidden
causal multiplicity, partially—statistically—accounted for by quantum
mechanics.

Under all conditions, general economy must, along with the loss in
representation and knowledge, always take into account the irreducibly
heterogeneous, although it is worth pointing out that not all theories of
heterogeneity, or of expenditure and loss, are general economies. Analogously to quantum physics, such aspects of general economy as heterogeneity, multiplicity, or configurational richness need not imply the presupposition of a hidden totality, existing outside or alongside general
economic configurations, but inaccessible to a given general economy by
virtue of its multiplicity or complexity. Such a presupposition would reinstate a restricted economy, commonly, of the Hegelian type. A general
economic loss signals the prohibition of both full representation and the
absolutely unrepresentable, including an unrepresentable totality. As it
complementarizes different representations and different models of representation, general economy also complementarizes the representable
and the unrepresentable, and various closures of representation.

Insofar as it can suggest the (restricted economic) configuration just
indicated, Derrida's terms 'remainder' (réstance) or 'iterability' may be
a bit misleading. Derrida's inscription itself of these terms in "Signature
Event Context" (*Margins*), "Limited inc," (*Limited Inc.*) and "Living On:
Border Lines" (*Deconstruction and Criticism*) does not appear to suggest
such a reading; and one must always take into account his other terms,
such as, in particular, 'dissemination,' which may be seen as most directly related to the radical multiplicity and heterogeneity at issue. There
is always a remainder, but, unlike the classical understanding of such
processes, there is no totality that leads to such a remainder in view of
partiality of account. Or rather, the latter economy is possible, too, and

often necessary. In any given field, beginning with physics, we constantly encounter very large statistical, or otherwise unencompassable, configurations. We can only approach them partially, statistically, by way of approximations. But such classical economies operate only under certain conditions, locally, within the limits where one can and must operate classically; and in a general economy global situations are always local. General economy, thus, makes locality and globality enter into a continuous interplay, a kind of complementarity. Bataille often invokes the global character of general economy; and, particularly in *The Accursed Share*, derives many of his conclusions from global considerations—literally from the economy of the globe, or even economies operating on a still broader, quite cosmic scale. One can, in principle, read Bataille's concept of general economy in this way, that is, as implying a global economy. Such a reading, however, would be too restricted (in either sense). The textual network in which Bataille's concepts are inscribed suggests a reading of the type offered here, positioning Bataille closer to Nietzsche and Derrida, on the one hand, and Bohr, on the other.[11]

Defining general economic multiplicity, the configuration just described is analogous to the radical, suprastatistical indeterminacy of quantum mechanics. One can metaphorize it by saying that we have an irreducible—indeed infinite—degree of multiplicity even locally, at each point. For, in contrast to classical theories, quantum mechanics gives an infinite degree of freedom to a single particle at each point. This is why it becomes necessary to use at each point the statistical apparatus similar to that applied in classical physics to large ensembles. Quantum mechanical statistics, however, at least in the standard complementarity (as opposed to the hidden-variables) interpretation, is more radical than classical statistical physics. It does not presuppose, indeed it prohibits a hidden, causal multiplicity—totality—of states or variables about which quantum mechanics would, in the manner of classical statistical physics, give partial, statistical information due to the lack of sufficiently precise measurement or inability to contain such a hidden multiplicity.

In terms of this analogy, which can be supported by Bataille's many elaborations on chance, particularly in *Guilty* and *On Nietzsche*, there can be even less a hidden-variables general economy in the field of social and human sciences than a hidden-variables interpretation of quantum mechanics—an interpretation that implies a hidden classical and, especially, causal multiplicity which is incompletely, statistically reflected in the quantum mechanical data. In the event—unlikely, I think—that a hidden variables or otherwise classical model will be reinstated in physics, Bohr's matrix would still retain its value as a metaphorical model in the social sciences and the humanities, where a return to classical models appears even less likely than in physics.

Conversely, more complex and more radically heterogeneous and indeterminate models are quite possible and may be necessary, particularly in view of the fundamentally interactive character of general economy as complementarily engaging various modes and fields but never unifying them in a Hegelian fashion. It is this dissemination that leads to the irreducible expansion of and the interaction between its fields—interpretive, theoretical, historical, cultural, social, political or still other, and one will not in fact be able to close this list once and for all—even though and because the same dissemination also prohibits the classical and specifically Hegelian synthesis of these fields. Derrida defines dissemination, or jointly *différance* and dissemination, through their incompatibility with the Hegelian (restricted) dialectical economy. General economies—theories never identical even to themselves—are theories in a plural style or genre, self-differentiating and self-disseminating, making the very concept of the self profoundly problematic.

In general economy and quantum mechanics alike, the complex appears always to precede the simple rather than follow it, as the order of classical logic would entail. This remarkable feature may be seen as a fundamental point of departure for Derrida's analysis from his early work on Husserl on, and it may well be a key point for Bohr's thinking on quantum mechanics and of all anti-epistemology. This reversal of the classical principles of theorizing must, however, be understood as a recomprehending rather than an absolute reversal. It redelimits, rather than abandons, the classical configurations that move from simplicity to complexity and makes the very economy of the relationships between the simple and the complex general.

It may be argued that Bataille's general economy deals essentially with global economies—that it is macroeconomic rather than microeconomic —while quantum mechanics is a "microeconomics" of matter, as opposed, for example, to Einstein's general relativity, particularly in its cosmological dimensions. At the outset of *The Accursed Share*, Bataille differentiates between physics and economics on the basis of the possibility or, conversely, the impossibility of localization:

> Between the production of automobiles and the *general* movement of the economy, the interdependence is rather clear, but the econ-

omy taken as a whole is usually studied as if it were a matter of an isolatable system of operation. Production and consumption are linked together, but, considered jointly, it does not seem difficult to study them as one might study an elementary operation relatively independent of that which it is not.

This method is legitimate, and science never proceeds differently. However, economic science does not give results of the same order as physics studying, first, a precise phenomenon, then all studiable phenomena as a coordinated whole. Economic phenomena are not easy to isolate, and their general coordination is not easy to establish. So it is possible to raise this question concerning them: Shouldn't productive activity as a whole be considered in terms of the modifications it receives from its surroundings or brings about in its surroundings? In other words, isn't there a need to study the system of human production and consumption within a much larger framework? (*The Accursed Share*, 19–20; *La Part Maudite*, 57–58)

The shift toward global economies is crucial to Bataille. General economy derives its conditions and results from the necessity of considering global configurations. As was just suggested, however, quantum mechanics implies very complex relationships between local and global economies in physics as well. Some of these complexities are apparent already in the earliest formulations of quantum mechanics. As quantum physics developed, it transformed all aspects and models of the interaction between local and global configurations. It is conceivable that these complexities will problematize even the distinction Bataille claims concerning the difference between physics and economics. One may, however, advance the following general economic reconfigurative principle: classical local models must be replaced with configurations following classical global models, such as statistical models, and under certain conditions by configurations that cannot conform even to the classical global model, including classical statistical models.

In this sense, one should perhaps speak of extended, rather than global, configurations, for the general economic loss in representation is also the loss of wholeness, whether this wholeness is conceived as representable or as unrepresentable. General economy thus, entails a loss in all totalization, even though Bataille speaks, as does Nietzsche, of the economy of the whole. This "whole" is itself general economic. Certainly, the global economy is not seen as an ideal model of conservation and presence— being-presence or becoming-presence—to which local economies then are required to conform as closely as possible. Globalization—globalization without totalization, one might say—necessitates instead the irreducible general economic loss. Local configurations must, however, in turn be considered general economically, which implies, among other things, that they can never be absolutely local either.

Means of Production

General economy must relate to unproductive losses and expenditures—expenditures without reserve. In every sense of this central politico-economic term "production," however, the production aspect of general economy is crucial, whether local or global production is at stake. The richness—"the incomparable richness"—of general economic configurations would be impossible without production. As conceived by Bataille, the general economy depends on a cluster of entropy and energy metaphors. To begin with, "[e]xcesses of energy," and therefore *energy* itself, "are *produced.*" This "energy," however, is also something that cannot exist in an ontological sense, whether pre-Heideggerian or Heideggerian. At issue is not what "is," since by this stage all ontology is suspended, but what we can—or cannot—say about this "efficacity" and how it can—or cannot—be configured. This dynamics makes a certain entropic production into an energy-like efficacity. General economy must relate to an *entropic* dynamism of loss. But this dynamism is also an *energic* dynamism of production, even of excessive production—production of excesses that can never be fully utilized. If we could still speak of time here, time would be defined as the "source"—a mutually inhibiting efficacity—of both energy and entropy, and thus both a productive and a dissipating force, and at times a destructive force. In both of these aspects, however—productive and disruptive—this efficacity has enormous antiepistemological potential. It implies a radical dislocation of the classical concept of "knowledge," particularly, *as* conscious and conceptual knowledge even though, to the extent that such forms are possible, the degree of "knowledge" may be just as great or even greater in a general economy. All conscious, particularly theoretical, knowledge is an effect of what proceeds by way of a loss in representation and knowledge.

A general economy thus *relates* consumption and expenditure, gain and loss, conservation and waste. It makes them complementary, by both differentiating and intermixing them, and doing so differently under different conditions. Logically or theoretically, although not ontologically, a general economy precedes any restricted economy, but it does not simply suspend the latter. As opposed to restricted economies—political, conceptual, or other—a general economy must relate to losses, unreserved expenditures. It is not the economy of losses alone, however, whether calculable or incalculable losses, reserved or unreserved expenditures. By the same token, the interplay of conservation, or accumulation, and expenditure in a general economy is not simply conflictual and oppositional, but instead multiply complementary. This precomprehending character of general economy is equally crucial for Derrida. An analogous configuration or *economy* of interplay of restricted and general economies defines Nietzsche's matrix, making Nietzsche a major precursor of Bataille and Derrida and a first practitioner of general economy. Bohr's complementarity is also the interplay of restricted—classical—and general-economic—quantum—theories, in part by virtue of Bohr's second great principle—the correspondence principle, which finds its analogy in Derrida's notion of the closure of metaphysics.

That the *excessive* energy is lost "without any meaning" does not mean that some energies *cannot be* utilized, via the production of meaning or value—conceptual, politico-economic, or other. Bataille is careful to point out that there is no more absolutely productive expenditure than absolutely unproductive expenditure, no more absolute losses than absolute gains: "This is regrettable in that the notions of 'productive expenditure' and 'nonproductive expenditure' have a basic value in all the developments of my book. But real life, composed of all sorts of expenditures, knows nothing of purely productive expenditure; in actuality, it knows nothing of purely nonproductive expenditure either" (*The Accursed Share*, 12; *La Part maudite*, 52). It follows that "real life" knows nothing about "real life" either. One must deal with a radical alterity that cannot be absolute and that requires the (general) economy of theoretical and interpretive closures to be considered in chapter 8. The suspension of either expenditure, productive or unproductive, is problematic, and such suspensions remain persistent even in some recent theories. For example, it may lead to the metaphysics, or the politico-economic utopias, of expenditure, difference, plurality, otherness, loss of meaning, and so forth, which never exceed the limits of restricted economy, even though they may overtly oppose more classical forms of restricted economy. Derrida sees configurations of that type as instances of unproblematized reversal—a reversal that is unaccompanied by a reinscription of the members of a given metaphysically established opposition or hierarchy. As a result it leaves the metaphysical base supporting the initial configuration untouched. One is best off seeing general economy as the economy of interaction or as a complementarity of losses and gains, which figures the diversity of their interplay. The inscription of loss, waste, expenditure without reserve, and meaninglessness, where classical theories—restricted economies—"see" gain, conservation, investment, and meaning remains, however, Bataille's great contribution. It transforms the theoretical and metaphorical horizons of modern thought. Throughout this study, I shall understand "general economy" as relating to the complementary interplay—as opposed to a full synthesis—of production, conservation, and expenditure. As such, it enacts a kind of displacement-translation, which is also a rigorous suspension, of Hegelian *Aufhebung,* which negates, conserves, and supersedes *simultaneously,* a concept that itself must be suspended and deconstructed in the process. Locally, within the refigured limits, various forms of synthesis can and must be utilized; and, as we have seen, general economy has a similar double relation of suspension and reutilization to Kantian absolute difference. Radical transgressions of general economy cannot be as absolute, even though and because they enact a general suspension of all absolutes—absolute incorporation, absolute suspension, or absolute transgression.

CHAPTER 2

General Economy 2:

Derrida

Différance

Derrida's work and his usage of general economy represent a major anti-epistemological development. The concept of general economy is crucial throughout his works, and Derrida often defines his matrix in general economic terms. The general economy of *différance*, Derrida's arguably most important and most famous rubric, is particularly significant in this respect, as *différance* itself becomes analogous, although not identical, to Bataille's sovereignty. Derrida's theoretical and textual strategies, plural even within any given text, cannot be contained within the rubric of *différance*, which itself requires other structures—trace, supplement, dissemination, *writing*, and so forth [1]—in order to be approached. These strategies cannot be contained by the rubric of general economy either; nor by any given rubric, for example, deconstruction. General economy, however, offers a comprehensive and possibly the most radically anti-epistemological approach to Derrida's theoretical economy. The latter may be seen as the analysis of the general-economic efficacity of the processes that classical theories understand in terms of restricted economies—meaning, presence, and truth; the full consciousness and self-consciousness; the possibility of unconditionally grounding or centering interpretation or theory; the possibility of interpretive and theoretical gains without accompanying losses; the possibility of a fully coherent unity of knowledge and of the projects based on these assumptions; and so forth. These configurations are not identical, but are all complicit within what Derrida sees as the metaphysics of presence—a powerful and systematic unity that defines the history of Western philosophy, but is operative far beyond its limits, whether in linguistics, anthropology, psychoanalysis, literary criticism, or elsewhere. One of Derrida's major contributions is the understanding and analysis of this commonality as operative across a broad manifold of texts and fields and across extended historical trajectories.

The perspective of general economy positions Derrida closer to Nietzsche, Freud, Bataille, and Lacan, than to Hegel, Husserl, Heidegger or Levinas. The role of history and text of philosophy, however, remains crucial and perhaps finally irreducible in Derrida. To begin with, philosophy and its metaphysical base is what is to be deconstructed. Even more significantly, a special, if not the privileged, role of the philosophical discourse in Derrida is defined by what Derrida sees as the closure of metaphysics, to be considered in detail in Part 3. One may say that the defining complementarity of Derrida's text, a text on the "margins of philosophy," is that between this text and the text of philosophy. Derrida's own writing and the economy of *writing* introduced by Derrida are, however, both processed via general economy. Grammatology is defined by Derrida as the "science"—a general economy—of *writing* in Derrida's sense, which he juxtaposes to a traditional, narrow concept of writing, conceived as a representation of speech and as hierarchically subordinated to speech within the metaphysical opposition of speech and writing. I shall consider Derrida's *writing* later in this chapter. In the meantime, I shall understand by Derrida's *writing* a transformation of all language, or what is classically designated as language—oral or written, theoretical or (so-called) ordinary—under the conditions of *différance* and accompanying structures—trace, supplement, dissemination, and so forth, which form, by definition, an interminable network.[2] Derrida's *writing* is itself part of this efficacious ensemble, rather than only an effect of Derrida's other structures, certainly not in the sense of classical causality. The general economy where this ensemble is inscribed—*written*—deconstructs and suspends all classical, causal efficacies. This noncausal efficacious dynamic necessarily affects the very shape of the discourse that must relate to it. According to Derrida:

> What I will propose here [in delineation of *différance*] will not be elaborated simply as a philosophical discourse, operating according to principles, postulates, axioms or definitions, and proceeding along the discursive lines of a linear order of reasons. In the delineation of *différance* everything is strategic and adventurous. Strategic because no transcendent truth present outside the field of writing can govern theologically the totality of the field. Adventurous because this

strategy is not a simple strategy in the sense that strategy orients tactics according to a final goal, a *telos* or theme of domination, a mastery and ultimate reappropriation of the development of the field. Finally, a strategy without finality, what might be called blind tactics, or empirical wandering if the value of empiricism did not itself acquire its entire meaning in its opposition to philosophical responsibility. If there is a certain wandering in the tracing of *différance*, it no more follows the lines of philosophical-logical discourse than that of its symmetrical and integral inverse, empirical-logical discourse. The concept of *play* keeps itself beyond this opposition, announcing, on the eve of philosophy and beyond it, the unity of chance and necessity in calculations without end. (*Margins*, 6–7; *Marges*, 7)

As a modification of the French word "différer" [to differ], *différance* connotes an economy of, jointly, difference and delay (or deferral). This aspect of *différance* plays a decisive role at its economy and, as shall be seen in chapter 8, at crucial junctures. Derrida, however, conceives of the economy of *différance* much more broadly. For "This correlation [between the different and the deferred], however, is not simply one between act and object, cause and effect, or primordial and derived" (*Speech and Phenomena*, 129).[3] This correlation thus entails a complex anticausal dynamics. "In a conceptuality adhering to classical strictures '*différance*' would be said to designate a constitutive, productive, and originary causality, the process of scission and division which would produce or constitute different things or differences." However, "that which lets itself be designated *différance* is neither simply active nor simply passive, announcing or rather recalling something like the middle voice, saying an operation that is not an operation, an operation that cannot be conceived either as passion or as the action of a subject on an object, or on the basis of the categories of agent or patient, neither on the basis of nor moving toward any of these *terms*. For the middle voice, a certain nontransitivity, may be what philosophy, at its outset, distributed into an active and a passive voice, thereby constituting itself by means of this repression" (*Margins*, 8–9, *Marges*, 9). The general economy of *différance* thus recomprehends and redelimits the classical causality, just as Bohr's complementarity does in physics. According to Derrida:

What is written as *différance*, then, will be the playing movement that "produces"—by means of something that is not simply an activity—these differences, these effects of difference. This does not mean that the *différance* that produces differences is somehow before them, in a simple and unmodified—in-different—present. *Différance* is the non-full, non-simple, structured and differentiating origin of differences. Thus, the name "origin" no longer suits it. . . .

We will designate as *différance* the movement according to which language, or any code, any system of referral in general, is constituted "historically" as a weave of differences. "Is constituted," "is produced," "is created," "movement," "historically," etc., necessarily being understood beyond the metaphysical language in which they are retained, along with all their implications." (*Margins*, 11–12, *Marges*, 12–13)

This dynamics is, then, translated into or interfused with a—general—economy of theoretical discourse:

The same, precisely, is *différance* (with an *a*) as the displaced and equivocal passage of one different thing to another, from one term of an opposition to the other. Thus one could reconsider all the pairs of opposites on which philosophy is constructed and on which our discourse lives, not in order to see opposition erase itself but to see what indicates that each of the terms must appear as the *différance* of the other, as the other different and deferred in the economy of the same (the intelligible as differing-deferring the sensible, as the sensible different and deferred; the concept as different and deferred, differing-deferring intuition; culture as nature different and deferred, differing-deferring; all the others of *physis—tekhnē, nomos, thesis*, society, freedom, history, mind, etc.—as *physis* different and deferred, or as *physis* differing and deferring. *Physis* in *différance*. And in this we may see the site of a reinterpreation of *mimēsis* in its alleged opposition to *physis*). (*Margins*, 17; *Marges*, 18)

This economy is reminiscent of Bohr's complementarity, not only insofar as the latter refers to physical representation and variables—such as waves and particles, position and momentum, or coordination and causality—but as it, as a matrix, employs more general concepts and conceptual structures—such as subject and object, interiority and exteriority, analysis and synthesis, concept and intuition, *physis* and *mimēsis*, and so forth—which Bohr sees as complementary as well. A very broad and radical reinterpretation of all classical concepts is thus at stake in the functioning of *différance;* and the differing-deferring of *différance* cannot be seen as presupposing some (in the classical sense) original or undisturbed presence or cause, differed and deferred by the representational process. *Différance* affects, or infects, all interpretive and theoretical processes, including its own inscription, so as to make them general economic.

Différance enacts an irreducible, general economic loss in all representation by ineluctably—always already—subtracting from the fullness of any presence, original unity, centrality, or plenitude—whether they are conceived of in terms of form, content, structure, history, logos or telos, or other concepts defining Western philosophy.[4] Derrida assembles these classical forms of governing interpretive, theoretical, or historical processes under the general rubric of 'presence.' Hence the corresponding theories—restricted economies—become forms of the 'metaphysics of presence,' although Derrida also uses rubrics such as 'logocentrism,' or, following Heidegger, 'ontotheology.' At the same time, *différance*, and its accompanying structures, must be conceived as *producing* these effects—presence, plenitude, unity, form, content, structure, history, and so forth. *Différance* connotes the joint dynamics of production-dislocation—an energy-like and an entropy-like process. Hence, the general economy of *différance* and accompanying structures recomprehends classical theories: it accounts for the conditions of their possibility and for the production of their concepts.

This precomprehending character of general economy is a crucial point for Derrida. His general economies are designed as much in order to deconstruct and precomprehend various restricted economies, as in order to introduce a new theoretical matrix. In this sense the balance of deconstructive and productive economies in Derrida may be seen as somewhat different from those in Bataille, or Nietzsche and Bohr, although the latter theories in turn incorporate various deconstructive agendas. The earlier program of grammatology as the 'science' of *writing* could be seen as more *positive* in this sense, although, as Bataille's general economy, such a "science" cannot be seen as "positive"—positivist or metaphysical—science.[5] This 'science' would remain characteristically Derridean insofar as Derrida gives a very broad and in many ways primary role to deconstructive readings, such as his reading of Rousseau in *Of Grammatology*.

Derrida's inscription or *writing* of *différance* in "Différance" conjoins Bataille with Hegel, Nietzsche, Freud, Saussure, Husserl, Heidegger, and Levinas. The general economic thematics, however, remain decisive throughout. Bataille enters, next to Hegel, at a crucial moment in the essay—at "the point of greatest obscurity, . . . the very enigma of *différance*":

> Elsewhere, in a reading of Bataille, I have attempted to indicate what might come of a rigorous and, in a new sense, "scientific" *relating* of the "restricted economy" that takes no part in expenditure without reserve, death, opening itself to nonmeaning, etc., to a general economy that *takes into account* the nonreserve, that keeps in reserve the nonreserve, if it can be put thus. I am speaking of a relationship between a *différance* that can make a profit on its investment and a *différance* that misses its profit, the *investiture* of a presence that is pure and without loss here being confused with absolute loss, with death. Through such a relating of a restricted and a general economy the very project of philosophy, under the privileged heading of Hegelianism, is displaced and reinscribed. The *Aufhebung—la relève*—is constrained into writing itself otherwise. Or perhaps simply into *writing* itself. Or, better, into taking account of its consumption of writing. (*Margins*, 19; *Marges*, 20–21)

Thus, general economy in Derrida entails, jointly, a deconstruction of Hegel and the introduction of *writing* in Derrida's sense. The concept of *Aufhebung* is based on the double or triple meaning of the term—negation, preservation or conservation, and supersession. Heidegger describes it as follows: "Th[e] sublating or *Aufhebung* must . . . be conceived in terms of the resonance of its threefold meaning: *tollere*, removing and eliminating the mere, initial illusion; *conservare*, preserving and including in the experience; but as an *elevare*, a lifting up to a higher level of knowing itself and its known" (*Hegel's Phenomenology of Spirit*, 28). Although one may engage other restricted economies with similar results, in both Bataille and Derrida, the movement from restricted to general economy proceeds via an encounter with Hegel. In this sense, the movement from restricted to general economy is a radical transgression or displacement of Hegel. According to Derrida, "If there were a definition of *différance*, it would be precisely the limit, the interruption, the destruction of Hegelian *relève* [i.e., *Aufhebung*] *wherever* it operates. What is at stake here is enormous [L'enjeu est ici énorme]. I emphasize the Hegelian *Aufhebung*, such as it is interpreted by a certain Hegelian discourse, for it goes without saying that the double meaning of *Aufhebung* could be written [in Derrida's sense] otherwise. Whence its proximity to all operations conducted *against* Hegel's dialectical speculation" (*Positions*, 40–41; *Positions*, 55). In fact, *différance* cannot be defined in view of this dislocation of Hegelian logic, or all classical logic. As other classical concepts, the very concept of definition becomes problematized and deconstructed in the process. It will not be discarded, but the limits of the possibility of classical definitions become refigured. The displacement of Hegel at issue is, according to Derrida, infinitesimal and radical at once (*Margins*, 14; *Positions*, 44).[6] Both, although not identically, the general economy of sovereignty in Bataille and the general economy of *différance* in Derrida are, in part, defined by this ambivalent displacement. At the same time, as Derrida argues ("From Restricted to General Economy," *Writing and Difference*, 274–76), general economy cannot be rigorously compatible with the *Aufhebung*, even though Bataille himself, at certain moments, claims otherwise, as in *Erotism* (*Erotism*, 36 n. 1; *L'Erotisme*, 42 n.) or, via Kojève, in *Theory of Religion* (123–24). Hegel marks a decisive moment in the history at issue: he sums up classical philosophy as ontotheology and the metaphysics of presence (*Of Grammatology*, 24–26). One may argue that this history culminated in Heidegger, a philosopher likewise of "uncircumventable [incontournable]" significance for Derrida (*Margins*, 22; *Marges*, 22) and his economy of the ontological difference in *Being and Time* or more complex, but still restricted, economies emerging in his later works. In *The Question of Being* (1951), Heidegger writes:

> The meaning-fullness [Mehrdeutigkeit: literally, the "more-meaning-ness," both in the sense of the fullness of the meaning and plurality and (controlled) ambiguity of meaning] of what is said [die Sage] by no means consists in a mere accumulation of meanings [Bedeutungen] emerging haphazardly. This meaning-fullness is based on a play [Spiel] which, the more richly it unfolds, the more strictly it is held (within the domain governed) by a hidden rule [Regel]. Through (the presence of) this rule, this meaning-fullness plays within the balance(d), whose oscillation we seldom experience. That is why what is said remains "bound into" the highest law [Gesetz]. That [this being bound into the highest law] is the freedom that "frees into" the all-playing structure [Gefüge: juncture] of never-resting transformations. (*The Question of Being*, 104–5; translation modified)

Derrida radicalizes this economy by replacing it with a general economy in which transformations can never be fully or unconditionally controlled. Conditionally such controls do take place: the play at issue is the *complementary* (inter) play of chance and necessity or randomness and causality, differently balanced at each point, and thus without a final or unique law of interaction between them. Derrida's many structures are introduced in order to account for various configurations of his general economy and, often correlatively, to enact deconstructions of classical, restricted economic concepts and fields. By the same token, this economy cannot be centered around or originate from *différance,* or anything else. Derrida's other structures—trace, supplement, dissemination, *writing,* and so forth—are rigorously necessary, and they cannot be seen merely as different aspects of *différance* or of any structure, overt or hidden, nameable or unnameable.

Trace

As enacted by *différance,* "the play of differences supposes, in effect, [non-Hegelian] syntheses and referrals which forbid at any moment, or in any sense, that a simple element be *present* in and of itself, referring only to itself. . . . Nothing, neither among the elements nor within the system, is anywhere ever simply present or absent. There are only, everywhere, differences and traces of traces" (*Positions,* 26; *Positions,* 37–38). This economy leads to the fundamental deferral of the first "origin" and to a deconstruction of absolute origin. This deconstruction is again a rigorous suspension: it does not eliminate origins, but instead refigures the whole thematics of origin. Once one wants to speak about origins, and one cannot avoid speaking about them, one *always* has to suspend the first origin, whether one speaks of the origin of language, as in Rousseau, of the origin of geometry, as in Husserl (two cases most specifically analyzed by Derrida), or of any other origin. However one thinks, speaks of or writes *the* origin, one always arrives at the necessity of suspending it. There is no text that could avoid this suspension. There are only texts that *claim* the possibility of an absolutely origin. If one could speak of anything originary, only *différance* could be originary. But, "to say that *différance* is originary is simultaneously to erase the myth of a present origin. Which is why 'originary' must be understood as having been *crossed out,* without which *différance* would be derived from an original plenitude. It is non-origin which is originary" (*Writing and Difference,* 203; *L'Écriture et la différence,* 302–3).[7] "The place of a problematic of the *trace*" in Derrida is "the question of meaning and of its origin *in difference*" (*Of Grammatology,* 70; *De la grammatologie,* 102; emphasis added), or better in *différance*, from which the trace is indissociable, without being identical to it. Derrida "call[s] *trace* that which does not let itself be summed up in the simplicity of a present." According to Derrida, one is "authorized" to use this name by virtue of "[the] impossibility of reanimating absolutely the manifest evidence of an originary presence," which "refers us therefore to an absolute past" (*Of Grammatology*, 66; *De la grammatologie*, 97). As he writes:

> if the trace refers to an absolute past, it is because it obliges us to think a past that can no longer be understood in the form of a modified presence, as a present-past. Since past has always signified present-past, the absolute past that is retained in the trace no longer rigorously merits the name "past." Another name to erase, especially since the strange movement of the trace proclaims as much as it recalls: *différance* defers-differs [*diffère*]. With the same precaution and under the same erasure, it may be said that its passivity is also its relationships to the "future." The concepts of *present*, *past*, and *future*, everything in the concepts of time and history which implies evidence of them—the metaphysical concept of time in general—cannot adequately describe the structure of the trace. And deconstructing the simplicity of presence does not amount only to accounting for the horizons of potential presence. . . . It is not a matter of complicating the structure of time while conserving its homogeneity and its fundamental successivity, by demonstrating for example that the past present and the future present constitute originarily, by dividing it, the form of the living present. . . . It is [instead] the problem of the deferred effect (*Nachträglichkeit*) of which Freud speaks. The temporality to which he refers cannot be that which lends itself to a phenomenology of consciousness or of presence and one may indeed wonder by what right all that is in question here should still be called time, now, anterior present, delay, etc. (*Of Grammatology*, 66–67; *De la grammatologie*, 97–98)

Hence "there are no 'conscious' traces" (*Margins*, 18, *Marges*, 19), as the unconscious itself must be refigured within this general economy. "The alterity of [this] 'unconscious' makes us concerned not with horizons of modified—past or future—presents, but with a 'past' that has never been present, and which never will be, whose future to come will never be a *production* or a reproduction in the form of presence. Therefore the concept of trace is incompatible with the concept of retention, of the

becoming-past of what has been present. One cannot think the trace—
and therefore, *différance*—on the basis of the present, or of the presence
of the present" (*Margins*, 21; *Marges*, 22).

It is not only the question of, jointly, the constitution of presence and
of the constitution and deconstruction of the metaphysical concept of
presence, but equally of difference and the metaphysical concept of difference. *Différance* is not more simply difference or transformability than
simple identity or presence, no more simply becoming than simply being,
although it refers to the dynamic efficacity of the production of all these
effects and the concepts, classical or deconstructive, accounting for them.
The "difference" of *différance* is too radical to be either absolute difference, as in Kant, or conversely an absolute overcoming of difference
or exteriority, even if by means of (controlled) economies of difference,
exteriority, transformation, as in Hegel. *Différance* is neither simply identity nor difference; neither presence not absence; neither plentitude nor
scarcity or emptiness; neither oneness nor multiplicity; neither order nor
chaos; neither transformation nor structure; neither randomness nor causality; neither determinacy nor indeterminacy; neither decidability nor
undecidability. *Différance* also renders the efficacity of these complementary effects as supplementary in Derrida's sense (to be defined below)
rather than as a classical, causal, efficacy. We can and must continue to
employ classical concepts in order to describe and analyze the effects
of general economic efficacities. A general economy will proceed within
the necessary closure or closures of classical theories, but it will have
to relate to an alterity, which cannot be conceived by means of classical theories, whether Kantian, Hegelian, Husserlian, or Heideggerian,
or still other. A similar economy defines Bohr's complementarity, since
there, too, classical descriptions can and must be used, often complementarily, in order to describe the effects of general economic efficacities,
but not these efficacities themselves. Such efficacities may be unrepresentable and inconceivable, whether by classical or restricted economic
means, including unrepresentable and inconceivable as the (absolutely)
unrepresentable and inconceivable. Hence Derrida relates, via Levinas,
the (a)temporality of the trace to the question of alterity: "A past that has
never been present: this formula is the one that Emmanuel Levinas uses,
although certainly in a nonpsychoanalytic way, to qualify the trace and
enigma of absolute alterity: the Other [autrui]" (*Margins*, 21; *Marges*, 22).
The radical alterity and efficacities at stake in general economy cannot be
absolute, however; and are both fundamentally material and fundamen-

tally unconscious, as both matter and the unconscious must be in turn refigured general economically.

At the same time, in order to inscribe the trace one must, Derrida argues, rigorously traverse a metaphysical and specifically transcendental text, such as that of Husserl's transcendental phenomenology. This is necessary in order to avoid "a scientifist objectivism, that is to say . . . another unperceived or unconfessed metaphysics. This is often noticeable in the work of the Copenhagen School."[8] As Derrida writes:

> It is to escape falling back into this naive objectivism that I refer here to a transcendentality [Husserl's] that I elsewhere put into question. It is because I believe that there is a short-of and a beyond of transcendental criticism. To see to it that the beyond does not return to the within is to recognize in the contortion the necessity of a pathway [*parcours*]. That pathway must leave a track in the text. Without that track, abandoned to the simple content of its conclusions, the ultra-transcendental text will so closely resemble the precritical text as to be indistinguishable from it. We must now form and meditate upon the law of this resemblance. What I call the erasure of concepts ought to mark the places of that future meditation. For example, the value of the transcendental arche [*archie*] must make its necessity felt before letting itself be erased. The concept of arche-trace must comply with both that necessity and that erasure. It is in fact contradictory and not acceptable within the logic of identity. The trace is not only the disappearance of origin—within the discourse that we sustain and according to the path that we follow it means that the origin did not even disappear, that it was never constituted except reciprocally by a nonorigin, the trace, which thus becomes the origin of the origin. From then on, to wrench the concept of the trace from the classical scheme, which would derive it from a presence or from an originary non-trace and which would make of it an empirical mark, one must indeed speak of an originary trace or arche-trace. Yet we know that that concept destroys its name and that, if all begins with the trace, there is above all no originary trace. (*Of Grammatology*, 61; *De la grammatologie*, 90)

Husserl's scheme must, thus, be deconstructed in turn, in part by using linguistics, Hjelmslev's or Saussure's, against it; and a similar procedure must be employed in relation to the Heideggerian economy of trace (*Margins*, 23–25, 63–67).

It is worth qualifying that, in relation to all these texts the term 'transcendental' should be understood in the Kantian or post-Kantian sense of exploring *the conditions of the possibility* of experiential knowledge. In *The Critique of Pure Reason,* Kant distinguishes in this sense between "transcendent," as that which lies absolutely outside of the sensible world, and "transcendental," as that which defines the totality of conditions in the sensible world. General economy also deals with the conditions of certain possibilities, or necessities. The conditions themselves, however, are fundamentally different from those arrived at by all transcendental philosophy hitherto. For at stake are also the conditions of the *impossibility* of the absolutely originary, grounding, centering, or totalizing presence that would control differential play. The latter economy has not only never been questioned, at least not anywhere radically enough, by classical philosophy, but has always grounded all philosophical conditions of possibility, such as the transcendental or posttranscendental philosophy, be it in Kant, Hegel, Husserl, Heidegger, Levinas, or elsewhere. Here, however, I have in mind primarily Derrida's general rubric of "transcendental signified," defining a broad spectrum of the metaphysics of presence. Thus, as Derrida writes on Heidegger:

> Heideggerian thought would reinstate rather than destroy the instance of the logos and of the truth of being as "primum signatum:" the "transcendental" signified ("transcendental" in a certain sense, as in the Middle Ages the transcendental—*ens, unum, verum, bonum*—was said to be the "primum cognitum") implied by all categories or all determined significations, by all lexicons and all syntax, and therefore by all linguistic signifiers, though not to be identified simply with any one of those signifiers allowing itself to be precomprehended through each of them, remaining irreducible to all the epochal determinations that it nonetheless makes possible, thus opening the history of the logos, yet itself being only through the logos; that is, *being nothing* before the logos and outside of it. (*Of Grammatology,* 20; *De la grammatologie,* 33)

Heidegger's philosophy may be seen as the culmination of this history, even though it also has considerable deconstructive dimensions. Derrida's statement would apply (with suitable modifications) to a very broad spectrum of philosophical economies, where analogous reinstatement takes place, in spite of the deconstructive potential that such economies might offer.[9] One could, particularly in view of Nietzsche's analysis, question the necessity of a kind of exhaustive traversal of transcendental or more generally classical texts—such as, in particular, Hegel's, Husserl's, or Heidegger's. An ultra-transcendental text may be produced by means of a more direct theoretical work; and Derrida to a degree does so himself, particularly in "Différance." As shall be seen, as it proceeds from the empirical—photographic—trace to the general economic, Derridean trace, Bohr's complementarity offers a comparable general economy, both ultratranscendental and ultraobjectivist, through the analysis of "the conditions of the possibility" of quantum mechanical traces themselves—the tracks of particles in cloud chambers or on photographic plates—and of their particular structures defined by uncertainty relations. Naturally, one must always guard one's analysis against reinstating restricted economic forms of determination, be they transcendental, empiricist, objectivist, positivist, or still other.

The joint dynamics of *différance*, trace, and *writing* deconstructs and precomprehends classical economies of the sign, in particular Saussure's concept of the sign as the conjoined structure of the signifier—the (mental image of the) phonic or graphic substance—and the signified—the concept or idea by means of which a given reference becomes possible. A meaning, then, is produced by means of a reduction of the signifying, spoken or written, substance, or expression, and attaining the plentitude of a concept, meaning or content—that is, the alleged plentitude claimed possible by means of this reduction. In many respects, Saussure's economy is itself proto-deconstructive, although it never sufficiently displaces the classical economies of the sign, such as Rousseau's or Hegel's. Derrida locates more radical possibilities in Peirce. As he writes:

> Peirce goes very far in the direction that I have called the de-construction of the transcendental signified, which, at one time or another, would place a reassuring end to the reference from sign to sign. I have identified logocentrism and the metaphysics of presence as the exigent, powerful, systematic, and irrepressible desire for such a signified. Now Peirce considers the indefiniteness of reference as the criterion that allows us to recognize that we are indeed dealing with a system of signs. *What broaches the movement of signification is what makes its interruption impossible. The thing itself is a sign. . . .* There is thus no phenomenality reducing the sign or the representer so that the thing signified may be allowed to glow finally in the luminosity of its presence. The so called "thing-itself" is always already a *representamen* shielded from the simplicity of intuitive evidence.

> The *representamen* functions only by giving rise to an *interpretant* that
> itself becomes a sign and so on to infinity. The self-identity of the
> signified conceals itself unceasingly and is always on the move. . . .
>
> From the moment that there is meaning there are nothing but
> signs. We *think only in signs.* Which amounts to ruining the notion of
> the sign at the very moment when, as in Nietzsche, its exigency is
> recognized in the absoluteness of its right. One could call *play [jeu]*
> the absence of the transcendental signified as limitlessness of play,
> that is to say as the trembling [ébranlement] of ontotheology and the
> metaphysics of presence. . . . Here one must think of writing as a
> play/game [jeu] within language. (The *Phaedrus* (277e) condemned
> writing precisely as play—*paidia*—and opposed such childishness to
> the adult gravity [*spoudē*] of speech). (*Of Grammatology*, 49–50; *De la
> grammatologie,* 71–72; translation modified)

It becomes logical that writing rather than speech becomes the model
of the originary meaning, or rather of the originary-nonoriginary meaning. From Plato, and before, to Saussure and beyond, writing has always
been defined as a secondary representation of and an exterior addition
to—a *supplement* of—speech, which would, in its closer proximity, represent the plentitude of thought. Derrida deconstructs both concepts—
origin and meaning—and the narrow concept of writing, classically and,
from this new perspective, unrigorously conceived as merely a representation of speech. Writing, which has been defined as at best a superfluous
exterior and at worse a dangerous supplement of speech, in fact manifests
and is a model of the efficacious dynamics of speech or thought itself.
Writing exposes the play within language that produces that to which it is
supposed to be simply added, just as difference—refigured through *différance* and trace—produces that original presence or plentitude to which
it is supposed to be added, or from which it allegedly derives or, it is often
claimed, deviates. The traditional function of writing is not erased. But,
whether at issue are its psychological, cultural, theoretical, or political aspects, or (as is in fact always the case) interactively all of them, the play of
writing can never be contained by the concept of writing as a representation of speech. The play defined by the absence of the transcendental
signified is also the play of what Derrida calls "the strange structure of
the supplement," which refigures the classical order of signification and
meaning.

The Supplement

In his reading of Husserl, Derrida describes "the strange structure of the supplement" as follows: "by delayed reaction, a possibility produces that to which it is said to be added on" (*Speech and Phenomena*, 89; *La voix et le phénomène*, 99).

The supplement does not imply that, for example, writing simply comes before, instead of after, speech, or speech before thought, or any signifier before its signified, although such direct reversals do take place under certain conditions. More generally, signifiers are never simply added to their signified, and the former just as often is affected and at times effected by the latter, as the latter, supplementarily, by the former. Signifiers and signifieds always supplement each other, and the (general) economy of the supplement is close to Nietzsche's critique of classical causality, which may be read as the exposure of supplementarity within causality.[10] The efficacities of that type cannot be conceived of in terms of some original presence—being-presence or becoming-presence—even if this presence is seen as different-deferred by a representation. One needs continuously to keep in mind both the trace and supplementarity rather than think in terms of absolutely originary (originarily present) structures, empirical or transcendental, from which something differs or in relation to which something is deferred. Any claim upon this efficacity can only be locally, interpretively supplemented upon its effects. The possibility of these effects will always produce what it is (classically) supposed to be added on—the form or the very possibility of any representation, or unrepresentability, of this efficacity. The same economy is at work in quantum mechanics. Complementarity is concerned with a supplementary efficacity, rather than causal efficacy. It is supplementary.

The logic of the supplement discloses that an allegedly imperfect or deficient supplementary signifier—such as a writing—of a more ideal signifier—such as speech—which represents, or *supplements*, an originary plentitude or presence—such as a signified content or idea—in fact manifests the efficacity by means of which the second, more ideal signifier and finally the (claimed) ideal presence of the signified are themselves produced as effects. The efficacity "behind" a signifier is—always already—a *différance*-like supplementary process, a text *written* in Derrida's sense. Derrida's famous proposition that "*there is nothing outside of the text* [there is no outside-text; *il n'y a pas de hors-texte*]" must be understood as refering to this dynamics, jointly described by Derrida's network of structures, rather than to any narrow, conventional concept of text, oral or written:

> [Reading] cannot legitimately transgress the text toward something other than it, toward a referent (a reality that is metaphysical, historical, psychobiographical, etc.) or toward a signified outside the text whose content could take place, could have taken place outside of language, that is to say, in the sense that we give here to that word, outside of writing in general. That is why the methodological considerations that we risk applying here to an example are closely dependent on general propositions that we have elaborated above; as regards the absence of the referent or the transcendental signified. *There is nothing outside of the text* [there is no outside-text; *il n'y a pas de hors-texte*]. And that is neither because Jean-Jacques' life, or the existence of Mamma or Thérèse *themselves*, is not of prime interest to us, nor because we have access to their so-called "real" existence only in the text and we have neither any means of altering this, nor any right to neglect this limitation. All reasons of this type would already be sufficient, to be sure, but there are more radical reasons. What we have tried to show by following the guiding line of the "dangerous supplement," is that in what one calls the real life of these existences "of flesh and bone," beyond and behind what one believes can be circumscribed as Rousseau's text, there has never been anything but writing; there have never been anything but supplements, substitutive significations which could only come forth in a chain of differential references, the "real" supervening, and being added only while taking on meaning from a trace and from an invocation of the supplement, etc. And thus to infinity, for we have read, *in the text*, that the absolute present, Nature, that which words like "real mother" name, have always already escaped, have never existed [as so named or conceived]; that what opens meaning and language is writing as the disappearance of natural presence. (*Of Grammatology*, 158–59; *De la grammatologie*, 227–28)

"Never existed" clearly refers to classical, restricted economies of existence, be they materialist or idealist, phenomenological, theological, ontological, psychological or psychoanalytic, or still others, in short to the metaphysics of presence. Rousseau's life, or life in general—or, at the limit, nature (matter)—must be seen as *différance*. It does not "exist" ontologically, but connotes an efficacity—and a certain "materiality"—as a radical alterity, which "exists" only insofar as the term can be divested from its determination by means of the metaphysics of presence. Matter is understood by Derrida as a radical alterity and a certain *différance* in a general economy (*Positions*, 64). Life, or "the history of life," is *différance*, "as the history of *grammē*" (*Of Grammatology*, 84; *De la grammatologie*, 125), or perhaps even a still more complex process. For "it is precisely the property of the power of *différance* to modify life less and less as it spreads out more and more. If it should grow *infinite*—and its essence excludes this a priori—life itself would be made into an impassive, intangible, and eternal presence: infinite *différance*, God or death" (*Of Grammatology*, 131; *De la grammatologie*, 191). At the same time, however, "death is the movement of *différance* to the extent that that movement is necessarily finite" (*Of Grammatology*, 143, *De la grammatologie*, 206).

Différance implies and is necessitated by a radical alterity that cannot be mastered by any given text, philosophical or other, and thus by any metaphysical concept of alterity, including absolute alterity. Such an alterity would be neither inside nor outside *a* text, or simultaneously both inside and outside *a* text, insofar as such classical terms and logic can apply. One must always keep in mind the joint logic of radical alterity and of the closure of classical theory. The logic of supplement is this logic. "Something promises itself as it escapes, gives itself, as it moves away, and strictly speaking it cannot even be called presence. Such is the constraint of the supplement, such, exceeding all the language of metaphysics, is this structure 'almost inconceivable to reason.' *Almost* inconceivable: simple irrationality, the opposite of reason are less irritating and disorienting for classical logic" (*Of Grammatology*, 154; *De la grammatologie*, 222; translation modified).

Dissemination

'Dissemination' relates to that which is opposed to unity or polysemy as the controlled plurality of meaning (such as that of the Hegelian *Aufhebung*), signification, history, or indeed anything. The irreducible plurality of dissemination prohibits a full or unconditional control of the multiple. It must allow for local, conditional structures (or strictures) controlling the multiple. Otherwise, through an unproblematized reversal, one would reinstate a restricted economy—that of absolute multiplicity. Dissemination is developed most specifically in the context of Plato and Hegel in Derrida's reading of Mallarmé in "The Double Sci-

ence" and of Sollers in "Dissemination" (both in *Dissemination*), but it
operates equally against Lacanian (*Positions*, 84–87) or other (restricted)
economies of controlled plurality, undecidability, or indeterminacy.[11]
These economies have (co)defined the metaphysics of presence in philosophy, anthropology, linguistics, and other human and social sciences
throughout their history. As a result, dissemination becomes perhaps the
most crucial counterpart of *différance*.

Dissemination also makes it impossible to close the network of Derrida's structures themselves. This irreducible proliferation of theoretical
terms and functions is a fundamental consequence of a general economic understanding of the theoretical process, applied by Derrida to his
"neither word[s] nor concept[s]" (*Margins*, 7; *Marges*, 7). Dissemination
is, however, operative within classical theories as well. The latter can only
claim to contain or control, in practice or in principle, their multiplicity
and indeterminacy (or undecidability) by restricted economic means, but
never actually do so, in practice or in principle. In fact, general economy would tell us that this dissemination cannot be controlled by any
means; or, again, it cannot be *fully* controlled. In any given situation, such
a proliferation will be terminated in one way or another. Under different conditions, however, one may need a very different array of terms,
concepts, or demarcations. There is no taxonomical closure that would
exhaust, saturate, or contain all such extensions once and for all. There
can, as I said, be no more absolute multiplicity than absolute unity or
any other form of absolute control of the multiple. While it may have a
certain strategic priority in Derrida or a certain preeminence after Derrida, *différance*, by definition, cannot be seen as primary in relation to
other Derridean structures. *Différance* and dissemination may necessitate
and define each other more directly;[12] but *différance* equally depends on
trace, supplement, *writing*, and other structures employed by Derrida.
These structures interact with and necessitate, but are not identical to,
each other. Indeed they are not identical to themselves. Any one of them
is the "same," that is not identical, is a *différance* (with an *a*) and dissemination of "itself."

The Unconscious

For both Bataille and Derrida, as for Nietzsche before them, the loss in
question in general economy is always related to a certain structural, irreducible unconscious. According to Derrida, "[the] deconstruction of

presence accomplishes itself through the deconstruction of consciousness, and therefore through the irreducible notion of the trace (*Spur*), as it
appears in both Nietzschean and Freudian discourse" (*Of Grammatology*,
70; *De la grammatologie*, 103). The inscription—*writing*—of *différance* in
"Différance" proceeds, therefore, via both Nietzsche and Freud: "[B]oth
of [them], as is well known, and sometimes in very similar fashion, put
consciousness into question in its assured certainty of itself. . . . *Différance*
appears almost by name in their texts, and in those places where everything is at stake. . . . I will only recall that for Nietzsche 'the great principal activity is unconscious,' and that consciousness is the effect of forces
whose essence, byways, and modalities are not proper to it" (*Margins*, 17;
Marges, 18).

This insight serves Derrida as a key entrance into the field of *différance*,
although, as shall be seen, a difference between Nietzsche and Derrida
also emerges along the way. "Is not all of Nietzsche's thought a critique of
philosophy as an active indifference to difference, as the system of adia-
phoristic reduction or repression? Which according to the same logic,
according to logic itself, does not exclude that philosophy lives *in* and *on*
différance, thereby blinding itself to the *same*, which is not the identical.
The same, precisely, is *différance* (with an *a*)" (*Margins*, 17; *Marges*, 18).
This Nietzschean juncture leads Derrida to his arguably broadest "definition" of *différance:* "Thus, *différance* is the name we might give to the
'active,' moving discord of different forces, and of differences of forces,
that Nietzsche sets up against the entire system of metaphysical grammar,
wherever this system governs culture, philosophy, and science" (*Margins*,
18; *Marges*, 19).

"What is at stake here is enormous," Derrida, we recall, says in "defining" *différance* against Hegel's *Aufhebung* and dialectic "*wherever* [they]
operate." Against Hegel, this manifold of processes and fields of inquiry
cannot be unified within one system or manifold—hence dissemination.
The structural unconscious subtracts from the plenitude of presence in
every process of representation, just as a kind of "material unconscious"
of quantum mechanics disables a full representation of a given quantum
system. For Bohr the problem of consciousness and self-consciousness
is the area where complementarity may be productively applied, and he
appears to have been skeptical about (uncomplementarized) conscious
determinations of anything.[13]

The unconscious constitutes a crucial dimension of general economy
or complementarity, but it must itself be inscribed—*written*—general

economically. One must *write* that radical difference and alterity—*différance*—and multiplicity—dissemination—to which, as Derrida puts it, "Freud gives the *metaphysical* name of the unconscious."

> For the economic character of *différance* in no way implies that the deferred presence can always be found again, that we have here only an investment that provisionally and calculatedly delays the perception of its profit or the profit of its perception. Contrary to the metaphysical, dialectical, "Hegelian" interpretation of the economic movement of *différance*, we must conceive of a play in which whoever loses wins, and in which one loses and wins on every turn. If the displaced presentation remains definitively and implacably postponed, it is not that a certain present remains absent or hidden. Rather, *différance* maintains our relationship with that which we necessarily misconstrue, and which exceeds the alternative of presence and absence. A certain alterity—to which Freud gives the metaphysical name of the unconscious—is definitively exempt from every process of presentation by means of which we would call upon it to show itself in person. In this context, and beneath this guise, the unconscious is not, as we know, a hidden, virtual, or potential self-presence. It differs from, and defers, itself; which doubtless means that it is woven of differences, and also that it sends out delegates, representatives, proxies; but without any chance that the giver of proxies might "exist," might be present, be "itself" somewhere, and with even less chance that it might become conscious. In this sense, contrary to the terms of an old debate full of the metaphysical investments that it has always assumed, the "unconscious" is no more a "thing" than it is any other thing, is no more a thing than it is a virtual or masked consciousness. This radical alterity as concerns every possible mode of presence is marked by the irreducibility of the aftereffect, the delay. In order to describe traces, in order to read the traces of "unconscious" traces (there are no "conscious" traces), the language of presence and absence, the metaphysical discourse of phenomenology, is inadequate. (Although the phenomenologist is not the only one to speak this language.) (*Margins*, 20–21; *Marges*, 21)

Even as it produces the effects of consciousness and self-consciousness, *différance* irreducibly subtracts from the plenitude of consciousness or self-consciousness, individual or collective; or from the metaphysically conceived plenitude or presence of the unconscious. The unconscious cannot in turn be thought of as existing by itself, in the fullness of its presence, absolutely outside consciousness or in a metaphysical opposition to it. Strategically, Derrida's deconstruction employs an opposition between consciousness and the unconscious. Theoretically, this deconstruction is a precomprehending general economic complementarity between them, which prohibits unconditionally privileging one member over another within either opposition. Hence, while general economy must deconstruct and to a degree destroy restricted economies of consciousness, it must consider the complementary functioning of consciousness within refigured limits. Consciousness, as Freud knew, is a most complex and enigmatic thing, perhaps more complex and enigmatic than the unconscious.[14] If one keeps these qualifications in mind, however, the movement from a restricted to a general economy is a movement from consciousness to the unconscious.

Matter

In *Positions*, Derrida speaks, via Bataille, of matter as a (general-economic) radical alterity: "if, and in the extent to which, *matter* in this general economy designates, as you said, radical alterity (I will specify: in relation to philosophical oppositions), then what I write can be considered 'materialist' " (*Positions*, 64; *Positions*, 87). In short, if matter is *différance*, then Derrida's general economy can be considered materialist. In this general economy, however, *différance is* matter; thus both, and often jointly, matter and the unconscious are refigured general economically. In Derrida's statement in "Différance" cited earlier, "radical alterity" (of the unconscious) is defined by an even stronger claim; it "concerns every possible mode of presence" (*Margins*, 21; *Marges*, 22). This alterity, again, cannot be seen as absolute. For then it would become defined by a metaphysical opposition of absolute identity and absolute difference, which would make it restricted-economic. Derrida's formulation just cited may be more directly indebted to Bataille. As early as 1933, around the time and perhaps in the wake of quantum mechanics and Bohr, Bataille offers the following extraordinary formulation, ". . . matter, in fact, can only be defined as the *nonlogical difference*, that represents in relation to the *economy* of the universe what *crime* represents in relation to the law" ("The Notion of Expenditure," *Visions*, 129; *OC* 1:320). Such a difference or alterity demands a different—general-economic—concept or neither a word nor a concept of matter and, as Bohr realized, a different—general—economy of physics and of the laws of nature, just as, in the social field, Bataille's general economy demands a very different understanding of crime, the law, and legal theory. Quantum mechanical nature is a kind of criminality that always escapes from the laws of physics. Or, rather, we never seem to be able quite to establish the law that would allow us fully to regulate its behavior. This is also the problem with criminality or humanity, to begin with, as Bataille and Kafka (who might have been on Bataille's mind here), or Nietzsche (who must have been on both Bataille's and Kafka's minds), profoundly understood.

Bohr was perhaps first to grasp fully that we can no longer speak of matter as an independent reality existing by itself, independent of observation, measurement, interpretation, or theory, even though, at the same time, this "matter" affects and constrains all observation, measurement, interpretation, and theory. The resulting anti-epistemological quantum *meta*-physics constrains physics. As such, it prohibits the classical *metaphysics*—epistemology and ontology—of matter and the corresponding ideology of physics, such as, and particularly, Einstein's. Complementarity becomes necessitated by a general economy of matter as a radical, but again not absolute, alterity. Whether the practitioners themselves accept or recognize this or not, the practice of physics must be seen as a kind of general economy of matter, which, let me stress, never simply dispenses with, but redelimits, classical physics. Metaphysical ideologies may not always inhibit physics itself, but that does not mean that they are always compatible with the findings of physics. For, as Bohr argued, it is the very nature of these findings that leads to complementarity. At the very least, the findings of physics impose some constraints upon metaphysics. Bohr was able to derive very radical anti-epistemological implications from these findings, although his thinking may have been helped by anti-epistemological ideas elsewhere. One can locate texts and theoretical and textual strategies that produce a similar concept, or neither a term nor a concept, of matter. Bohr's momentous achievement is that it is produced within the field of physics itself, by rigorously taking into account the irreducible interaction between quantum objects and measuring instruments.

Metaphor

General economy or complementarity must be seen as tropes or figures, or, better, catachreses—figures whose constituents are themselves metaphors. Such is in fact always the case. For, as Derrida shows, most specifically in "White Mythology: Metaphor in the Text of Philosophy" (*Margins*), this general metaphoricity is irreducible and is irreducibly catachrestic, since, in principle, it entails an interminable metaphoric play. This metaphoric or catachrestic play is in fact correlative to Derrida's *writing* (*Of Grammatology*, 15). Metaphor or (and as) *writing* in Derrida's sense is irreducible even in an attempt to define (the concept or metaphor of) metaphor itself; for there can be no nonmetaphoric constituents out of which such a definition can be constructed. In practice, in any given case, such a play will, of course, always be terminated in one way or another, and any given configurations, such as a given definition of metaphor, can be put into circulation within either a restricted or a general economy. This local terminability or reduction of catachresis cannot, however, suspend the irreducible *writing*-metaphoricity as the noncausal efficacity it entails. Once refigured as *writing* this general metaphoricity deconstructs the classical understanding of the metaphoric just as much as the classical understanding of the literal and the proper, and the unproblematized, metaphysical opposition between them. By making catachresis irreducible, *writing* "explode[s] the reassuring opposition of the metaphoric and the proper, the opposition in which the one and the other have never done anything but reflect and refer to each other in their radiance" (*Margins*, 270–71; *Marges*, 323). *Writing* makes the field of this light and this reflection uncertain, quantum.

Positioned on the opposite sides of this economy, and reversing each other, metaphysics, idealist or materialist, and positivism, or empiricism, are, as Derrida shows, defined by this forgetting of *writing*-metaphoricity. "As Hegel says somewhere, empiricism always forgets, at the very least, that it employs the words to be. Empiricism is thinking *by* metaphor without thinking the metaphor *as such*" (*Writing and Difference*, 139; *L'Écriture et la différence*, 204). By reversing empiricism without thinking *writing*, however, metaphysics and philosophy, including Hegel's, also does not think metaphor *as such*. This forgetting often manifests itself by a negative attitude toward both writing and metaphor in their more conventional roles. A much broader front of forces, however, defines the metaphysics of presence, in which both "philosophical-logical discourse" and "empirical-logical discourse" are implicated and complicit (*Margins*, 7; *Marges* 7). The general economic navigation of *différance* must both use these two discourses as pathways and circumvent them as obstacles.

Without naming it, Bohr appears to have realized that metaphor is irreducible—irreducible, one might say, technologically. Derrida, too, relates *writing* and technology throughout his writing. Philosophy has always seen writing as, in principle, a dispensable auxiliary *technique,* just as classical physics sees the experimental arrangements as, in principle, reducible—as not measurably affecting the physical processes themselves—which is never possible in quantum mechanics. As anti-epistemology, complementarity is defined by the irreducible mutual and, as Bohr grasped, "uncontrollable" interactions, between *physis* and *tekhnē*—between physical processes and the technologies of experiment.

Writing

Derrida's economy of *writing* inevitably emerges through a general economic deconstruction of the classical (and, as Derrida shows, unrigorous) concept of writing as a representation of speech. A general economic science of *writing* was originally proposed by Derrida under the name 'grammatology' in *Of Grammatology* and other earlier texts, where it is juxtaposed to classical, particularly Saussurean, linguistics as the science—the restricted economy—of language, specifically as the science of speech conceived of in the metaphysical opposition to writing. Privileging speech over writing, this opposition characterizes philosophy as the metaphysics of presence, with which linguistics becomes thus complicit. Philosophy customarily subordinates to the logos and to truth all language and thought, rather than only theoretical, such as philosophical, language and thinking, although the latter have a privileged position by virtue of their alleged closest proximity to the logos and to truth. If, however, this conventional concept or field of concepts of writing is thereby shown to be uncritical, the same is also true of the classical concept of speech. Derrida's economy of writing refigures both. Borrowing its name from the subordinate member of the classical opposition, Derrida demonstrates how what he calls *writing* emerges in the place to which classical theories and fields assign the denomination of language.

The economy, by definition general, just described offers a paradigmatic example of deconstruction, particularly as practiced in Derrida's earlier texts, but important throughout his work. The operation can and must apply to other classical oppositions, indeed, as we have seen, to "all the pairs of opposites on which philosophy is constructed and on which our discourse lives" (*Margins,* 17; *Marges,* 18). As I have stressed from the outset, Derrida's deconstruction does not dispense with or simply reverse these oppositional pairs, which is never sufficient to transform a given metaphysical field radically enough; it recomprehends the necessity of such oppositions within classical discourse and redelimits them in general economic fields. In order to deconstruct effectively the classical opposition of speech and writing—or the signified and the signifier, form and content, and so forth—it is not enough simply to reverse the opposition and the hierarchy which privileges speech over writing by virtue of its closer proximity to thought, logos, or truth. One must produce a new concept, possibly by using a reversal as a phase and, strategically, borrowing a name, such as writing, from a subordinate member of a given hierarchy. By means of such a new concept, or a network of concepts, the whole preceding configuration—the members of the opposition, the relationships between the concepts involved, and the whole system that produces them—is recomprehended. The old configuration is deconstructed and refigured rather than simply abandoned. In this sense, one can speak of a rigorous suspension in juxtaposition to an uncritical negation or unproblematized reversal.[15]

Derrida pursues precisely this type of project and this set of strategies, "conser[ving] the *old name*," the subordinate name, of "writing" for his new concept (*Margins*, 329; *Marges*, 392). This concept, or neither a word nor a concept, of *writing* can no longer be understood conventionally as a representation of speech; and the latter concept and all other classical concepts involved are, in turn, transformed and reinscribed. "It is not a question of resorting to the same concept of writing and of simply inverting the dissymmetry that now has become problematical. It is a question, rather, of producing a new concept of writing" (*Positions*, 26; *Positions*, 37). Derrida specifies the "nuclear traits of all writing" as follows:

(1) the break with the horizon of communication as the communication of consciousnesses and presences, and as the linguistic or semantic transport of meaning; (2) the subtraction of all writing from the semantic horizon or the hermeneutic horizon, at least as a horizon of meaning, lets itself be punctured by writing; (3) the necessity of, in a way, *separating* the concept of polisemia [as a controlled plurality of meaning] from the concept I have elsewhere named *dissemination*, which is also the concept of writing; (4) the disqualification or the limit of the concept of the "real" or "linguistic" context, whose theoretical determination or empirical saturation

are, strictly speaking, rendered impossible or insufficient by writing. (*Margins*, 316; *Marges*, 376)

In addition, as we have seen, a network of structures is produced, which, by definition, cannot be exhausted. The reinscription or recomprehension at issue amounts to the production of a general, as opposed to a restricted, economy of writing, which becomes *writing* in Derrida's sense. This economy transforms and recomprehends a much broader restricted economy, including, as we have seen, specifically the Hegelian dialectic.

The general economy of writing so conceived acquires tremendous theoretical potential and allows one to attach the reconfigurative operator *writing* to other classical denominations. They may be *writing*-speech, *writing*-writing, *writing*-thinking, *writing*-philosophy, *writing*-literature, *writing*-theory, *writing*-criticism, *writing*-reading, *writing*-practice, *writing*-painting, or even *writing*-dancing, as in Mallarmé, where according to Derrida's analysis, all these forms of *writing* participate and interact.[16]

Writing-science and *writing*-mathematics become possible and necessary as well. Derrida relates the question of *writing* to the question of mathematical formalism from the outset of *Of Grammatology*. Mathematical symbolism offers an example of nonphonetic writing, and the possibility of such a writing helps to undermine the metaphysics of presence. For, as follows from the analysis just given, from Socrates to Saussure, logocentrism is always phonocentrism. Such an undermining does, to a degree, take place in Leibniz's project of a universal characteristic, creating a deconstructive stratum of his text. In the same movement, however, Leibniz reinstates the logos, presence, truth, proximity to thinking, in short, everything that is in question in the question of *writing* in Derrida. Thus, this project in turn requires a deconstruction (*Of Grammatology*, 76–81; *Positions*, 35).

Derrida's most important treatment of the question of mathematics is his analysis of Husserl, in his *Introduction* to Husserl's "The Origin of Geometry," although the related discussion of Leibniz and Hegel concerning mathematical formalism remains important, along with comments on mathematical discourse in "White Mythology" (*Margins*). According to Husserl, the origin of geometry is *not* geometry; it is "philosophy" in the general sense of that which thinks on the essentiality of essences; and not all philosophy is truly philosophical in this sense. As Derrida shows, however, this is precisely the kind of claim that Husserl is unable to sustain. It may even be suggested that mathematical logic is more rigorous than any other form of logic, formal or transcendental. Gödel may well be right in stating that "mathematical logic . . . is nothing else but a precise and complete formulation of formal logic" ("Russell's Mathematical Logic," *Philosophy of Mathematics*, 447), and, one might add, perhaps the only precise—fully rigorous—and complete logic available. But, in view of Gödel's theorem, it may not be claimed to be absolutely rigorous—fully precise or (classically) complete—either. Certainly it cannot be liberated from *writing* in Derrida's sense and all that it would imply—the suspension of originary presence and originary truth within the economy of trace, supplement, *writing*, and so forth. This suspension could not be a theoretical or historical deferral to the philosophical, and specifically transcendental (in whatever sense), origin and presence, as in Hegel, Husserl, and Heidegger. There are philosophical genealogies of geometry or mathematics, just as there are mathematical genealogies of philosophy. But there is no fundamentally philosophical origin of geometry or mathematics. Frege, at one point, said:

> Strictly speaking, it is really scandalous that science has not yet clarified the nature of number. It might be excusable that there is still no generally accepted definition of number, if at least there were general agreement on the matter itself. However, science has not even decided on whether number is an assemblage of things, or a figure drawn on the blackboard by the hand of man; whether it is something psychical, about whose generation psychology must give information, or whether it is a logical structure; whether it is created and can vanish, or whether it is eternal. It is not known whether the propositions of arithmetic deal with those structures composed of a calcium carbonate or with non-physical entities. There is as little agreement in this matter as there is regarding the meaning of the word "equal" and the equality sign. Therefore, science does not know the thought content which is attached to its propositions; it does not know what it deals with; it is completely in the dark regarding their proper nature. Isn't this scandalous? [17]

This scandal is the scandal of trace; and the word scandal continuously resurfaces and is used in analogous situations, in relation to the problem of writing, trace, or supplement throughout the history of the metaphysics of presence.[18] Most philosophical or intellectual scandals of the type invoked by Frege are those where one type of *différance* or another would inevitably emerge, for example, the scandal of quantum mechanics. No less than all mathematical writing or thinking, "*merely* a sign that a man's hand traces on the blackboard" is always, always already, *writing* in Derrida's sense; and it entails all that Derrida's *writing* entails. Frege's scandal is, then, the scandal of the irreducible *différance* of mathematical writing, and thus the irreducibility of *writing* within mathematics and within all natural or exact—that is, mathematical—sciences.

CHAPTER 3

From the Quantum

Postulate to Anti-

Epistemology to

Complementarity

**Complementarity and the
General Economy of
the Quantum Postulate**

The principle and then the framework
of complementarity were introduced by
Niels Bohr in the wake of quantum mechanics, or as it is sometimes called, new
quantum theory, developed in the works
of Werner Heisenberg, Max Born, Erwin
Schrödinger, Wolfgang Pauli, Paul Dirac, and others, in contrast to the
old quantum theory, to which Bohr's own earlier theory of the atom
(1913) was a major contribution. Bohr's aim was to account for such
paradoxical features of quantum processes as the wave-particle duality,
the difficulties of simultaneous determination of coordination and causality, and related problems. According to Bohr, complementarity is an
inevitable consequence of the quantum postulate, which introduces an
essential discontinuity or, as Bohr also calls it, individuality in processes
at the subatomic level, or rather in our *representation* of such processes.
The quantum postulate reflects or, as Bohr's puts it, symbolizes a major
experimental finding, perhaps unique in its significance, that has defined
twentieth-century physics—from Planck's, Einstein's, and Bohr's initial
approaches to postmodern physics. Planck's law, the first manifestation
of quantum processes, was, coincidentally, discovered by Max Planck
in 1900.

The quantum postulate makes problematic the application of the strict
causality implied by classical physics and classical meta-physics—*metaphysics*—with which classical physics is complicit. Einstein's view may
manifest this complicity most dramatically and most poignantly in view
of his resistance to quantum mechanics. But this complicity has shaped

the views and the work of a great many, some among the greatest, physicists, beginning with Kepler, or Aristotle. The revolutionary character of Bohr's thinking is defined by his realization that one must abandon both classical physics and classical metaphysics. This radical departure was necessary for a comprehensive account of the situation defined by the quantum postulate—a situation "completely foreign to the classical theories" (*The Philosophical Writings of Niels Bohr* [hereinafter *PWNB*] 1:53).[1] In "The Quantum Postulate and the Recent Development of Atomic Theory" (1927), in which he introduced complementarity, Bohr writes:

> The quantum theory is characterized by the acknowledgment of a fundamental limitation in the classical physical ideas when applied to atomic phenomena. The situation thus created is of a peculiar nature, since our interpretation of the experimental material rests essentially upon the classical concepts. Notwithstanding the difficulties which, hence, are involved in the formulation of the quantum theory, it seems, as we shall see, that its essence may be expressed in the so-called quantum postulate, which attributes to any atomic process an essential discontinuity, or rather individuality, completely foreign to the classical theories and symbolized by Planck's quantum of action. (*PWNB* 1:53)

The concluding formulation is decisive. It suggests that quantum discontinuity, or even complementarity, has only a symbolic character; it is an idealization. This economy redefines the relationships between the concepts of experimental finding and of the product of theorizing, or event and observation, to begin with. As both Bohr and, with a very different attitude, Einstein realized, the consequences of Planck's discovery for both physics and meta-physics and for our whole interpretive and theoretical economy are "far-reaching," revolutionary. According to Bohr:

> This postulate implies a renunciation as regards the causal space-time co-ordination of atomic processes. Indeed, our usual description of physical phenomena is based entirely on the idea that the phenomena concerned may be observed without disturbing them appreciably. . . . Now, the quantum postulate implies that any observation of atomic phenomena will involve an interaction with the agency of observation not to be neglected. Accordingly, *an independent reality in the ordinary physical sense can neither be ascribed to the phenomena nor to the agencies of observation.* After all, the concept of observation is in so far arbitrary as it depends upon which objects are

included in the system to be observed. Ultimately, every observation can, of course, be reduced to our sense perceptions. The circumstance, however, that in interpreting observations use has always to be made of theoretical notions entails that for every particular case it is a question of convenience at which point the concept of observation involving the quantum postulate with its inherent "irrationality" is brought in.

This situation has far-reaching consequences. On one hand, the definition of the state of a physical system, as ordinarily understood, claims the elimination of all external disturbances. But in that case, according to the quantum postulate, any observation will be impossible, and, above all, the concepts of space and time lose their immediate sense. On the other hand, if in order to make observation possible we permit certain interactions with suitable agencies of measurement, not belonging to the system, *an unambiguous definition of the state of the system is naturally no longer possible, and there can be no question of causality in the ordinary sense of the word.* (*PWNB* 1:53–54; emphasis added)

The propositions I stress here—"*an independent reality in the ordinary physical sense can neither be ascribed to the phenomena nor to the agencies of observation,*" and, as a result, "*an unambiguous definition of the state of the system is naturally no longer possible, and there can be no question of causality in the ordinary sense of the word*"—may be seen as the central anti-epistemological implications of quantum mechanics as understood by Bohr. I shall explore various aspects and implications of Bohr's extraordinary formulations throughout this study. For the moment, I shall follow Bohr's elaborations in the essay cited, proceeding from the *quantum postulate* to *anti-epistemology* to *complementarity* and connecting all three.

It is from the propositions just cited that Bohr derives his arguably most refined formulation of complementarity: "The very nature of the quantum theory thus forces us to regard the space-time co-ordination and the claim of causality, the union of which characterizes the classical theories as complementary but exclusive features of the description, symbolizing the idealization of observation and definition respectively. . . . [I]n the description of atomic phenomena, the quantum postulate presents us with the task of developing a 'complementarity' theory the consistency of which can be judged only by weighing the possibilities of definition and observation" (*PWNB* 1:54–55).

Similar relationships characterize other complementarities of quantum theory, such as waves and particles, or continuous and discontinuous processes:

> The two views of the nature of light are . . . to be considered as different attempts at an interpretation of experimental evidence in which the limitation of the classical concepts is expressed in complementary ways.
>
> The problem of the nature of the constituents of matter presents us with an analogous situation. The individuality of the elementary electrical corpuscles is forced upon us by general evidence. Nevertheless, recent experience, above all the discovery of the selective reflection of electrons from metal crystals, requires the use of the wave theory superposition principle in accordance with the original ideas of L[ouis] de Broglie. Just as in the case of light, we have consequently in the question of the nature of matter, so far as we adhere to classical concepts, to face an inevitable dilemma which has to be regarded as the very expression of experimental evidence. In fact, here again we are not dealing with contradictory but with complementary pictures of the phenomena, which only together offer a natural generalization of the classical mode of description. In the discussion of these questions, it must be kept in mind that, according to the view taken above, radiation in free space as well as isolated material particles are abstractions, their properties on the quantum theory being definable and observable only through their interaction with other systems. Nevertheless, these abstractions are, as we shall see, indispensable for a a description of experience in connection with our ordinary space-time view. (*PWNB* 1:56–57)

Wave-particle complementarity is, thus, defined in anti-epistemological terms, again by fundamentally relating it to the experimental arrangements in which specific observations are made and specific questions are asked concerning a given quantum system. The latter feature and, more generally, the question of the relationships between the object and the measuring instruments becomes crucial to Bohr's approach.

Complementarity appears to have been introduced by Bohr in response to the wave-particle *duality*, which becomes the wave-particle complementarity in his framework. The discovery of the wave-particle duality by Einstein, in the case of light, and by de Broglie, in the case of particles, preceded the introduction of Heisenberg's and then Schrödinger's quantum mechanics in 1925 and uncertainty relations in 1927.[2] As we have just seen, however, the quantum postulate and the problem of causality that it poses were crucial to Bohr's thinking from 1913 on and thus to the genesis of complementarity. The complementarity of coordination and causality, which results from these considerations, appears to be the most fundamental for Bohr's matrix. As correlative to Heisenberg's uncertainty relations, it also enables the continuing consistency between all physics available so far and complementarity as a framework. The key complementary features are clearly present in Bohr's formulation of the wave-particle complementarity.[3] Bohr himself does not seem to have considered in detail the interconnections between two complementarities, although some suggestions concerning these interconnections can be found in his works.[4] Within the quantum mechanical formalism, the wave-particle complementarity can be interpreted as a manifestation of quantum anticausality and of the complementarity of coordination and causality. This interpretation is made possible by Max Born's interpretation of Schrödinger's wave-function as mapping the probability-distribution defining statistical predictions of quantum mechanics. This interpretation suspends the physical significance of quantum waves, and Bohr appears to have accepted it all along.[5] The wave-picture remains for Bohr an idealized visualization, related in a complex way to observed traces and their efficacity. Bohr's overall view implies that neither wave nor particle picture has a realistic significance.[6]

Neither the wave-particle complementarity nor the kinematic-dynamic complementarity nor the complementarity of coordination and causality nor any other complementarity, however, appears to be seen by Bohr as *causing* other complementarities. Specific complementarities form instead an interacting ensemble within the overall matrix. They become effects, whose efficacity cannot be conceived in classical causal terms, or perhaps in any terms. Whatever is observed can be understood only in terms of effects without classical causes—whether open or hidden, interpretable or uninterpretable, nameable or unnameable. Bohr appears at times to use the term 'effect' in this sense, in speaking, for example, of "the individuality of the typical quantum effects" or of "observable effects obtainable by a definitive experimental arrangment" (*PWNB* 2:40, 57). Bohr defines all specific complementary relations and his framework as a whole by means of the same (general) economy. This economy is fundamentally conditioned by the irreducible dependence of quantum processes on the experimental arrangements, where quantum effects are observed, and the mathematical formalism—in particular, uncertainty relations—that accounts for them.

The complementarity of coordination and causality is correlative to the kinematic-dynamic complementarity, the complementarity of position and momentum, and to quantum mechanical indeterminacy and Heisenberg's uncertainty relations. The latter are a mathematical expression of the limits on the possibility of *simultaneous* exact measurement of complementary or, in terms of the quantum mechanical formalism, conjugate variables—such as position and momentum, or time and energy. In the mathematical formalism of quantum mechanics, all such variables—'observables,' as they are also called—are represented by mathematical symbols called operators (in a Hilbert space)—P (momentum), Q (coordinate), T (time), and so forth—to which standard mathematical operations, such as addition and multiplication, can be assigned. The state of a quantum system at a given point is described by another mathematical object in a Hilbert space, associated with the system, the so-called state vector. Numerical values of observables can then be calculated and its state described or determined, including determined as undetermined. For the peculiar feature of this formalism is that the multiplication of such operators do, in general, not commute—PQ may not, and usually does not, equal QP. This noncommutativity represents the fact that corresponding operators cannot be applied and corresponding variables or observables—such as momentum or position—measured or determined, or even be defined simultaneously. It is important that complementarity and uncertainty relations limit only a *simultaneous joint* measurement, applicability and definability of complementary features within the *same* experimental arrangement. Either variable by itself can be measured with full precision (available to us) and be well-defined at any given point. In contrast to classical theories, however, at no point can the values of both variables be measured with full precision. Therefore variables themselves cannot be *simultaneously* well-defined; for, according to Bohr, in quantum mechanics only that which can be measured can be considered well-defined. This impossibility prevents one from defining a physical state of a particle at any point in the way the classical theory would do. Furthermore, it disallows the claim that a particle can have a well-defined state at any point—a state that possesses properties, whether such properties are conceived of as overt or hidden, or as ones that can or cannot be measured, fully or approximately, statistically. Once one returns to classical limits, the formalism can be adjusted accordingly, and the problem of simultaneous observation and measurement does not arise. Quantitatively, uncertainty relations establish precisely these limits.

Uncertainty relations and the mathematical formalism that produces them allow for and have received a variety of physical and meta-physical interpretations, including with respect to the very terms uncertainty and indeterminacy. The interpretations defined by the formalism just considered are sometimes assembled under the rubric of orthodox interpretation, which can be juxtaposed to other interpretations of the experimental results at issue in quantum mechanics, such as, for example, hidden variables interpretations. Even within the orthodox interpretation differences may arise in view of other features introduced in a given interpretation consistent with orthodox mathematical formalism. One can, in principle, define orthodox interpretation simply by associating the formalism just described with every quantum system considered. Bohr's interpretation—complementarity—is much richer in this respect. It is, however, fully consistent with orthodox formalism. According to Bohr, "an adequate tool for a complementary way of description is offered precisely by the quantum-mechanical formalism" (*PWNB* 2:40).

Under the conditions of quantum mechanics, then, momentum and position not only cannot be measured simultaneously, but corresponding variables cannot be observed simultaneously or even unambiguously defined so as to be applied simultaneously. This impossibility would prohibit "the definition of the state of a physical system, as ordinarily understood." The point is central to Bohr's argument against Einstein, particularly in his analysis of the Einstein-Podolsky-Rosen (EPR) argument. As Bohr stresses throughout his writing, the impossibility at issue arises by virtue of the irreducible interactions between the object and the measuring instruments. This irreducibility is reflected in the formalism of quantum mechanics and uncertainty relations, which cannot meaningfully apply independently of considering these interactions. As Bohr writes:

> These circumstances [of the irreducible interaction between the object and the measuring instruments] find quantitative expression in Heisenberg's indeterminacy relations which specify the reciprocal latitude for the fixation, in quantum mechanics, of kinematical [position] and dynamical [momentum] variables required for the definition of the state of a system in classical mechanics. In fact, the limited commutability of the symbols by which such variables are represented in the quantal formalism corresponds to the mutual exclusion of the experimental arrangements required for their unambiguous definition. In this context, we are of course not concerned with a restriction as to the accuracy of measurement, but with a limitation

of the well-defined application of space-time concepts and dynami-
cal conservation laws, entailed by the necessary distinction between
measuring instruments and atomic objects. (*PWNB* 3:5)

The final sentence and particularly Bohr's "of course" are rather striking. The point, however, is logical, even inevitable, if seen, as it must
be, as reflecting the fact that quantum indeterminacy is structural, irreducible. This indeterminacy, that is, cannot be seen as giving partial,
statistical information about some complete system hidden from quantum measurements or as implying a concept of reality independent of
observation, interpretation, or theory; or, by implication of mathematico-
technological and socio-political conditions under which physics operates. In quantum mechanics, one must always deal with the fact that irreducible, irrecoverable losses in the representation of the behavior of
quantum systems do take place and that one must relate both one's interpretation and theory to these losses, which can only be done by means
of general economy. In Bohr's theory this situation leads to a radical
reconsideration of the concepts of observation, measurement, and interpretation under quantum conditions. The relationships between description and event and the very notions, classically conceived, of 'event'
or 'object' and of description and interpretation are subjected to a radical deconstruction and reinterpretation. This reinterpretation makes description and event in turn reciprocal and complementary. Quantum
events become the effects of efficacity without causes, or without *classical*
causes, except when we return to classical limits. This efficacity makes
a corresponding theoretical economy a general economy. I again use
the term "efficacity," in contrast to "efficacy," to designate the dynamics which suspends or better redelimit classical causality, while allowing
one to retain necessary classical "effects." "Efficacity" itself is a metaphor designed to undermine traditional philosophemes that might be
employed here.

Bohr offers many brilliant and precise formulations together with a
general framework that extends well beyond the domain of quantum
physics. He speaks of the "epistemological lesson" of quantum mechanics, although "anti-epistemological lesson" may be a better phrase; the
implications of these designations will be developed in the course of this
study. The meaning, or rather framework, of complementarity as conceived by Bohr is as broad as it is profound and revolutionary in its implications, both in the field of physics itself and in more general conceptual

and metaphoric terms. Complementarity can be extended into theoretical aspects of the humanities and social sciences. One needs, however, to develop it more comprehensively than Bohr does in his attempts (it is true, very preliminary) to apply complementarity elsewhere. One might say that one should do so more in the spirit—and the letter[7]—of complementarity as practiced by Bohr in his physics and his meta-physics as anti-epistemology—a general economy of physics.

Extensions

As Abraham Pais observes, "Complementarity can be formulated without explicit reference to physics, to wit, as two aspects of a description that are mutually exclusive yet both necessary for a full understanding of what is to be described." He adds, "Personally, I found the complementary way of thinking liberating" (*Niels Bohr's Times*, 24). The goal of this section is to introduce a broader understanding of complementarity, extending Bohr's ideas and the principles of general economy.

According to this understanding, a complementarity theory must employ diverse—and at times conflicting or mutually incompatible (particularly from the classical perspective)—configurations, double or multiple, operative within the same framework, but without lending themselves to a full synthesis, Hegelian or other. Such a matrix entails introducing and accounting for both heterogeneous and interactive operations of pairs or clusters of concepts, metaphors, or of conceptual and metaphoric networks. Complementary relations emerging in the process may, as I have suggested, be described as heterogeneously interactive and interactively heterogeneous: at times making their constituents act jointly, at times complementarily, at times conflicting with or inhibiting each other, at times mutually exclusive; but never allowing for a full synthesis. Local economies of synthesis must be engaged.

Complementarity, in this extended sense, entails a multiple parallel processing of terms, concepts, metaphors, problems, texts, frameworks, or even fields. I borrow the latter metaphor from modern computer technology, where the term 'parallel processing' refers to the systems—software and hardware—that allow one to process multiple data and solve many problems simultaneously. Such data and problems may or may not be related to each other; and systems of that type are designed primarily to solve problems arising in processing heterogeneous information and tasks. But such systems also allow one to solve mathematical problems whose complexity makes their sequential processing impossible and demands multilinear arrangements of the data and procedures involved. In the present context, 'parallel processing' refers to the concurrent consideration of concepts, metaphors, or frameworks always necessary under the joint conditions of general economy and complementarity.

The complementary functioning can thus be extended to any conjunction or clustering, either double or multiple, of terms and concepts, or as in Derrida, neither terms nor concepts. Many complementarities addressed by this study relate to the efficacities that cannot be seen as concepts in any of the classical senses of this term (such as Hegel's or Saussure's) and are irreducibly distanced, via *différance* or otherwise. Such complementarities, and at a certain level perhaps all complementarities, become complementarities of complementarities.

The relationships between Bohr's complementarity as a quantum mechanical general economy and broader interpretive, theoretical, social, or historical general economic paradigms, such as those explored by Nietzsche, Bataille, and Derrida, can be both metaphoric and metonymic. On the one hand, Bohr's complementarity provides a metaphoric model that can be effectively utilized elsewhere. On the other hand, the complementary general economy of matter emerging in quantum mechanics generates powerful, if highly mediated, constraints on general economic theories. Insofar, however, as any specific articulation of such constraints is concerned—or insofar as one can speak of constraints or use any name or concept—a certain generalized metaphoricity remains, as we have seen, irreducible.

The economy of complementarity may, as I said, be extended to entire theoretical matrices or fields, or other broader forms of enclosure. Such an extension is actually inevitable, although it may be only implicit in a given case; for no term or concept can exist otherwise than as inserted into a given conceptual chain or matrix, and often into networks of matrices or fields that are complementary in the present sense. One can, therefore, and often must, employ the complementarity of interpretation and history, history and theory, theory and literature, and so forth, or their multiple complementary conjunctions.

The complementary functioning may often be simultaneous, but, as I stressed, it does not proceed, at least not always, by way of synthesis or within a uniformly or globally controlled system or process, or system-process, as in Hegel. In David Bohm's formulation, "a given system is capable, in principle, of demonstrating an infinite variety of properties that cannot all exist in simultaneously well-defined forms . . . [and] is potentially capable of an endless variety of transformations in which the old categories figuratively dissolve, to be replaced by new categories that cut across the old ones" (*Quantum Theory*, 160–61). One can in fact no longer speak of one system either.[8]

Within the scheme just delineated, complementary constituents are not always mutually exclusive, as in Bohr's definition cited earlier. At a certain level, however, the same is the case in Bohr's complementarity, viewed as a general matrix and overall interpretation of quantum physics. Particles and waves, or coordination and causality, are concepts or idealizations that must, under certain conditions, be used jointly. They are multiply complementary in the present sense.

Complementarities themselves may be as often multiple as paired, which may well be the case with different and multiply related complementary pairs in quantum mechanics—such as waves and particles, continuity and discontinuity, or causality—all of which multiply interact, although, in this case, they are still organized through dualities. In general, however, complementary relationships may be extended into triple or more multiple configurations, some of which cannot be controlled by dualities. This complementary multiplicity allows one to exceed the binary without uncritically dispensing with it or ignoring its extraordinary resources. Complementarity is a very broadly conceived interconnectivity, except that it equally implies, under certain conditions, the possibility of mutual exclusivity, conflictuality, irreconcilable features of description, and other forms of discontinuity, both from without and from within.

As in Bohr, complementarity itself as understood here functions as a matrix—a theoretical economy—whose constituents may, and at a certain level must, include matrices and frameworks, or other complementarities and complementarities of complementarities. This economy is a general economy, while, conversely, general economies in turn continually develop and deploy complementary configurations. Bohr's complementarity as matrix and general economy demand each other and may be said to be parts of the same economy, were it not for the fact that such an economy can never be the same. It is never identical to itself; and is the same only as a certain *différance*, a household—*oikonomia*, economy in Greek—that is always divided against, or is always complementary, to itself. In this sense, complementarity and general economy are not complementary: they always operate together. One can credit Bohr with introducing general economy in the field of science, which defines his difference from Einstein—or perhaps his *différance* from Einstein. For, on the one hand, their views are not without some commonalities, and, on the other, both philosophies are not without being divided against themselves. It is only that, divided against itself, Einstein's house falls and, complementary to itself, Bohr's stands, in part because Bohr's house is built upon this self-division or self-complementarity.

Interconnections

This study argues for the general economic character of quantum mechanical complementarity understood as a general framework.[9] This argument, however, continuously involves other general economies. Such a joint or complementary approach allows one to explore more effectively the relationships between different general economies and to develop new general economic and complementary configurations. Bohr's matrix and strategies themselves offer rich metaphorical possibilities for general economies, which often engage complementary procedures, extending them to parallel processing of different theories and fields.

 In part, the approach taken by this study is necessitated by the fact that the genealogy of the models at issue is itself mixed. The nonscientific models considered here have scientific lines of descent, while the scientific models trace some of their lineage to literature and art, philosophy, psychology, and still other fields. The genealogy of Bohr's complementarity would offer an extraordinary example of this complementary genealogy. Bohr's initial interests were in psychological epistemology, and these efforts already contain ideas suggestive of those that would later constitute the architectonics of complementarity. Beyond Kant, Hegel, Kierkegaard, William James, Harald Høffding, and other philosophical connections, one can suggest interactive links to Nietzsche and Freud, on the one hand, and to modern science and mathematics, such as Bernhard Riemann's ideas, on the other. An elaboration of these connections would require an historical analysis on a much broader scale than the limits of this study permit. It becomes clear, however, that this history, or any history, requires a general economic and complementary model and, specifically, a complementarity of historical and theoretical analyses.[10] The present discussion concentrates on theoretical interactions among the fields at issue. This theoretical analysis, however, cannot avoid—no analysis of that type can—its complementary historical counterparts.

Constrained by physics and rigorously taking its constraints into account in his meta-physics—his philosophy or anti-philosophy of nature—Bohr arrived at a theoretical economy radically undermining all previous philosophies of nature. This is why his matrix not only offers a rich and effective metaphorical model, but also establishes powerful, if mediated, constraints, especially insofar as the general economy of matter is concerned. These two functions, metaphorical and constraining, are interactive: first, the constraints at issue themselves give a theory the character of general economy and complementarity; and second, as a metaphorical model, wherever applied, complementarity is also constraining. Such is in fact always the case, however productive a given model may be. Conversely, constraints may be as enabling as they are inhibiting. Thus, from their introduction to the present, uncertainty relations have proven to be extremely productive constraints, generating positive propositions, often of great importance. Indeterminacy has been used as a versatile tool for theoretical construction: it constrains and inhibits, but also produces new configurations. It is worth pointing out, however, that quantum physics does not consist of uncertainty relations alone. There are plenty of equations, descriptions, and "pictures" beyond indeterminacy.

Most major literature on Bohr and on quantum mechanics, particularly more recent studies, would allow for many claims advanced by this study, even though this literature does not always explore, and often resists the anti-epistemological implications of Bohr's ideas, in part because it customarily reads Bohr from epistemological, restricted-economic perspectives. The situation is, of course, not uncommon elsewhere. The oscillations between epistemological—restricted economic—and anti-epistemological—general economic—forces and the textual stratifications they produce are found throughout the history of the metaphysics of presence, whether in primary texts or commentaries. These oscillations make the deconstruction of the metaphysics of presence possible both inside and outside the text of philosophy. According to Derrida, in view of the closure of metaphysics, such interactions between epistemological and anti-epistemological strata are unavoidable also within an anti-epistemological or deconstructive discourse, although the latter, naturally, entails a different balance of such strata. This balance, while, in the end, always anti-epistemological, is not simple or always unequivocal in Bohr either. This complexity is, in part, responsible for the double —epistemological and anti-epistemological—stratifications of commentaries on Bohr, although the epistemologies extraneous to Bohr play, I think, a more decisive role in a classical reenclosure of Bohr's complementarity in most commentaries. One encounters oscillations between anti-epistemological and epistemological possibilities in most treatments of Bohr and quantum mechanics, specifically in four recent full-scale studies of Bohr—by John Honner, Dugald Murdoch, Henry Folse, and Jan Faye. It may be useful to comment briefly on these studies from this perspective.

Thus, John Honner's *The Description of Nature: Niels Bohr and the Philosophy of Quantum Physics* (1987) correctly identifies many key ingredients of Bohr's logic of the complementary, which are presented within what he sees as Bohr's "transcendental philosophy." Honner uses the term 'transcendental' in a Kantian or post-Kantian sense, considered earlier, as, in Honner's words, "signify[ing] a concern with the necessary conditions of the possibility of experiential knowledge, which includes unambiguous reports of that knowledge" (13). One cannot, in principle, object to this formulation, insofar as it reflects Bohr's understanding that quantum mechanics redefines the conditions of possibility, necessity, and limits of physical and meta-physical knowledge. Nor can one ignore Kant's and other classical contributions to posing, within the classical limits, the question of the conditions and the limits of the possibility of knowledge. It was, interestingly, Nietzsche—the sharpest and the most uncompromising critic of Kant—who offered perhaps the most astute description of this contribution in his comments on Kant and causality (an issue, interestingly, not considered by Honner). As Nietzsche writes: "Let us recall, . . . *Kant's* tremendous question mark that he placed after the concept of 'causality'—without, like Hume, doubting its legitimacy altogether. Rather, Kant began cautiously to delimit the realm within which this concept makes sense (and to this day we are not done with this fixing of limits)" (*The Gay Science*, 305; *KSA* 3:598: translation modified). Causality is the site of Bohr's, or Nietzsche's own, even more tremendous question mark. Nietzsche's, Bohr's, and other anti-epistemologies explore and redelimit causality and epistemology far deeper and more fundamentally than Kant or philosophy has ever done. They do so, let me stress, not by arbitrarily renouncing classical theories, but instead by giving them new significance. Bohr in fact sees complementarity "as a rational generalization of the very ideal of causality" (*PWNB* 2:41).

Much closer to Nietzsche's, Bataille's, and Derrida's anti-epistemologies, Bohr's economy of the conditions of the possibilities and limits

at issue, and specifically of causality, is so different from Kant's philosophy—or Hegel's, Husserl's, Heidegger's, or other transcendental or
post-transcendental philosophies—that the comparison with Kant, while
possible and often made in literature on Bohr, nearly loses its meaning.
Bohr's is anti-epistemological—general-economic—as opposed to epistemological or—restricted-economic—questioning of the conditions of
the possibility and of the concepts of knowledge and experience. Specifically, Kant's economy does entail the possibility, first, of a totality of
the conditions of experience and knowledge and, secondly, of the transcendental object behind the phenomenon, as opposed to a general economic efficacity of the phenomenon. Both of these—totality and the transcendental object—are prohibited by Bohr's (general) economy. Kant's
choice of the term 'transcendental' is not accidental; and Kant defines
specific types of the conditions of the possibility of knowledge and experience, and of experience and knowledge themselves. As a result Kantian
transcendentality is, as I indicated earlier, irreducibly metaphysical—a
form of the metaphysics of presence, which cannot be subtracted from
the Kantian economy. It would be just as unacceptable to Bohr, as it is to
Nietzsche. As Faye points out, Bohr in fact associates this Kantian claim
with Einstein's views, specifically in the context of the EPR argument:
"Einstein 'simply took the view of old-fashion philosophy, took the view
of Kant'" (*Niels Bohr*, xix).[11] The very choice of the term 'transcendental'
is ineffective in view of its history and its other connotations, even though
Honner does specify it so as to avoid some possible confusions. Honner
also points out that one cannot identify Bohr's and Kant's views. Honner's reading itself, however, displaces Bohr's *anti*-epistemology toward
Kant's transcendental *epistemology* and other classical epistemologies. In
this sense his term "transcendental philosophy" is in accord with his interpretation. The interpretation itself, however, becomes problematic as a
result. Honner ends up by inferring, untenably, from Bohr's propositions
a physical reality as a Kantian transcendental object.

Equally problematic is Honner's appeal to holism, although Bohr's is
claimed to be a case of "moderate holism" (14–22), which does not make
the claim any less problematic. Honner favorably compares such moderate holism to Richard Rorty's "thoroughgoing holism," which he finds
too radical (17–21, 170–72, 187–89). In fact Honner would have done
well to consider Rorty's critique of the transcendental argument.[12] If anything, Bohr's anti-epistemology is more radical than Rorty's. Honner's

association of Bohr's ideas with those of Habermas and his "transcendental defence of reality" (20) is particularly problematic and misses the radical character of Bohr's thinking.

This epistemological or restricted-economic, as opposed to anti-epistemological, re-framing of Bohr's ideas results in a number of claims made by Honner that cannot, I think, be compatible with Bohr's complementarity as anti-epistemology—such as, to cite just a few, "the asymptotic convergence of theory and reality" (17, 21) or the very concept of reality (or equally the metaphysical concept of truth) reintroduced by Honner; Bohr's alleged belief "in infinite and eternal harmony [or coherence] in nature," to which "science is moving towards [asymptotically], if never arriving at" (21) and the resulting claims of proximity to Einstein (221–22); an emphasis, pronounced throughout the book, on "unity-in-difference" (rather than, which would be much more to the point, difference-in-unity), bringing complementarity closer to Einstein. In short, Honner finally re-encloses Bohr's vision within classical, and indeed transcendental, epistemology.

In his *Niels Bohr's Philosophy of Physics* (1987), while recognizing Bohr's contribution and effectively rendering many of Bohr's positions, Dugald Murdoch finally philosophically sides with Einstein, or certainly closer to Einstein than to Bohr (236–58). Murdoch rejects most key aspects of Bohr's "philosophy of physics"—in a way rightly, for Bohr's thinking is neither a philosophy of physics nor a philosophy in general, in the sense Murdoch understands it—again rightly, for this is how philosophy has for the most part understood itself throughout its history. Murdoch's philosophical view may well be responsible for some of the more problematic aspects of his reading of Bohr, for example, his claim that Bohr held that "successful observation or measurement reveals the objective, preexisting value of an observable" (107).

Henry Folse's reading of Bohr in *The Philosophy of Niels Bohr: The Framework of Complementarity* (1985) does not appear to claim any philosophical position from which Bohr's philosophy is read or evaluated. Folse does not read Bohr in anti-epistemological terms, although his reading, at certain points, comes close to general economy. Folse, however, diminishes the radical implications of Bohr's anti-epistemology when he invokes "the *reality* of the system considered as an object existing independently of observational interaction" (*Philosophy of Niels Bohr*, 151), which is similar, although not identical, to Murdoch's claim. This and surrounding claims cannot, I think, be sustained, and Folse's analysis at its best need not rely on them. It appears that this claim results not from metaphysical necessity but from his critically motivated attempt to argue against idealist, phenomenological, or positivist interpretations of Bohr. Folse appears to sense something like a (general-economic) radical alterity in Bohr, but he does not follow this idea to the point where it becomes apparent that one cannot under these conditions reintroduce, as he does, the economy of reality independent of observational interaction.

In his *Niels Bohr: His Heritage and Legacy: An Anti-Realist View of Quantum Mechanics* (1991), Jan Faye criticizes Folse's interpretation on similar grounds (*Niels Bohr*, 203–11), in part by pointing out changes of Bohr's view in the wake of the EPR argument, not sufficiently considered by Folse. Faye also offers a criticism of Murdoch's metaphysical claims concerning Bohr's epistemology (229–30). In some of its aspects, Faye's interpretation is consistent with the present reading, particularly insofar as Bohr's antirealism is seen by Faye as "den[ying] the realist idea that the aim of quantum mechanics (or of any other physical theory) is to explain the phenomena [in Bohr's sense of the term] in terms of an underlying, hypothetical reality" (217). Faye, too, however, reintroduced what may be seen as metaphysical determinations into Bohr's views (225–36), which prevents him from exploring general economic dimensions of Bohr's matrix. He assigns Bohr "a form of [objective] anti-realism which [he is] attributing to Høffding" (216). Faye shows that Bohr's interactions with Høffding were extensive, especially during the genesis of complementarity. He considers Høffding's ideas and his reaction to complementarity, which influenced Høffding's later work. Høffding, I think, reads complementarity epistemologically rather than anti-epistemologically. In my view, Bohr's complementarity entail a far more radical revision of classical philosophy than anything Høffding ever approaches. Faye's reading diminishes the anti-epistemological potential of Bohr's matrix by bringing it too close to Høffding.

Finally, Faye reintroduces the notion of "an objective reality" (236). The latter is defined and does function against other forms of realism— such as, antipositivist, or antiphenomenological, forms of empiricist or scientific (physical or mathematical) objectivist realism—found in interpretations of Bohr and of quantum mechanics itself. But it in turn reinstates a metaphysical, and specifically phenomenological, restricted economy. This economy could be seen, in terms defined earlier, as an unproblematized reversal of scientific or empiricist realism or objectivism. One could argue that the resulting concepts of objectivity and truth, and, as a result, Faye's interpretation of complementarity as a whole are closer to Husserl's phenomenology than to Bohr's anti-epistemology. One would need instead mutually to deconstruct and exceed both types of the metaphysics of presence along the lines of Derrida's analysis as considered earlier. A radical alterity—the alterity inaccessible to philosophical oppositions—is missing from Faye's analysis. Even when Faye considers the elements of Bohr's anti-epistemology, they are still described in terms of classical epistemological and ontological predicates, such as "an object in itself" (235). These predicates are never quite taken by Faye to the points where they can be used against each other in the deconstructive or anti-epistemological registers. These predicates and the fields they define are, however, so deconstructed by Bohr.

In fact, most, perhaps all analyses of Bohr so far, appear to rely on and, in contrast to Bohr himself (in the present reading), to ground their reading in classical epistemology or ontology of one type or another, rather than to deconstruct them, for example, by using various forms of the metaphysics of presence against each other. As shall be seen, Bohr's usage of classical concepts, such as 'reality' and 'phenomenon' conforms to this deconstructive (general) economy. The fact that Bohr does use such terms and concepts cannot, therefore, be used against the claims advanced by the present reading of Bohr, if one takes into account the radical displacement to which Bohr subjects classical concepts within the complementary field he introduces. The failure to take this displacement fully into account is one of the reasons why most of the treatments of complementarity resist or fall short of Bohr's anti-epistemology.

It may well be that the power of classical epistemology—or ontology, phenomenology, and other forms of the metaphysics of presence—has been more dominant in fields where Bohr's philosophy (rather than physics) have been studied. The metaphysics of presence is the product of the history and institution of philosophy, even though it extends its functioning and power well beyond philosophy, specifically to modern or even postmodern science.[13] That (some) physicists are constrained more by physics than epistemology may allow one to ignore or to transgress its limits, as Bohr did. But, then, physics easily offers many contrary examples as well, beginning with Einstein, although Einstein is hardly a beginning. Anti-epistemological ideas are, conversely, found elsewhere than in science, beginning with Nietzsche—and this may well be something like a beginning, to the degree that beginnings are possible.

Quantum mechanics offers a broad spectrum of interpretive possibilities, and I shall comment on some of them throughout this study. It goes (almost) without saying that in the anti-epistemological field, the very difference between a given data or mathematical formalism (or a theory) and its interpretation can only be provisional or conditional. Neither of them can exist in itself or by itself, independently of an interpretation, any more than quantum objects can in Bohr's anti-epistemology. These conditions, however, do not eliminate the possibility of—and the necessity of accounting for—differences between specific interpretations, perspective, or positions. One must do so, however, anti-epistemologically— general economically—rather than by means of one restricted economy or another, which would do so, for example, by unconditionally separating reality, truth, theory, or text from interpretation. The situation in quantum mechanics is not different, *in principle,* from that which one encounters in the spectrum of reading of other historico-theoretical junctures (in either direction, toward or against metaphysics), such as in the cases of Nietzsche, Bataille, or Derrida, or Hegel, Marx, or Heidegger. *In practice,* of course, there are important differences. For experimental data and mathematical formalism make it possible to maintain different interpretations simultaneously; and insofar as their functioning in physics is concerned, there are no differences among the relevant results of Heisenberg, Schrödinger, Dirac, or Bohr.

The *relative* insignificance of such differences allows one to speak of the orthodox interpretation as considered earlier, or, sometimes simultaneously, of "the Copenhagen interpretation," in part as a tribute to Bohr. These designations are imprecise, however, amalgamating at times quite different physical and meta-physical interpretations, such as Born's, Heisenberg's, Pauli's, Wigner's, and still others.[14] It would be more precise to speak of mathematically-experimentally equivalent interpretations, which are equally constrained by interactively experimental data and a given mathematical formalism, such as uncertainty relations. Many of the meta-physical consequences derived, often uncritically, from this equivalence would not follow, however; and not all meta-physics can be seen as consistent with physics. Bohr's complementarity did not initially receive much attention among his fellow physicists partly because it did not introduce any new mathematical formalism or derive any new physical consequences of quantum data. Einstein, however, reacted immediately. He sensed the momentous significance of both quantum physics and Bohr's interpretation. It was the end of the classical era in physics and meta-physics alike; and that nature or matter itself (if one could still speak of either) behaved so strangely has had, and continues to have, a profound impact on modern intellectual history across different fields—be it science and mathematics, the history and sociology of science, the philosophy of science, philosophy, or critical theory, or literature and art—and their interactions.

Bohr's own orientation appears to have been strongly pragmatic, insofar as physics was concerned. As Murdoch writes: "Bohr was agreeing [with Philipp Frank] that whether or not electrons have such conjunctive property [simultaneously existing position and momentum] (even though we cannot measure it) is a metaphysical question in the pejorative sense which positivists are wont to give this term, that is, it is a vacuous question, devoid of factual content since an affirmative answer has no practical consequences. The basis of Bohr's agreement with Frank, however, was not positivism [like Frank's], but pragmatism" (*Niels Bohr's Philosophy*, 235). Murdoch offers an important qualification: "[T]he foundation of Bohr's instrumentalist realism is pragmatism, and a pragmatism, it is important to stress, of a sort that is weaker than the very forthright doctrine of James" (232).[15] One must equally distinguish various positivist or logical-empiricist positions, which suspend or claim to suspend metaphysical concerns and presuppositions, within the Copenhagen interpretation—such as Born's, Pauli's, Jordan's, Wigner's, or Heisenberg's (to the degree that the rubric applied in all these cases). For these positions do have pragmatist—or realist or idealist—dimensions. These terms themselves can shift their meaning, although positivism or logical empiricism often functions as an uncritical reversal that reinstates metaphysics rather than transgresses it. One would need a specific analysis of a given case in order to make strong claims to that effect. It would not be possible to consider here the cases and different readings of major figures involved. The differences in their philosophical positions have been extensively discussed by these physicists themselves and by commentators. In particular, Heisenberg's views of quantum theory, which evolved during his long career, would require a separate discussion.[16] Bohr's position is different from those of all the figures just mentioned, and it remains the only radical anti-epistemology of quantum mechanics. It may be defined as a general economic pragmatism. At one point, Derrida invokes "*pragrammatological*" analysis, "at the intersection of a pragmatics and a grammatology" ("My Chances/Mes Chances," *Taking Chances*, 27), to which Bohr's attitude and practice are very close.

Bohr's meta-physical conclusions are always grounded in experimental evidence, even though the very concept, as classically understood, of experimental evidence (or of grounding and fundamentality) is fundamentally undermined by Bohr's and other anti-epistemologies. Bohr's meta-physics, however, is as much experimentally grounded as any other and more so than most. Physics, one might say, constrains Bohr into both complementarity and a general economy; and while the practice of physics may not depend on a given meta-physics, that does not mean that all meta-physics is consistent with physics. Pragmatics appears to lead to a general economy, no less in physics than elsewhere. As Murdoch suggests: "Someone who holds a more realist theory of models [Murdoch's own position] would find Bohr's practice very unsatisfactory, for the complementary use of the dual models provides no intelligible conception of the real nature of electron at all; indeed it makes its nature highly mysterious. Adopting a pragmatist approach, however, Bohr is content, since the complementary use of disparate models is logically consistent and enables *all* empirical data to be subsumed" (232).

The last proposition is to the point. It is, however, the "conception of *the real nature* of electron," or of "real nature," that was problematic for Bohr (and "content" is hardly a word to describe Bohr's attitude). It became problematic not only because it is questionable in the domain of meta-physics rather than physics, but also because for Bohr physics itself prohibits it. This is why "realism" is no more an effective rubric to describe Bohr's attitude than is idealism or positivism. Of course, the conditions do exist that lead to the (metaphysical) concepts of reality, some of whose features may need to be retained and have been retained in Bohr's matrix.

The practice of physics itself may or may not be affected by the difference in meta-physical positions. We do have, however, in Bohr's complementarity, an interpretation that is reasonably free of the metaphysical assumptions characterizing its rival interpretations and that is fully compatible with experimental data and mathematical formalism of quantum physics. To apply Occam's Razor: to the degree that we can avoid metaphysical assumptions or consequences, and metaphysical (restricted) economies, we should avoid them, in part because they have proven ineffective just about everywhere else. Of course, since the economy of Occam's principle must itself be refigured as a general economy, the minimality of such conditions becomes a complex issue, as does the very designation "we."

The interaction between Bohr's complementarity and general economy remains an extraordinary example of the relationships between the natural and human sciences, both by virtue of the multiple traffic between them and by virtue of the analogous responses and analogous problems emerging in different fields.[17] It remains important to keep in mind the metaphorical status of all parallels thus suggested. Applicability of such parallels is limited and the economy of transfer of metaphorical models or constraints from one field to another is complex. Such differences and their demarcations are, of course, never unconditional. They are subject to a complex interplay of boundaries, internal and external. Modern science multiply affects the social and human sciences, or literature and art; and is in turn affected by these fields. For psychological, cultural, and political reasons, the scientific status and value of a given scientific model may affect both its metaphorical value and its constraining force in other fields. Given how we view things at the moment, there are only metaphorical models, fictions, or fables. The question is what specific layers of metaphoricity are engaged in a given field and how they are engaged. It is true that in fields of the natural and exact sciences many descriptions often function "as such," that is, the metaphoricity at issue loses its significance, however provisionally. One can, however, never be either absolutely "inside" or absolutely "outside" any given field, and the power of such constraints to operate *as* constraints always emerges in a stratified theoretical ensemble. A full formalization might remain an impossible task in any field or form of discourse. This impossibility, however, would not make any less desirable or necessary an analysis of the (anti-)epistemological problems at issue in various fields and through a variety of approaches. In this sense, the exploration and problematization of the boundaries between fields, such as the natural or human sciences, or literature and science, or the practical and political spheres and the aesthetic sphere—or for that matter, all boundaries—would not entail their elimination. Such explorations could even lead to the introduction of new boundaries, within and without.

The specificity of a given field remains a crucial factor, however, particularly insofar as the mathematical character of modern science is concerned. As Heisenberg writes: "This necessity of constantly shuttling between the two languages [ordinary and mathematical] is unfortunately a chronic source of misunderstanding, since in many cases the same words are employed in both. The difficulty is unavoidable. But it may yet be of some help always to bear in mind that modern science is obliged to make use of both languages, that the same word may have very different meanings in each of them, that different criteria of truth apply and that one should not therefore talk too hastily of contradiction" (*Across the Frontiers*, 120). Thus complementarity in physics is meaningless outside the rigorous mathematical formalism that supports quantum physics or science in general. As Heidegger grasped, from Galileo or Kepler on, modern physics is experimental because of "the mathematical project" (*What is a Thing?*, 93).[18] Galileo speaks of the book of the universe written "in the language of mathematics:" "Philosophy is written in this grand book— I mean the universe—which stands continually open to our gaze, but it cannot be understood unless one first learns to comprehend the language and interpret the characters in which it is written. It is written in the language of mathematics, and its characters are triangles, circles, and other geometrical figures, without which it is humanly impossible to understand a word of it; without these, one is wondering about in a dark labyrinth" (*Assayer, The Controversy on the Comets of 1618*, 183–84). In his preface to Newton's *Optics*, Einstein said that for Newton nature was an open book, and he appears to have meant that this book was written in the language of mathematics (*Optics*, vii), a view shared by Einstein himself.[19] Perhaps dark labyrinths are uncircumventable. One must traverse even stranger landscapes; labyrinths are still decidable, are finally calculable and determinable. Once anything is written, in whatever language—which is to say, in whatever *writing*—one always encounters what the classical philosophy of mathematics or physics, such as Frege's or Einstein's, or any classical philosophy in general, sees as the scandal of numbers—or the scandal of geometry or the scandal of quanta or the scandal of writing— and what Derrida reads or *writes* as trace, *différance*, or *writing*.[20]

From Kepler to Einstein to the present, physics was indissociable from metaphysical demands. As he introduced his mathematical explanation for planetary motion, Kepler also posed the question of the relationships among mathematics, physics, and meta-physics—and metaphysics—or interpretation and language. Quantum mechanics can be seen as the site of this question. Different levels of theorizing at times exhibit very close proximity and offer great possibilities of mutual translations, but at other times they diverge no less radically and appear to allow for no translation at all. Quantum mechanics brings this double economy into the foreground. To cite Heisenberg again, "in the last resort, even science must rely upon ordinary language, since it is the only language in which we can be sure of really grasping the phenomena" (*Across the Frontiers*, 120).[21] Bohr expresses similar views, and I shall consider his view on the significance of ordinary language later. As Derrida shows in relation to the question of philosophical languages, a more complex—more undecidable and more complementary—relationship between different languages and more complex deconstructions must be pursued.

The situation becomes still more complicated when a reverse traffic—metaphoric transfer of scientific or mathematical models into other fields—becomes engaged; and, as Derrida argues in "White Mythology: Metaphor in the Text of Philosophy," the reverse traffic has always been a major metaphoric source of philosophy (*Margins*, 220). This transfer can be rigorous in the sense of establishing theoretically and historically grounded metaphoric parallels and interactions. The problems of the formalization of nonformal, nonmathematical, or nonexperimental requirements of rigor are formidable, for example, in relation to the question of philosophical rigor. As it complementarizes the formal and the informal, however, the general economy of this transfer exceeds all formalisms, formal or transcendental, although it does not simply erase, but recomprehends and redelimits them. By the same token, however, one must distinguish this general economic excess from the excess of formal logic characterizing, or rather claimed by, restricted philosophical economies and the transcendental logic of philosophy—whether in Kant, Hegel, Husserl, Heidegger, or elsewhere.[22] For, as Bohr tells us, classical philosophy offers us no logic, formal or transcendental, that "really understands what is meant by the complementary descriptions."

PART II

Quantum

Anti-Epistemology

This part of the book considers Bohr's complementarity as a general-economic matrix.

Chapter 4 offers a discussion of the defining experimental-theoretical configuration of quantum mechanics and its anti-epistemological implications.

Chapter 5 continues to describe major features of Bohr's complementarity. The first section, "Complementarities," considers several key complementary junctures of Bohr's matrix. The sections that follow, "Correspondences" and "Asyntheses," are concerned, respectively, with Bohr's correspondence principle and with the question of theoretical synthesis and asynthesis, explored through a juxtaposition of Bohr's and Einstein's views.

Chapter 6 considers the Einstein-Podolsky-Rosen argument, aimed at proving the incompleteness of quantum mechanics and Bohr's response, hidden variables, and Bell's theorem.

CHAPTER 4

The Age

of Quantum

Mechanical

Reproduction

Photographs 1: Photomena

The subject of this chapter is the experimental-theoretical configuration—the "scene"—defining quantum physics. It becomes quickly apparent that this scene, the scene of photographs and traces—and the photographs of traces and of traces of traces—may be seen or read, or *written*, as "a scene of *writing*" in Derrida's sense. Whether as landscape, stage, or drama, "scene" is a metaphor which one should use with caution, even though it is effective and will be utilized here. Particles seen as theater actors, appearing in masks and disguises or in complex post-cubist landscapes, offer a *dramatic* means of representation. Bohr has been associated with Picasso by several commentators, and, according to Pais, "among the paintings hanging in [Bohr's] house was one by a founder of cubism [Jean Metzinger]" (*Niels Bohr's Times*, 25, 335). Honner also comments, although in a different context, that "Bohr found a kindred spirit in Picasso" (*The Description of Nature*, 165). Einstein, Pais reports, by contrast, did not appear to care for cubist landscapes, any more than for the landscapes of quantum mechanics—the landscapes, to use Wheeler's phrase, "of Sibyline strangeness"—although, according to Einstein's stepdaughter Margot Einstein, " 'sometimes [Einstein] surprised [her] by looking at the *early* period of Picasso (1905, 1906). . . . Words like *cubism, abstract painting* . . . did not mean anything to him . . .' " (*"Subtle is the Lord,"* 16; emphasis in the original). Einstein, as Wheeler points out, was by no means a stranger to "the Sibyline strangenesses of the landscapes" of modern physics, such as the grand landscapes of general relativity or, "as a grandfather of complementarity," of quantum mechanics, however much he resisted the latter.[1]

Bohr, too, relates his complementary view to a theater metaphor: "in the drama of existence we are ourselves both actors and spectators" (*PWNB* 2:63). Bohr may well be alluding to Shakespeare's "All the world's a stage, / And all the men and women merely players" (*As You Like It*, II, vii). Rousseau, citizen of Geneva, argued in his "Letter to D'Alembert on the Theatre" how detrimental establishing a theater would be for the Republic of Geneva (and D'Alembert's work in mathematics and science or philosophy has considerable pertinence for the many themes of the present study). Neither *role*—that of actors or that of spectators—would be acceptable to Rousseau, any more than writing and its supplementary economy. Bohr's—or Shakespeare's—vision of the world and life entails, complementarily, both. One must be careful, however, to respect the limits of such dramatic or graphic metaphors.

Photography, my main metaphor in this chapter, imposes itself more easily, in part because it is also a metonymy. In quantum mechanics we deal with photographs of quantum phenomena—with photo-phenomena or photon-phenomena or photomena, as one might call them —for example, the complementary phenomena of (the traces of) photons, themselves the main agents of photography. One cannot, however, help thinking of metaphorical analogies provided by modern and postmodern photography or by computer-generated imagery—from the computer-generated portrait of Einstein, arguably the most famous image of that type, to the photographs illustrating chaos theory, another recent icon. The—complementary—pair of photographs of Einstein and Bohr, sometimes accompanied by photographs picturing them together, adorn virtually every physics department in the world. The use of photographs of Einstein and Bohr in books on quantum theory and the history of science is abundant.[2] *Quantum Theory and Measurement* opens with four photographs (taken by Paul Ehrenfest, a friend of both Bohr and Einstein) and a section entitled "Bohr-Einstein Dialogue," thus framing the history of complementarity by the Bohr-Einstein dialogue. The framing is historically justified, but is a bit too "complementary." The history of complementarity itself becomes a complementarity of Bohr and Einstein. Honner's comments on Ehrenfest's photographs are equally interesting from this perspective:

> Their characters were very different in many ways. Einstein was solitary in his work, Bohr gregarious. Einstein sought simplicity, order, and clarity where Bohr, who certainly sought the same order and

clarity, seemed to relish paradox and profundity. Einstein showed greater faith in mathematical purity, while Bohr, on the other hand, gave priority to actual physical observations. There are several marvelous photographs of the two of them, taken by their mutual friend Paul Ehrenfest, and in nearly every one their attitudes and expressions contrast with each other: one sits forward and frowns, the other leans back and holds forth; one looks up at the heavens, almost in intercession, the other stares despondently at the carpet; one gestures vigorously, the other has his fist glued to his jaw. A telling photograph shows the pair of them walking together out of step, with Einstein slightly ahead, as if trying to flee from Bohr's inexorable dialectic. Bohr has his mouth open, his finger pointing; Einstein's hands are still, his eyes hooded, his mouth fixed in a whimsical, half-unbelieving smile. Bohr is looking up, his hat brim turned up, his shirt collar turned down, his coat on his arm. Einstein is the reverse: eyes down, brim down, collar up, coat on. (*The Description of Nature*, 109)

Honner's reading—a verbal "photograph," as it were—again clearly modeled on complementarity, may or may not correspond to its object— the photographs at issue, which may or may not in turn correspond to its object, which is to say, to some other "photograph," some other image of an image. For while Bohr and Einstein existed and discussed complementarity, there is not and has never been at any point, even for Einstein and Bohr themselves, any other account of these discussions than a *written* record (in Derrida's sense)—a photograph—which can be only read, interpreted, or (re)photographed by one or another technology of *writing*. In many ways, quantum mechanics is a response to this very situation—the irreducibility of trace and *writing*—in the case of (the traces of) quantum processes.

In his account of the genesis of uncertainty relations, Heisenberg describes his thinking at the time as follows: "There was not a real path of the electron in the cloud chamber. There was a sequence of water droplets. Each droplet determined inaccurately the position of the electron, and the velocity could be deduced inaccurately from the sequence of droplets. Such a situation could actually be represented in the mathematical scheme; the calculation gave a lower limit for the product of the inaccuracies of position and momentum" (*The Uncertainty Principle and the Foundation of Quantum Mechanics*, 8). This "mathematical scheme" led

Heisenberg to uncertainty relations. Bohr's account of the same situation led him to complementarity.

One deals here only with traces, traces of traces, and photographs of traces as the effects of a certain *différance*-like efficacity and "the strange structure of the supplement" invoked by Derrida: "by delayed reaction the possibility [here an experimental possibility], produces that to which it would be said to be added on." One will need, therefore, a Derridean economy of trace, which is not compatible with an objectivist or empiricist—or, conversely, phenomenological or transcendental—economy, or any restricted economy, of trace. Bohr sees these "strange" effects as resulting from "the finite [i.e., quantum] and uncontrollable [i.e., indeterminate] interaction" between the quantum object and the measuring instruments.[3]

This (general) economy need not, and cannot, mean that there is no material efficacity to the empirical or experimental quantum traces. It is just that this efficacity cannot be approached by means of a restricted economy. No classical origin can be assigned to such traces, and supplementarity here may be even more crucial than the delay and difference in representation one always encounters in dealing with traces left by particles in one medium or another. This is why we need the Derridean trace (irreducible to an empirical mark) and supplementarity. The efficacity at such a trace cannot be conceived of in terms of some originary presence—being-presence or becoming-presence—even if this presence is seen as differed-deferred by a given representation. There is no escape from this loss in origin and representation. All claims upon the nature and structure of this efficacity can only be supplementarily derived from the effects at issue, via a complex mathematical, technological, conceptual, metaphorical, and institutional process. The intervening nature of this process is, therefore, no longer reducible, as it would be in classical physics or classical metaphysics.

Derrida (or Nietzsche and Bataille before him) explores this anticausal supplementarity throughout his writing. The problematics of quantum mechanics quite possibly affected Heidegger's conceptions of the lost trace of Being, which play a major role for Derrida, particularly in "Différance" and "*Ousia* and *Grammē.*" *Being and Time* dates around 1927. *Time and Being* (1962) opens with the invocation of Heisenberg (along with Paul Klee and Georg Trakl), albeit in the Heideggerian terms of the search for a cosmic formula, and references to Heisenberg are found throughout Heidegger's writings. Quantum physics was an important point of reference for Heidegger, particularly in *What is a Thing?*, *What is Called Thinking?*, and "The Question Concerning Technology" and related essays.

Derrida's matrix, however, or some of his key structures—such as trace, supplement, and *différance*—may exemplify or be exemplified by quantum "photomenology" the most graphically. This matrix was developed most directly via Nietzsche's ideas, Freud's theory of memory traces and deferral, several major concepts in Heidegger and Levinas, and Bataille's general economy. But the proximity of quantum physics to Derrida's conceptions appears to be significant, however indirect the influence of quantum physics upon Derrida may be in textual and historical terms. Nor would this significance be contradicted by the fact that, as shall be discussed in chapter 7, Derrida himself dissociates his matrix from the economy of indeterminacy. In both theories one deals only with traces or traces of traces—translations without the original. All putative origins of such traces-translations—that is, all possible representations of processes whose effects appear as traces—can only be seen as supplements in Derrida's sense. Complementarity is theory in the age of quantum mechanical reproduction; and, at a certain level, all reproduction is quantum mechanical, for example, that to which Benjamin refers to as "mechanical reproduction" in his famous essay, to whose title the title of this chapter alludes.[4]

As Derrida suggests, in reading Freud, but also referring to Heidegger, "the question concerning *technology* (a new name must perhaps be found in order to remove it from traditional problematics)" would have to be posed very differently from the way Heidegger poses it (*Writing and Difference*, 228; *L'Écriture et la différence*, 337). The question is central to Derrida, beginning with his earliest works, and the (general) economy of *writing* is also a recomprehension of Heideggerian thematics via the new "technologies" of reproduction.[5] These new technologies are both conceptual and more strictly technological, and we can no longer unequivocally dissociate these two forms of technology either. Bohr's concept of "the finite [quantum] and uncontrollable [indeterminate] interaction" between the object and the measuring instruments leads to an analogous economy.

There is a variety of experiments describing particles—such as electrons or photons—passing throughout slits and showing their strange capability of behaving either as waves or as particles. Most standard books on quantum mechanics contain descriptions of such experiments.[6]

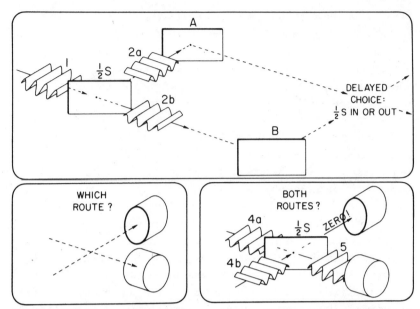

Figure 1. The beam splitter experiment. (Source: Wheeler, John Archibald and Wojciech H. Zurek, eds. *Quantum Theory and Measurement.* Princeton, N.J.: Princeton University Press, 1983. Copyright 1983 by Princeton University Press. Reproduced by permission of Princeton University Press.)

The following discussion uses Wheeler's analysis in "Law without Law" (*Quantum Theory and Measurement*). Wheeler considers the following experiment (fig. 1):

> An electromagnetic wave comes in at 1 and encounters the half-silvered mirror marked "½S" which splits it into two beams, 2a and 2b, of equal intensity which are reflected by mirrors A and B to a crossing point at the right. Counters (lower left) located past the point of crossing tell by which route an arriving photon has come. In the alternative arrangement at the lower right, a half-silvered mirror is inserted at the point of crossing. On one side it brings beams 4a and 4b into destructive interference, so that the counter located on that side never registers anything. On the other side the beams are brought into constructive interference to reconstitute a beam, 5, of the original strength, 1. Every photon that enters at 1 is registered in that second counter in the idealized case of perfect mirrors and 100 per cent photodetector efficiency. In the one arrangement (lower left)

one finds out by *which* route the photon came [in a particle-like manner]. In the other arrangement (lower right) one has evidence that the arriving photon came by both routes [in a wave-like manner]. (*QTM*, 183)[7]

There is no situation in which a photon can behave as both a particle and a wave at one and the same time, and there is no "picture" and no classical "logic" available to synthesize both patterns. According to Bohr:

> The extent to which renunciation of the visualization of atomic phenomena is imposed upon us by the impossibility of their subdivision is strikingly illustrated by the following example to which Einstein very early called attention and often has reverted. If a semi-reflecting mirror is placed in the way of a photon, leaving two possibilities for its direction of propagation, the photon may either be recorded on one, and only one, of two photographic plates situated at great distances in the two directions in question, or else we may, by replacing the plates by mirrors, observe effects exhibiting an interference between the two reflected wave-trains. In any attempt of a pictorial representation of the behavior of the photon we would, thus, meet with the difficulty: to be obliged to say, on the one hand, that the photon always chooses *one* of the two ways and, on the other hand, that it behaves as if it had passed *both* ways. (*PWNB* 2:50–51)

We have no possibility of knowing in advance which way a photon will choose or, to be more precise, which of two counters will register a photon, although we can be certain that a large amount of photons will be equally distributed between two counters. As will be seen, this ineluctable strangeness of the quantum world manifests itself even more dramatically in the so-called delayed-choice version of the experiment just described. In that version the half-silvered mirror is inserted at the last moment and a photon's "choice" of trajectory could be differently determined "*after*" it "has already taken place." One cannot, however, speak of any dynamic properties and thus trajectories of particles prior to an act of observation. While more dramatic, the delayed-choice experiment is, fundamentally, no different from other quantum experiments.[8] Bohr was the first to realize that any re-presentation of this behavior meets with difficulty and demands a kind of general economy as a result:

> [T]he elucidation of the paradoxes of atomic physics has disclosed the fact that the unavoidable interaction between the objects

and the measuring instruments sets an absolute limit to the possibility of speaking of a behavior of atomic objects which is independent of the means of observation.

We are here faced with an epistemological problem quite new in natural philosophy, where all description of experiences has so far been based upon the assumption, already inherent in ordinary conventions of language, that it is possible to distinguish sharply between the behavior of objects and the means of observation. This assumption is not only fully justified by all everyday experience but even constitutes the whole basis of classical physics, which, just through the theory of relativity, has received such a wonderful completion. As soon as we are dealing, however, with phenomena like individual atomic processes which, due to their very nature, are essentially determined by the interaction between the objects in question and the measuring instruments necessary for the definition of the experimental arrangements, we are, therefore, forced to examine more closely the question of what kind of knowledge can be obtained concerning the objects. In this respect we must, on the one hand, realize that the aim of every physical experiment—to gain knowledge under reproducible and communicable conditions—leaves us no choice but to use everyday concepts, perhaps refined by the terminology of classical physics, not only in all accounts of the construction and manipulation of the measuring instruments but also in the description of the actual experimental results. On the other hand, it is equally important to understand that just this circumstance implies that no result of an experiment concerning a phenomenon which, in principle, lies outside the range of classical physics can be interpreted as giving information about independent properties of the objects, but is inherently connected with a definite situation in the description of which the measuring instruments interacting with the objects also enter essentially. This last fact gives the straightforward explanation of the apparent contradications which appear when results about atomic objects obtained by different experimental arrangements are tentatively combined into a self-contained picture of the object. (*PWNB* 2:25–26)

This is a remarkable description. Everyday experience is indeed hardly a good guide, even within classical limits, as was shown already by Einstein's relativity, which Bohr sees, rightly, as a completion of classical physics. As he writes, "in dealing with the task of bringing order into an entirely new field of experience, we could hardly trust in any accustomed principles, however broad, apart from the demand of avoiding logical inconsistencies and, in this respect, the mathematical formalism of quantum mechanics should meet all requirements" (*PWNB* 2:56).

The main requirement is that rigorously verifiable results are produced. All theoretical speculations must be correlated with experimental, here quantum, data, which can only be done by means of mathematical formalism. Quantum theory was extensively confirmed by experiment and proved to have extraordinary predictive power.[9] Einstein understood this aspect of quantum theory very well, and on that basis he had very little to object to Bohr. He saw it as a theory of great explanatory power but, according to his criteria, an incomplete one. As he says, "There is no doubt that quantum mechanics has seized hold of a beautiful element of truth and that it will be a test stone for any future theoretical basis, in that it must be deducible as a limiting case from that basis" (*Out of My Later Years*, 92). The incompleteness, however, was claimed on metaphysical, not experimental or mathematical grounds. For Bohr complementarity was necessitated by experimental results. An agreement with experiment was for him a necessary condition of an interpretation of quantum mechanics. Heisenberg's comments on his first encounter with Bohr are revealing in this respect:

> Thus I understood: knowledge of nature was primarily obtained in this way [of intense occupation with the actual phenomenon], and only as the next step can one succeed in fixing one's knowledge in mathematical form and subjecting it to complete rational analysis. Bohr was primarily a philosopher, not a physicist, but he understood that natural philosophy in our day and age carries weight only if its every detail can be subjected to the inexorable test of experiment ("Quantum Theory and Its Interpretation," 95).

The emphasis on "the inexorable test of experiment" as defining Bohr's approach is crucial. Bohr's intense occupation with the actual quantum phenomena led him to his knowledge that all our knowledge about quantum world is subject to an irreducible loss of knowledge. By fixing this knowledge in mathematical terms, Heisenberg derived uncertainty relations. Penrose directly appeals to a necessary "lack of knowledge" in his discussion of the two-slit experiment and of the uncircumventable strangeness of the quantum world—of "quantum magic and quantum mystery"—where particles-waves easily circumvent the barriers of our classical ideas. As he writes:

> As support for the view that the particle does not partly go through one slit and partly through the other, the modified situation may be considered in which a *particle detector* is placed at one of the slits or the other. Since when it is observed, a photon—or any other particle—always appears as a single whole and not as some fraction of a whole, it must be the case that our detector detects either a whole photon or no photon at all. However, when the detector is present at one of the slits, so that an observer can *tell* which slit the photon went through, the wavy interference pattern at the screen disappears. In order for the interference to take place, there must apparently be a "lack of knowledge" as to which slit the particle "actually" went through. (*The Emperor's New Mind*, 236)[10]

Bohr, too, speaks of "the inevitable loss of knowledge" at the same juncture (*QTM*, 147), which disallows a single, unified picture or account. There can be no synthesis in any of the senses previously available, but only complementarity. One is ineluctably faced with the choice, always unavoidable and always limited to either one or another, but never simultaneously both, types of experimental arrangements. As Bohr writes, "To my mind, there is no other alternative than to admit that, in this field of experience, we are dealing with individual phenomena and that our possibilities of handling the measuring instruments allow us only to make a choice between the different complementary types of phenomena we want to study. . . . [W]e must realize that in the problem in question we are not dealing with a *single* specified experimental arrangement, but are referring to *two* different, mutually exclusive arrangments" (*PWNB* 2:51, 57). The situation demands "a radical revision of our attitude towards the problem of physical reality" (*QTM*, 146), if this radical revision will allow us to retain the term reality. According to Wheeler:

> The dependence of what is observed upon the choice of experimental arrangement made Einstein unhappy. It conflicts with the view that the universe exists "out there" independent of all acts of observation. In contrast Bohr stressed that we confront here an inescapable new feature of nature, to be welcomed because of the understanding it gives us. In struggling to make clear to Einstein the

central point as he saw it, Bohr found himself forced to introduce the word "phenomenon." In today's words Bohr's point—and the central point of quantum theory—can be put into a single, simple sentence. "No elementary phenomenon is a phenomenon until it is a registered (observed) phenomenon." It is wrong to speak of the "route" of the photon in the experiment of the beam splitter. It is wrong to attribute a tangibility to the photon in all its travel from the point of entry to its last instant of flight. A phenomenon is not yet a phenomenon until it has been brought to a close by an irreversible act of amplification such as the blackening of a grain of silver bromide emulsion or the triggering of a photodetector. In broader terms, we find that nature at the quantum level is not a machine that goes its inexorable way. Instead what answer we get depends on the question we put, the experiment we arrange, the registering device we choose. We are inescapably involved in bringing about that which appears to be happening. (QTM, 184–85)

It is important to keep in mind, however, that we cannot fully control the outcome of experiments we have arranged. Strictly speaking, what Wheeler refers to as registered (observed) phenomena are already inferences made from traces left on photographic plates. These traces are "always already" processed by a given interpretive economy, which defines the phenomenon of any given trace and the very concept of trace.[11] Hence the complexity of Derrida's economy of trace, and, once again, one needs this type of economy to comprehend quantum traces. These qualifications nuance and amplify, rather than weaken, Wheeler's and Bohr's conclusions.

Bohr's concept of phenomenon is hardly phenomenological in the classical sense, whether Kant's, Hegel's, Husserl's, or still other, although one can locate common features in Bohr's and these and other classical phenomenologies. Bohr's is an anti-epistemologically—general-economically—displaced concept. It undermines and deconstructs classical concepts and restricted economies of the phenomena (in either sense) at issue in quantum mechanics. Bohr uses his concept of 'phenomenon' against classical objectivity, which would conceive of the possibility of quantum objects existing by themselves, independently of interpretation. His usage, analogously displaced, of terms such as 'objective' and 'reality' is aimed, conversely, against idealist, positivist, or phenomenologist interpretations of quantum "phenomena." Bohr's view would not suggest, as some forms of positivism would, that what is not observed, or even what cannot be observed, does not exist. One might even see Bohr as claiming that much of what exists, or how it exists, cannot be observed, to the extent that the term "existence" (or "alterity") can apply to this alterity. Bohr does argue as to what can or cannot be inferred about this alterity on the basis of what is experimentally observed—which is the only evidence we have, at least insofar as physics is concerned. We cannot, however, on these experimental grounds, ascribe to this alterity the kind of reality that Einstein wanted.

The observed or measured (registered) phenomenon in Bohr's sense always involves the 'phenomenon' of observation and measurement and of the apparatus involved. For "while, within the scope of classical physics, the interaction between object and apparatus can be neglected or, if necessary, compensated for, in quantum physics this interaction thus forms an inseparable part of the phenomenon" (*PWNB* 3:4). Terms such as "object" and "apparatus" are used here neutrally, without assigning an object an independent metaphysical, and in particular metaphysically independent, status. According to Bohr, "*the finite magnitude of the quantum of action prevents altogether a sharp distinction being made between a phenomenon and the agency by which it is observed*, a distinction which underlies the customary concept of observation and, therefore, forms the basis of the classical ideas of motion . . . an independent reality *in the ordinary physical sense* can neither be ascribed to the phenomena [i.e., 'object'] nor to the agencies of observation" (*PWNB* 1:11–12, 54; emphasis added). In contrast to the preceding quotation (where 'phenomenon' subsumes the measuring apparatus), here the term "phenomenon"—relating to a more conventional form of inference from observed traces—corresponds to Bohr's earlier usage, prior to the EPR argument. This difference does not affect the main point at issue: the impossibility of assigning an observed object an independent physical reality. Our inferences—such as particles or waves and variables that define their motion—from these traces may, of course, be shaped by some ideas borrowed from theories grounded in such a concept of reality.

Bohr's statements need not mean that the object and apparatus form an indivisible whole, although Bohr does speak of wholeness in this respect on some occasions. Earlier in the same paragraph, Bohr says that "the essentially new feature in the analysis of quantum phenomena is . . . the introduction of a *fundamental distinction between the measuring apparatus and the objects under investigation*. This is a direct consequence of the necessity of accounting for the functions of the measuring instruments in purely classical terms, excluding in principle any regard to the quantum of action" (*PWNB* 3:3–4; Bohr's emphasis). The *interaction* itself between the object and the instrument is, of course, quantum, as Bohr has stressed throughout his writings, although, "*however far the phenomena transcend the scope of classical physical explanation, the account of all evidence must be expressed in classical terms*" (*PWNB* 2:39). It is the *interaction* between the object and the apparatus that is an *inseparable* part of quantum phenomenon. Bohr speaks of the "*impossibility of any sharp separation between the behavior of atomic objects and the* interaction *with the measuring instruments which serve to define the conditions under which the phenomena appear*" (*PWNB* 2:39–40). This always irreducible interaction forms not a unity, governed by a classical economy of synthesis, but a complex and shifting complementarity.

The economy just considered corresponds to Bohr's later usage of the term 'phenomenon' after the discussions around the EPR argument in 1930s. Bohr's earlier usage, as Folse observes, "refer[s] to the object of observation as distinguished in the description of the interactions from 'agencies of observation' which are described as the physical system with which the 'observed phenomena' interact in the observation" (*The Philosophy of Niels Bohr*, 110). Eventually, Bohr came to use the term 'phenomenon' as referring to that which must "involve a complete description of the experimental arrangement as well as the observed results" ("Newton's Principle and Modern Atomic Mechanics," 59–60). This view, as Folse argues, does not represent a fundamental change in Bohr's anti-epistemology, but rather a change, significant and important, in emphasis (*The Philosophy of Niels Bohr*, 154). Faye agrees with this assessment (*Niels Bohr*, 186), although he stresses more than Folse does the significance of modifications introduced by Bohr in view of both the EPR argument and the diminished significance of Høffding's influence. Faye criticizes Folse's interpretation for not sufficiently taking these modification into account (*Niels Bohr*, 203–11). Even Bohr's earlier understanding can be interpreted in more radically anti-epistemological terms than either Folse or Faye suggests. Bohr's modifications do, however, articulate these anti-epistemological dimensions more effectively.

Bohr's later understanding of the term phenomenon as referring to the experimental arrangement does not suspend the possibility or necessity of speaking of electrons, photons, positions, momenta, and so forth. It does redefine and redelimit the status and functioning of all these terms. In

principle, one can render quantum (or classical) physics in terms of numerical data and mathematical formalism, without referring to any such
concepts or metaphors. While such a recasting would modify the "text"
of quantum mechanics, it would not mean that metaphor in general (as
writing in Derrida's sense) or even specific metaphors can in fact be suspended in the course of the processing of such a text, or that mathematical language itself is free from metaphoricity, free from "the scandal of
the trace."

Photographs 2: Delayed Choice

The quantum *scene* becomes even more *dramatic* in view of the version
of the experiment described earlier, known as the delayed choice experiment, which can be enacted on a literally cosmic scale. As Bohr observes: "it obviously can make no difference, as regards observable effects
obtainable by a definite experimental arrangement, whether our plans of
constructing or handling the instruments are fixed beforehand or whether
we prefer to postpone the completion of our planning until a later moment
when the particle is already on its way from one instrument to another"
(*PWNB* 2:57). According to Wheeler, "In the new 'delayed-choice' version of the experiment one decides whether to put in the half-silvered
mirror or take it out at the very last minute [i.e., the very last picosecond].
Thus one decides whether the photon 'shall have come by one route, or by
both routes' after it has '*already done* its travel.' . . . In this sense, we have
a strange inversion of the normal order of time. We, now, by moving the
mirror in or out have an unavoidable effect on what we have a right to say
about the *already* past history of that photon" (*QTM*, 183–84).[12] Wheeler's
elaborations become actually reminiscent of Derrida's on *différance*:

> Of the signs that testify to "quantum phenomenon" as being the
> elementary act of creation, none is more striking than its untouch-
> ability. In the delayed-choice version of the split-beam experiment,
> for example, we have no right to say what the photon is doing in all
> its long course from point of entry to point of detection. Until the
> act of detection the phenomenon-to-be is not yet a phenomenon.
> We could have intervened at some point along the way with a dif-
> ferent measuring device; but then regardless whether it is the new
> registering device or the previous one that happens to be triggered
> we have a new phenomenon. We have come no closer than before

to penetrating to the untouchable interior of the phenomenon. For a process of creation that can and does operate anywhere, that reveals itself and yet hides itself, what could one have dreamed up out of pure imagination more magic—and more fitting—than this? (189)

Wheeler's choice of the expression "the phenomenon-to-be" is apt, for at no point does quantum data reflect a reality independent of representation. "The phenomenon-to-be" is that which will be registered as a "photographic" trace or effect at a certain point, but the efficacity of which can never—either in the past, present, or future—be seen as *present*, whether as representable or as unrepresentable, existing in itself or by itself, independent of and inaccessible to any interpretation. This loss in presence make the quantum theoretical economy a general economy and the efficacity at issue analogous to Derridean alterity-efficacity which "makes us concerned not with horizons of modified—past or future—present, but with a 'past' that has never been present, and which never will be, whose future to come [l' 'a-venir'] will never be a *production* or a reproduction in the form of presence" (*Margins*, 21; *Marges*, 21). There are only "photographs," which would have to be described as always—always already—taken too late to allow one to describe or even to speak of a reality behind quantum phenomena. These phenomena are always incomplete and, from the classical point of view, contradictory. The degree, to which one could speak in classical terms at this point is very limited, however, as Bohr understood, although classical terms remain, at least for now, effective and even indispensable.

At times, this situation makes one appeal to the terms that are used in transcendental, theological (particularly, negative theology), or mystical discourses. One encounters the terms of and proximities to these discourses in Bataille, Derrida, and Bohr. Some among such proximities are structural, that is, analogously determined by the respective conceptual networks; and these proximities are considered by Bataille and Derrida. The differences, however, are far more crucial. General economy is not only not mystical, but is opposed to every form of mysticism, even though and because one may need to consider, as Bataille does, various forms of mystical experience from the perspective of and place them within a general economy.[13] Although more mystical interpretations of quantum mechanics are possible and have been advanced, one can also say that there is nothing mystical or mysterious in quantum mystery and quantum magic. As Bohr writes: "It may perhaps appear at first sight that such an attitude towards physics would leave room for mysticism which is contrary to the spirit of natural science. However, we can no more hope to attain to a clear understanding in physics without facing the difficulties arising in the shaping of concepts and in the use of the medium of expression than we can in other fields of human inquiry" (*PWNB* 1:15). Bohr even speaks of complementarity as "a *rational* utilization of all possibilities of unambiguous interpretation and measurement" (*QTM*, 148), or more directly: "far from containing any mysticism foreign to the spirit of science, the notion of complementarity points to the logical conditions for description and comprehension of experience in atomic physics" (*PWNB* 2:91).[14]

Wheeler also considers the perhaps most striking example of quantum *différance*—"delayed-choice at the cosmological scale":

> [The delayed-choice experiment] reaches back into the past in apparent opposition to the normal order of time. The distance of travel in a laboratory split-beam experiment might be thirty meters and the time a tenth of a microsecond; but the distance could as well have been billions of light years and the time billions of years. Thus the observing device in the here and now, according to its last minute setting one way or the other, has an irretrievable consequence for what one has the right to say about a photon that was given out long before there was any life in the universe.
>
> Two astronomical objects, known as 0957+561 A,B, once considered to be two distant quasistellar objects or "quasars" because they are separated by six seconds of arc, are considered now by many observers to be two distinct images of one quasar. Evidence has been found for an intervening galaxy, roughly a quarter of the way from us to the quasar. Calculations indicate that a normal galaxy at such a distance has the power to take two light rays, spread apart by fifty thousand light years on their way out from the quasar, and bring them back together at the Earth. This circumstance, and evidence for a new case of gravitational lensing, make it reasonable to promote the split-beam experiment in the delayed-choice version from the laboratory level to the cosmological scale. . . .
>
> We get up in the morning and spend the day in meditation whether to observe by "which route" or to observe interference between "both routes." When night comes and the telescope is at last usable we leave the half-silvered mirror out or put it in, according to

our choice. The monochromatizing filter placed over the telescope makes the counting rate low. We may have to wait an hour for the first photon. When it triggers a counter, we discover "by which route" it came with the one arrangement; or by the other, what the relative phase is of the waves associated with the passage of the photon from source to receptor "by both routes"—perhaps 50,000 light years apart as they pass the lensing galaxy G-1. But the photon has already *passed* that galaxy billions of years before we made our decision. This is the sense in which, in a loose way of speaking, we decide what the photon *shall have done* after it has *already* done it. In actuality it is wrong to talk of the "route" of the photon. For a proper way of speaking we recall once more that it makes no sense to talk of the phenomenon until it has been brought to a close by an irreversible act of amplification. (*QTM*, 191–92)

The scale of the delayed-choice experiment can be extended to the earliest history of the universe (*QTM*, 203), although we might not be able to speak of either an origin or history prior to the Big Bang or early—pre-Big Bang—universe or prior to the moment when it becomes possible to use such concepts. Wheeler's qualification that "in actuality it is wrong to talk of the 'route' of the photon" is crucial, and his quotation marks are very much to the point. It is only "in a loose way of speaking," that we can say "that we decide what the photon *shall have done* after it has *already* done it." Rigorously speaking, we deal with a radical alterity inaccessible to any interpretation, including an interpretation as something absolutely inaccessible, or any conceivable form of alterity. The experimental data just described disallows us to conceive of this "alterity" by any interpretive and conceptual means available to us, unless, in view of Bell's theorem, other fundamental constraints of physics, such as the finite speed of light are violated. Wheeler adds: "What we have the right to say of past spacetime, and past events, is decided by choices—of what measurements to carry out—made in the near past and now. The phenomena called into being by these decisions reach backward in time in their consequences, . . . back even to the earliest days of the universe. Registering equipment operating in the here and now has an undeniable part in bringing about that which appears to have happened. Useful as it is under everyday circumstances to say that the world exists 'out there' independent of us, that view can no longer be upheld. There is a strange sense in which this is a 'participatory universe'" (*QTM*, 194).

It is, thus, not a question of somehow modifying a past that has already existed. Were such the case, one would reinstate metaphysical—present —reality, whether as being or as becoming, which would exist in itself and by itself, independently of interpretation. Claims advanced by Wheeler would, then, lead to standard logical problems, which Bohr's and, following Bohr's, Wheeler's interpretations avoid. Such interpretations of Wheeler's analysis of the delayed-choice experiment or of the experiment itself are possible, but they would be neither rigorous nor effective.[15] From the anti-epistemological point of view it is this, Einsteinian, concept of reality that becomes impossible.

One might do well to abandon the term 'reality' altogether, provided that one takes precautions against positivist, idealist, phenomenologist, or transcendentalist interpretations that would reverse this concept without sufficiently displacing the metaphysical base grounding it. The history of its usage makes the term 'reality' difficult to adjust to anti-epistemological agendas, and in most studies of Bohr or elsewhere it has always functioned so as to inhibit anti-epistemological possibilities. Rhetorically or strategically, alterity is a much better term, although it needs, naturally, to be (re)inscribed within a general economy. Both Bohr and Wheeler use the term 'reality.' In both cases, however, one encounters a reciprocal or complementary economy, complementarizing the inside and the outside. This economy is an economy of an—reciprocal—alterity, radical but not absolute, rather than any form of classical reality, or less metaphysically charged concepts of reality found in some interpretations of Bohr and quantum mechanics referred to here. Wheeler's overall interpretation does contain some metaphysical predicates, for example, in his discussion of "nothingness" and the early universe (*QTM*, 205–7). In contrast to most other cases, however, his logic here can be easily modified so as to produce a general economic field. Wheeler often appeals to concepts which are close to Derrida's "neither terms nor concepts." His subsequent views become more problematic.

The delayed-choice experiment only amplifies the fact that in quantum physics one always deals with "absolute past" as considered earlier—a past that is incompatible with the category of present, whether as now-present, past-present, or future-present. The irreducible "finite and uncontrollable" indeterminate interaction with the measuring devices, irreducibly and uncontrollably delays—differs and defers—all quantum events or phenomena, such as particles or waves, and their dynamic properties. Or rather it "delays" that to which we relate by means of our mathematical, conceptual, and metaphorical constructs developed from traces and traces of traces registered by the measuring devices. This interaction places the "events" "themselves" into the absolute past, a past that has never been present, by means of which one relates to a radical alterity in the differing-deferring movement—drift-derivation—of *différance*. As shall be seen in chapter 7 the alterity at issue may not even conform to the Derridean economy of delay or deferral, or *différance*. Under all conditions, however, absolute past suspends the possibility of objects existing by themselves and in themselves, independently of interpretation, as much as the possibility of full representation. Bohr rejects the possibility of both creation and distortion through observation; and his concepts of "phenomenon," "observation," and "measurement" are not subject to either interpretation. He writes: "It is certainly not possible for the observer to influence the events which may appear under the conditions he has arranged. . . . I warned especially against phrases, often found in the physical literature, such as 'disturbing of phenomena by observation' or 'creating physical attributes to atomic objects by measurement.' Such phrases, which may serve to remind of the apparent paradoxes in quantum theory, are at the same time apt to cause confusion, since words like 'phenomena' and 'observation,' just as 'attributes' and 'measurements,' are used [by Bohr] in a way hardly compatible with common language and practical definition" (*PWNB* 2:51, 63–64, 73).

This is not to say that what is approached by means of this radical alterity does not "exist." The material traces are effects of this—material—alterity-efficacity. The radical alterity at issue may not, however, be defined by means of any modes and concepts of existence available within our interpretive and theoretical closure or closures, especially the closure of classical concepts defining either an absolute difference from any interpretation or, conversely, a reality that may be mapped or approached, for example asymptotically, by observation, interpretation, or theory. Even the Derridean economy may not be radical enough in this sense, insofar as it delimits the theoretical closures involved by the closure of philosophy.

It is the potential of complementarity as a metaphorical model for the social sciences and the humanities and its significance in modern intellectual history that are most important for this study. The concept of general economy may, however, be useful, at least, for the meta-physics of quantum theory. Derrida's economy of trace is especially relevant here. For this economy not only makes the economy of trace and the suspension of all absolute origins inevitable, but, as we have seen, also complicates the structure of trace itself. In both quantum mechanics and Derridean deconstructed field alike, "nothing, neither among the elements nor within the system, is anywhere ever simply present or absent. There are only, everywhere difference and traces of traces" (*Positions*, 26; *Positions*, 38). Such a trace, however, and the efficacity that produces it prohibit both an original presence and an original absence of which a trace would be a trace, or a trace of a trace, however remote—or however empirical or however transcendental—such a presence or absence might be. Quantum photography and particularly the delayed-choice experiment equally suggest that there is no classical, anywhere present metaphysical reality, or phenomenality, of which the traces left in the cloud chamber or on photographic plates would be traces or traces of traces. There is instead an efficacity and an economy of trace, analogous to that developed by Derrida. These *material* effects displace and problematize classical phenomenality, but they make equally problematic all concepts —objectivist, subjectivist, materialist, idealist, positivist, transcendentalist, or still other—of reality hitherto conceived. The delayed-choice experiment only manifests what is found in all quantum experiments: the structural, irreducible deferral of presence or absence of the photon's actual trajectory. This delay makes all these terms—photon, actual, trajectory, delay—provisional and inadequate, if necessary within our closure of representation. All quantum experiments exemplify "the strange structure of the supplement," where "by delayed reaction, a possibility produces that to which it is supposed to be added on."

In quantum mechanics all our reactions are "always already" delayed, and so are all our choices. All quantum experiments are delayed-choice experiments, and unlike classical physics this delay cannot be reduced or compensated for, except within classical limits. We are always already too late to make it possible for us to know what a photon's identity—or difference, difference-*différance*, or multiplicity-*dissemination*—or trajectory is. We have no choice, or one might say, we only have a delayed choice. Derrida speaks of the category of choice as "particularly trivial" under the condition of *différance* (*Writing and Difference*, 293; *L'écriture et la différence*, 428), except that the category of necessity may well become equally trivial. We need, instead, a kind of *différance* of both—chance and necessity— in short a complementarity of chance and necessity; or chance, choice, and necessity. The always already delayed-choice experiment defining the scene of quantum mechanics, creates what I called earlier the scandal of trace. As other anti-epistemologies, however, quantum mechanics makes the scandal of trace into the possibility for a new theory.

Photographs 3: Cuts, Disturbances, Distortions

The cut, distortion, and disturbance are other concepts commonly used in discussions of quantum physics that I want to consider. The cut designates the borderline that separates that which observes from that which is observed, while disturbance and distortion refer to the (claims of) displacement of quantum objects and data by observation or measurement. "Cut" and "distortion" may again be seen as photographic metaphors— "cut," more obviously, as representing a frame which separates the inside from the outside and "distortion" as referring to the inevitable transformation of an object by photographic representation. One can think of André Kertész's "Distortions"—a series of photographs of distorted images of the naked female body taken from their images in a fun-house mirror. While the topology of many images *reflects* continuous, smooth— Riemannian or Einsteinian—transformations of the "original" form, in some cases the interplay of the surface of the mirror and light produces fantastic twisting and dislocations, complementarily continuous and discontinuous. The body can in principle spread, twist, and fracture itself across the surface of the mirror, forming multiply complementary pictures. In quantum mechanics (in Bohr's interpretation) there is finally no original form distorted in a mirror, but only effects of a more "twisted" play—an irreducibly suspended efficacity. As Kertész's "Distortions" photographs and other deconstructions of phenomenology teach us, however, in the final account such is always the case—for any (so-called) original perception of any "phenomena."

In quantum mechanics our mirrors and photographs are constrained by the continuous and discontinuous—particle-like and wave-like— effects that we cannot observe simultaneously or at least without mutually inhibiting asynthesis. Any image, however twisted or complementary, can be only an image—an always already "distorted" photograph—an effect, the radical alterity of whose efficacity cannot be photographed by any technological or conceptual-metaphorical equipment available to us, even by means of Derrida's *writing*. In this sense, distortion, like repetition, would precede the original, which, however, destroys all three concepts. *Différance* connotes this originary distortion-repetition. The concept and metaphor of trace, even if it is processed via Derridean economy, and the matrix as a whole can only imperfectly, vaguely relate to a quantum mechanical "process itself." As a result, the latter expression in turn becomes impossible. Process *itself* can, under these conditions, only be read as implying not only local interpretive conditions and therefore reciprocity and complementarity, but also the final indeterminacy or undecidability of relationships between the "exterior" and the "interior" of any interpretive configuration. Derrida has pursued analyses of these conditions beginning with his earliest writings, although more along the lines of undecidability than indeterminacy. The section "The Outside [Is] the Inside" ("Le dehors [est] le dedans") in *Of Grammatology* defines them by its very title. One could speak of complementarity of the inside and the outside, as opposed to their unequivocal, metaphysical definability, at however deep a level it may be assumed. Bohr does not appear to do so directly. Complementarity as matrix, however, allows for and in fact implies such a complementarity. According to d'Espagnat:

> [I]n Bohr's view, the conditions of observation influence in a fundamental way physical reality itself, that is, anything that we can call "physical reality." In other words, Bohr does not consider the arbitrariness of the object-subject separation as merely reflecting a set of technical possibilities which enables us to simplify the calculations whenever we are not interested in complex correlations between object and instrument. On the contrary he attributes to that arbitrariness in the separation—and, in particular, to the possibility of putting the instrument on the same side as the subject—a fundamental significance. Following Shimony, we can state that Bohr introduces a complementarity between object and subject and that this generalized complementarity, far from being a mere appendix to the physical theory, is, on the contrary, the most essential part of it. (*Conceptual Foundations of Quantum Mechanics*, 254)[16]

This assessment is not incorrect, but several qualifications are in order. Given the history of these terms and the history of the critique they have elicited, one might not want to retain the conceptuality of the objective and subjective. Bohr does use these terms, both in his discussion of quantum mechanics and his his attempts to extend complementarity elsewhere, particularly to psychology and the problem of consciousness. Thus he writes: "I hope . . . that the idea of complementarity is suited to characterize the situation, which bears a deep-going analogy to the general difficulty in the formation of human ideas, inherent in the distinction between subject and object" (*PWNB* 1:91). As I have indicated, this analogy has a genealogy in Bohr's thinking that preceded complementarity, and it has been extensively discussed by many commentaries on Bohr. Bohr's usage of the terms on this occasion is partly a reflection of his conceptual vocabulary and syntax, and partly rhetorical and strategic, as it displaces the classical opposition of subjective and objective. Bohr's formulation itself just cited suggests this type of displacement. Bohr similarly uses and displaces the terms "objective theory" and "objective description." Were one to apply his complementary anti-epistemology rigorously in this context (which Bohr has never quite done), it would problematize the distinction between and the very terms subject and object as much as it does in Bohr's analysis of the relationships between the object and the measuring instruments in quantum mechanics. Most interpreters of the remark just cited and of other comments made by Bohr to that effect, fail to follow these implications to their anti-epistemological limits, in part by retaining and metaphysically resolidifying the subject-object opposition.

The relationships between that which interprets and that which is interpreted may, then, be seen as complementary. The cut between them is arbitrary, as was immediately understood by Bohr. We recall that he sees "the concept of observation . . . in so far arbitrary as it depends upon which objects are included in the system to be observed" (*PWNB* 1:54). As Murdoch points out, "the cut may be made either between the original object and instrument, or between the composite object consisting of the original object *cum* instrument and some further instrument, and so on *ad infinitum*" (*Niels Bohr's Philosophy*, 96).

On the one hand, this arbitrariness may be seen as analogous to that of the subject-object distinction in psychology. Bohr illustrates this parallel by his famous example of "attempting to orient [oneself] in a dark room by feeling with a stick. When the stick is held loosely, it appears to the sense of touch to be an object. When, however, it is held firmly, we loose the sensation that it is a foreign body, and the impression of touch becomes immediately localized at the point where the stick is touching the body under investigation. It would scarcely be an exaggeration to maintain, purely from psychological experiences, that the concepts of space and time by their very nature acquire a meaning only because of the possibility of neglecting the interaction with the means of measurement" (*PWNB* 1:99).[17]

On the other hand, the situation *incorporates* the human observer metonymically. As John von Neumann was perhaps first to point out (although

Bohr makes similar intimations), the "cut" may be made between the brain and the consciousness of the observer, where quantum effects may in fact operate.[18]

One thus encounters the movable and arbitrary "cut." Such a "cut" is arbitrary or " 'unmotivated'['immotivée']" "but not capricious," as Derrida describes 'trace' (*Of Grammatology*, 46; *De la grammatologie*, 68). Derrida speaks of "the instituted trace [la trace instituée]," which implies an instituted "cut" in the present sense. As the preceding analysis would show, "cut" and "trace" are a part of the same mediating economy, the same *différance*. Bohr insists that indeterminacy affects the interaction, and thus the possibility of sharp distinction, between the measured object and the measuring instrument, since both must be treated as quantum systems (*PWNB* 1:11; *PWNB* 2:25–26, 72–74). Quantum indeterminacy would remain regardless of where the "cut" was made. No "cut" can erase uncertainty relations (*PWNB* 1:54, 66–68) unless one returns to classical limits, where one can also see the observed object and the measuring equipment as separate. The "cut" is sufficiently determined by experimental arrangements so as to make results sufficiently independent of a specific observer—a fact which Bohr persistently stresses and which appears to define for him the objective character of quantum mechanics.

The shifting "cut" further problematizes the concept of independent physical reality and complicates the possibility of, on the one hand, "creation" and, on the other, "disturbance" and "distortion" by observation or measurement in quantum physics. Bohr, as we have seen, rejects both possibilities. The disturbance-distortion interpretation would presuppose an object and, thus, a metaphysically conceived reality existing independently of observation. It is the rejection of either theory that enables Bohr to argue, against Einstein and others, that one cannot assign any form of "independent properties" to the object that we observe, which properties would afterward be disturbed by observation. Quantum conditions, according to Bohr, disallow the concept of undisturbed reality, which could then be disturbed or distorted by observation. Some disturbances and distortions of certain "previous" configurations can, of course, take place under certain conditions. But they must be seen as superimposed upon *structural* distortions, prohibiting one from speaking of an undisturbed reality or matter existing 'by itself,' independently of interpretation, or of their metaphysical opposition or, conversely, unity. It becomes impossible to see any given distortion as unconditionally primary or to claim the unconditional primacy of distortion as structure.

Nor can we comprehend this economy by any form of classical causality. Hence Derrida's deconstruction of both concepts—distortion and primacy—and their unequivocal, metaphysical opposition. One can thus speak neither of a "creation" of quantum events by experiment nor of an independent, "undisturbed" or "undistorted," quantum event, or of an "event," to begin with. One *cannot* speak of uninterpretable or uninterpreted particles, or matter, even if one assigns the name "matter" to the difference, or *différance*, at issue here and its radical alterity in a general economy, which applies to matter as well. Were one to do so, undisturbed intrinsic properties and states independent of interpretation and interaction would reemerge, implying a metaphysical reality, instead of the radical alterity of general economy. Such a reality may be assigned either a classical—deterministic, causal, or statistical—character or a complementary character. Complementarity, however, makes no such presuppositions and suspends any form of independent (physical) reality.

To the extent that it is a materialist theory, Bohr's complementarity implies a material "remainder [*réstance*]" in Derrida's sense. Such a remainder cannot, however, be seen as being assigned any definite form, known or unknown, or absolutely unknowable; any form of alterity, difference, or exteriority, whether simple or absolute; or any form any identity. A very different relation—if it is even a relation—is at stake, a relation that is contradictory or impossible from the classical point of view. This remainder cannot be seen in terms of the Kantian or materialist objectivist economy of matter, existing independently of interpretation. It cannot be a thing-in-itself or an objective reality existing independently of interpretation. The "remainder" at issue must be seen as productive of further interpretive iterability at any point, or after any "cut," but not in the sense that there is anything that can exist as undisturbed at any point and then be disturbed or differently observed, measured, or interpreted. Hence one can no longer speak either of preexisting and disturbed states or features or of creating by observation or measurement.

Bohr insists on this double (general) economy, along with and as part of what he calls the "objective" character of quantum mechanics and complementarity, which "objectivity" may, as I said, be seen as defined by this economy. He defends it both against accusations of subjectivism—or idealism or positivism—throughout his life. Complementarity is anti-subjectivist by virtue of its general economic character. Any general economy is, by definition, anti-subjectivist, being incompatible with the (metaphysical) category of the subject. As Derrida writes, "Constituting and dislocating it at the same time, writing [in Derrida's sense] is other than the subject, in whatever sense the latter is understood. Writing can never be thought under the category of the subject; however it is modified, however it is endowed with consciousness or unconsciousness, it will refer, by the entire thread of its history, to the substantiality of a presence unperturbed by accident, or to the identity of the selfsame [le propre] in the presence of self-relationships" (*Of Grammatology*, 69; *De la grammatologie*, 100). This proposition is generalizable to any general economy, be it in Nietzsche, who offered the first and in many ways a still unsurpassed critique of classical subjectivity, Bataille, or Bohr. By the same token, general economy is anti-idealist. It is a materialist theory in the sense that the unutilizable excesses of material energy are produced by alterity-efficacity, which could be seen as defining matter itself, except that it does not exist by itself or in itself. These excesses cannot be fully utilized by any subjective process using material resources, whether materiality is defined in terms of physics, biology, psychology, or history.

No general economy, however, including Bohr's, can be seen as 'objective,' either, given the history of that term and concept. The choice or necessity of any given term is always strategic and historical. The term 'objective' is problematic, even though Bohr himself uses it, particularly in his argument with Einstein, who saw quantum mechanics as lacking in objectivity. Bohr's emphasis is on "the *conditions* for objective description" (*PWNB* 1:2). Rather than implying objectivity or reality in the classical understanding of these terms, Bohr's phrase refers to the conditions of possibility of unambiguous communication of the experimental results, the possibility of making experimental results independent of a particular observer under the arranged conditions, and the impossibility for any observer to influence the results under the arranged conditions. One might say that, on Einstein's own terms, complementarity allows for a description that is more "objective" than is possible within Einstein's own scheme of independent objective reality. One can, and many commentators do, cite formulations in Bohr's texts in which he uses 'objectivity,' 'reality'—or, conversely, 'phenomenon'—and other classical terms against Einstein and other critics of complementarity, (mis)interpreting Bohr's views as subjectivist or positivist—or, conversely, metaphysically objectivist. Such terms and Bohr's complementarity itself may be read in terms of and reabsorbed by various classical, metaphysical frameworks, which would inhibit anti-epistemological possibilities of Bohr's matrix. From the anti-epistemological perspective, one is much better off exploring the differences from and displacements of classical frameworks in Bohr's text, rather than the affinities with them. In such a reading, Bohr's classical terms and the concepts or the nonconcepts they designate operate *against* corresponding concepts as classically conceived. Bohr's anti-epistemology itself renders ineffective the terminology of objectivity, the object-subject opposition, 'reality', and most other classical concepts as they have been developed throughout their history.[19]

Bohr avoids the logic of restricted economy, even when he uses its terms and concepts. In this respect, too, he is much closer to Nietzsche and Bataille, who both proceed in a rigorous but nonphilosophical mode, insofar as we identify all prior philosophy with a restricted economy. Bohr may have, intuitively, sensed this difference. Perhaps this was why he said that "no man who is called a philosopher really understands what is meant by the complementary description," even though one of his reasons appears to be that "they [philosophers] did not see that it was an objective description, and that it was the only possible objective description" (*AHQP*, interview 5, page 3 of transcript). Philosophers may have been right from their perspective; for complementarity is not an objective description according to any definition of objectivity hitherto produced or required by the institution of philosophy as the metaphysics of presence. What philosophy as the metaphysics of presence fails to grasp or refuses to accept is that in order to be "objective" one needs a general economy—a theory that cannot be seen as objective from a classical, restricted economic standpoint.

Bohr appears to have seen the necessity of a fundamental, but rigorous, suspension of classical concepts and their implications much better than his commentators when he speaks of and pursues "a radical revision of our attitude toward the problem of physical reality" (*QTM*, 146). "Problem" may well be the key word here. In Bohr's matrix, no independent physical reality or object can exist, and both concepts are "meaningless," or at least, according to Bohr, "it is difficult for [him] to associate any meaning with the question of what is behind the phenomenon," which may be best read as fully independent of the phenomenon.[20] As we have seen, Bohr's displaced usage of the term "phenomenon" nowhere implies classical phenomenology; and would equally operate against an identification of quantum efficacity with phenomena. A radical suspen-

sion of reality independent of interpretation and related notions, along
with their idealist or phenomenologist opposites, may be the greatest
(anti-)epistemological lesson of quantum mechanics.

One can, of course, attempt to define "reality" by way of or as the
radical alterity or *différance* in the general economy, as Derrida defines
matter. In most, perhaps all, interpretations of Bohr so far, however, the
term 'reality' and the concept(s) it designates inhibit rather than open
anti-epistemological possibilities of the interpretation of Bohr and quantum physics. The loss in representation defining general economy cannot
imply a "reality" that is anywhere present by itself and that cannot be
fully represented or even partially represented, or conceived of—represented—as absolutely unrepresentable, by an ontotheology, positive or
negative, any more than by any form of scientific, objectivist, or empiricist
realism. The radical alterity that emerges cannot be accessed by way of
the "unrepresentable," or the opposition of the representable and the unrepresentable, even though we may have to continue to operate within the
closure of such oppositions and continue to use them against the metaphysics of presence which they govern. This alterity cannot be governed
by any single structure, nameable or unnameable (or a containable cluster
of structures). In this, too, alterity appears to be a rhetorically better term
than reality, or ideality, would be, but alterity (or efficacity) is not meant
here as the only term governing the efficacity at issue. Instead, alterity so
conceived minimizes metaphysical claims upon this efficacity. In fact it
makes no such claims in any form that the metaphysics of presence could
hitherto conceive of, including via various forms of scientific empiricism
or objectivism. By retaining this alterity-like material efficacity, general
economy suspends and allows one to deconstruct the opposite forms of
metaphysics—idealist, phenomenologist, transcendentalist, or positivist.

Of course, whatever its historical, theoretical, rhetorical, or strategic
economy, any given term, such as "matter," or "alterity," may pose problems similar to those posed by the term "reality." In order to avoid these
problems one must follow a general economic chain of analysis. Complementarity must be seen as a general economy of matter, which, to return to Derrida's formulation, in this general economy designates radical
alterity in relation to philosophical oppositions, including the oppositions
that would imply an absolute alterity of matter.

Complementarity entails a radical critique or deconstruction of classical concepts, models, and frameworks, or the entire processes and technologies of measurement and observation, and finally, while not their

wholesale replacement, a redefinition and redelimitation of their functioning. Specifically, it makes the functioning of classical concepts and models *complementary*, and within certain limits, necessarily complementary. As a result, a certain closure of classical concepts emerges as well, although one might need to consider stratifications and transformations of all such closures. Bohr's understanding of quantum physics entails both a dependence on classical physics, by virtue of the correspondence principle, and a dependence on, interactively, philosophical concepts and ordinary language. Bohr eventually reformulates the correspondence principle itself so as to reflect this latter dependence.

Bohr's complementarity, thus, suggests, specifically against Einstein but with many consequences elsewhere in physics and beyond, that no mathematical, conceptual, or metaphorical model—continuous, as Einstein would want, discontinuous, or complementarily continuous and discontinuous—and no properties of such models can be assigned the status of physical reality. There is no "reality" in the following sense: there is no conglomerate of structural properties that can be postulated even as partially representable or displaced by means of mathematical, conceptual, or metaphorical models. Nor, conversely, can one speak of reality as that which is absolutely unrepresentable, but which exists or is present (statically or dynamically) in itself or by itself somewhere, either outside or alongside its partial or displaced representations, or as absolutely inaccessible to any representation. The latter concept is in fact a representation—as an absolute difference or absolute alterity—and it would conform to what can be seen generally as negative ontotheology. This is why the radical alterity of general economy cannot be absolute. This is also why, while the denomination "realist" cannot be effectively applied to Bohr's matrix, it is even more difficult to claim this matrix as idealist or subjectivist or phenomenologist or positivist. Once one suspends the absolutely unrepresentable, it seems logical that some partial or displaced representation of some "reality" existing independently of observation or interpretation—and therefore such reality itself—must be presupposed. Such a presupposition, however, need not follow. One can and must apply a different logic, the logic of "neither, nor" or "either, or" or both at once. This logic implies a complex economy, and all propositions just advanced are subject to the qualifications offered by the preceding analysis (and further nuances will be considered throughout this study). Within this economy, Bohr's complementarity may be seen as functioning within the closure of (certain forms of) realism—or conversely, of (certain forms of) phenomenology—while mutually deconstructing both and other forms of metaphysics of presence and transforming the previous closure of theory. With these qualifications in mind, one can say that complementarity spells the end of all realism—mathematical, physical, or other—along with all idealism, hitherto.

CHAPTER 5

Complementarities,

Correspondences,

Asyntheses

Complementarities

The analysis in this section is arranged under the headings of several complementary rubrics: idealizations and deidealizations, continuity and discontinuity, randomness and causality, completeness and incompleteness. These rubrics are not and cannot be exhaustive. Beyond the standard quantum mechanical complementarities—the wave-particle complementarity, the kinematic-dynamic (position-momentum) complementarity, and the complementarity of coordination and causality—such complementary relations as the inside and the outside, difference and identity (or similarity), and localization and globalization, which play key roles throughout this study, pervade the discussion in this chapter as well. All these rubrics continuously interpenetrate each other and generate subrubrics and new complementarities.

Idealizations and Deidealizations

According to Bohr, all classical (and by implication, all) concepts and descriptions, through which we approach quantum physics, can only be seen as idealizations. Even before the introduction of complementarity, Bohr realized that quantum physics entails a suspension of classical spatiotemporal descriptions. He writes in 1925: "in the general problem of the quantum theory, one is faced not with modification of the mechanical and electrodynamic theories describable in terms of the usual physical concepts, but with essential failure of the pictures in space and time on which the description of natural phenomena has hitherto been based"

(*PWNB* 1:34–35). Or "the possibility of obtaining a space-time picture based on our usual conception becomes ever more hopeless" (*Collected Works* 5:297). In his letter to Born, he argues that quantum experiments "preclude the possibility of a simple description of the physical occurrences by means of visualizable pictures . . . such pictures are of even more limited applicability than is ordinarily supposed. This is of course almost a purely negative assertion, but I feel that . . . one must have recourse to symbolic analogies to an even greater extent than hitherto. Just recently I have been racking my brains to dream up such analogies" (*Collected Works* 5:311).[1] He also writes: "[The wave theory's] 'visuability' . . . is both its strength and its weakness, and in stressing the symbolic character of the treatment I have thought to remind of the great difference (brought about by the quantum postulate) from the classical theories, which has not always been kept sufficiently in mind" (*NBA: BSC*, 14).[2]

In Einstein's relativity the (four-dimensional) space-time is a unity, not a complementarity. It is a unified continuum that was given mathematical grounds by Hermann Minkowski, who introduced the term 'space-time,' and earlier by Bernhard Riemann, whose geometry is the basis of relativity. As a unity, the concept of space-time is close to the Hegelian *Aufhebung*. It offers a kind of deconstruction of Newtonian space-time, and in particular of the concept of simultaneity. While an extraordinary achievement, anti-epistemologically it is well short of complementarity. It remains a classical theory by retaining the space-time continuum as its underlying continuous and fully causal economy, even if relativized with respect to a given perspective. It may, as I said, acquire a certain "Sibyline strangeness" and surrealistic features. But even in general relativity, the Einsteinian landscape falls well short of the quantum mechanical landscapes. Bohr's complementarity, as we have seen, not only deconstructs and deunifies the classical unities, such as coordination and causality, but also complementarizes classical disunities, such as between particles and waves, or continuities and discontinuities. What must be separate in classical theory appears jointly in complementary descriptions, although it cannot be unified in terms of a classical synthesis. Conversely, that which was classically unified now must be seen as mutually exclusive, except to the extent that classical configurations can be retained within new limits assigned to them. Bohr's usage of descriptions and concepts, together with his analysis of such usage, has been a major revolutionary aspect of his matrix and is central in defining its proximity to general economy. Bohr himself speaks of "a thoroughgoing revolution in the concepts upon which the description of nature has rested up to now" ("Über die Wirkung von Atomen bei Stossen," 155).

Continuity and Discontinuity

Conceptually and metaphorically, the complementarity of continuity and discontinuity is central to Bohr's matrix. It affects all specific complementarities at issue in quantum mechanics, in particular, the wave-particle complementarity, but also the complementarity of coordination and causality, for at a certain level causality is always continuity. The interaction of continuous and discontinuous processes has been crucial to Bohr's thinking, beginning with his early encounters with the work of Høffding and Riemann's mathematical ideas.[3] He writes, "The more precise formulation of the content of the quantum theory appears, however, to be extremely difficult when it is remembered that all concepts of previous theories rest on pictures which demand the possibility of *continuous* variation" (*PWNB* 1:29; emphasis added).

As we have seen, the quantum postulate has defined Bohr's understanding of quantum physics since his work on the old quantum theory in 1913. Bohr's earlier work on atomic theory itself engages complex forms of conceptual and discursive discontinuity with preceding physics. In 1913 he states that for his hypothesis, which is essentially equivalent to the quantum postulate, "there will be given no attempt at a mechanical foundation," that is, explaining it in classical or continuous terms, and he adds an extraordinary parenthesis—"(*as it seems now hopeless*)" (*Collected Works* 2:135).[4] The greatness of Bohr's step lies in his proceeding onward without offering such a foundation. Einstein famous remark is arguably the best and, made as late as 1949, the most poignant commentary: "That this insecure and contradictory foundation was sufficient to enable a man of Bohr's unique instinct and tact to discover the major laws of the spectral lines and of the electron shells of the atom together with their significance for chemistry appeared to me like a miracle—and appears to me as a miracle even today. This is the highest musicality [höchste Musikalität] in the sphere of thought" ("Authobiographical Notes," *Albert Einstein: Philosopher Scientist,* 45–47; translation modified). The quantum postulate cannot be justified in classical—causal or continuous—terms. At the same time, however, an extraordinarily rich and productive theory can be developed on what, from the classical perspective, appears as an "insecure and contradictory foundation."

Bohr understood the great role of the idea of continuity and its relation to causality in all perception, interpretation, conceptualization, and theory. As he says: "[E]very notion, or rather every word, we use is based on the idea of continuity, and becomes ambiguous as this idea fails."[5] Bohr, however, saw an even greater significance of the introduction of discontinuity into physics, in turn leading to a radical break—a radical, but not absolute, discontinuity—with classical theories in both physics and philosophy. Given that such a departure cannot be absolute, classical physics or philosophy retain their significance, or acquire a new significance, by virtue of their relation to the closure of (the concept of) continuity. There is, of course, also the closure of discontinuity. One must function within and proceed by complementarizing both. While one can speak of "causal" connections between the process and the effects under observation and measurement, these connections are neither strictly continuous (or deterministic), nor strictly discontinuous (or random). These are effects without causes in the classical sense; but as we have seen, they have complex, general economic efficacities. The implications are profound for physics and philosophy alike. We may no longer be constrained by the necessity of an uncompromised continuity. The failure of classical theories is not a failure of the idea of continuity as such. It is a failure to engage the *complementarity* of the continuous and discontinuous, and complementarity in general.

Randomness and Causality

The wave-particle complementarity and indeterminacy—and, thus, the complementarity or coordination and causality—may be mathematically connected within the framework of quantum physics by way of probability. In Max Born's formulation: "The motion of particles follows the probability law but the probability itself propagates according to the law of causality."[6] Probabilities can be gauged in a reasonably deterministic manner by Schrödinger's equation. The "picture" itself is never fully predictable, since it is constrained by uncertainty relations, which are inherent in Schrödinger's equation. One cannot quite say that Schrödinger's equation is completely deterministic, as, for example, Penrose suggests (*The Emperor's New Mind*, 250–51). It is true that it *mathematically* determines "the evolution of the wave function" (250), which may be all that Penrose intends to claim, and 'deterministic' may simply be too strong a term. Given the nature of Schrödinger's wave-function—

the famous Ψ-function—it can only *determine* what it determines *as undetermined,* stochastic. There is no way to reduce this indeterminacy. The very representation of this indeterminacy in terms of probability or statistics may be inadequate conceptually, however effective or necessary the corresponding mathematical apparatus may be in the actual practice of physics.

The irreducibility of chance was a major vexation for Einstein. He found it very difficult, and finally impossible, to accept the necessity of the suspension of strict causality, along and interactively—or even codefinitionally—with strict continuity. In the famous rendition of his objection, Einstein did not believe that God would throw dice in that way. Bohr's reply is interesting: "On his side, Einstein mockingly asked us whether we could really believe that the providential authorities took recourse to dice-playing ('ob der liebe Gott würfelt'), to which I replied by pointing at the great caution, already called for by ancient thinkers, in ascribing attributes to Providence in everyday language" (*PWNB* 2:47).

Nietzsche offers extraordinary elaborations on the pre-Socratics in *Philosophy in the Tragic Age of the Greeks.* Invoking "a free undetermined [willkürlichen] *nous,* . . . guided by neither cause nor effect [weder von Ursachen noch von Zwecken geleitet]" in Anaxagoras, he says that in guessing such attributes "the answer is difficult. Heraclitus supplied: a game [die Antwort ist schwer, Heraclit würde ergänzen—ein Spiel] . . . the final solution, the ultimate answer, that ever hovered on the lips of the Greeks" (*Philosophy in the Tragic Age of the Greeks,* 117, 112; *KSA* 1:872, 869; translation modified). Game, play—and the (inter)play of chance and necessity—may still be our best chance or bet, too.[7]

For Bataille chance is a major theme throughout his work, particularly in *Inner Experience, On Nietzsche* and *Guilty,* his most Nietzschean works. His elaborations on God and chance in *On Nietzsche* and through the chapter "Games of Chance" in *Guilty* might have been written with Einstein's comments in mind, although Bataille has many other concerns and reference frames. He sees chance as the richest concept, in contrast to the concept of Being, which is the most impoverished one (*Guilty,* 84; *Le Coupable,* 114).

From Democritus to Nietzsche and beyond, at stake in all these approaches is the play and the complementarity of chance and necessity and, interactively but not simply correlatively of continuity and discontinuity. The calculus of this interplay under the conditions of general economy may, as Derrida argues, be finally interminable. For Derrida chance is as crucial a theme as it is for Nietzsche, Bohr, and Bataille, and he explore it throughout his writing. This writing itself, being *writing* in Derrida's sense, must obey the economy of chance or of complementarily chance and necessity and their undecidable and interminable calculus, although, as I shall discuss in chapter 7, Derrida juxtaposes this undecidable *determination* to, according to him, all forms of indeterminacy or indetermination.[8] It is, however, impossible to speak of absolute indeterminacy or absolute, uncomplementarized chance—chance without complementary necessity, although other complementarities may be needed as well. Like all other absolutes, an absolute chance is not radical enough.[9]

While Einstein was troubled by the absence of an underlying deterministic configuration in quantum mechanics, he understood profoundly the significance of statistical behavior in the case of large ensembles, and he made important contributions to the physics, including the quantum physics, of such ensembles. It is only that there are always irreducibly large, infinite ensembles, even in the case of a single particle. A radical indeterminacy is built in even in the case of the smallest ensemble consisting of one particle, which would in effect prohibit the oneness of particles. Bohr, as we have seen, insists on the radical nature of this "statistics" and its difference from classical statistical physics throughout his writing. One is dealing not so much with statistical determination *in practice* (due to large ensembles), but *in principle*. As Bohr writes:

> [I]t is most important to realize that the recourse to probability laws under such [quantum] circumstances is essentially different in aim from the familiar application of statistical considerations as practical means of accounting for the properties of mechanical systems of great structural complexity. In fact, in quantum physics we are presented not with intricacies of this kind, but with the inability of the classical frame of concepts to comprise the peculiar feature of indivisibility, or 'individuality,' characterizing the elementary processes. . . . [T]he situation presents no analogue to the application of statistics in dealing with complicated mechanical systems, . . . [and] in quantum mechanics, we are not dealing with an arbitrary renunciation of a more detailed analysis of atomic phenomena, but with a recognition that such an analysis is *in principle* excluded (*PWNB* 2:34, 42, 62).

Dirac was the first to suggest that one always needs infinite ensembles of particles and complementarities within each rubric. In fact such ensembles are always generated by a given quantum mechanical, or rather quantum electrodynamical, event.[10] Quantum electrodynamics and its subsequent extension in quantum field theory form a more comprehensive theory, which incorporates the effect of special relativity and introduces an even broader and more complex transformational field than that of the nonrelativistic quantum mechanics. As Bohr comments, again stressing the difference from classical statistics: "Dirac's ingenious quantum theory of the electron offered a most striking illustration of the power and fertility of the general quantum-mechanical way of description. In the phenomena of creation and annihilation of electron pairs we have in fact to do with new fundamental features of atomicity, which are intimately connected with the non-classical aspects of quantum statistics expressed in the exclusion principle, and which have demanded a still more far-reaching renunciation of explanation in terms of a pictorial representation" (*PWNB* 2:63).

Dirac's pairs imply irreducible, infinite multiplicities. Quantum statistics redefines the conditions of both identity and multiplicity of elementary particles and the unity or disunity of their ensembles, making unity, or identity, and multiplicity themselves complementary. Single particles themselves become statistical ensembles, and classical structure of identity such as spatial separation no longer obtain by virtue of wave-particle complementarity, since the particles spread out like waves (to the extent that classical concepts and images may be used even in complementary descriptions). The "dissemination" enacted by Dirac's theory is, however, also a new economy of connectibility. Quantum field theory moves even further away from the Parmenidean one toward the Heraclitean many, assuming that this "many" can still be called Heraclitean. As Michael Readhead notes, "quantum field theory has more affinity with the Heraclitean flux than with the Parmenidean One" ("A Philosopher Looks at Quantum Field Theory," 22). Much would depend, however, on how one interprets the Heraclitean multiplicity and flux, and particularly whether one does so through a restricted or a general economy.

Completeness and Incompleteness

Quantum mechanics, Bohr argues, is a complete theory. Under the conditions of Bohr's quantum anti-epistemology or any general economy, completeness does not entail a full unity or synthesis. It connotes instead what may be described as rigorous comprehensiveness. Insofar as it is measured against and prohibits the classical models of completeness, complementarity entails incompleteness—structural, irreducible incompleteness. To borrow Bataille's formulation in *Theory of Religion*, "rigor demands a clear recognition of these conditions" [of incompleteness] (13). The theory complementarity offers is, however, not incomplete. On the contrary, it is a complete theory of its data, even though, and because, it deconstructs the classical concepts of completeness, such as that held by Einstein. Complementarity is as complete as a theory can be under the available conditions and constraints, such as those of incompleteness that make it impossible to have a complete picture in the classical sense.

We must thus reconceive the very notion of a complete theory, via the complementarity of completeness and incompletenesss. Such a reconception would not mean that there are no limits on what a comprehensive description or theory can offer—the limits established within and between the fields, which limits can, of course, be transformed by new theories. These limits entail the fundamental incompleteness of quantum mechanical descriptions in the classical sense of wholeness, coherence, or causality and demand a redefinition and redelimitation of all such concepts.

In view of Gödel's theorem, an analogous but not identical incompleteness characterizes modern mathematics, more or less;[11] and in both these cases a certain completeness is implied. As I have suggested, it is possible that Gödel's theorem, discovered in 1930, influenced the development and refinement of Bohr's work on complementarity. The consistency of quantum mechanics had been a major issue from its inception. Complementarity was also Bohr's response to the demands for a consistent theory, and it resolved the paradoxes implied by preceding conceptions.[12]

The question of completeness of quantum mechanics is central to Bohr's debate with Einstein, particularly in the context of the EPR argument. The word "complementarity" is used by Bohr to suggest both a mutual exclusiveness of the features involved and a completeness of description. According to Murdoch: "Mutual exclusiveness is frequently thought to be the sole condition of Bohr's notion of complementarity. . . . This is a mistaken view: the notion of mutual exclusiveness and of joint completion are equally necessary, indeed complementary, ingredients in the meaning of Bohr's conception. In the genesis of the conception the notion of joint completion came first (in the acceptance of wave-particle duality); the notion of mutual exclusiveness came later (in the acceptance of the uncertainty principle)" (*Niels Bohr's Philosophy*, 61).

The information on the state of the quantum system cannot be more complete than that provided by the inherent indeterminacy and incompleteness and, thus, a certain complementarity of completeness and incompleteness of quantum theory. The radical indeterminacy of quantum mechanics does not, according to Bohr, reflect some hidden non-statistical configuration, implying a (classically) complete, causal theory of which quantum mechanics would be a limited incomplete, statistical case, as Einstein would want. There would, therefore be no new correspondence principle relating quantum mechanics and such a theory, analogous to the correspondence principle between classical physics and quantum mechanics. Quantum mechanics offers as *complete* a description as possible under quantum conditions. Both Bohr's complementarity and anti-epistemologies elsewhere are comprehensive theories, if in, and by virtue of, the absence of classical synthesis. Classical—and classically complete—theories are less complete than theories, such as quantum mechanics, that are incomplete from the classical point of view. Bohr's correspondence principle reflects this reversal of the relative potential for completeness—for comprehensiveness of description—of classically complete and classically incomplete theories.

Correspondences

Bohr's correspondence principle reflects the fact that within classical limits the results of quantum and classical theory coincide. This principle finds an important analogy in Derrida's concept of the closure of philosophy (as the metaphysics of presence), which may be seen as analogous to classical physics in the general economic field engaged by Derrida. Bohr eventually formulated the correspondence principle in very general terms: "the necessity of making an extensive use, nevertheless, of the classical concepts, upon which depends ultimately the interpretation of all experience, gave rise to the formulation of the so-called correspondence principle which expresses our endeavours to utilize all the classical concepts by giving them a suitable quantum-theoretical reinterpretation" (*PWNB* 1:8).[13] The last qualification is extremely important, suggesting that correspondence does not quite correspond, but instead reflects a complex complementarity of continuity and discontinuity with classical theories. One can take advantage here of another meaning of the word 'correspondence.' We continue to maintain our connection, and continuity, with classical theories and its founders by way of what Derrida sees as a postal economy, which extends, to use Derrida's subtitle to *The Post Card*, "From Socrates to Freud and Beyond." Heraclitus, Parmenides, and other pre-Socratics, however, had already sent their messages, which this postal economy continues to circulate. Since this economy is general, the circulation cannot be encircled by any name or field, such as philosophy, and no field is absolutely uncircumventable or, conversely, absolutely outside it. There are areas with a complex complementary topology of proximities and distances, or continuities and discontinuities, which pervade any given field and within which we cannot avoid correspondence, in either sense. Letters, however, may never arrive at their destinations, and even when they do seem to "arrive," they always simultaneously arrive and do not arrive. One thus needs the complementarity of arrival and nonarrival—and of remaining, or returning, and departing.[14]

Bohr always maintained the relative indispensability of classical concepts and descriptions, for both historical and theoretical reasons; and he conceives of this type of closure in very broad terms, well beyond the domain of physics or natural science. This "closure" also relates to observing and measuring instruments, since we must "read" measured results classically, and to the correspondence principle, but it extends beyond these relations and indeed beyond physics alone. As Bohr writes:

> [I]t would be a misconception to believe that the difficulties of the atomic theory may be evaded by eventually replacing the concepts of classical physics by new conceptual forms. Indeed, . . . the recognition of the limitation of our forms of perception by no means implies that we can dispense with our customary ideas or their direct verbal expressions when reducing our sense impressions to order. No more is it likely that the fundamental concepts of the classical theories will ever become superfluous for the description of physical experience. The recognition of the indivisibility of the quantum of action, and the determination of its magnitude, not only depend on an analysis of measurements based on classical concepts, but it continues to be the application of these concepts alone that makes it possible to relate the symbolism of the quantum theory to the data of experience. At the same time, however, we must bear in mind that the possibility of an *unambiguous* use of these fundamental concepts solely depends upon the self-consistency of the classical theories from which they are derived and that, therefore, the limits imposed upon the application of these concepts are naturally determined by the extent to

which we may, in our account of the phenomena, disregard the element which is foreign to classical theories and symbolized by the quantum of action. (*PWNB* 1:16)

Bohr's point here is double. First, he warns against Einstein's hope that some new concepts or theories will lead to a classically causal and complete theory. The second point relates more directly to the question of transformations of theory and the problematics of closure (perceptual, interpretive, or theoretical). Bohr's formulations here are close to Derrida's ideas concerning closure. As I shall discuss later, one can argue for more radical transformations of the classical fields—and of theoretical closures themselves—than are suggested by Derrida, or by Bohr here. (Bohr's overall views in this respect appear to be complex and shifting.) Certainly, new, at times very radically "new conceptual forms," even forms that can no longer be assigned the denomination "conceptual," have been produced in the process, in part *because* one can no longer "disregard . . . element[s] foreign to classical theories," such as those "symbolized by the quantum of action."

Arthur Fine argues that "in the end Einstein was more radical in his thinking than were the defenders of the orthodox view of quantum theory, for Einstein was convinced that the concepts of classical physics will have to be replaced and not merely segregated in the manner of Bohr's complementarity" (*The Shaky Game*, 24). It would, of course, depend on how one views the radicality of such new concepts. Even leaving aside the problem of unconditional departures or reversals, Einstein put stringent *old* demands—metaphysical and mathematical—upon such new concepts. This claim is well supported by Fine's own analysis of Einstein's views, which is one of the more nuanced treatments available, in some contrast to his treatment of Bohr's ideas, even here. One can hardly see Bohr's complementarity as "merely segregat[ing]" old concepts, or doing anything "merely."

The correspondence principle is not an exact quantitative law, but a complex and equivocal tool—a "link between the old and the new," which Bohr used with great effectiveness even before he formulated it.[15] As Bachelard argued, we must be careful to speak in terms of approximation in relating classical physics and the new physics;[16] and even in the case of the nonrelativistic quantum mechanics, the point that it can be approximated by classical physics should be made with considerable caution. The economies of correspondence become even more complex in the fields at issue in this study. At stake are multifaceted stratifications of proximities and differences between classical and new theories, or different languages of description—ordinary, philosophical, mathematical, metaphorical, various jargons, and so forth. We can neither fully separate them, establishing some fully or purely philosophical, theoretical, or mathematical language, nor suspend the difference between them. A very complex economy of correspondences, differentiations, and closures emerges as a result. Bohr was acutely aware of this complexity. He understood the necessity and effectiveness of so-called "ordinary" language and description in the domain of physics, in part since he claimed that "the aim of every physical experiment [is] to gain knowledge under the reproducible and communicable conditions" (*PWNB* 1:25–26). The statement is a bit idealistic, given how complex the economy—theoretical, psychological, and, importantly, political—of such aims is. As we have seen, however, the economy of reproducibility and communication in the experimental-mathematical sciences is profoundly understood by Bohr, and constraints of that type are formidable. Bohr also insists on the significance of "ordinary" concepts and language, alongside theoretical concepts and language.[17] This insistence suggests, first, the stratifiction of the economy of closure operative in any given theory, be it in science or elsewhere. Secondly, it points toward the necessity of problematization and deconstruction of the concept of scientific or theoretical, such as philosophical language, and its uncritical opposition to the so-called "ordinary" language. The latter project has been pursued by Derrida throughout his works.

The principle or economy of the closure of philosophy introduced by Derrida is analogous to Bohr's correspondence principle. Moreover, there may be proximities between them with respect to the resulting views of theoretical transformation, specifically the caution as concerns the introduction or the very possibility of absolutely new concepts. According to Folse, "Bohr's method required searching for a breakthrough by cumulatively compiling the then known difficulties which any theory had to confront" (*The Philosophy of Niels Bohr,* 60). Bohr's complementarity is a complementarization of classical concepts and modes of description, along with and as deconstruction of these concepts and their classical unions or disunions, compatibilities and incompatibilities, and possibilities of simultaneous applications. Classical physics appears to be irreducible, for, while all measuring interactions are always quantum, the measurements themselves must proceed by using classical physics and by classically reading the results from measuring devices. The theoretical and historical closure of classical physics is much broader, given the shared mathematical apparatus and the historical continuity of the ideas of classical and quantum physics. While, however, continuities are irreducible, very radical transformations are also at stake.

The point is of great importance in general, and the issue has complex nuances and ramifications. I shall explore them in detail later, along with the stratification of closures that one must consider—the interactive but heterogeneous closures of perception, conceptualization, language, theory, and possibly still other closures. One can point out briefly that, analogous to the case of classical and quantum physics, there are workable and effective limits of classical theories and concepts. Such limits are one of the main concerns of general economy. These are not the only limits, however; and the interaction between complementary features, which by extension can again be multiple, takes different forms within different limits. A recomprehension of that type already transforms both classical concepts and their limits, as the complementarity of quantum mechanics also points out. Bohr understood that very well. Even within the limits of their applicability, classical theories and models can no longer be given their full classical sense under new conditions, thus refiguring both the classical concepts and the classical limits and suggesting the transformation of our theoretical closure. Such a transformation also transforms correspondences between all senders and receivers of letters, or between postal stations or still broader systems involved. The actual correspondence between the founders of quantum mechanics is of much interest and perhaps a unique importance, in particular the letters between Einstein and Bohr, directly or via the letters of other correspondents—Born, Schrödinger, Heisenberg, Pauli, Dirac. Einstein's letters to Bohr finally transmit or *continue* the letter, and spirit, of Newton, or Kant or Hegel: the letter and spirit of continuum. Bohr's great letter to Einstein, the letter and spirit of complementarity, may never have arrived, although Einstein no doubt read all of Bohr's mail very carefully. There must have been a quantum gap or a quantum leap in the system and history.

Asyntheses

The argument between Bohr and Einstein contains many important nuances, which I shall consider here and in the next chapter. My main concern in this section is the question of theoretical (a)synthesis. It is worth to begin, however, by describing the main features of Einstein's philosophy of physics and by considering the key elements of Bohr's response to Einstein. Einstein's main philosophical requirements upon physical theory can be summarized as follows:

(a) the *causality* of and the absence of randomness in all physical interactions—at bottom, if not in all overt manifestations, which, Einstein agrees, may be statistical;

(b) the *continuity* of all mathematical representations, beginning with the space-time continuum;

(c) the *completeness* of theory, defined in classical terms, via Einstein's concept of a physical reality;

(d) the concept of physical *reality*, defining it as existing independently of observation or interpretation, to which reality the concepts and laws of physics must conform.

Every one of these features is fundamentally, at its very core, threatened by quantum mechanics.

Determined by the conditions discussed in the preceding analysis, the logic of Bohr's argument with Einstein is exquisite and, in a way, simple. All Bohr's questions concern the conditions of meaning and the possibility of such expressions as 'physical reality', 'independent physical reality', 'intrinsic properties', and other concepts of that type. Complementarity as matrix is the exploration of such conditions—the conditions of the possibility and necessity of observation and measurement, of defining variables or observables themselves, of assigning single or complementary features, of physics itself (experiment and theory), and finally of human knowledge. Bohr often likens this exploration to Einstein's own examination of the conditions of applicability of the notion of simultaneity in the theory of relativity. The parallel, although not invalid, is deceptive, given a far more radical character of Bohr's questioning; and, as Bohr notes (*PWNB* 2:36, 41), this questioning is also a critique of Einstein's demands upon a successful physical theory—continuity, causality, classical completeness, and consistency with his concept of physical reality as independent of observation.

Bohr, as it were, continually asks in reply to Einstein: What does it mean that something is independent or has a given value, or even is defined as a variable or observable, such as position or momentum? It means that certain experimental conditions can be arranged so that a given variable or set of variables can be defined, and if such variables were measured, which can only be done within such arrangements, they would have this or that value. Once such is the case, however, one cannot suspend the measuring process. For what does it mean to assume that a particle, or a wave, possesses a state or a real state, definite or given coordinate or momentum? Or what does it mean that 'coordinate' and 'momentum'— or particle or wave—can be defined so as to relate a theory rigorously to experimental data, which data itself and the very concepts of data must be similarly scrutinized? It would mean that, if such a coordinate or momentum were measured, it would have a certain value, which in turn must mean that specific arrangements and procedures of observation and measurement would always have to be involved and, thus, are necessary in order to define such variables. Moreover, beyond the impossibility of measuring both with full precision due to uncertainty relations, one cannot meaningfully speak of either or both as being well defined or of an "object" possessing them, or thus of an object, outside these arrangements. The latter consideration does not appreciably affect classical physics, but it is, Bohr argues, crucial in quantum mechanics. Unlike the case of classical physics, we can neither decouple the impact of experimental arrangements nor compensate for this impact.

We can thus never speak rigorously of suspending such arrangements and, through them, the irreducible locality of interpretation and constitution of whatever is engaged—matter, spatio-temporal continuum, and so forth. Such local arrangements allow one to observe a certain class of quantum effects, usually defined as 'elementary particles,' such as, under one set of conditions and arrangements, waves and, under the other set, particles, but never as simultaneously both, or at least never as both without a loss in one type of representation as against the other. Unless such effects are observed—registered—within a given arrangement as either a particle or a wave, one cannot, strictly speaking, refer to them by any idealization or metaphor, including 'objects' or 'phenomena' (or 'effects'), even though their "materiality," or rather the interaction of this materiality with experimental apparatus, can leave traces of both types. In addition, under all experimental arrangements, one encounters the irreducible indeterminacy conditions, with respect to measurement and the very definition of conjugate variables (such as position and momentum) or of coordination and causality. One encounters this indeterminacy only *within* given arrangements. As will be seen, under certain conditions, such as those of the EPR experiment, it is possible, by means of the formalism of quantum mechanics and standard experimental arrangements, to calculate and predict *both* a coordinate and momentum of a particle and to verify such predictions with respect to either variable by measuring such a variable at a later point. It is never possible, however, to perform a *simultaneous* exact measurement of both variables *within the same experimental arrangement,* and thus simultaneously to verify such a prediction with respect to both variables or to ascertain that a particle possesses both at any given point.

Bohr continuously uses the argument just summarized in order to counterargue and undermine Einstein's presuppositions, arguments and claims. The goal of this argument is to show that quantum mechanics is incompatible with (the metaphysics of) Einstein's meta-physics and demands a different meta-physics—a de facto general economic anti-epistemology. The data at issue in this debate and all quantum data are the results of experiments. Uncertainty relations establish uncircumventable constraints, leading to the suspension of such notions as "independent reality," "intrinsic properties," "wholeness," and various specific unities and disunities of classical theory. In fact indeterminacy increases, rather than decreases with the precision of measurement. Experimental confirmation was provided already by Jean-Baptiste Perrin's early work.[18] As Folse comments: "The mistake of the disturbance interpretation becomes apparent the moment we note that according to it, we could approach the classical ideal of strict determinism if only our instruments of observation were approximately the same size as atoms. However, in fact it is only the immense *difference* between the dimensions of ordinary human experience and those involved in atomic processes that ever made strict determinism a nearly attainable ideal. Were we of the same dimensions as atoms, then the role of the quantum in an interaction would be ever more *increased* rather than decreased, as the disturbance interpretation maintains" (*The Philosophy of Niels Bohr,* 133–34, emphasis added).

One can, thus, again speak of a kind of quantum mechanical *différance,* which can never be reduced, but would increase if one could reduce the difference—another immense *différance*—between the macroscopic —classical—and microscopic—quantum—worlds. This multileveled *différance* underwrites (also in Derrida's sense) the fundamental difference between the calculable, at least in principle, disturbance or distortion of classical statistical physics and the disturbance or distortion of quantum physics, which is in principle irreducible. These considerations also suggest that, while they must be seen as produced within a certain mathematical, conceptual, and interpretive closure, uncertainty relations reflect a structure that—*within this closure* and *within this interpretation*—must be seen as operative in the absence of observation at the time of the process, for example, at the earlier stages of the universe, possibly prior to the Big Bang itself. All recent theories of subnuclear processes are constrained by and depend upon them.[19] That is, we continue to account for such events by using uncertainty relations, even though we could not possibly have observed them at the time of their occurrence. All our deductions do depend on observable traces left by these events, from which certain inferences are derived by using, among other things, uncertainty relations. But then again, we can only observe delayed traces and supplement our inferences upon them, even in the most "immediate" experimental situations, which makes all classical economies of immediacy—and all classical mediation—inapplicable in quantum physics.

We can no more apply quantum considerations fully to classical configurations than classical logic to quantum configurations, even though, in the final account, all classical processes and the interactions between quantum objects and the measuring instruments appear to be quantum.[20] The processes just described suggest a pervasive and perhaps irreducible classical closure as a complex interpretive, conceptual, and psychological—or even biological—conglomerate of constraints. This closure determines conceptual, mathematical, and technological fields of classical physics and, as a closure, even of quantum physics, insofar as classical physics continues to function there. Under these conditions and within this closure or closures, we have a double economy of constraints—some general-economic and others restricted-economic. This economy extends to philosophy and its classical ideals; and many of the classical ideals of physics and philosophy are the same or are mutually complicit.

Synthesis is one of the oldest and the most enduring such ideals in physics and philosophy alike, including the synthesis of the microscopic and macroscopic pictures of the world, which was made so difficult and, it appears, impossible by quantum physics. Quantum physics undermines and dislocates the classical economy of synthesis at every level of its application. Under the conditions of complementarity, there may and must be, alongside mutual exclusivities, relations between different counterparts and specific complementarities. There is, however, no full conceptual or causal synthesis. The complementary information obtained in the quantum domain "cannot," according to Bohr, "be combined into a single picture by means of ordinary [i.e., classical] concepts," but, Bohr adds, "[these kinds of information] represent indeed equally essential aspects of any knowledge of the object in question which can be obtained in this domain" (*PWNB* 2:26). The underlying structure may be seen as finally indeterminate or undecidable in relation to a given pair or cluster. There is in fact no single underlying structure—determinate or indeterminate, decidable or undecidable, known or unknown, nameable or unnameable—any more than a single "surface" picture; and this opposition must itself be deconstructed and complementarized. Such structures cannot be seen as underlying in the sense of an underlying reality independent of the interpretive process, as Einstein would require.

Einstein's position has proximities to both, or oscillates between, Kant and Hegel, between whom, too, there are many, at times infinitesimal, proximities, along with radical differences. Murdoch sees Einstein's position not as "some sort of naive" realism, but a "realism of a sophisticated sort, containing as it does elements of neo-Kantian conceptual idealism," whereby "a physical theory of physical reality" existing "independently of our observation of it" is "mediated" and "determined" by "our concepts" and "conceptual schemes." "The notion of reality is primarily explanatory, an idea which we create to make sense of our experience. No *particular* concept—not even the concept of physical reality—is absolutely binding" (*Niels Bohr's Philosophy*, 198–99). One should not, of course, oversimplify Einstein's position, the complexity of which is correctly argued by Murdoch and has been shown by several recent studies, perhaps particularly by Fine's *The Shaky Game*. In "Reply to Criticisms," Einstein himself says that

> [T]he "real" in physics is to be taken as a type of program, to which we are, however, not forced to cling *a priori*. No one is likely to be inclined to attempt to give up this program within the realm of the "macroscopic" (location of the mark on the paper strip [is?] 'real'). But the "macroscopic" and the 'microscopic' are so inter-related that it appears impracticable to give up this program in the "microscopic" alone. Nor can I see any occasion anywhere within the observable facts of the quantum-field for doing so, unless, indeed, one clings *a priori* to the thesis that the description of nature by the statistical scheme of quantum-mechanics is final. (*Albert Einstein: Philosopher Scientist*, 674)

Einstein notes that "the theoretical attitude here advocated is distinct from that of Kant only by the fact that we do not conceive of the 'categories' as unalterable (conditioned by the nature of the understanding) but as (in the logical sense) free conventions. They appear to be *a priori* only insofar as thinking without the positing of categories and of concepts in general would be as impossible as is breathing in a vacuum" (674).

Einstein's concept of reality is far more than "primarily explanatory." Or, since Einstein does realize the explanatory nature of all our concepts, as do most major philosophical figures—certainly, Kant, Hegel, Husserl, and Heidegger—one might say that his concept of reality is the *primary* explanatory concept of his philosophy. The grounding role of this concept firmly positions Einstein's philosophy of physics within the metaphysics of presence. As we have seen, the (apparently "real") location of the mark on the paper strip is a much more complicated *matter* (in either sense) than Einstein suggests. For one deals here with writing and thus one must confront everything that the question of writing entails— the deconstruction of all classical philosophy, including Einstein's, on the one hand, and Derrida's general economy of *writing*, on the other. As has been pointed out by his most informed coworkers and commentators, Einstein's concept of reality appears to be even more primary for him than causality or continuity. This concept may be the main reason why Einstein's statement misses Bohr's main anti-epistemological point, namely, that the suspension of physical reality (in Einstein's sense) is necessitated by "the observable facts of the quantum field," even though and because one must also deconstruct the concept of the observable fact. This point is also missed by Einstein, perhaps for the same reason. This suspension has nothing to do with "cling[ing] *a priori* to the thesis that the description of nature by the statistical scheme of quantum-mechanics is final," and along with all terms of this phrase—thesis, description, nature, final, or statistics—complementarity deconstructs the concept of a priori far more radically than Einstein's qualification cited above would suggest.

As Fine writes, again from an Einsteinian, realist position: "In charging the instrumentalist Copenhagen theorists with playing a shaky game with reality, Einstein was certainly correct. But it would be an error of judgment on our part to suppose that when the realist moves beyond the truth of the quantum theory to construct its interpretation, he is doing anything other than playing a game himself, and one rather *too* shaky because, granted truth, the rules of this realist game have now been cut loose from any ongoing scientific practice" (*The Shaky Game*, 171). Fine's qualifications here and elsewhere in the book notwithstanding, the metaphysical appurtenances of this position are irreducible: the uncritical difference between the truth of the quantum theory and its interpretation or between interpretation and scientific practice or the truth and interpretation or, which is the main point, of the existence of truth and reality independent of interpretation. In Bohr's case, "the truth of the quantum theory" cannot be unequivocally opposed to "the shaky game" of "construct[ing] its interpretation." Commonalities—or a certain *différance*—notwithstanding, at issue are two very different shaky games.

"The concept of physical reality . . . independent of our observation of it," invoked by Murdoch (*Niels Bohr's Philosophy*, 198), and several other equally metaphysical assumptions are just about "absolutely binding" for Einstein, as they are for Murdoch himself, whose metaphysical position is Einsteinian, rather than Bohrian (*Niels Bohr's Philosophy*, 196, 232, 236, 241–45). The fact that Einstein did believe that "theory determined what can be observed" (198) is not enough to substantiate Murdoch's claim concerning Einstein's view of physical reality. Einstein's understanding is certainly very different from radical theories—anti-epistemologies—of science. Einstein's claims to that effect are based on the success of Riemann's geometry and, or here *as*, general relativity. They may be seen more as a claim upon the determination of the nature of reality by mathematical representation[21]—a kind of mathematical realism. One must be attentive both to the complexities and diversities of this determination, as well as the complexities of Einstein's vision, which, just as Bohr's, can be related to different rubrics.[22]

Murdoch actually notes the decisive difference in this respect between Einstein and Bohr, whom he sees as an "empirical realist." "Unlike Bohr, Einstein was inclined toward a Platonist conception of applied mathematics—the 'mathematics is the language of the Creator' view—according to which physical reality has a structure that may be faithfully reproduced by some mathematical theory" (217). He qualifies: "Einstein believes, [that] some of the mathematical concepts which we freely invent may in fact provide true representation of the intrinsic properties of physical reality. The fact that many of the concepts which we invent seem to fit reality as well as they do is for Einstein something awesomely mysterious" (221). These qualifications are again well taken. Specifically, one should not see Einstein's position simply as Kantian (which is not a simple position either); and one can use conceptual economies of that type against Kant. One cannot, however, finally say, as Murdoch does, that Bohr in turn believes "that our experience is of an independently existing physical world" (221). As the preceding analysis shows, all the terms of this sentence must be questioned, and some suspended, given Bohr's anti-epistemology. Beyond the richer conceptual and metaphorical potential of Bohr's model and its appeal elsewhere, Einstein's claims are problematic in terms of physics itself. We are, Bohr argues, constrained against them by quantum evidence. As Folse writes: "Regarding the quantum postulate as axiomatic, Bohr believed Einstein dogmatically refused to accept its logical consequence that we must abandon the classical presupposition that the classical state of the system refers to properties possessed by an independent physical reality. In fact Einstein was far from regarding the quantum 'postulate' as axiomatic. For him the quantum mechanical description of the discontinuous change of the atomic system from one stationary state to another must be controlled by as yet undiscovered physical laws which he expected would eventually be discovered and allow a return to the classical ideal of describing change of state *continuously*. Since all of Bohr's argumentation was erected on the quantum postulate, it all bypassed Einstein" (*The Philosophy of Niels Bohr*, 152; emphasis added).

In 1931, well after the introduction of quantum mechanics and after Dirac's quantum electrodynamics, Einstein wrote: "Since Maxwell's time, Physical Reality has been thought of as represented by *continuous fields* . . . not capable of any mechanical interpretation. This change in the conception of Reality is *the most profound and the most fruitful* that physics has experienced since the time of Newton" (*James Clerk Maxwell*, 66; emphasis added).[23] He then adds a key comment: "I incline to the belief that physicists will not be permanently satisfied with . . . an indirect description of Reality [implied by quantum theory], even if the theory can be fitted successfully to the General Relativity postulates. They would then be brought to the attempts to realize that programme which may suitably be called Maxwell's: the description of Physical Reality by fields which satisfy without singularity [that is absolutely continuous fields] a set of partial differential equations" (66). Pais correctly sees this program as "uniquely Einstein's" (*"Subtle is the Lord,"* 463), and he stresses the causality aspect of it (15). So does Einstein himself: "field-theory does exist as a program: 'Continuous functions in the four-dimensional [continuum] as basic concepts of the theory.' Rigid adherence to this program can rightfully be asserted of me" (*Albert Einstein: Philosopher-Scientist*, 675).

The "Newton" referred to by Einstein is, on the one hand, the theory of particles—the *continuous* motion of *discrete* particles—and on the other, Newton's optics.[24] Pais comments: "No consequence of the new theory was more profound than the unification of light with electromagnetism: light composed of electromagnetic waves. No part of the new theory appeared to be better understood than the wave nature of light as it travels through empty space. Consequently no part of the old quantum theory appeared more dubious than Einstein's idea that under certain circumstances light behaves as if it has particle structure" (*Inward Bound*, 244). Einstein was responsible for the introduction of light quanta. On mathematical and philosophical grounds alike, however, his agenda was to eliminate quanta as a singularity, which cannot be approached by means of causality, synthesis, unity, and other standard metaphysical machinery.

Einstein, whom Pais calls, "the godfather of complementarity" (*Inward Bound*, 248), clearly searched for this unity, in physical and in philosophical terms, through the idea of continuity and continuum, that had worked so well for him in relativity. In this, he remained a classicist, both in microphysics—the physics of elementary particles—and macrophysics—cosmology. There is another curious historical *continuity* with Newton in Einstein's case. Newton did maintain the corpuscular nature of light, as Einstein did by introducing light quanta. It may be that what Einstein resisted to an even greater extent than discontinuity was *complementarity*—and for good reason, for from it stems the prohibition on conceptual synthesis in any form available hitherto.

The question of the mathematical representation of "reality" has been crucial to the metaphysics and the very concept of "reality." Mathematical, physical, and metaphysical realism are fundamentally connected. One can speak of the mathematical representation by means of quantum mechanical mathematical models, taking into account the discontinuous and complementary, for example, by using Hilbert spaces. This approach may lead to what may be called mathematical metaphysics or Platonism, based on the mathematics of quantum fields, as opposed to the continuums of Riemann's geometry, as in Einstein. The attitude can be found in Heisenberg, particularly his later work, or again in Penrose.[25] In this respect, too, Bohr's position is decisively anti-metaphysical. As Murdoch writes, "It is probable also that Bohr intended to construe the state vector in non-realist terms, regarding it not so much as providing a description of the physical state of an individual object as a mathematical device that generates the correct probability function for the results of measurement. He says that the wave function is a purely symbolic device which specifies the statistical laws governing observations obtainable under specified conditions" (*Niels Bohr's Philosophy*, 214).[26]

Anti-epistemologically understood, materiality can no more be represented by means of mathematics or formal logic than by means of metaphysical or, to remain with Husserl's terms, of transcendental logic. In this context, the philosophical critique of mathematical formalism, from Kant to Hegel to Husserl to Heidegger, is important, although it is not or is no longer sufficient. A radical critique entails a simultaneous deconstruction of transcendental logic.[27] Bohr's anti-epistemology enacts a deconstruction of both formal and transcendental logic of physics. In this case, science operates against formalism—formal or transcendental—not, as does classical theory from Newton to Einstein, in support of it.

Multiple traces of Hegelianism (if not of Hegel himself) can be detected in many of Einstein's philosophical positions and his overall philosophical vision. Hegel's analysis sums up the type of mediation and determination by way of concepts that Einstein wants in the case of physics. Hegel undertakes an unprecedented exploration of these problematics, most pertinently, in the present context, in *The Science of Logic,* but in truth throughout his writing. He asks and in great measure answers Einstein's philosophical questions within much more comprehensive limits than does Einstein himself, specifically with respect to the historical character of the processes at issue.[28]

Einstein's requirements upon physical theory conform to the metaphysics of presence or restricted economy. A general economy, such as Bohr's complementarity, would have, therefore, to suspend these requirements and the determinations resulting from them, including those of theoretical unification or synthesis. The latter are never given primary, if any, significance by Bohr—at least not in their metaphysical form. Bohr does occasionally speak in terms of synthesis, or the opposition of analysis and synthesis, but always displacing these concepts, in the sense considered earlier.[29] Classical unities become de facto deconstructed already by a different economy of the questions to be asked under the conditions of quantum mechanics, and, as we have seen, the question about what kind of questions one can ask is key to Bohr's approach. Quantum physics makes this question irreducible. The question of theoretical synthesis is at the heart of the argument between Bohr and Einstein, since one of the key reasons why Einstein rejected complementarity was that it made a conceptual synthesis impossible. In addition, for Einstein, such a synthesis had to be grounded in a specific conception of physical reality. According to Bohr, however, both become impossible under the quantum conditions, which demand both a very different epistemology or ontology, finally an anti-epistemology and an anti-ontology, and a very different notion of completeness of description. Supplementing the mathematical continuum of Newton, Maxwell, and Riemann, Einstein's vision demanded a synthesis in terms of the conceptual and causal continuum and homegeneity, following Spinoza, Kant, and inescapably, if imperceptibly, Hegel, although Aristotle can, of course, be included in both of these chains. As Murdoch writes:

> Although Einstein was inclined to doubt whether the aim of achieving the greatest possible conceptual unity is attainable, he believed that the aim should be maintained as a regulative principle. He was greatly troubled by the lack of conceptual unity in the foundations of contemporary physics, at the heart of which lie the two disparate concepts of discrete mass and continuous field, according to which energy is conceived of as being now discontinuously, now continuously, distributed in space. The difficulty of uniting quantum theory with relativity theory was, he believed, due largely to a lack of conceptual unity: what was needed was a unified conceptual scheme subsuming the schemes of mechanics and electrodynamics, and uniting the notions of the electromagnetic and gravitational fields. Here Einstein differs from Bohr, for whom conceptual homogeneity *per se* was not one of the main goals of science. (*Niels Bohr's Philosophy*, 196)

The principle of conceptual unity and homogeneity as the main goal of science could not be more Hegelian. Hegel gave this concept more complexity than anyone ever had before—and within these classical limits, arguably more than anyone after him. This is the reason why one is compelled to see these limits themselves as Hegelian. To see conceptual unity as a regulative principle is also problematic, and such a view in no way departs from Hegel. It is not that the principle of unification—aesthetic, mathematical, or other—has not had a pragmatic value in the history of physics. On the contrary, its role has often been extraordinarily productive; and that it may guide physicists effectively has been demonstrated by the history of physics from Newton to Einstein to the most recent developments. Pragmatically speaking, however, suspending this principle or using the opposite principle at certain points is equally effective. Many examples can be offered, beginning, naturally, with Bohr. In this sense, too, Einstein's position may be seen as closer to Hegel's than to Kant's.

To a degree, Kant, or Kierkegaard, William James, and Høffding, can be used against Hegel; and Bohr's position may be seen as closer to theirs, as some commentators suggest. As anti-epistemology, however, complementarity radically questions all these philosophies along with Einstein's. Bohr's matrix not only makes "conceptual homogeneity *per se*" questionable "as the main goal of science" or as a primary principle, regulative or other, but also radically questions the possibility of conceptual homogeneity *as such*.

Einstein's main agenda was, however, continuum as synthesis, both in physical or mathematical and in conceptual terms. Einstein, let me stress, thought that quantum mechanics would have its place within a broader (classically defined) theory. It would emerge as a statistical theory based on incomplete information about quantum mechanical systems, just as Newton's physics is based on incomplete information about relativity. Indeterminacy and complementarity appear to be intrinsic to these systems, however. They must always be factored in and have in fact productively shaped all modern physics. Such, as we have seen, would be the case even for one-particle systems, except that one can no more speak of one particle than of a complete system, thus undermining the very concepts of oneness and completeness. Einstein's comment on Maxwell cited above was made in the immediate aftermath of Dirac's work, which provided the quantum mechanics version of Maxwell's theory and was a crucial part of "*the most profound and the most fruitful change* that physics has experienced since the time of Newton," possibly even more so than Maxwell's. Dirac's theory relates special, *not* general, relativity as a "continuum" theory and quantum mechanics as complementarity. It forces us to think in terms of always many, even infinitely many particles at any given point. A more complex complementarity than ever enters the scene, and Bohr, as we have seen, invokes Dirac's theory in this context. Such a theory puts into question, all the more radically, Reality, Physical Reality, or indeed conceptuality. Even though Einstein, as Pais notes, had "a brief flirtation with Dirac's equation" ("*Subtle is the Lord,*" 466), Dirac's theory, which is the foundation of modern physics, seems to have given Einstein the most difficulty, and it marks the most radical break between Einstein and quantum theory. In physics and philosophy alike, Einstein resisted the disruption of causality and continuum no less than had Hegel, Kant, Spinoza, Descartes, or Aristotle and Plato.

Such attitudes—physical, mathematical, conceptual, metaphorical, or ideological—are not easy to change, and not only for psychological or sociopolitical reasons. New interpretations are difficult to construct. As Dirac commented: "Interpretation was rather more difficult than to play with equations."[30] Of course, one should not assume that playing with equations is an easy matter, either. Commenting in 1936 on the theoretical difficulties of quantum electrodynamics, Wolfgang Pauli said in one of his customary witticisms: "Success seems to have been on the side of Dirac rather than logic."[31] The difficulties to which Pauli refers have not been fully resolved yet, despite significant progress. Dirac's nonlogic, however, remains more logical than any preceding logic. A different logic of theoretical thinking and a different form of theoretical and experimental rigor are at stake in quantum physics and, by implication, in general.[32] Astutely juxtaposing quantum mechanics and relativity, Feynman comments that "nobody understands quantum mechanics" (*The Character of Physical Laws*, 129).[33] He means, I think, that one cannot understand quantum behavior by means of classical representations and theories, and thus by way of the kind of synthesis that Einstein wanted. We cannot achieve such synthesis by classical means, nor, in a certain sense, given the constraints of various classical closures, by any means. We must live with and build upon the shaky foundations of quantum mechanics. That we can do so is remarkable enough, as Feynman also says, and so, as we have seen, does Einstein, referring to Bohr's 1913 theory of the atom.

Einstein's heroic efforts to reinstate "continuum" may be seen as a kind of Hegelian overcoming of rupture, in theory and in history. Bohr, conversely, may be seen as one of the greatest revolutionaries in this century's intellectual history and one of the most anti-epistemological thinkers. Bohr does have his continuities, in the field of physics and elsewhere, specifically with Einstein himself—Einstein against Einstein—or Max Born, who was the first to speak of abandoning "the classical continuum theory," by which he also seems to mean causality, "to retain only formalism and to fill in the new physical content."[34]

Both cases, Bohr and Einstein, would thus differently play out the complementarity of continuities and breaks as the structure of scientific revolution. Einstein's greatest continuity with the old, in physics and metaphysics, appears to be the idea of continuum itself. While in a different manner, this is in great measure the case for Hegel, with Aristotle as his Maxwell and Newton together, and Kant, Spinoza, Leibniz, and Descartes, with whom Hegel both has continuities and breaks, proximities and differences, from infinitesimal to radical. Interactively with the mathematics and physics of continuum, this continuum is Einstein's continuity as well.[35] By contrast, Bohr's complementarity breaks radically

with continuum at all levels—in its mathematics, its physics, its thinking, and in its understanding of how physics works. Strictly speaking,
by virtue of complementarity Bohr breaks with classical discontinuity as
well, interestingly, against Einstein's idea of the light quantum at the
earlier stages of their debate. First, as Folse notes, "Bohr resisted according any 'reality' to this [Einstein's] particle-like model of radiation" (*The
Philosophy of Niels Bohr*, 71), which is consistent with his general antireal-
ist attitude. Second, more interestingly, Bohr insisted on the necessity
of simultaneously engaging continuous fields, and thus complementary
descriptions, which define quantum fields of the quantum mechanics of
Born, Heisenberg, Schrödinger, and Dirac. According to Oscar Klein,
"[Bohr] always stressed the necessity of looking into the deep abyss between the classical way of looking at things . . . while Einstein tried in
some way to have a *continuous* development with the classical ideas" (emphasis added).[36] "The bottomless abyss" was in fact one of Bohr's favorite phrases, reflecting his philosophy of nature and further suggesting a
proximity between Bohr and general economic theories, and specifically
deconstruction.[37] Einstein's conceptual continuity with classical theory—
now Newton's corpuscular theory of light—may take precedence over the
continuous mathematical model. It is true and of some importance that
this specific encounter takes place before Einstein develops general relativity. The conceptual and psychological pattern, however, is interesting.
Throughout his career what takes precedence is continuity as conceptuality and causality, physical and historical. It is, then, the acausal complementarity of the continuous and discontinuous and a movement toward
asynthesis that Einstein rejects and Bohr introduces and develops in both
physics and meta-physics.

    Thus, at a metalevel, the relationships of Bohr's complementarity to
history are complementary. Like all radical breaks, Bohr's is not absolute.
Mirroring the structure of complementarity itself, it has both continuities
and breaks. By engaging the question of writing, Freud, as Derrida shows,
himself *writes* in every sense conceivable, finally in Derrida's sense of
writing.[38] By introducing complementarity, Bohr complementarizes various classical, or classical and quantum, theories. Einstein, by contrast,
continues the classical tradition in physics and philosophy by retaining
the continuum of classical physics and of classical metaphysics. These
meta-economies have been in great fashion over the last two decades,
and they are interesting and important; and their role in Freud, Einstein,
Bohr, or other economies of scientific revolution cannot be overlooked.
In my estimate the emerging theories are more significant, however, even

leaving aside the fact that the complexity of the genealogies at issue cannot be subsumed by metaconfigurations of that type.

Bohr's break is both toward the complementarity of continuities and breaks and toward complementarity as matrix—a non-Hegelian conglomerate of conceptual and mathematico-experimental (or technological) structures. Such structures can, of course, be seen as unified in Hegelian fashion, and powerful (non-Hegelian) unities within and between them are formed and must be taken into account. To think in these terms is, however, against the spirit, if not the letter (unless in Lacan's sense or in Derrida's sense of writing) of complementarity in Bohr and as understood here. As we have seen, complementarity offers comprehensive and, under the conditions of radical incompleteness, complete descriptions of its data. To say so, however, is quite different from claiming a unifying epistemological, ideological, or aesthetic principle or hope—Einstein's hope, Husserl's hope in "The Origin of Geometry," Heidegger's hope, of which Derrida speaks (*Margins*, 27).[39]

Bohr's complementarity suggest a massive anti-epistemological agenda, operating against continuum and against synthesis. Along with other anti-epistemologies, it constitutes "the epistemological lesson" that we are far from having exhausted. Complementarity is *practiced*, as against, and *against*, the underlying, given or established once and for all, philosophical or aesthetic principle, such as continuum, or prohibition that *der Alte*, "the old one," "subtle but not malicious" should play dice.[40] Continuum and this prohibition may in fact be the same, if one understands continuum as a principle, "the principle of all principles," as that introduced by Husserl in *Ideas* (83). It may in fact be seen as the principle of continuum and presence at the level of "the immediate intuition of consciousness," based on the model of temporality as the continuum of presence, the model that, as Derrida shows, is unsustainable, even within the logic of Husserl's own text. As a general economy, Bohr's complementarity is not and by definition cannot be claimed as such a principle.[41] Uncertainty relations are a law, as are specific complementarities. Bohr does not attempt by a single argument to cover all cases—this is why one speaks of a framework or strategic play or even a working method. By definition, complementarity cannot even be *always* complementarity. Other relations than complementarity can *always* be multiply involved. Anti-epistemology entails a kind of general economy (in either sense) or a double constraint of "always"—nothing can always be (present), but something else can always become involved.

CHAPTER 6

Locality and

Causality

Bohr's argument for complementarity is developed with particular effectiveness and force in his reply to the Einstein-Podolsky-Rosen (EPR) argument. The exchange, as it happens, represents the last full-fledged attack mounted by Einstein against quantum mechanics. It is also one of the best examples of the physics and meta-physics of complementarity at work, and it played a key role in helping Bohr to refine his understanding of and argument for complementary. Einstein conceded that the argument failed to prove its main thesis—*the incompleteness of quantum mechanics*—in physical or logical terms. He never relinquished the metaphysical views that informed it, however, and continued to hope that quantum mechanics would be replaced by a theory that would reinstate (classical) continuity, causality, completeness, and reality to physics. The EPR argument has continued to generate ideas and to provoke debates of major significance, especially in the contexts of the hidden variables theories and Bell's theorem. This chapter considers these developments. The first section gives a general summary. The sections that follow offer detailed analyses of the EPR argument and Bohr's response to it, the question of hidden variables, and Bell's theorem and his philosophical views.

Summary

The EPR argument concerns a situation in which both the position and momentum of a particle could be predicted definitively—without uncertainty—in view of the following considerations. Although, due to uncertainty relations, in quantum mechanics one can never simultaneously

measure both the momentum and position of any particle with full precision, quantum mechanical formalism does allow one to calculate without uncertainty the combined momentum of and the relative distance
between two particles. If these particles are, then, allowed to interact,
the possibility of measuring *either* the position *or* momentum of one of
them at any given point (which is always allowed by quantum mechanics)
and the law of momentum conservation (which applies under all conditions) allow one to *calculate* and *predict* with certainty the position and
momentum of the other particle. Since, EPR claims, in quantum mechanics such predictions of the exact value of conjugate variables (variables
subject to uncertainty relations) are impossible, their argument would
show the incompleteness of quantum mechanics by a certain—in their
view, reasonable—criterion of completeness based on a certain—equally
reasonable—criterion of physical reality.

As was shown by Bohr and others, the application of the assumptions
of the argument, particularly in its initial form, to quantum mechanics,
was problematic, beginning with the claim that quantum mechanics never
allows for exact *predictions* of the values of both conjugate variables, such
as position and momentum. Quantum mechanics claims only that, due
to uncertainty relations, the *exact simultaneous measurement* of both is impossible at any given point within any given experimental arrangement.
In the EPR case, too, such simultaneous measurements or even simultaneous predictions are impossible: *two separate* measuring procedures are
required in order to measure with certainty the position and the momentum of one particle, which are necessary in order to calculate the position
and momentum of the other. EPR do introduce the question of the simultaneous measurement of conjugate variables at the end of their article,
without, however, realizing its implications for the possibility of applying
their criteria of reality and completeness in the case of quantum mechanics. It is the impossibility of that simultaneous measurement and only
this impossibility—rather than the impossibility of predicting both on the
basis of other data and calculations—that defines quantum mechanical
complementarity and its (anti-)epistemology. Joint predictions of both the
momentum and the position of a given particle are possible under certain
conditions, such as those specified by the EPR argument; exact measurement of both simultaneously is *never* possible, under any conditions—for
example, if one wanted to verify such predictions. This double point was
not fully considered by EPR, who did not appear sufficiently to differentiate between prediction and measurement. The absence of such differ-

entiation was possible by ascribing simultaneous reality to both position and momentum without simultanously measuring both of them—and, in the case of the second particle of the EPR experiment, without measuring either of them—which is not possible in the case of quantum mechanics.

Bohr uses all these considerations in his critique: he argues that one is constrained as to what can and cannot be asked and predicted concerning the second particle at any given moment. He shows that measuring the momentum, or conversely the position, of one particle disallows the necessary conditions for measuring or meaningfully ascribing position, or conversely momentum, to *both* the first and the second particles (*QTM*, 147–48). These conditions must include specific experimental arrangements. The interactions between the objects and measuring instruments in quantum mechanics are, Bohr argues, not taken into account by EPR. A rigorous analysis of these interactions would disallow their key assumptions and expose what Bohr sees as "an essential ambiguity" in the EPR argument, resulting from two assumptions: first, that an element of reality can be meaningfully ascribed to each of the quantities represented by the variables defined as position and momentum, and, second, that the predictions and ascriptions at issue can be done "without in any way disturbing the system" (associated with the second particle) (*QTM*, 148).

The EPR argument was based on classical concepts (the concept of physical reality independent of interpretation, intrinsic properties, and the like) and criteria of completeness and on the unexamined preconditions for the rigorous use of such concepts in the quantum situation. The same features characterize most subsequent versions of the argument, although many corrections and modifications have been made throughout its history, beginning with Einstein's own. In his reply, Bohr says that "the apparent contradiction [claimed by EPR] in fact discloses only an essential inadequacy of the customary viewpoint of natural philosophy for a rational account of physical phenomena of the type with which we are concerned in quantum mechanics. Indeed the *finite interaction between object and measuring agencies* conditioned by the very existence of the quantum of action entails—because of the impossibility of controlling the reaction of the object on the measuring instruments if these are to serve their purpose—the necessity of a final renunciation of the classical ideal of causality and a radical revision of our attitude towards the problems of physical reality" (*QTM*, 145–46).

The assumptions of the EPR argument were exposed by Bohr as problematic and finally inapplicable under the conditions of quantum mechanics. Quantum mechanics, Bohr argues, does not depend on these assumptions or that logic. It cannot, therefore, be judged incomplete by criteria based on them, insofar as the data itself is derived from quantum mechanics. The physical data of the EPR argument is not only consistent with quantum mechanics, but it cannot be obtained otherwise, and the EPR predictions are possible only on the basis of the quantum-mechanical formalism. This point is crucial for Bohr's critique of the EPR argument and his claims concerning the completeness of quantum mechanics. He argues that both EPR's definition of reality and their criteria of completeness are inapplicable in the case of quantum mechanics. One cannot, therefore, claim that quantum mechanics, which is *not* a classical theory, is an incomplete theory by criteria defining the completeness of classical theories, insofar as it fully accounts for its data and insofar as this data cannot be accounted for by classical theories. Even if a classical theory could do so, the result would be two equally valid theories, assuming that neither violated other physics (which consideration becomes crucial in view of Bell's theorem). The conditions proposed by EPR may be indispensable in view of the metaphysical or ideological (in the broad sense of the term) positions of the authors. They may be indispensable or workable in classical theories (where role of the measuring instruments can be disregarded), suggesting the complicity, perhaps irreducible, between classical physics and classical metaphysics. They have, however, no mathematico-theoretical or experimental basis in quantum mechanics.

The EPR argument was an important contribution to the development of quantum theory and the philosophical debates around it, although the topic receded into the background in the aftermath of Bohr's response. It was, however, revived and widely discussed after Bohm introduced his hidden variables interpretation of quantum theory in 1952, and, then, in the wake of Bell's theorem, discovered in 1964.

Hidden variables theories seek to supplement quantum-mechanical statistical data by additional variables affecting physical states, unobtainable by means of—"hidden" from—quantum mechanics, although operative within a nonstatistical, causal theory and possibly eventually experimentally obtainable. Quantum mechanics, then, would be subsumed by a classically complete and fully causal theoretical framework consistent with quantum mechanics within the latter's limits. Einstein expressed skepticism concerning Bohm's hidden variables theory. He hoped that quantum mechanics would prove to be wrong at some critical limit and (rather than be supplemented by additional variables) be replaced by a completely new theory of a classical, causal type, accounting for the data that could not be accounted for by quantum mechanics. A successful new theory, as conceived by him, would be a new classical theory by virtue of its desired features—(classical) completeness of description, causality, continuity, and reality—all suspended by quantum mechanics. Einstein, however, can still be seen as a proponent of the hidden variables view in the form of his intrinsic-properties doctrine.

Bell's theorem introduced a new dimension into this problematics. It offered an unexpected answer to the hidden variables argument by stating that no hidden variables theory, which is both causal, nonstatistical *and* local, can be compatible with the statistical predictions of quantum mechanics. Any classical theory whose predictions would be compatible with such predictions would have to be, in Bell's phrase, "grossly non-local," as is Bohm's hidden variables theory. This "gross non-locality" implies an instantaneous action at a distance and propagation with a speed higher than the speed of light, forbidden by Einstein's relativity. It would violate one of the most fundamental experimental constants in all physics. One cannot, thus, simultaneously maintain quantum mechanical and relativity data within a classical theory. Insofar as quantum mechanical data remains valid, therefore, Bell's theorem places severe constraints upon the possibility of hidden variables or any classically complete and causal theory accounting for quantum data—the data violating local causality. The result is ironic, and disappointing to the proponents of the Einsteinian philosophy of physics, including Bell himself: locally causal theories violate the locality requirement, while a locally noncausal theory—quantum mechanics—allows one to maintain it.

The EPR Argument and Bohr's Response

The EPR article opens with and uses throughout its argument a number of meta-physical (and metaphysical) claims and concepts, which, in view of the preceding analysis, must be seen as inapplicable to quantum mechanics (in Bohr's interpretation) and problematic in general. According to EPR's opening statement:

> Any serious consideration of a physical theory must take into account the distinction between the objective reality, which is independent of any theory, and the physical concepts with which the theory operates. These concepts are intended to correspond with the objective

reality, and by means of these concepts we picture this reality to ourselves.

In attempting to judge the success of a physical theory, we may ask ourselves two questions: (1) "Is the theory correct?" and (2) "Is the description given by the theory complete?" It is only in the case in which positive answers may be given to both of these questions, that the concepts of the theory may be said to be satisfactory. The correctness of the theory is judged by the degree of agreement between the conclusions of the theory and human experience. This experience, which alone enables us to make inferences about reality, in physics takes the form of experiment and measurement. It is the second question that we wish to consider here, as applied to quantum mechanics. (*QTM*, 138)

The EPR argument is based on the assumption that the data itself described by and accounted for by quantum mechanics is correct. This point is crucial to their argument and to the subsequent history of the questions posed by it. EPR, then, introduce what they see as a necessary criterion of completeness and a "reasonable" criterion and "as a sufficient condition of reality," which, according to their view, are "in agreement with both classical and quantum mechanical ideas of reality":

Whatever the meaning assigned to the term *complete*, the following requirement for a complete theory seems to be a necessary one: *every element of the physical reality must have a counterpart in the physical theory*. We shall call this the condition of completeness. The second question [of completeness] is thus easily answered, as soon as we are able to decide what are the elements of the physical reality.

The elements of the physical reality cannot be determined by *a priori* philosophical considerations, but must be found by an appeal to results of experiments and measurements. A comprehensive definition of reality is, however, unnecessary for our purpose. We shall be satisfied with the following criterion, which we regard as reasonable. *If, without in any way disturbing a system, we can predict with certainty (i.e., with probability equal to unity) the value of a physical quantity, then there exists an element of physical reality corresponding to this physical quantity*. It seems to us that this criterion, while far from exhausting all possible ways of recognizing a physical reality, at least provides us with one such way, whenever the conditions set down in it occur. Regarded not as a necessary, but merely as a sufficient, condition of reality, this criterion is in agreement with classical as well as quantum-mechanical ideas of reality. (*QTM*, 138–39)

EPR then consider the basic quantum-mechanical situation in order to establish the following alternative: "(1) *the quantum-mechanical description of reality given by the wave function is not complete* or (2) *when the operators corresponding to two physical quantities do not commute the two quantities cannot have simultaneous reality*" (*QTM*, 139). The second possibility is equivalent to the claim that when two physical quantities cannot be established with full precision simultaneously, they cannot have simultaneous reality. EPR argue that the first assumption "leads to a contradiction," but, which is crucial, only when taken "together with the criterion of reality given above" (140).

The authors consider a possible quantum experiment from a standpoint based on two considerations. First is the law of the conservation of momentum in any physical motion and in (i.e., before and after) any physical interaction. Second is the fact that, while quantum mechanical formalism disallows the simultaneously measurement of momentum (p) and position (q) of a given particle since corresponding operators do not commute, it does allow one to establish, simultaneously, the combined momentum (p_1+p_2) and the relative distance (q_1-q_2) between two particles, because the corresponding operators do commute. The latter fact results from a simple calculation known as the transformation theorem. To use Pais's account:

> Two particles with respective momentum and position variables (p_1, q_1) and (p_2, q_2) are in a state with definite total momentum $P=p_1+p_2$ and definite relative distance $q=q_1-q_2$. This, of course, is possible since P and q commute. The particles are allowed to interact. Observations are made on particle 1 long after the interaction has taken place. Measure p_1 and one knows p_2 without having disturbed particle 2. Therefore (in their [EPR] language), p_2 is an element of reality. Next, measure q_1 [without simultaneously measuring p_1] and one knows q_2 again without having disturbed particle 2. Therefore q_2 is also an element of reality, so that both p_2 and q_2 are elements of reality. But quantum mechanics tells us that p_2 and q_2 cannot simultaneously be elements of reality because of the noncommutativity of the momentum and position operators of a given particle [and thus both cannot be measured simultaneously]. Therefore quantum mechanics is incomplete. (*"Subtle is the Lord,"* 455–56)

It is crucial that at no point are position and momentum measured—or predicted—simultaneously; these predictions are made possible solely by virtue of the momentum conservation law. Pais comments: "It should be stressed that this paper contains neither a paradox nor any flaw of logic. It simply concludes that objective reality is incompatible with the assumption that quantum mechanics is complete. . . . This conclusion has not affected subsequent developments in physics, and it is doubtful that it ever will. . . . 'It is only the mutual exclusion of any two experimental procedures, permitting the unambiguous definition of complementary physical quantities which provides room for new physical laws,' Bohr wrote in his rebuttal. He did not believe that the Einstein-Podolsky-Rosen paper called for any change in the interpretation of quantum mechanics" (456). One cannot quite say that the EPR argument "has not affected subsequent developments in physics." Pais does, however, cite here arguably the single most important statement of Bohr's reply. It defines complementarity in relation to experimental conditions and "provides room for new physical laws" (*QTM*, 148).

Bohr's counterargument is profound and is the product of a highly nontrivial way of thinking, although the problematic nature of EPR's assumptions and, specifically, of their concept of reality should be apparent in view of the analysis given earlier. In the course of his reply Bohr actually refutes the EPR claims concerning the incompleteness of quantum mechanics many times and at many levels. One would, of course, need Bohr's or analogous interpretation in order to produce such a counterargument. Some of Bohr's major ideas are intimated in his short note, "Quantum Mechanics and Physical Reality" (*QTM*, 144). Bohr's full reply, published under the same title as the EPR article, "Can Quantum-Mechanical Description of Physical Reality Be Considered Complete?," is a great conceptual and rhetorical document of both Bohr's work and modern anti-epistemology. Bohr proceeds as follows. After a brief summary of the EPR argument, he points out first the key metaphysical elements of the EPR definition of reality and its criteria of completeness. Both will have to be shown to "disclose only an essential inadequacy of the customary view of natural philosophy for a rational account of physical phenomena of the type we are concerned with in quantum mechanics" (*QTM*, 146). Bohr inserts a key footnote explaining that the EPR predictions are derived on the basis, and only on the basis, of "a coherent mathematical formalism covering automatically any procedure of measurement" in quantum mechanics. While the fact that the EPR predictions are based on this formalism is an obvious point, Bohr's qualification that the formalism at issue "covers automatically any procedure of measurement" is decisive because such procedures are not rigorously considered by the EPR argument (145). These procedures, however, must be taken into account by any definition of reality and by all criteria of completeness that one applies to quantum mechanics. Bohr then offers one of his best accounts of the interaction between the object and the measuring instruments in quantum mechanics. It is through this analysis that he argues for what he sees as "an essential ambiguity" of the EPR criteria. He concludes with the rhetorical move, which he often uses, of comparing quantum mechanics and relativity. On this occasion, he refers to general relativity— Einstein's most radical theory: while both complementarity and general relativity "[uphold] an ordinary description of all measuring processes," "the very essence" of both theories is "the establishment of new physical laws, in the comprehension of which, we must renounce" customary ideas concerning physical reality (*QTM*, 150–51). The comparison may again be misleading, in view of the more radically anti-epistemological character of complementarity, made quite pronounced in Bohr's formulation of this comparison. But it is a brilliant rhetorical move aimed both directly at Einstein and at a broader audience, who was by that time reconciled (although originally resistant) to relativity. The point is also well taken substantively: "this new feature [the finite and uncontrollable interaction between objects and measuring instruments] of natural philosophy means a radical revision of our attitude as regards physical reality, which may be paralleled with the fundamental modification of all ideas regarding the absolute character of physical phenomena, brought about by the general theory of relativity" (*QTM*, 151).

Bohr immediately understood the key physical assumptions of the EPR argument derived from the main facts of the EPR experiment: the fact that the system consisting of two interacting particles may be assigned a combined momentum and a difference of positions, the fact that either conjugate variable—position or momentum—by itself can be measured with full precision for both particles at any point, and the fact that the other conjugate variable can be calculated with full precision in the EPR situation. In view of these facts, EPR made a—meta-physical and metaphysical—assumption that both particles continue to possess both positions and momenta as intrinsic properties after the interaction and, by implication, possess them before the interaction or indeed at all points. These considerations, in the authors' view, imply that quantum mechanics is an incomplete theory, since it disallows the possibility of determining these properties simultaneously. Quantum interactions disallow the EPR assumptions, however, in view of considerations that prevent one from assigning or, again, defining any physical variables *prior* to the local process of measurement, defined by the interaction, itself quantum, between the object and the measuring instruments. The facts of the EPR experiment change nothing in this respect. Not carefully considered by EPR, the quantum and indeterminate ("finite and uncontrollable") interaction between the object and the measuring instruments becomes a major point in Bohr's counterargument.

The EPR argument and their very criteria of completeness and reality are, Bohr argues, based on "ascrib[ing] an element of reality to each of the quantities, represented by quantum mechanical variables" (*QTM*, 145), which are exactly *predicted* for the second particle through measurement performed in S_1 (the local system associated with the first particle), but are not measured simultaneously at any point in their local system (S_2). Such an ascription is, according to Bohr, impossible under the conditions of quantum mechanics, within which the EPR argument operates and on which it depends in deriving its data. In order to make it possible, one would have to measure both the position and momentum simultaneously in S_2, which cannot be done. This absence of simultaneous measurement and prediction introduces a further "disturbance" into or "influence" upon what actually happens in the local system (S_2) associated with the second particle. For we become constrained as to what can be measured and what kinds of questions can be asked about the second particle. As EPR themselves point out, the position and momentum of the second particle are not even predicted simultaneously (*QTM*, 141). If not the impossibility of the simultaneous definition of these variables, the impossibility of their simultaneous measurement or prediction is never contested by EPR, who concede that their criterion of reality would be affected by this impossibility. These are the changes in the concept of reality resulting from this impossibility, possibly the necessity of abandoning this concept altogether, that they find unacceptable and that Bohr finds uncircumventable (*QTM*, 145).

The impossibility of unambiguously defining and applying these variables, or all concepts involved, becomes crucial at this juncture. As Bohr says: "Indeed we have in each experimental arrangement suited for the study of proper quantum phenomena not merely to do with an ignorance of the value of certain physical quantities, but with the impossibility of defining these quantities in an unambiguous way" (*QTM*, 149). One cannot, therefore, speak of ascribing reality to both position and momentum of either the second or the first particle, as EPR do. Nor, by the same token, can one claim that this can be done "without in any way disturbing a system," even the second system, for it is only within—and thus by inevitably disturbing—that system that one can meaningfully speak of values and of variables themselves in relation to the second particle of the EPR pair. Hence one can only measure with full precision and thus unambiguously ascribe either momentum or position, but never both, either in the case of the first or the second EPR particle (*QTM*, 147–48). Bohr argues this point by carefully examining the interactions (themselves quantum and subject to uncertainty relations) between the particles and the measuring instruments. This examination is a major part of Bohr's reply. It allows him to expose complications and ambiguities unperceived by EPR—certainly those concerning the possibility of the simultaneous measurement and definition of the positions and momenta of both particles at any point, but also more subtle complications concerning the possibility of treating two particles as separate quantum systems, or even the possibility of unambiguously applying the law of the conservation of momentum in view of the complications emerging at every step of the measuring procedures involved. To cite the concluding elaboration of this part of Bohr's analysis:

> By allowing [in measuring the distance between the EPR particles] an essentially uncontrollable momentum to pass from the first particle into the mentioned support [of the measuring device], however, we have by this procedure cut ourselves off from any future possibility of applying the law of conservation of momentum to the system consisting of the diaphragm and the two particles and therefore have lost our only basis for an unambiguous application of the idea of momentum in predictions regarding the behavior of the second particle. Conversely, if we choose to measure the momentum of one of the particles, we lose through the uncontrollable displacement inevitable in such a measurement any possibility of deducing from the behavior of this particle the position of the diaphragm relative to the rest of the apparatus, and have thus no basis whatever for predictions regarding the location of the other particles. (*QTM*, 148)

In "The Causality Problem in Atomic Physics" (the Warsaw lecture) Bohr remarks that "the [EPR] paradox finds its complete solution in the frame of quantum mechanical formalism, according to which no well defined use of the concept of 'state' can be made as referring to the object separate from the body with which it has been in contact, until the external conditions involved in the definition of the concept are unambiguously fixed by a further suitable control of the auxiliary body" (21). This crucial point of quantum mechanics, at least in Bohr's interpretation, is never considered by EPR. As both Faye (*Niels Bohr*, 183), in commenting on this passage, and Murdoch (*Niels Bohr's Philosophy*, 191) observe, one of the EPR particles can be treated as such an auxiliary body—a measuring instrument—while the other is treated as an object. I shall comment on the significance of this possibility below. Einstein's subsequent (1949) comments on Bohr's reply are of some interest here:

> Of the "orthodox" quantum theoreticians whose position I know, Niels Bohr's seems to me to come nearest to doing justice to the problem. Translated into my own way of putting it, he argues as follows:
>
> If the partial systems A and B form a total system which is described by its Ψ-function $\Psi/(AB)$, there is no reason why any mutually independent existence (state of reality) should be ascribed to the partial system A and B viewed separately, *not even if the partial systems are spatially separated from each other at the particular time under consideration.* The assertion that, in this latter case, the real situation of B could not be (directly) influenced by any measurement taken on A is, therefore, within the framework of quantum theory, unfounded and (as the paradox shows) unacceptable.
>
> By this way of looking at the matter it becomes evident that the paradox forces us to relinquish one of the following two assertions:
>> (1) the description by means of the Ψ-function is *complete*
>> (2) the real states of spatially separated objects are independent of each other.
>
> On the other hand, it is possible to adhere to (2), if one regards the Ψ-function as the description of a (statistical) ensemble of systems (and therefore relinquishes [1]). However, this view blasts the framework of the "orthodox quantum theory." ("Reply to Criticism," *Albert Einstein: Philosopher-Scientist*, 681–82)

As will be seen, it is actually possible to adhere to the independence aspect of (2) without blasting the framework of the orthodox quantum theory, insofar as one also adheres to Bohr's interpretation of the orthodoxy.[1] In Bohr's interpretation of the EPR experiment, the situation "*B* need not be (directly [or, in Bohr's terms, 'mechanically,' physically]) influenced by any measurement taken on A," thus preserving the prohibition upon action at a distance, entailed by relativity. One would have to suspend "state of reality," "real states," "real situation," or the existence of anything independent of observation and measurement, and so forth—all of which are inapplicable under the conditions of quantum mechanics (in Bohr's interpretation). This is one of the key points of both Bohr's response to EPR and of his interpretation of quantum mechanics, the point largely missed by EPR and not fully understood or, at least, not adequately considered by Einstein here or elsewhere. Bohr's argument is indeed here "translated into [Einstein's] own way of putting it." Bohr's position allows him to retain the "independence" at issue, but prohibits the possibility of "real states." The alternative, thus, is between the completeness of quantum mechanics and the possibility of real states, rather than the independence or separability of the two systems at issue.

Einstein is not incorrect (except again for the "state of reality" parenthesis) in suggesting that, in Bohr's view, "if the partial systems A and B form a total system which is described by its Ψ-function $\Psi/(AB)$, there is no reason why any mutually independent existence (state of reality) should be ascribed to the partial system A and B viewed separately." Insofar as one applies, as EPR do, the formalism describing the combined system, one cannot claim, as EPR do, that one can predict "with certainty" the value of physical variables for the second particle "without *in any way* disturbing a system" (*QTM*, 138; emphasis added), although, as Bohr stresses, "there is [in this case] no question of a mechanical disturbance of the system under investigation." This is one of several reasons why Bohr says that EPR's criterion of physical reality "contains an ambiguity as regards the meaning of the expression 'without in any way disturbing a system'" (*QTM*, 148). Bohr offers a meticulous analysis of the experimental situation involving both systems of the EPR experiment (*QTM*, 147–50). Nowhere, however, does this analysis imply a physical action at a distance and a physical—direct (in Einstein's terms) or mechanical (in Bohr's terms)—disturbance of one of the two systems of the EPR argument by the measuring procedures performed on the other. As will be seen, such would not be the case even when one of the particles of the EPR pair is itself treated as a measuring instrument and another as an object. As would follow from the preceding analysis, however, Bohr's argument would expose the EPR logic as problematic, even if one considers the systems associated with two particles as separate after the par-

ticles interact. That the EPR particles must perhaps be seen as a combined
system after the interaction actually appears to be less significant than
other key aspects of Bohr's argument.[2] Bohr brilliantly utilizes the fact
that two separate measuring procedures are required for establishing and
even defining the position and momentum of the second particle. To cite
Murdoch's commentary:

> Einstein was inclined to argue that since either the exact momen-
> tum of (particle) S_2 or the exact position of S_2 can be determined
> in this case without physically disturbing it in any way, S_2 must be
> said to *have simultaneously* an exact position and an exact momentum,
> contrary to Bohr's interpretation of the uncertainty relations. As
> Bohr remarks, it might seem, as it does to Einstein, that the two pos-
> sible determinations (or predictions) must refer to the same physical
> state of S_2 and ought therefore to be included in "an exhaustive ac-
> count of physical reality": it might seem that we are "able to assign
> to one and the same state of the object two well-defined physical at-
> tributes in a way incompatible with the uncertainty relations" ["The
> Causality Problem in Atomic Physics," 21]. Bohr maintains, how-
> ever, that this is not the case; for we are concerned here with "*a
> discrimination between different experimental procedures which allow of
> the unambiguous use of complementary classical concepts*" [*QTM*, 148].
>   Although a measurement on [the particle] S_1, Bohr admits, could
> not physically disturb S_2, nevertheless the experimental arrange-
> ment required for the measurement determines both for S_1 and for
> S_2 the necessary conditions for the meaningful ascribability of the
> physical property concerned. For the properties of exact position and
> exact momentum, moreover, these conditions mutually exclude each
> other. If the momentum of S_1 were measured, then the necessary
> conditions for the meaningful ascribability of an exact position to S_1
> and S_2 (or even of meaningful talk of such a property) would not be
> satisfied. *Mutatis mutandis* the same holds for a measurement of the
> position of S_1. Hence, Bohr holds, Einstein is mistaken in assum-
> ing that S_2 must have both an exact, though unknown, simultaneous
> position and momentum. An object cannot meaningfully be said to
> have certain properties in the absence of the conditions which make
> such talk meaningful. . . .
>   Although S_2 is not physically disturbed in the EPR experiment, it
> would be wrong to think that the notion of the measurement distur-
> bance plays no significant role in the argument, for S_1 is inevitably

disturbed by whichever measurement is performed upon it, and it is this disturbance, among other factors, which prevents us from assigning to S_2, without disturbing it, a well-defined position and momentum at the same time. (*Niels Bohr's Philosophy*, 169–71)

These considerations enable Bohr to argue that, as applied to the conditions one encounters in quantum mechanics, the EPR criteria of reality and completeness, and specifically the expression "without in any way disturbing a system," contain "an essential ambiguity," (*QTM*, 144, 148) and to refute the EPR claim concerning the incompleteness of quantum mechanics:

> [W]e now see that the wording of the above-mentioned criterion of physical reality proposed by Einstein, Podolsky and Rosen contains an ambiguity as regards the meaning of the expression "without in any way disturbing a system." Of course there is in a case like that just considered no question of a mechanical disturbance of the system under investigation during the last critical stage of the measuring procedure. But even at this stage there is essentially the question of *an influence on the very conditions which define the possible types of predictions regarding the future behavior of the system.* Since these conditions constitute an inherent element of the description of any phenomenon to which the term "physical reality" can be properly attached, we see that the argumentation of the mentioned authors does not justify their conclusion that quantum-mechanical description is essentially incomplete. On the contrary this description, as appears from the preceding discussion, may be characterized as a rational utilization of all possibilities of unambiguous interpretation of measurements, compatible with the finite and uncontrollable interaction between the objects and the measuring instruments in the field of quantum theory. In fact, it is only the mutual exclusion of any two experimental procedures, permitting the unambiguous definition of complementary physical quantities, which provides room for new physical laws, the coexistence of which might at first sight appear irreconcilable with the basic principles of science. It is just this entirely new situation as regards the description of physical phenomena, that the notion of *complementarity* aims at characterizing. (*QTM*, 148)

To ascribe a state to a quantum particle or system, according to the EPR procedure, would imply that the position or momentum could be simultaneously assigned, as in the classical situation which does not depend on interactions with the measuring instruments and which is not defined by the finite (quantum) and uncontrollable character of these interactions. But in quantum mechanics, including the EPR situation, one never deals with cases governed by the protocol of classical physics, even leaving aside the metaphysical protocol at work in the EPR argument. One cannot, therefore, claim the incompleteness of quantum mechanics according to the classical protocol, insofar as there is no data for which quantum mechanics does not account. No such data is presented by EPR. Their argument is based on the quantum mechanical character of their data, unobtainable by means of classical theory. It is the concept of reality implied by EPR that becomes suspect. The question becomes not only whether the EPR criterion of reality is reasonable, but whether any philosophical concept or criterion of reality hitherto conceived can be reasonable under the condition of quantum mechanics.

Bohr uses the criteria of completeness under the conditions of the quantum postulate, uncertainty relations, and dependence on the interaction with measuring instruments, none of which conditions EPR consider with sufficient rigor. The EPR argument presupposes a physical reality independent of interpretation as a necessary condition for completeness. For Bohr, however, quantum mechanics can and must be seen as a complete theory, which is capable, and is the only source, of exact predictions of the EPR type. Bohr does not argue against the possibility of exact predictions, which, as he stresses from the outset, are obviously possible, but only against the EPR argument against the incompleteness of quantum mechanics. Quantum mechanics is incomplete only if viewed from a classical perspective, since it entails an irreducible loss of knowledge, as classically understood, concerning the systems it considers. In actuality it delivers all knowledge possible. Bohr writes: "In the phenomena concerned we are not dealing with an incomplete description characterized by the arbitrary picking out of different elements of physical reality at the cost of sacrifying [sacrificing] other such elements, but with a rational discrimination between essentially different experimental arrangements and procedures which are suited either for an unambiguous use of the idea of space location, or for a legitimate application of the conservation theorem of momentum" (*QTM*, 149). We recall that any given variable by itself can be measured with full precision, which fact may tempt one to see the impossibility of the simultaneous joint measurement of conjugate variables as a sign of the incompleteness of quantum mechanics as a whole.

As I have indicated, EPR do not ignore the fact that the requirement of simultaneous measurement or prediction would render their argument invalid. They, however, see this requirement as incompatible with any reasonable definition of reality. They write, in closing their article:

> One could object to this conclusion [concerning the incompleteness of quantum mechanics] on the grounds that our criterion of reality is not sufficiently restrictive. Indeed, one would not arrive at our conclusion if one insisted that two or more physical quantities can be regarded as simultaneous elements of reality *only when they can be simultaneously measured or predicted.* On this point of view, since either one or the other, but not both simultaneously, of the quantities P [coordinate] and Q [momentum] can be predicted, they are not simultaneously real. This makes the reality of P and Q depend upon the process of measurement carried out on the first system, which does not disturb the second system in any way. No reasonable definition of reality could be expected to permit this. (*QTM,* 141)

Pais sees the final sentence as the "key to Einstein's philosophy," which "so poignantly summarizes Einstein's view on quantum mechanics in his later years" (*"Subtle is the Lord,"* 456). From the point of view of classical physics and classical metaphysics, quantum mechanical reality is not reasonable and may in fact not be a "reality." But, which is Bohr's main point, this need not mean that quantum mechanics and its anti-epistemology are unreasonable or incomplete by other, possibly more reasonable, criteria. On this particular occasion, however, "in saying that no reasonable definition of reality can permit this," EPR refer to a kind of action at a distance which affects the state of the second system by means of a physical process carried out in the first, spatially separated system. This type of influence would, as I said, be also unacceptable for Bohr, although mainly because it would violate the experimentally confirmed results (here of relativity), rather than because it might or might not be permitted by some metaphysically reasonable definition of reality. EPR's statement is predicated on ascribing reality to either position or momentum, or, in the case of the second particle, to both without actually measuring them within their local system. The "finite and uncontrollable" interaction between quantum objects and measuring instruments makes such an ascription impossible, however. Once this fact is taken into account, the direct, physical influence of "the process of measurement carried out on the first system" on the second, spatially separated, system need not follow. No action at a distance or any other violation of physical laws would be implied. Hence Bohr says that it is not a question of "a mechanical disturbance" of the second system.[3]

The relationships between "predicted" and "measured" become crucial in this context, along with the fact that the position and momentum of the first particle are never measured and the position and momentum of the second are never predicted simultaneously. The momentum conservation law allows one to argue that the prediction of momentum or position, or, when (separately) *measured,* position and momentum themselves will not be affected by this nonsimultaneity. In this sense, EPR correctly state that "one would not arrive at our conclusion if one insisted that two or more physical quantities can be regarded as simultaneous elements of reality *only when they can be simultaneously measured or predicted."* Actually, even if both the position and momentum of a given particle could be simultaneously predicted, in order to be simultaneously defined—or to be simultaneously "real"—and in order to verify this prediction, they would still have to be simultaneously *measured,* with full precision which can never be done.[4] This need not mean that one cannot make or utilize EPR-type predictions and calculations, but only that one cannot speak, as EPR do, of assigning simultaneous reality to both position and momentum of either particle at any point. There emerges a very different (from EPR's) picture of reality or of the impossibility thereof. This difference is defined by Bohr's understanding that in quantum mechanics nothing can be defined unless it is measured. Thus nothing can be defined outside a given local experimental arrangement where such a measurement can be performed. The "reality" of both position or momentum is always defined by and depends on processes performed within a local system—in this case associated with the second particle. The EPR argument legitimately uses this fact in order to measure—sequentially, rather than simultaneously— the position and momentum of the first particle. The seeds of Bohr's argument can be traced to earlier discussions with Einstein in 1927. In Paul Ehrenfest's account: "By faintly illuminating a small, freely moving body, one may determine its position rather nicely every hour and evaluate the intermediate velocity and momentum with enormous accuracy. Thereby the uncertainty relation APPEARS to be violated. This is, however, merely a misunderstanding. One has here only EVALUATED the momentum for the intermediate time, *not actually measured it. . . .* Altogether the notion of a 'conceptual tracking of the particle between the moments of observation' should be rejected just as the notion of a 'tracking of a light corpuscle through the wave field between emission and absorption' " (*Collected Works of Niels Bohr* 6:415; emphasis added).[5]

The rejection of the EPR claim concerning the incompleteness of quantum mechanics does not thus contradict the locality of all measuring procedures. This locality is, if anything, more radical than that demanded by Einstein, insofar as it irreducibly individualizes every experimental procedure. Nothing that is done in one system needs physically—"mechanically"—affect the procedure that determines the values of physical variables and defines the variables themselves in another spatially separated system. This assertion is not contradicted by the fact that a previous interaction between two particles affects and correlates their motions, as all such interactions do in classical and quantum physics alike, nor by the fact that what can or cannot be measured and what questions can or cannot be asked concerning the second particles are affected by a measurement performed on and questions asked concerning the first particle. Hence, again, at issue is not the "mechanical" interaction between two systems under consideration, but the conditions of the possibility or impossibility of description, measurement, and definition within each, even though, and because, in the EPR situation, what we do within the first system and what kinds of questions we ask concerning it do affect what can and cannot be done within the second and what kind of questions can be meaningfully asked about it at a given point. Thus, the requirement of the locality of physical (inter)action need not be violated. A correlation between the EPR particles implies neither any physical—"mechanical"—disturbance or influence, nor any action at a distance prohibited by relativity. One cannot say, thus, as Murdoch does, that Bohr "held no strong view on the question of locality" (*Niels Bohr's Philosophy*, 185). Murdoch himself argues for the compatibility of Bohr's interpretation of the EPR experiment and the locality requirement by using Bohr's rejection of creation by measurement doctrine, the rejection in part prompted by the EPR argument (176, 191–95). As he writes:

As Bohr clearly saw, one of the two particles of an EPR pair may be treated as an object and the other may be treated as an instrument; after they have interacted, the states of the two particles are correlated in the same way as the states of the object and the instrument are correlated by the measurement interaction; hence a suitable observation of the one particle (the instrument) enables us to infer the correlated value of an observable of the other (the object). Moreover, just as the process of measurement does not create the value that is measured, so the observation made on one particle (the instrument) does not create the correlated value of the other particle (the object). Hence EPR-type correlations do not involve any action at a distance. Bohr, then, wished to reject the [Einsteinian] condition of value independence and to uphold what might be called "the principle of local action," which forbids action at a distance. (191–92)[6]

One can also question Murdoch's guess concerning Einstein's attitude toward locality: "Einstein wished to uphold the intrinsic-properties theory, the objective-values theory [in which successful observation reveals the objective, preexisting value of an observable] and a locality condition. Which of these conditions would he have chosen to relinquish? No doubt the locality condition, since he held the latter to be more dispensable than the intrinsic-properties/objective value conditions" (193–94). There may be some doubt, however. Einstein strongly maintained the indispensability of the locality condition throughout his scientific life.[7] He hoped that one could develop the kind of theory he wanted without sacrificing the well established laws of physics, particularly those upon which his theory of relativity was based.

Hidden Variables

The hidden variables theories seek to replace quantum mechanics by a (classically) complete and causal framework. Thus they address the question central to the Einstein-Bohr debate and the exchange around the EPR argument, namely: whether, as Einstein hoped, the statistical character of quantum mechanics is due to the fact that the results of quantum mechanical measurements are averages over "hidden" states (for which such results could be fully determined in the manner of classical statistical mechanics), or whether, as Bohr maintains, quantum indeterminacy is irreducible in principle and quantum mechanics itself is irreducible to a classical statistical theory.

The "motivation" for the hidden variables argument arises naturally, once an Einstein-like position is adopted. As Bell writes: "Once the incompleteness of the wave function description is suspected, it can be conjectured that the seemingly random statistical fluctuations are determined by the extra 'hidden variables'—'hidden' because at this stage we can only conjecture their existence and certainly cannot control them"

(*Speakable and Unspeakable in Quantum Mechanics* [hereinafter *SUQM*],
30). The genealogy of this hypothesis is clearly Einsteinian. In "Reply
to Criticisms," Einstein writes: "I am, in fact, firmly convinced that the
essentially statistical character of contemporary quantum theory is solely
to be ascribed to the fact that this [theory] operates with an incomplete
description of physical systems. . . . Assuming the success of efforts to ac-
complish a complete physical description, the statistical quantum theory
would, within the framework of future physics, take an approximately
analogous position to the statistical mechanics within the framework of
classical mechanics. I am rather firmly convinced that the development of
theoretical physics will be of that type; but the path will be lengthy and
difficult" (*Albert Einstein: Philosopher-Scientist*, 666, 672). Bohm's work
and then Bell's own have been guided by the same ideas, before and after
Bell's theorem, which made the task of fulfilling this type of program all
the more difficult.[8]

A hidden variables theory need not contain all of the Einsteinian features. The relationships between hidden variables theories and the intrinsic properties theories are complex. Hidden variables may be "located"
in the measuring equipment or be conceived of through an interactive
theory. Completeness, too, may be defined more generally through an
appeal to a nonstatistical hidden states system behind the quantum mechanical picture, rather than by an appeal to the reality corresponding
to standard measured variables, such as position and momentum. Most
classical, metaphysical features, however, are customarily (re)introduced,
once hidden variables are introduced, often for philosophical and ideological reasons, by proponents of the approach. Some such features appear inevitable in any hidden variables framework—for example, the deterministic, causal character of theory and the presence of a complete
system as a reality behind quantum effects. The very appeal to "hidden"
completeness and determinacy behind incompleteness and indeterminacy may be seen as a metaphysical move. Naturally, the hope of the hidden variables theorists is that hidden states will at some point be revealed
or confirmed by means of experiments. Einstein's intrinsic properties
framework and Bohm's and several other theories of hidden variables are
all subject to Bell's theorem, deduced from an analysis of the EPR-type
experiment.[9]

As follows from the preceding analysis, the implications of the questions at issue in the hidden variables argument are momentous. Obviously, Einstein would find "that the hidden variables problem has some
interest," as Bell says (*SUQM*, 12 n.2). Bell argues, against Max Jam-

mer, that Einstein's views suggest "a rather clear commitment to what is usually meant by hidden variables. . . . It seems to me then beyond dispute that there was at least one Einstein, that of the EPR paper and the Schilpp volume, who was fully committed to the view that quantum mechanics was incomplete and should be completed—which is the hidden variables programme" (*SUQM*, 90). Bell notes "negative reactions by Einstein to the very particular 1952 hidden variables of Bohm. This scheme reproduced completely, and rather trivially, the whole of nonrelativistic quantum mechanics. It had great value in illuminating certain features of the theory, and in putting in perspective various 'proofs' of the impossibility of a hidden variable interpretation. But Bohm himself did not think of it as in any way final" (*SUQM*, 91).

Following de Broglie's earlier attempts, Bohm's hidden variables interpretation is the best known, and it has been presented and discussed in, by now, voluminous literature by Bohm himself and many commentators.[10] By adding (hidden) mathematical variables to Schrödinger's wave mechanics, Bohm is able to assign a given particle a "real" position alongside a "real" momentum at each point. The standard quantum mechanics probabilities are recovered as a result. Bohm's theory is mathematically different from the standard model, whether described by the Schrödinger equation or by (mathematically equivalent) Heisenberg's matrix mechanics. Bohm's scheme is deterministic. It presupposes real, if hidden, states and a model of physical reality, analogous to Einstein's. Mathematically, the initial conditions determine all subsequent states of the system. That one cannot predict where a given elementary particle will appear in a given experimental arrangement is due to the fact that complete information about the system is not available—hidden. That one cannot arrange for a given state to be registered is due to the fact that we cannot fully control the experimental arrangements themselves.

This interpretation is obviously very different from Bohr's complementarity or, more generally, from the standard model, which sees indeterminacy as irreducible in principle. It is crucial that the standard model does allow one to measure with full precision any given variable within any conjugate pair, such as position or momentum, at each point of any trajectory, but at no point simultaneously both (although both can be fully *predicted* or *calculated* under certain conditions, such as those specified in the EPR experiment). The standard model contains a built-in indeterminacy and incompleteness by classical criteria, which disallows the application of classical epistemology—whether classically deterministic or classically statistical. The description, however, is complete with respect to any given variable, such as position, that can in principle be defined or measured at any given moment insofar as it is not defined or measured simultaneously with its conjugate, such as momentum. Bohr, as we have seen, simultaneously differentiates quantum mechanics from classical statistical physics and sees it as a complete theory. There appears to be no need and no room for hidden variables in quantum mechanics. While Bohm is forced to introduce that which cannot be measured, Bohr deals only with what can be measured. That which can be measured, however, allows for no classically complete picture at any point. It may very well be that "nature (*physis*) hides itself" (*physis kryptesthai philei*), as Heraclitus said; but it may have no hidden variables or anything else that is hidden as existing—present—in or by itself. *Physis* plays a more complex game.

In contrast to the standard interpretation, where they represent probability distributions, in Bohm's theory the waves suggested by Schrödinger's equation are, in Bell's approving words, "conceived, in the tradition of Maxwell and Einstein, as an objective field, and not just as some 'ghost wave' of information (of some presumably well-informed observer?)" (*SUQM*, 112). The wave aspect in Bohm's theory is constructed by means of de Broglie-Bohm's pilot wave, which, as it were, "guides" a given particle. The pilot wave provides the synthesis of particle and wave picture at each point, which feature is actually admired by Bell (*SUQM*, 112, 171, 192), who sees the "wave or particle" of complementarity as a conundrum (171). "To the question 'wave or particle?' [de Broglie and Bohm] answer 'wave *and* particle'" (112). De Broglie-Bohm's interpretation, thus, strongly contrasts with the standard one, where the wave function has, as we have seen, no physical meaning. It is used to calculate the probabilities related to uncertainty relations.

Unlike quantum mechanics, Bohm's scheme is manifestly nonlocal because "the guiding wave, in the general case, propagates not in ordinary three-space, but in a multidimensional-configuration space" (*SUQM*, 114). As a result, "the behavior of a given variable . . . is determined by the conditions in the immediate neighborhood (in ordinary three-space) but also by what is happening at all the other positions" (*SUQM*, 36). The theory acquires signals that propagate instantaneously. Thus, it violates the finite limit upon all interactions in actual space, established by Einstein's relativity—the speed of light, one of the most fundamental experimental constants in all physics.

Einstein's attitude to Bohm's theory was and perhaps had to be ambivalent because of its nonlocality, and possibly because it lacked the kind of mathematical elegance that Einstein came to admire so much. In addition, Bohm's theory was still too close to quantum mechanics, rather than a new different theory, as, say, Einstein's own general relativity was with respect to Newtonian gravitation. According to Pais, "in regard to Einstein, I know the following. That in regard to Bohm, he thought the work was very interesting, but it is not what he had in mind, it was not what he really wanted" (*Some Strangeness in the Proportion*, 267).[11] Einstein would have preferred to see quantum mechanics, even combined with special relativity by means of quantum electrodynamics, proved wrong in a critical situation and replaced by a new theory. He wrote: "Have you noticed that Bohm believes (as de Broglie did, by the way, 25 years ago) that he is able to interpret the quantum theory in deterministic terms? That way seems too cheap to me." Bell cites the remark, as well as Max Born's comment on it: "Although this theory was quite in line with his own ideas" (*SUQM*, 91). Einstein, as I said, saw a kind of future correspondence, perhaps modeled on Bohr's correspondence between quantum and classical theory. His aim was not to restore classical physics, but to restore to physics the classical metaphysics—the metaphysics that preserves and unites continuity, causality, completeness, and reality.

Much of Bell's work is devoted to exposing the problems of the so-called "impossibility proofs" for hidden variables interpretations, such as those by Gleason, Von Neumann, and Jauch and Piron. Bell exposes the *hidden* assumptions of these arguments, that appear self-evident but are not required by experimental data, although they may be, as in Gleason's case, built into a particular mathematical apparatus used by the standard model. Bell shares his agenda with Einstein and Bohm, even though his theorem appears to point in Bohr's direction. Bell concedes that "It is easy to find good reasons for disliking the de Broglie-Bohm picture. Neither de Broglie nor Bohm liked it very much; for both of them it was only a point of departure. Einstein also did not like it very much. He found it 'too cheap.'" He adds, however: "But like it or lump it, it is perfectly conclusive as a counter example to the idea that vagueness, subjectivism, or indeterminism, are forced on us by the experimental facts covered by nonrelativistic quantum mechanics" (*SUQM*, 163).

This latter claim is contestable, even leaving aside that Bell made the statement well after his theorem (in 1982) and his rather indiscriminate lumping together of quantum mechanical ideas: certainly Bohr's complementarity is not subjectivist. The expression "perfectly conclusive"

is hardly applicable either. Bell's readings of Bohr are far from sufficiently rigorous, which can be in part explained, but not justified, by
his professed inability to understand and his dislike of Bohr's argument
and complementarity. In addition, "nonrelativistic" may well be a crucial qualification here. Well before Bohm's interpretation, and even before the debate around the EPR argument, quantum electrodynamics and
Dirac's relativistic equation of the electron were developed, which incorporated quantum mechanics, but also conformed to and enhanced the
anti-epistemology of complementarity. They are fully consistent with the
data both of quantum mechanics and of special relativity, and thus with
the conditions of local action. One cannot, therefore, exclude these "experimental facts" from the views of Bohr, Heisenberg, Born and others,
including, on the opposite side of the argument Einstein, concerning experimental support for quantum theory, which is really at stake in this
debate, rather than only the elementary nonrelativistic version of theory.
Bohr, as we have seen, makes this point directly, as he invokes Dirac's
contribution (PWNB 2:63). Nothing in subsequent theories and experiments—modern field theory, gauge theories, quarks, chromodynamics,
and so forth—contradicts quantum mechanics and much depends on it,
particularly on uncertainty relations. All these theories are consistent with
complementarity. In part, these considerations answer Bell's questions in
the same article, the questions that he himself does not "attempt . . . to
answer":

> But why then had Born not told me of this "pilot wave"? If only
> to point out what was wrong with it? Why did von Neumann not
> consider it? More extraordinarily, why did people go on producing
> "impossibility" proofs, after 1952, and as recently as 1978? When
> even Pauli, Rosenfeld, and Heisenberg, could produce no more dev-
> astating criticism of Bohm's version than to brand it as "metaphysi-
> cal" and "ideological"? Why is the pilot wave picture ignored in text
> books? Should it not be taught, not as the only way, but as an antidote
> to the prevailing complacency? To show that vagueness, subjectivity,
> and indeterminism, are not forced on us by experimental facts, but
> by deliberate theoretical choice? (SUQM, 160)

Physics, both relativity and quantum mechanics, and its "experimental
facts" appear to be against de Broglie-Bohm's interpretation and define
"theoretical choices" and "complacencies," which is hardly an applicable
term here. To a considerable degree, Bohm's theory has "devastated"

itself by its, in Bell's own terms, "*gross* non-locality," which, as Bell's theorem shows, is unavoidable in all theories of that type. It is true that Bohr's analysis of the EPR argument, which powerfully questioned (if one does not accept that it has refuted) claims of the incompleteness of quantum mechanics, and Bohr's ideas in general had a great influence on all figures mentioned by Bell. The reasons for these influences are many and complex, but Bohr's physics was always fully grounded in experiment, at least as much as anything can be so grounded. Even if there were two equally applicable models, it would be natural to select the one that does not violate the main principles of physics and in particular relativity. Were quantum mechanics or relativity proven wrong, it would be different, of course, but such was not and still is not the case. The main "advantage" of Bohm's theory for Bell appears to be that it is classical and deterministic.

One cannot, therefore, ignore the "metaphysical" and "ideological" forces shaping Bohm's, Einstein's, or Bell's visions, although these visions were undoubtedly shaped by physical considerations as well. Naturally, metaphysical, or, in Bohr's case, anti-metaphysical, and ideological reasons shape the argument of the opposite side, and within an equally complex economy. Bell is a great deal more insistent on ideology in the latter case, and he sees Bohr's interpretation as the one that went beyond pragmatism and as "romantic" (*SUQM*, 189–90). By contrast, Bohm's and de Broglie's work is seen as "natural and simple" (91), as "the unromantic, 'professional,' alternatives," and, "measure[d] up to professional standards," as "undoubtedly show[ing] the best craftsmanship among the pictures [of quantum mechanics]." A somewhat pious conclusion is added: "But is that a virtue in our time?" (*SUQM*, 194–95).

Bell's claim that "the conventional [i.e., complementary] formulations of quantum theory, and of quantum field theory in particular, are unprofessionally vague and ambiguous" ("Beables for Quantum Field Theory," *SUQM*, 173) can, I think, only be made if one does not read Bohr carefully, even leaving aside the extraordinary mathematical and physical craftsmanship of both the founders of quantum mechanics and the subsequent work, "in quantum field theory in particular." "Professional theoretical physicists ought to be able to do better. Bohm has shown us a way"—Bell says in speaking, rather naively, of his "strictly professional [as opposed to philosophical] concerns" (*SUQM*, 173), particularly since he continuously invokes philosophical concerns in many of his works. One would be hard pressed to accept this assessment not only of physics, but also of philosophy. Vague and ambiguous the formulations at issue may be, but only structurally, irreducibly so and, as such, allowing for as much precision and professionalism—in mathematics, physics, and meta-physics—as is possible. They are more precise than Bell's meta-physical notion of "beable"—"be-a-Bell," perhaps—which is introduced in the article just cited and which implies the intrinsic-properties doctrine: "we will exclude the notion of 'observable' in favour of that of 'beable.' The beables of the theory are those elements which might correspond to elements of reality, to things which exist. Their existence does not depend on 'observation'" (174). One wonders whether such "beables" can in fact exist in view of the "observations" we have. Bell does offer a qualification: "I use the term 'beable' rather than some more committed term like 'being' or 'beer' to recall the essentially tentative nature of any physical theory. Such a theory is at best a *candidate* for the description of nature. . . . In fact 'beable' is short for 'maybe-able'" (174). The latter is a much better and much more quantum-mechanical, more indeterminate term. Bell, however, wants and hopes to have "beables"— maybeables, but hopefully beables; may-be-a-Bell, but hopefully be-a-Bell. There is a big difference between maybe-able beables and maybe-able observables, which are also observable maybe-ables. Mathematically and physically the observable-maybeables of quantum mechanics are extraordinarily precise. They offer the best "maybe-able" available, at least for now. Perhaps, finally, it is Bohr who has shown us the way by his physics and meta-physics alike, without demanding that they conform to a given form of metaphysics. Bohr's complementary physics and meta-physics are as rigorous and professional as both can be.

The search for alternatives need not, of course, and in truth cannot be precluded, for whatever reasons it is pursued. The results are never quite predictable; and Bell's own work, leading to his theorem, is a case to the point. One cannot help thinking, however, that Bell does not perceive the degree to which metaphysics and ideology shape Einstein's, Bohm's, or his own vision of the world and science. In his earlier "On the Problem of Hidden Variables," Bell does refer to the major metaphysical features— such as causality—of Bohm's model as "prejudices." These prejudices are, however, "reasonably desired" (*SUQM*, 9–10), as opposed to, one presumes, the nondesirable "prejudices" of anti-metaphysical complementarity. By (almost) any criteria, in view of their insistence on completeness, causality, and reality Bohm's (and Bell's) attitudes are vastly more metaphysical. For those ideas have defined metaphysics throughout its history. Very little in Bohr's complementarity has a similar complicity.

It is complementarity that has been and, as Bohr realized, had to be a problem for philosophy, rather than Einstein's or Bohm's philosophy, which are complicit with classical metaphysics.

The logic of Bell's criticism is curious, although not uncommon: quantum mechanics and especially complementarity are simultaneously both too ideological and too philosophical (rather than professional) and, by not conforming to classical metaphysics, not philosophical enough. This view would be less surprising were it not for the implications of Bell's theorem. Bell concedes that he has no physical argument against Bohr, whose "intuition" could be "right" after all (*SUQM*, 155). It is clear from the preceding analysis why Bohr was not likely to be attracted to hidden variables theories on physical grounds. In this, Bohr's intuition appears to have been correct. Subsequent developments of physics have shown that a return to a classical, causal form of thinking is unlikely; quite possibly, a still more complex physics and meta-physics of matter could await. Bohm's reinterpretation of quantum mechanics in 1952 (after the recent progress in quantum field theory) was not likely to impress Bohr, particularly since it introduced instantaneous action at a distance. For Bohr, the experimentally confirmed data of quantum mechanics and relativity constrain all physics and all meta-physics.[12] Bell's theorem makes it impossible for hidden variables models to satisfy the requirements of both theories. As such it may be seen as a great physico-mathematical confirmation of complementarity and its anti-epistemology.

The Physics and Metaphysics of Bell's Theorem

Examining the experiments of the EPR type, Bell's theorem states that a nonstatistical, causal hidden variables theory cannot be consistent with the statistical predictions of quantum mechanics, insofar as the locality requirement is maintained. According to Bell's original communication:

> The paradox of Einstein, Podolsky and Rosen was advanced as an argument that quantum mechanics could not be a complete theory but should be supplemented by additional variables. These additional variables were to restore to the theory causality and locality. In this note that idea will be formulated mathematically and *shown to be incompatible with the statistical predictions of quantum mechanics.* It is the requirement of locality, or more precisely that the result of a measurement on one system be unaffected by operations on a distant

system with which it [the first system] has interacted in the past, that creates the essential difficulty. (*SUQM*, 14; emphasis added)

Bell's theorem, thus, may be seen as consistent with both Bohr's views and his reply to the EPR argument. It follows from the preceding analysis that the locality part of the theorem is consistent with Bohr's reply to the EPR argument and with complementarity, which is recognized by Bell (*SUQM*, 155). The locality condition is, as we have seen, also the essential requirement for Einstein, as Bell notes, citing Einstein: "on one assumption we should, in my opinion, insist without qualification: the real factuality (state) [der reale Sachverhalt (Zustand)] of the system S_2 is independent of any manipulation of the system S_1, which is spatially separated from the former" (*Autobiographical Notes*, 81).[13] One can only have a complete, hidden variables theory at the cost of abandoning locality: "[Bohm's] interpretation has . . . a grossly non-local structure. This is characteristic, according to the result to be proved here, of any such theory which reproduces exactly the quantum mechanical predictions. . . . In a theory in which parameters are added to quantum mechanics to determine the results of individual measurements, without changing the statistical predictions, there must be a mechanism whereby the setting of one measuring device can influence the reading of another instrument, however remote. Moreover, the signal involved must propagate instantaneously" (*SUQM*, 14, 20).

Bell subsequently observes that: "The question then arises: can we not find another hidden-variable scheme with the desired local character? It can be shown [by means of the argument of Bell's theorem] that this is not possible. The demonstration moreover is in no way restricted to the context of nonrelativistic wave mechanics, but depends only on the existence of separated systems highly correlated with respect to quantities such as spin" (*SUQM*, 36). This is a very large class of quantum systems. In his original paper, Bell adds: "Of course, the situation is different, if the quantum mechanical predictions are of limited validity" (20). The locality or separability requirement acquires, thus, a particular significance in view of Bell's theorem. Physics appears to present much stronger reasons against than for hidden variables, since the locality requirement is consistent with quantum mechanics and complementarity—which lack local causality. Murdoch, who correctly sees Bohr's complementarity as independent of the concept of action at a distance (*Niels Bohr's Philosophy*, 194), argues that while Bell's theorem shows that "Einstein's position cannot be sustained" (193), "it leaves Bohr's position intact" (185) because "he does not hold the intrinsic-properties theory" (194). With regret and with hope that nature may eventually prove differently, Bell, too, admits that "if nature follows quantum mechanics in these [EPR] correlations [i.e., locality], then Einstein's conception of the world is untenable," (*SUQM*, 86),[14] while quantum mechanics and Bohr's view may be justified (*SUQM*, 155).

In his formulation, Bell does not rely on all the metaphysical features that characterize Einstein's vision, de Broglie-Bohm's theory, and Jean-Pierre Vigies's and other hidden variables interpretations—such as full separation of an object and the measuring instruments, intrinsic properties, real states, absolute wholeness, or certain forms of causality. He reformulates both the EPR argument and the hidden variables theory in terms of a very general, mathematically defined scheme, rather than in terms of these features, although some among these features are seen as desirable by him. The locality requirement can be formulated, too, without appealing to intrinsic properties or states, by stating that measurements in one system do not (physically) affect measurements in another spatially separated system. This generalization allows one to make subject to Bell's theorem a very broad class of theories—such as (some of) the EPR-type theories, Bohm's and other hidden variables interpretations, and several other theories.[15] Bell's theorem, however, remains fully consistent with Bohr's interpretation or with a class of interpretations, which share their key nonclassical features.

While some metaphysical features may thus be absent from a hidden variables theory, all such theories presuppose a nonstatistical, causal economy, "hidden" behind quantum indeterminacy. This presupposition makes these theories restricted economies—ontological-epistemological metaphysics of matter—in contrast to the anti-epistemological general economy of Bohr's complementarity. From a Bohrian perspective, Bell's theorem would imply, simultaneously, conditions of irreducible incompleteness of physical knowledge and, under these conditions, the completeness of quantum mechanics. While Bell acknowledges the possibility of such an understanding of his theorem (*SUQM*, 155), this is not quite the way he himself sees the situation. For him, de Broglie-Bohm's picture offers advantages over Bohr's interpretation, first of all, by "dispos[ing] of the necessity to divide the world somehow into system and apparatus." "But another problem is [also] brought into focus": "For me then this is the real problem with quantum theory: the apparently essential conflict between any sharp formulation and fundamental relativity. That is to say, we have an apparent incompatibility, at the deepest level, between the two fundamental pillars of contemporary theory" (*SUQM*, 172). It depends on how one defines "sharpness," or conversely "vagueness" (*SUQM*, 155). For one may also say that, to borrow Bell's own expression, a certain "fundamental vagueness" is the sharpness of quantum mechanics.

From this perspective, Bell's theorem may be compared to Gödel's theorem. The analogy is all the more interesting in that both Gödel's and Bell's own views were classical, while their findings would offer powerful arguments in support of an anti-epistemological understanding of, respectively, mathematics and physics. Gödel's theorem precedes the EPR argument only by a few years and, as I indicated, Gödel's and other contemporary investigations into the foundation of mathematics might have influenced its aims and conceptual framework—completeness, consistency, and so forth.[16] We must, of course, keep in mind the differences between the functioning of these theorems in their respective fields and between their anti-epistemological implications. For one thing, quantum mechanics might be proven to be wrong, which would change the field of physics, while keeping its mathematics more or less intact. Gödel's theorem appears to pose a more fundamental anti-epistemological limit, one that, by virtue of the theorem, cannot be transgressed within the same field. This circumstance does not prevent various metaphysical interpretations of mathematics, as by Gödel himself and, it appears, by most mathematicians who have commented on the issue, such as, recently, Penrose. Penrose also maintains the metaphysical concept of reality associated with quantum physics, although based on the standard model rather than a hidden variables theory. The absence of an experimental field can even make a metaphysics of undecidables easier to maintain. Analogies between Gödel's and Bell's theorems are thus qualified. The parallel, however, is instructive, as is Bell's strong resistance to a quantum mechanical view of nature and to complementarity.[17]

Bell traces his resistance to his earliest encounters with quantum mechanics. He writes in "On the Impossible Pilot Wave" (an impossible but still desirable idea in 1982—or even in 1987, two decades after his theorem and into the continuing successes of "incomplete" quantum theory): "When I was a student I had much difficulty with quantum mechanics. It was comforting to find that even Einstein had had such difficulties for a long time. Indeed they led him to the heretical conclusion that something was missing in the theory" (*SUQM*, 159). Bell's motivations for the exploration of hidden variables are very much those of Einstein, Bohm, de Broglie, Schrödinger, and others who wanted to dispense with its undesirable anti-epistemological features—the statistical character of quantum mechanical predictions, indeterminism, (perceived) incompleteness, complementarity, or, in Bell's words, "the peculiar character of some of quantum mechanical predictions [of the EPR type], which seem almost to cry out for a hidden variable interpretation" and "make it hard to believe in the completeness of quantum mechanics" (*SUQM*, 30). Bell admits that these features are not required by the experimental data. He introduces, however, another set of considerations, which he sees as making a search for alternatives to quantum mechanics even more compelling.[18] These considerations, which again go back to Einstein's views (*Albert Einstein: Philosopher-Scientist*, 674), relate to the apparently irreducible dichotomy and "the moving boundary" between the quantum and classical worlds. All information about the quantum world is, we recall, obtained through classically read experimental data. As Bell writes:

> [I]n contemporary quantum theory it seems that the world must be divided into a wavy "quantum system," and a remainder which is in some sense "classical." The division is made one way or another, in a particular application, according to the degree of accuracy and completeness aimed at. For me it is the indispensability, and above all the shiftiness, of such a division that is the big surprise of quantum mechanics. It introduces an essential ambiguity into fundamental physical theory, if only at a level of accuracy and completeness beyond any required in practice. It is the toleration of such an ambiguity, not merely provisionally but permanently, and at the most fundamental level, that is the real break with the classical ideal. It is this rather than the failure of any particular concepts such as "particle" or "determinism." (*SUQM*, 188)[19]

As we have seen, and as Bell points out here and elsewhere (*SUQM*, 29–30), while this dichotomy is irreducible there is no absolute boundary that can be determined once and for all. The arbitrariness of the cut leads to a shifting complementarity of the inside and the outside of quantum interpretation. Bell sees such a theory as "surely of provisional nature" in part because the demonstration of the movability of the boundary is founded only on approximations, albeit very good ones (29). His search for a (classically) "objective" and "homogeneous account of the world" leads him to hidden variables. As he writes:

A possibility is that we find exactly where the boundary lies. More plausible to me is that we find that there is no boundary. It is hard for me to envisage intelligible discourse about a world with no classical part—no base of given events, be they only mental events in a single consciousness, to be correlated. On the other hand, it is easy to imagine that the classical domain could be extended to cover the whole. The wave functions would prove to be a provisional or incomplete description of the quantum-mechanical part, of which an objective account would become possible. It is this possibility, of a homogeneous account of the world, which is for me the chief motivation of the study of the so-called "hidden variable" possibility. (*SUQM*, 30)

This argument is hardly compelling, and it is continually made by Bell well into the 1980s. It is not clear why it is more plausible that there is no boundary, or why it is easier to imagine, at this point, that the classical domain could be extended to the whole rather than the other way around. The reliance on common-sensical concepts seems hardly a good guide, particularly given Einstein's relativity, a theory which Bell never questions in the same fashion. Why not suspend relativity, too, on the grounds that it violates many of our intuitions and a good deal of the classical views of the world? Why not insist on Newtonian nonrelativistic mechanics, to which most of the classical world conforms? Einstein's theory is, of course, classical, insofar as continuity, determinism, and (classical) completeness are concerned. This program, according to Bell, should guide our choice of hidden variables theories, and it guides all his work, in spite of his theorem. One can actually argue that there is really no division between the two worlds in the sense suggested by Bell. According to quantum mechanics, the underlying economy of all physical interactions is quantum.[20] This economy may entail a suspension of any form of uniquely underlying reality, metaphysically understood, be it classical or quantum, which is what appears to be most troubling to Einstein, or Bell. Quantum mechanics may instead be seen as suggesting an economy defined by radical difference and a closure or closures of representation, classical and quantum, and with a classical closure affecting all measurements. This classical closure need not imply, however, that one must seek its extension in order to eliminate its nonclassical counterparts. The experimental results make the two worlds—classical and quantum—complementary, within a closure which may no longer be seen as classical, but is itself complementarily classical and quantum.

Bell says that "for [him] the possibility of determinism is less compelling than the possibility of having one world instead of two" (30). "But," he adds, "by requiring it [determinism], the programme becomes much better defined and more easy to come to grips with" (30), or "in following what seems to be a minimal programme for restoring objectivity [by means of objective properties—*beables*], we were obliged to restore determinism also" (43). As we have seen, Bell speaks of the deterministic character of de Broglie-Bohm's synthesis in very positive terms. In fact, the classical domain in terms of which he wants to achieve "a homogeneous account of the [physical] world" would imply determinism, and historically speaking all accounts of that type, from or before Newton to Einstein and beyond, have been guided by the requirement of classical causality. Bell is not wrong in saying that "it is important to note that to the limited degree to which *determinism* plays a role in the EPR argument, it is not assumed but *inferred*," as against "the principle of 'local causality'—of 'no action at a distance,'" which is "held sacred" (143); and his qualifications concerning Einstein's position are pertinent (143–45). The significance of determinism for Einstein, as against other aspects of his positions— such as realism, continuity, completeness, or locality—is at times overstressed. The point, however, is relatively minor. For determinism is an inevitable counterpart of Einstein's views of reality and completeness, as emphasized by Bell in his analysis of Einstein's exchanges with Born; and presupposed or inferred, deterministic causality is equally significant for Bohm and Bell. Moreover, in physical and philosophical terms, all their key ideas are derived from classical deterministic models, and it is difficult to suspend the metaphysical determination of their views of physics, all the claims for pragmatism notwithstanding.

If anything, Bohr's interpretation is more pragmatic. One cannot, of course, suspend the anti-epistemological (in contrast to metaphysical), psychological, or ideological factors—"prejudices"—shaping his ideas either; and the complexity of the interaction between all such factors is itself general economic and complementary in the broader sense of this study. One should, however, consider "prejudice" equally in epistemological or anti-epistemological ideologies and the scientific pragmatism they accompany. When this is done, one finds, I think, a greater degree of pragmatism in Bohr than in Bell or Bohm. Bell does not deny the significance of pragmatic considerations for Bohr, nor Bohr's contribution to physics, in particular, indicatively, prior to the introduction of complementarity in 1925. To Bell, this contribution is especially significant "in clarifying the way in which the theory should be applied in order to avoid contradiction at the practical level" and, predictably, in Bohr's emphasis on the continuing significance of descriptions "*in classical terms*" and "ordinary language" and "logic" (*SUQM*, 189; emphasis added). According to Bell, however:

> Bohr went further than pragmatism, and put forward a philosophy of what lies behind the recipes. Rather than being disturbed by the ambiguity in principle, by the shiftiness of the division between "quantum system" and "classical apparatus," he seemed to take satisfaction in it. He seemed to revel in the contradictions, for example between "wave" and "particle," that seem to appear in any attempt to go beyond the pragmatic level. Not to resolve these contradictions and ambiguities, but rather to reconcile us to them, he put forward a philosophy which he called "complementarity." He thought that "complementarity" was important not only for physics, but for the whole of human knowledge. The justly immense prestige of Bohr has led to the mention of complementarity in most textbooks of quantum theory. But usually only in a few lines. One is tempted to suspect that the authors do not understand the Bohr philosophy sufficiently to find it helpful. Einstein himself had great difficulty in reaching a sharp formulation of Bohr's meaning. What hope then for the rest of us? There is very little I can say about "complementarity." But I wish to say one thing. It seems to me that Bohr used this word with the reverse of its usual meaning. Consider for example the elephant. From the front she is head, trunk, and two legs. From the back she is bottom, tail, and two legs. From the sides she is otherwise, and from top and bottom different again. These various views are complementary in the usual sense of the word. They supplement one another, they are consistent with one another and they are all entailed by the unifying concept of "elephant." It is my impression that to suppose Bohr used the word 'complementary' in this ordinary way would have been regarded by him as missing his point and trivializing his thought. He seems to insist rather that we must use in our analysis elements which *contradict* one another, which do not add up to, or derive from, a whole. By "complementarity" he meant, it seems to me, the reverse: contradictoriness. Bohr seemed to like aphorisms such as: "the opposite of a deep truth is also a deep truth": "truth and clarity are complementary." Perhaps he took a subtle satisfaction in the use of a familiar word with the reverse of its familiar meaning. (189–90)

Elsewhere Bell confesses, rather proudly, that he "never got the hang of complementarity" (194) or, one might say, the "elephant" of complementarity. It may be that in order to describe the elephant well one needs a picture much more *complementary* in Bohr's sense than the one presented by Bell here. A cubist—quantum-field-like and complementary—elephant by Picasso would perhaps do. Instead, what we can perhaps no longer afford are the elephants of unifying concepts. Bell is right to say that to use "the word 'complementarity' in this ordinary way would have been regarded by [Bohr] as missing his point and trivializing his thought." But he ignores the complex context of Bohr's statements on "deep truths," concluding "Discussions with Einstein" (*PWNB* 2:66), and Bohr's complex attitude toward such "deep truths." Bell's arguments against Bohr do not appear to be based either on a careful reading or an analysis of the logic of complementarity, which he claims not to understand. He does, however, understand, just as does Einstein, some of this logic, such as "the shiftiness of the division between 'quantum system' and 'classical apparatus'." His objections are clearly motivated by his resistance to Bohr's anti-epistemology.

Bell's statement is in fact more interesting in its extraphysical aspects. Even as he hints that it is Bohr's authority more than anything else that is responsible for the success of complementarity, Einstein's authority appears here, and throughout his work, to be central to Bell's own arguments. A touch of humility—"What hope then for the rest of us?"—is curious: as if there were no physicists who by that time (1987) could understand Bohr's ideas, whether they would agree with them or not. I do not want to overemphasize the significance of the rhetorical aspects of Bell's argument. The point remains, however, that this argument is far from free of nonpragmatic aspects—be they philosophical, ideological, rhetorical, or institutional-political. Of course, as we know now, no argument can be free of such aspects. This crucial qualification is, however, absent in Bell, who never considers the nonpragmatic arguments of the proponents on the opposite side, beginning with Einstein. Einstein's popular impact, too, was, if anything, vastly greater than Bohr's; and if one chooses, as Bell does (194–95), to condemn journalistic appeal, nothing rivals Einstein's relativity. In actuality, Bohm's theory and Bell's theorem rival complementarity in this respect. Nor can one really say that so-called "romantic" interpretations, complementary or other, are any less pragmatic or professional—or any more "romantic"—than their "unromantic" counterparts. To define as "unromantic" that which "requires mathematical work by theoretical physicists, rather than interpretation by philosophers, and does not promise lessons in philosophy for philosophers" (190) and to juxtapose this to Bohr's approach are at the very least disingenuous, even leaving aside that Bell often characterizes his own arguments as philosophical, as they are. Bell's views are, ironically, much more likely to find support among philosophers than physicists—for *pragmatic reasons*—and his views are also more likely be used for "lessons in philosophy for philosophers" than Bohr's anti-epistemology.

Bell is clearly inspired by and follows Einstein's philosophy of physics based on the three great capital "C"s and one "R" of classical physics and metaphysics—Completeness, Continuity, Causality, and Reality—destroyed or deconstructed by Bohr's revolution. Bell is particularly close to Einstein in arguing that a unified vision of the physical world should be classical. As he says in 1986: "It may be that a real synthesis of quantum and relativity theories requires not just technical developments but a radical conceptual renewal" (*SUQM*, 172). This position is, as we have seen, Einstein's. In view of where physics stood in 1986 and how it has continued to develop since, such a conceptual renewal seems unlikely to lead to "a real synthesis," clearly conceived classically by Bell. Bell's views imply a return to classical conceptuality rather than a radical renewal, unless this is a renewal of classical theories, as was in fact Bell's hope, just as it was Einstein's. Bell suggests four positions (although he qualifies that others are possible):

> First, and *those of us who are inspired by Einstein would like this best,* quantum mechanics may be *wrong* in sufficiently critical situations. Perhaps Nature is not so queer as quantum mechanics. But the experimental situation is not very encouraging from this point of view. . . .
>
> Secondly, it may be that it is not permissible to regard the experimental settings *a* and *b* in the analyzers [in the EPR-type situations] as independent variables, as we did. . . . But this way of arranging quantum mechanical correlations would be even more mind boggling than one in which causal chains go faster than light. Apparently separate parts of the world would be deeply and conspiratorially entangled, and our apparent free will would be entangled with them.
>
> Thirdly, it may be that we have to admit that causal influences *do* go faster than light. The role of Lorentz invariance in the completed theory would then be very problematic. An "aether" would be the

cheapest solution. But the unobservability of this aether would be disturbing. So would the impossibility of "messages" faster than light, which follows from ordinary relativistic quantum mechanics in so far as it is unambiguous and adequate for procedures we can actually perform. . . .

Fourthly and finally, it may be that Bohr's intuition was right— in that there is no reality below some "classical" "macroscopic" level. Then fundamental physical theory would remain fundamentally vague, until concepts like "macroscopic" could be made sharper than they are today. (154–55; emphasis added)

Bell adds a remarkable appendix on Bohr's views of the EPR argument, of which, unlike that of Einstein's position, Bell claims "to have very little understanding." "Yet," he adds in a rather peculiar phrasing, "most contemporary theorists have the impression that they themselves share Bohr's views" (155). Bell does not adhere carefully to Bohr's argument. The strategies of his appendix are, however, of much interest; and I shall conclude this chapter by considering it at some detail. Bell writes:

As an indication of [Bohr's] views I quote a passage from his reply to Einstein, Podolsky and Rosen. It is a passage which Bohr himself seems to have regarded as definitive, quoting it himself when summing up much later. Einstein, Podolsky and Rosen had assumed that ". . . if, without in any way disturbing a system, we can predict with certainty the value of a physical quantity, then there exists an element of physical reality corresponding to this physical quantity." Bohr replied: ". . . the wording of the above mentioned criteria . . . contains an ambiguity as regards the meaning of the expression 'without in any way disturbing a system.' Of course there is in a case like that just considered no question of a mechanical disturbance of the system under investigation during the last critical stage of the measuring procedure. But even at this stage there is essentially the question of *an influence on the very conditions which define the possible types of predictions regarding the future behavior of the system* . . . their argumentation does not justify their conclusion that quantum mechanical description is essentially incomplete. . . . This description may be characterized as a rational utilization of all possibilities of unambiguous interpretation of measurements, compatible with the finite and uncontrollable interaction between the objects and the measuring instruments in the field of quantum theory."

Indeed I have very little idea what this means. I do not understand in what sense the word "mechanical" is used, in characterizing the disturbances which Bohr does not contemplate, as distinct
from those which he does. I do not know what the italicized passage
means—"an influence on the very conditions. . . ." Could it mean
just that different experiments on the first system give different kinds
of information about the second? But this was just one of the main
points of EPR, who observed that one could learn *either* the position *or*
the momentum of the second system. And then I do not understand
the final reference to "uncontrollable interactions between measuring instruments and objects," it seems just to ignore the essential
point of EPR that in the absence of action at a distance, only the first
system could be supposed disturbed by the first measurement and
yet definite predictions become possible for the second system. Is
Bohr just rejecting the premise—"no action at a distance"—rather
than refuting the argument? (155–56)

Bell clearly misses Bohr's point. Indeed, as is clear from the analysis
given earlier, he misses most of Bohr's points. First of all, Bell extracts—
and further truncates—the passage which may have been seen as central by Bohr, but which depends on and is a conclusion to an extended
argument considered earlier. This argument is not mentioned and does
not appear to have been taken into account by Bell. Even Bohr's original
communication makes this point, when Bohr points out that "the procedure of measurement has an essential influence on the conditions on
which the very definition of the physical quantities in question rests" and
that "these conditions must be considered as an inherent element of any
phenomenon to which the term 'physical reality' can be unambiguously
applied." EPR fail to take this factor into account, allowing Bohr to argue
that their "conclusion" that quantum mechanics is incomplete "would
not appear to be justified" (*QTM*, 144). Thus, a more careful reading even
of this shorter text, quoted by Bell nearly in its entirety—but again with
some interesting omissions—would lead one to different conclusions.

Bohr does not refute the possibility of an exact prediction of both position and momentum in the EPR situation by means of quantum mechanical formalism, by using which and only by using which is the prediction
possible in this situation. What he is refuting is that the incompleteness
of quantum mechanics follows from the possibility of such exact predictions—based on calculations and not on the possibility of a simultaneous
exact measurement of both position and momentum within the same

experimental arrangement. By the same token, Bohr's elaborations are aimed at exposing the insufficiency of the classical philosophical assumptions and criteria (such as those of the EPR argument) in the case at issue, thus requiring "a final renunciation of the classical ideal of causality and a radical revision of our attitude towards the problem of physical reality" (*QTM*, 146).

Bell's theorem in fact reinforces the difference between classical and quantum mechanical cases, as Bell himself shows (*SUQM*, 83–86). His reading of Bohr's argument, however, misses the point of this difference which, while made easier by Bell's theorem, need not depend on it. For, as was considered in detail earlier, it does not follow from the possibility of an exact prediction on the basis of the transformation theorem and the experimental measurements performed, that both position and momentum of the second particle can be simultaneously measured or defined, and thus assigned, at any subsequent point. EPR's criteria of physical reality and completeness becomes inapplicable, and the conclusion that quantum mechanics is incomplete does not follow.

The simultaneous ascribability of position and momentum is impossible precisely by virtue of "the finite [i.e., quantum] and uncontrollable [i.e., indeterminate] interaction between the object and the measuring instruments in the field of quantum theory," which Bell "does not understand" or does not want to understand. Bohr describes this interaction in great detail immediately prior to the passage with which Bell begins his quotation. The statement cited by Bell states the *consequences* derived by Bohr from this analysis, not considered by Bell. The interaction at issue, specifically analyzed by Bohr in the case of the EPR situation (*QTM*, 147–48), shapes Bohr's argument as to why "there is essentially the question of *an influence on the very conditions which define the possible types of predictions regarding the future behavior of the system*," rather than a "question of a *mechanical* disturbance of the system under investigation during the last critical stage of measuring procedure," that is, something directly— physically, mechanically—affecting the system (i.e., the overall measuring arrangement) from outside. This is "the sense in which the word 'mechanical' is used," and this is what "the italicized passage means— 'influence on the very conditions.'" The latter phrase has nothing to do with the meaning proposed by Bell to the effect that "different experiments on the first system give different kinds of information about the second." This is indeed "just one of the main points of the EPR," clearly understood by Bohr from the outset of his argument.

It is difficult to understand why Bell does not understand all these points. Perhaps it is because he refuses *to read* the argument as fully stated by Bohr, particularly Bohr's analysis of the interaction between an object and the measuring instruments and his argument for the impossibility of ascribing simultaneous reality to both position and momentum. These are crucial, defining points of Bohr's argument missed or ignored by Bell. Once one considers this argument fully, it is not surprising that Bohr finds that "the wording of the above mentioned criterion of physical reality proposed by Einstein, Podolsky, and Rosen contains an ambiguity as regards the meaning of the expression 'without in any way disturbing a system.'" Bohr's targets are the EPR criteria of *completeness* and of *physical reality*—the point clearly missed by Bell. In citing the passage Bell in fact skips the phrase "physical reality," crucial to Bohr's argument insofar as the incompleteness of quantum mechanics is concerned.

Another passage omitted by Bell in the citation is even more decisive for the argument, no matter what Bohr himself cites in his subsequent summary in the Schilpp volume; and one cannot, in general, rely on that type of summary in a rigorous argument. What Bohr actually says is that "these conditions constitute an inherent element of any phenomena to which the term 'physical reality' can be properly attached" [in quantum mechanics]. That is, if one wants to speak of "physical reality" in the case of quantum mechanics, as EPR (not necessarily Bohr himself) do, these are conditions that must be considered, which the EPR article does not do. Hence, quite logically, "we see that the argumentation of the mentioned authors does not justify their conclusion that quantum-mechanical description is essentially incomplete. On the contrary this description, as appears from the preceding discussion, may be characterized as a rational utilization of all possibilities of unambiguous interpretation of measurements, compatible with the finite and uncontrollable interaction between the objects and the measuring instruments in the field of quantum theory" (*QTM*, 148–49). The expression "preceding discussion" is also omitted by Bell, as is this discussion itself, from his argument. The last reference to "uncontrollable interactions between measuring instruments and objects" would, thus, contrary to Bell's assertion, in no way "ignore the essential point of the EPR that in the absence of action at a distance, only the first system could be supposed disturbed by the first measurement and yet definite predictions become possible for the second system." Nor, therefore, "is Bohr just rejecting the premise—'no action at a distance'," insofar as one speaks of physical action. Bohr is, thus, "refuting," precisely "the [EPR] argument" itself, by showing the inapplicability of the EPR criteria of physical reality and completeness in the case of quantum mechanics.

Bell can say, of course, as he does in the statement allegedly supported by his argument in the appendix just considered: "It would be wrong to say 'Bohr wins again' (Appendix 1); the argument [Bell's theorem] was not known to the opponents of Einstein, Podolsky, and Rosen" (*SUQM*, 150). In truth, however, Bell's theorem does say that "Bohr wins again," and the argument appended by Bell does nothing to disprove it. To the extent that Bell's general argument modifies the EPR argument by reducing its metaphysical overload, one can argue that Bohr, by using specific features of the EPR original argument, wins a somewhat different case. But in fact Bohr's reply is applicable to most forms of the EPR argument and can also be used against Bell's metaphysics.

It is not, of course, that one cannot disagree with Bohr's views or criticize his understanding of the EPR experiment. Profound critical points have been raised, beginning with Einstein, which helped Bohr to refine his ideas and develop the EPR argument itself. It is just that Bell's does not do so in his reading, to the extent that he reads Bohr. What Bell's argument does prove, without realizing it, is that physics is also reading. For Bell's analysis (or the lack of thereof) of Bohr's reply to EPR— Bell's refusal to read—involves much physics, too. Bohr appears to be a much better reader—classical or deconstructive—than Bell, whether at issue is his reading of the defining configurations of quantum mechanics or his reading of EPR's text. Bohr, a proponent of structural vagueness, ambiguity, and indeterminacy reads precisely; Bell, who seeks to avoid vagueness, ambiguity, and indeterminacy reads, at least Bohr's text, rather vaguely. Bohr's reading of the EPR text enables an extraordinary refinement of physics and meta-physics—anti-epistemology—enacted by complementarity. Of course, physics or meta-physics cannot be reduced to reading in this sense. But neither can reading, or *writing* (in Derrida's sense), be subtracted from theory. Bohr profoundly understood their interconnection at all levels of quantum physics and brilliantly utilized this interconnection in his own practice.

PART III

Complementarity

and

Deconstruction

This part of the book analyzes the relationships—the affinities, differences, and interactions—between complementarity and Derridean deconstruction.

Chapter 7 discusses a distinction between the two shaped by their relations to their respective paradigmatic models—the complementarity and indeterminacy of quantum mechanics, on the one hand, and Gödelian undecidability, on the other. Thoralf Skolem's findings on nonstandard models in arithmetic are also introduced leading to a supplementary metaphorical model that mediates between undecidability and complementarity.

Chapter 8 considers the question of theoretical and interpretive closures, in part by juxtaposing Derrida and Nietzsche. The discussion extends complementarity to the economy of closure, thus conjoining the principles of complementarity and correspondence. It also suggests the possibility of refiguring the field and history of philosophy, from Plato to Heidegger and Derrida, via Hegel, as the metaphysics of closure.

Chapter 9 extends this analysis to the question of the transformation of closure.

CHAPTER 7

Undecidability and

Complementarity

Undecidability, Complementarity, and Nonstandard Models

In "Différance," Derrida relates *différance* to key "themes in Nietzsche's work":

> [O]n the basis of this unfolding of the same as *différance*, we see announced the sameness of *différance* and repetition in the eternal return.

Themes in Nietzsche's work that are linked to the symptomatology that always diagnoses the detour or ruse of an agency disguised in its *différance;* or further, to the entire thematic of active interpretation, which substitutes incessant deciphering for the unveiling of truth as the presentation of the thing itself in its presence, etc. Figures without truth, or at least a system of figures not dominated by the value of truth, which then becomes only an included, inscribed, circumscribed function. (*Margins*, 17–18, *Marges*, 18–19)

Nietzsche's view of the classical concept(s) of truth is effectively rendered here by Derrida. The last proposition is consonant with Nietzsche's view of truth and most so-called truths—moral, religious or theological, or philosophical—as at best undecidable but mostly untrue. Derrida further considers this thematics in *Spurs: Nietzsche's Styles* in relation to Heidegger and the question of woman. The functioning of truth becomes for Nietzsche supplementary in Derrida's sense, thereby also implying a certain complementarity of truth and nontruth. From this economy, Nietzsche derives the consequences that philosophy, from Socrates to Heidegger, has failed to derive. The truths of philosophy are, in Gödel's and Derrida's terms, at best undecidable. According to Nietzsche him-

self, the truths of philosophy are mostly untrue, but one must also recognize and accept the necessity of these errors, and of error in general,
thereby refiguring the relationship between truth and error. Naturally,
Nietzsche's own truths, while very likely more "true" than philosophical truths, must in turn be seen—and are seen by Nietzsche—as undecidable and possibly constituting one more error among others (*On the
Genealogy of Morals*, 18). Nietzsche introduces what, metaphorically ap-
propriating another concept from mathematical logic via Thoralf Skolem,
may be called nonstandard models of truth—or morality, aesthetics, and
other economies of meaning and value. Nonstandard models may function as the efficacities of standard models or interact with them or, implying more remote efficacities, lead to mutually exclusive complementarities similar to those of quantum mechanics.

In terms of analytic practice, Derrida's description just cited fits Derrida's own project much more closely than Nietzsche's; and while speaking of Nietzsche's *themes*, Derrida may well play out Derrida's *variations*.
The process he describes is much closer to his own practice of interminable analysis—"incessant deciphering"—of often, perhaps always, undecidable relations than to Nietzsche's practice. Nietzsche's economy of
active interpretation operates more by actively positing and, as it were,
experimentally testing "truths" and "fictions," or complementarily both,
rather than, and often *against*, engaging incessant deciphering or unveiling. Derrida's psychoanalytic metaphor suggests that the latter is modeled
on Freud's concept of interminable analysis, introduced in his late essay
"Analysis Terminable and Interminable," suggesting a continual return
of the patient to the analysis. Nietzsche's "eternal return," a complex and
equivocal conception, is plugged into this Freudian economy, which is
one of Derrida's key models, correlative to his own (interminable) exploration of philosophical undecidables.

At the same time, the *same* as *différance* that Derrida invokes at this point
is very close, although not identical, and clearly alludes, to the Heideggerian economy of the same, especially as developed in later essays in *Early
Greek Thinking*. One of these essays, "The Anaximander Fragment," is
considered by Derrida in "Différance." Derrida's theoretical project or
process may, thus, be seen as a triple conjunction of Freudian, Heideggerian, and Gödelian thematics. As such, it can to a degree be juxtaposed
to Nietzsche's or Bohr's (or Bataille's) practice, marked more decisively
by the exploration and engagement of complementary, rather than undecidable, economies. Freud's own practices—the practices of theory and

the practices of *practice*—may be seen in proximity to both Heidegger, on the one hand, and Derrida, on the other.[1] One must keep in mind that, as opposed to Heidegger's, Derrida's analysis remains general economic, specifically by virtue of the fundamental significance of the unconscious in his post-Freudian matrix.

Nietzsche proceeds by transformative complementarizations that more actively engage exterior, or in Deleuze's terms, more radically re-territorialized, theories and fields, such as psychology or contemporary science. He often creates new continuities, proceeding along psychological, social, political, or historical—genealogical—lines of analysis, which lead him to nonstandard models of various configurations defined within classical fields. One could even suggest that Nietzsche attacks the interminable analysis *of truth*, for example, in "How the 'True World' Finally Became a Fable: The History of an Error" (in *Twilight of the Idols*). On another occasion he says: "I approach deep problems like cold baths: quickly into them and quickly out of them" (*The Gay Science*, 343 n. 381; *KSA* 3:634). That does not mean that Nietzsche did not spend a long time—"live with"—his problems—"postponing judgment, learning to go around and grasp each individual case from all sides" (*Twilight of the Idols, The Portable Nietzsche*, 511; *KSA* 6:108). In his Preface to *Daybreak*, Nietzsche speaks of similar demands upon himself and his readers (1–5). He spends many "short sessions" with his cases—the case of Kant, "the case of Socrates," "the case of Wagner" (the last two are Nietzsche's titles). In this respect, Nietzsche anticipates psychoanalytic approach, which, however, would not erase the differences between Nietzsche's style and interminable analysis, either in Freud or, via "undecidables," in Derrida.[2]

Nor would this difference be suspended by the fact that, conversely, Derrida at certain points proceeds in a more Nietzschean way. New things, decidable and undecidable, are produced, while at the same time old things undergo deconstruction, and undecidability is exposed. In the first place, the undecidable or the deconstructable has to be constructed as such both by de-constructing and re-*constructing*, by carefully disassembling and reassembling, previous constructions and by engaging new ones. In addition, Derrida's deconstruction uses complementarization, for example, as we have seen, that of the differing-deferred opposites of classical philosophy, even though Derrida's main goal may be the exploration of their interaction and undecidability. Conversely, in Nietzsche or Bohr, more deconstructive explorations of the relationships between the components of the complementary pairs or clusters and various forms of undecidability may be involved as well. The difference between complementarity and (Derrida's) deconstruction is then rather that of the relative orientation and balance of different projects and procedures, or a theoretical process or style. One might say that the common constituents of both approaches are differently complementarized, and this complementarization is itself at times undecidable or indeterminate. (We must keep in mind differences, operative at various conceptual and metaphoric levels, between undecidability and indeterminacy, or between indeterminacy and uncertainty.) At the same time, however, the differences between such theoretical projects may be equally important, at times crucial.

To summarize, the difference between "deconstruction" and "complementarity" may be defined by way of their relations to the two major conceptions in modern mathematics and physics at issue here—Gödel's *undecidability* and Bohr's *complementarity*.

Undecidability deals with questions of truth and completeness, or incompleteness, of formal systems in mathematical logic and, in Derrida's case, with *analogous* configurations in philosophy. In Penrose's formulation: "What Gödel showed was that any precise ('formal') mathematical system of axioms and rules of procedure *whatever*, provided that it is broad enough to contain descriptions of simple arithmetical propositions . . . and provided that it is free from contradiction, must contain some statements which are neither provable nor disprovable by means allowed within the system. The truth of such statements is thus 'undecidable' by approved procedure. In fact, Gödel was able to show that the very statement of the consistency of the axiom system itself, when coded into the form of a suitable arithmetical proposition, must be one such 'undecidable' proposition" (*The Emperor's New Mind*, 102). Hence a proof of the consistency of a formalized system (provided that it is rich enough to contain arithmetic) cannot be contained within the formalism of this system itself, which statement constitutes Gödel's incompleteness theorem. Derrida's formulation gives undecidability an anti-Hegelian spin: "An undecidable proposition (Gödel demonstrated this possibility in 1931) is a proposition which, given a system of axioms governing a multiplicity, is neither an analytical nor deductive consequence of those axioms, nor in contradiction with them, neither true nor false with respect to those axioms. *Tertium datur*, without synthesis" (*Dissemination*, 219; *La Dissémination*, 248–49; translation modified). Philosophy, according to Derrida, can never make all its propositions or the delimitation of its own field decidable, or its systems complete.

Complementarity deals with complementary relations of terms and concepts, under the conditions of indeterminacy, on the model of Bohr's complementarity as considered here. The practice of complementarity in analysis or description, historical or theoretical, establishes an agenda of complementarization rather than deconstruction as the practice of undecidability. Theory as complementarity is thus analogous to quantum mechanics, and specifically Bohr's complementarity, in contrast to the undecidability and incompleteness matrix of mathematical logic.

Quantum (or analogous) indeterminacy may at times imply ultimate undecidability, in the extended conceptual and metaphorical sense of the term, between complementary components in quantum mechanics or elsewhere, and the semantic or metaphoric fields of both terms may themselves overlap. This undecidability is different from Gödelian—mathematically provable—undecidability and its effects, such as incompleteness, within formal systems where they are established. Unlike Gödelian undecidability, "undecidability" in quantum mechanics can change in view of new experimental evidence or new interpretations consistent with old evidence. It is, of course, possible that certain questions of physics—for example, whether the universe is open or closed—may remain forever undecidable. This undecidability would, however, still be different from Gödelian undecidability in the sense just described.

In general, there are many interactions between both frameworks, especially along the lines of general economy, required by both complementarity and undecidability, in the latter case perhaps only as an extended deconstructive paradigm. For in contrast to Bohr, Gödel's interpretation of mathematical undecidability appears to be metaphysical, restricted economic; and as such it may be juxtaposed to Derrida's antiepistemology. The two approaches—(the deconstructive) undecidability and complementarity—interpenetrate each other and may be multiply combined. In the first case, new, and often complementary, configurations may and often must be produced, along with and as part of the exploration of undecidability; in the second, an exploration of undecidability may be engaged alongside complementarity. The differences in orientation and balance of emphasis between complementarity and deconstruction may, however, have far-reaching implications, and, as shall be seen in the next section, Derrida himself opposes his economy of undecidability to indeterminacy, which may be associated with complementarity.

Thus, the indeterminacy (or again certain undecidability) of the particle and wave representations is an important part of the matrix, although as a practical and constructive instrument of theory it is less decisive than the complementarity of these two representations. It may well be more decisive that "particles" are both—particles and waves—rather than that they are perhaps finally neither. As we have seen, indeterminacy, too, functions largely as a constructive constraint and, as such, has proven to be extraordinarily effective. (To a degree, undecidability operates similarly in deconstruction.) As I indicated, indeterminacy itself is *determinate* or *decidable*, as are Gödelian or Derridean undecidables, as Derrida emphasizes. It is determined not only in the sense, more or less obvious, that certain relations are determined to be indeterminate (and possibly undecidable), but also in the sense that these relations engage specific complementarities of their constituent "idealizations" as mathematical, experimental, conceptual, and metaphoric complexes. Such complementarities can be used in the deconstructed or undecidable field, or more directly in what may be called the complementary, or complementarized field. In the first case, they would relate classical oppositions—such as signifier and signified, consciousness and the unconscious, the immediate and the mediated, or continuity and discontinuity—or more mediated terms and clusters, analogous to the complementarity of space-time coordination and the claim of causality in quantum mechanics. All such terms, moreover, are themselves complex conceptual and metaphoric conglomerates, leading to further complementarities.

Undecidability is a key element of Derrida's matrix, and, in the wake of Derrida's analysis, the concept had a major impact elsewhere. Derrida addresses the thematics of undecidability beginning with his early work on Husserl, specifically in his *Introduction* to Husserl's "The Origin of Geometry," Derrida's first published book (1962). Gödel's theorem is mentioned only briefly, but its significance is decisive, since, as Derrida points out, it contradicts the "ideal . . . clearly defined by Husserl, notably in [*Logical Investigations*]": "Starting from a system of axioms which 'governs' a multiplicity, every proposition is determinable *either* as analytic consequence *or* as analytic contradiction. That would be an alternative we could not get beyond. Such confidence did not have long to wait before being contradicted: indeed its vulnerability has been well shown, particularly when Gödel discovered the rich possibility of '*undecidable*' propositions in 1931" (*Introduction*, 53).

At the same time, as Derrida explains, however unsurmountable the fact of Gödel's theorem may be, it would not in itself, at least on the surface, be sufficient to undermine the primordial philosophicometaphysical project—and, historically, the process or history—that, according to Husserl, ground the project and history (or at least the origin) of mathematics and make them possible (53–55). This fact would not undermine even a certain primordial axiomatico-mathematical project, within which "the notion of the un-decidable—apart from the fact that it only has such a sense by some irreducible reference to the ideal of decidability—also retains a mathematical value derived from some unique source of value vaster than the project of *definiteness* itself" (53). Gödel's theorem was certainly not seen as undermining the mathematical or again, philosophico-mathematical project (of a rather Husserlian type) by Gödel himself, who appears to have been influenced and inspired by Husserl's philosophy. Much more complex conceptual and historical deconstructions or, as Derrida would see them at the time (1962), desedimentations must be engaged in order to problematize the core of Husserl's philosophy sufficiently radically and fundamentally. Derrida successfully accomplishes that goal here, particularly (but not exclusively) with respect to "The Origin of Geometry," and in his subsequent writings on Husserl; and the *Introduction* clearly anticipates and prepares his subsequent deconstructive work.[3] In fact, although Derrida does not pursue this line of questioning, in view of these deconstructions, Gödel's theorem can be seen as, in the end, fundamentally problematizing the possibility of an originarily or primordially fundamental mathematical or proto-mathematical (philosophical) project, be it Husserl's or Gödel's. If so, it would have to receive an interpretation analogous to Bohr's anti-epistemology of quantum mechanics, for example, via a Derridean or post-Derridean matrix, perhaps amalgamated by Skolem's ideas.

It is certainly not accidental that Derrida introduces undecidability into his matrix, which deconstructs and anti-epistemologically recomprehends Husserlian project, including in "The Origin of Geometry." At the same time, one can locate in Derrida's treatment in the *Introduction* signs of a certain proximity or rapprochement with classical philosophy, albeit at a very complex level of reengagement and accompanied by significant differences, specifically from Husserl. As shall be seen, this rapprochement reemerges—as a kind of delayed effect—with some rather direct echoes to the language of the elaborations in the *Introduction* (1962), just referred to (53–55), in Derrida's much more recent (1988) thinking on undecidability, which he, on that occasion, opposes to indeterminacy. These proximities become further reinforced by Derrida's economy of closure, to be discussed in the next two chapters.

In spite of these reconnections, there remains a fundamental difference between Gödelian and Derridean undecidability, the first being, at the philosophical level, epistemology or metaphysics, and the second anti-epistemology and a deconstruction of metaphysics. For, as I indicated, Gödel's own philosophy of mathematics was fundamentally metaphysical—a form of Platonism. In this sense, even as he discovers undecidability he remains a classicist, similarly to Einstein, who, as the discoverer of the light quanta may be seen as "the godfather of complementarity," but who never accepted it, particularly its anti-epistemological aspects. The parallel, we recall, can be grounded historically, as well as conceptually. Einstein and Gödel were both in Princeton, where they developed close intellectual ties. These ties were reinforced by the proximities in their philosophical outlook and their views of science. While there are differences between their epistemological positions, both belong to the *continuum* of the metaphysics of presence, which is also the metaphysics of the continuum. Gödel also made decisive mathematical, as well as philosophical, contributions to the mathematical problem of the continuum and to the problem of time in relativity. Thus, Einstein and Gödel, as classical, epistemological thinkers, can be juxtaposed to Bohr and Derrida, as anti-epistemological thinkers.[4] Einstein's and Gödel's philosophical positions need not undermine the significance of their scientific and mathematical findings. Whatever the case may be for Einstein or Gödel themselves, mathematics and physics, including the classical ones, are, as I said, not *absolutely* indissociable from metaphysics, and they can function within an anti-epistemological, general-economic framework and be used against metaphysics, as in Bohr.

While, then, metaphorically associating Derrida's project with Gödelian undecidability, the present analysis in no way implies the identity or even similarity of Gödel's and Derrida's philosophical positions, which must be juxtaposed. One can find proximities between them and, as I said, along certain lines, Derrida is closer to Gödel than to Bohr or Nietzsche—but only along certain lines, for Derrida's theoretical economy is general, while Gödel's is restricted. In view of the proximities between Husserl's (who was, next to Leibniz, Gödel's favorite philosopher) and Gödel's philosophical views, one could pursue a deconstruction of Gödel's philosophy analogous to Derrida's deconstruction of Husserl. Hao Wang suggests, cogently, that Gödel "values Husserl's work because [Husserl's procedure of] 'bracketing' promises for him a method of finding the right perspective to perceive concepts more directly" (*Reflections on Kurt Gödel*, 193). He also suggests that Husserl's 'bracketing' mediates the proximity between Gödel and Leibniz (196). The problematization of 'bracketing' as part of Husserl's phenomenological reduction is a key aspect of Derrida's deconstruction of Husserl in *Speech and Phenomena* and elsewhere.

It is worth mentioning that both Gödel and Wittgenstein were present at and influenced by Luitzen Egbertus Jan Brouwer's lecture in Vienna on March 10, 1928, on "Mathematics, Science and Language." Brouwer, the founder of intuitionism, spoke of, among other things, the inexhaustibility of mathematics within any formal system. According to Wang (*Reflections on Kurt Gödel*, 80–88), this lecture "is said to have caused Wittgenstein to return to philosophy" (80)—the philosophy of his later period. Gödel appears to have been influenced specifically by the lecture, according to Rudolf Carnap, and by Brouwer's ideas. He refers to Brouwer's work in his dissertation. Unlike Brouwer's more general or, one can say, philosophical formulations to that effect, and similarly to Bohr's in physics, Gödel's are rigorous mathematical results: within a formal system specific propositions are constructed that are undecidable in this system. Such a rigor is perhaps unattainable in philosophical discourse, as Gödel perhaps came to realize in his own philosophical work.[5]

In addition, the relations between Einstein and Bohr, on the one hand, and Gödel and Derrida, on the other, are far from strictly parallel in historical, conceptual, or institutional (field-specific) terms. In the first case, one encounters a direct debate within a given field (although both physics and philosophy are at stake) and, in the second, a partial and qualified transfer of undecidability as a metaphoric model from one field to another. Also, while he was one of the creators of quantum physics and a discoverer of complementarity or duality of light, Einstein rejected the subsequent development of the theory, even though the latter could be, in principle, interpreted more metaphysically. Perhaps he saw that physics was against such metaphysical interpretations of quantum theory and perceived the effectiveness of Bohr's interpretation from its inception. As we have seen, he believed that a different physics was possible and necessary, and he continued to pursue the framework offered by his general relativity theory, which was, as opposed to quantum physics, consistent with both his physical and metaphysical views. By contrast, for Gödel, his metaphysical position always remained consistent with the incompleteness and undecidability he discovered in the field of mathematical logic.

The present study both positions Bohr's and Derrida's matrixes symmetrically and juxtaposes them, by way of Nietzsche and Bohr himself, as complementarity and deconstructive undecidability. They are, however, juxtaposed as two forms of *anti*-epistemology rather than as an epistemology and an anti-epistemology, as in the case of Einstein and Bohr.

From this perspective, it may be that Thoralf Skolem's work on model theory suggests a more radical overall anti-epistemological model than Gödel's undecidability, both within the field of mathematical logic itself and, via metaphorical transfers, elsewhere. Skolem demonstrated the uneliminable existence of nonstandard models of arithmetics and exhibited such a model in 1933, in the wake of Gödel's theorem, although he had already suggested such a possibility in 1922. The existence of such models is actually a consequence of Gödel's theorem, according to which any consistent formal system S containing arithmetics would contain an undecidable proposition or formula P. Then, two formal systems—S_1 and S_2—which extend S by adjoining formula P, or conversely its negation, to their axioms will both be consistent, once S is consistent. By the completeness theorem of first-order logic (which Gödel proves as part of his incompleteness theorem), both extended systems have models—M_1 and M_2—which are also the models of the original system S. But (as the models of S) M_1 and M_2 are different, since the proposition P is true in M_1 and false in M_2. Applied to this situation, Gödel's theorem implies the existence of nonstandard models in arithmetics—the models that contain individuals other than numbers (or more precisely than those that represent numbers in a predicate calculus of first order, by means of which Gödel's theorem is proved). In Hilary Putnam's formulation,

> "[T]he argument that Skolem gave, and that shows that "the intuitive notion of a set" (if there is such a thing) is not "captured" by any formal system, shows that even a *formalization of total science* (if one could construct such a thing), or even a *formalization of all our beliefs* (whether they count as "science" or not), could not rule out denumerable interpretations, and, *a fortiori*, such a formalization could not rule out *unintended* interpretations of this notion. . . . What Skolem really pointed out is this: no interesting theory (in the sense of first-order theory) can, in and of itself, determine its own objects up to isomorphism. Skolem's argument can be extended . . . to show that if theoretical constraints do not determine reference, then the addition of operational constraints will not do it either. ("Models and Reality," *Philosophy of Mathematics*, 423, 442)

The anti-epistemological implications of Skolem's findings are unmistakable. As Putnam adds, "in some way, it really seems that the Skolem Paradox underlies the *characteristic* problem of 20th century philosophy" (435). Putnam's own response is hardly anti-epistemological. He is extremely uneasy with the possibilities of " 'Skolemiz[ing] absolutely everything' " (436). He also says, with obvious regrets, that "it is, *unfortunately*, the *moderate* realist position [which seeks to preserve the centrality of the classical notions of truth and reference without postulating nonnatural mental powers] which is put into deep trouble by the Löwenheim-Skolem Theorem [which leads to Skolem's nonstandard models] and related model-theoretic results" (422; emphasis added). "Verificationism" Putnam proposes "as a way of preserving the outlook of scientific or empirical realism" (422) remains fully within classical limits, both in general or in relation to mathematical logic and physics, to which Putnam gives a considerable space in his essay.[6] Although Putnam does make some suggestions to that effect, he never really explores the consequences of the possibility of extrapolating the nonstandard models matrix into other fields. From the present perspective, one can say that the original system *S* of the above description becomes epistemologically complementarized in the process. Skolem's findings introduce a kind of complementarity into the Gödelian field and by extension a metaphorical model—one may call it destandardization—that extends and enriches Gödel's. In a certain sense, this study would argue for "Skolemization"—destandardization and complementarization—of everything. This model, as will be seen, has further implications for the question of closure.[7]

As the preceding analysis would suggest, metaphorical analogies of this situation are found in Bataille's and Derrida's theories or Bohr's complementarity. In many ways, general economy may be seen, metaphorically, as a nonstandard or multistandard model, or a field of multistandardization, analogous to that opened by Skolem's findings in the field of mathematical logic. As I have indicated, however, Nietzsche's analysis and strategies offer the most striking analogy, thus also suggesting a new perspective on Nietzsche. All Nietzsche's works aim at exposing the nonstandard and multistandard regimes of various classical systems by showing that the latter can be extended by adding to them configurations that are undecidable by their rules. The interactions between these regimes are, of course, more multiple and complex than in mathematical logic; and one must, again, adhere to the possible limits of such transfers. Thus, in *The Birth of Tragedy*, the interplay of the Apollinian and the Dionysian becomes a kind of nonstandard model of tragedy, as opposed to the Aristotelian mimetic model or other classical models of tragedy. Nietzsche as "a 'subterranean man' at work, one who tunnels and mines and undermines" (*Daybreak*, 1; *KSA* 5:11) is again a discoverer of nonstandard models, here of both morality and of the logic that governs the philosophy of morality. *On the Genealogy of Morals* further develops these ideas by offering the nonstandard model of morality as in the interaction of active ("good and bad") and reactive ("good and evil") morality and a nonstandard model of philosophy as asceticism. The Dionysian economy as understood by Nietzsche's later works can be seen as a very general nonstandard model or a field of destandardization and multistandardization. The approach may be traced throughout Nietzsche's work, which may, thus, be characterized as a complementarization by means of nonstandard models. As such, it can be contrasted with Derrida's deconstructive undecidability, although deconstruction involves destandardization as well, analogously to the way Gödel's theorem implies it in mathematical logic.

Undecidability, Indeterminacy, and Determinations of Theory

Most explicitly, undecidability is played out by Derrida in *Dissemination*, via Mallarmé and then in a kind of "arithmetics"—"numbers"—in his reading of Sollers's *Nombres*.[8] It is worth noting that in Derrida and elsewhere, these are—and not without reasons—theoretical texts, such as philosophical or psychoanalitical, that tend to be treated as problematic, while the major new matrices are played out more freely in literary texts.[9] Although this analytic asymmetry is the outgrowth of a long intellectual history, it is also part of the economy of and the complementarity between literature and theory, and specifically philosophy, in the text of deconstruction, be it in Derrida, de Man, or most other practitioners. *Dissemination* and *Glas* present it perhaps the most graphically: between [*inter*] Mallarmé and Hegel, or Mallarmé and Plato, and in *Glas* between Hegel and Jean Genet. As I have suggested from the outset, the metaphorics of quantum physics have also affected Derrida's framework. The preference for undecidability, however, clearly reflects the character, or style, of Derrida's project(s). As will be seen presently, this preference is directly stated by Derrida and even claimed by him as necessary, in opposition to indeterminacy, or, at least, a certain indeterminacy.

Deconstruction, thus, can be seen as oriented toward, although not being reducible to, the construction of undecidable or aporetic configurations, at times by way of specific conceptual undecidables (in contrast to indeterminates) or, as in de Man, aporias, at times emerging on a broader scale of interaction between different fields, such as philosophy and literature. Derrida invokes undecidables throughout his work. The analysis in "The Double Session" and "Dissemination" (both in *Dissemination*) is structured directly through incompleteness, undecidability, and related logico-mathematical metaphors. It may be seen as an analysis of undecidability and construction of undecidable propositions and as a kind of spelling out of Derrida's "incompleteness theorem" of philosophy. One of the main tasks of most of Derrida's analyses, however, especially (but not exclusively) in his earlier works, is to mark the interval of undecidability. This move is necessary also in order to bring about "the irruptive emergence of a new 'concept,' a concept [*différance*] that can no longer be, and never could be, included in the previous regime" (*Positions*, 42; *Positions*, 57). One must, thus, mark "the interval between inversion" and open and produce the matrix of *différance*, dissemination, *writing*, and other Derridean "neither terms nor concepts." This matrix imposes powerful but productive constraints, which affect this matrix itself by radically pluralizing it. "If this interval, this biface or biphase, can be inscribed only in a bifurcated writing . . . , then it can only be marked in what I would call a *grouped* textual field: in the last analysis it is impossible to *point* it out, for a unilinear text, or a punctual *position*, an operation signed by a single author, are all by definition incapable of practicing this interval" (*Positions*, 42; *Positions*, 57–58). New matrices are thus generated, along with and, crucially, *by means of* exposing the undecidability of the theses of philosophy and above all the thesis of thesis itself, and through what Derrida calls the movement of athesis.[10] That movement includes the techniques of *writing* undecidability and of locating the space or interval of undecidability as *différance* and dissemination, but is not restricted to it. The process also produces, specifically as *writing*, new economies of interpretation, history, theory, or literature, as in particular in Mallarmé, Blanchot, Jabès, Genet, Artaud, or Ponge. The logic and exploration of undecidability, however, whether used deconstructively or in order to produce new "concepts," structures Derrida's work throughout. As he writes:

> Henceforth, in order better to mark this interval . . . it has been necessary to analyze, to set to work, *within* the text of the history of philosophy, as well as *within* the so-called literary text (for ex-

ample, Mallarmé), certain marks, shall we say, . . . that *by analogy* (I underline) I have called undecidables, that is, unities of simulacrum, "false" verbal properties (nominal or semantic) that can no longer be included within philosophical (binary) opposition, but which, however, inhabit philosophical opposition, resisting and disorganizing it, *without ever* constituting a third term, without ever leaving room for a solution in the form of speculative dialectics (the *pharmakon* [in Plato] is neither remedy nor poison, neither good nor evil, neither the inside nor the outside, neither speech nor writing; the *supplement* is neither a plus nor a minus, neither an outside nor the complement of an inside, neither accident nor essence, etc.; the *hymen* is neither confusion nor distinction, neither identity nor difference, neither consummation nor virginity, neither the veil nor unveiling, neither the inside nor the outside, etc.; the *gram* is neither a signifier nor a signified, neither a sign nor a thing, neither a presence nor an absence, neither a position nor a negation, etc.; *spacing* is neither space nor time; the *incision* is neither the incised integrity of a beginning, or of a simple cutting into, nor simple secondarity. Neither/nor, that is, *simultaneously* either *or;* the mark is also the *marginal* limit, the *march*, etc.). (*Positions*, 42–43; *Positions*, 58–59)[11]

"Either or" is added here by Derrida almost as an afterthought. To a degree against "neither/nor" (although the latter is in turn irreducible), however, it is this "either or" that marks the space of difference between deconstruction—as undecidability—and complementarity. Given the joint operation of "either or" and "neither nor," one cannot fully separate them either. They become complementary instead. Rather than complementarity, Derrida's "either or" implies an agenda of undecidability and suggests production and engagement of new "concepts" either by pursuing and playing out the undecidables or by (de)constructing the undecidables. A given configuration must often be shown to conform to either one denomination or determination or another, or to both at once in order to be shown to be undecidable. Such configurations may be complementary; and, in practice, undecidability often necessitates complementarity. Undecidability and complementarity can themselves be seen as complementary. Their complementarity, however, does not eliminate the differences between them. It figures this difference. The difference, as I have suggested, lies in the relative balance of undecidability, indeterminacy or uncertainty (including potential nuances of and differences

between these terms), and complementarity. This difference has important ramifications for projects that may result—such as Bohr's and Nietzsche's, oriented toward complementarity; or Derrida's, oriented toward
undecidability; or Bataille's, oscillating between the two—although none
of these projects can be reduced to either aspect or a single form of interaction between both.

Derrida's list just cited assembles the "undecidable propositions" of
philosophy, which are constructed and given rigorous sense as undecidable, partly in order to deconstruct the proposition of the previous
regime—"le régime antérieur." This project has been pursued at various levels—conceptual, ideological, institutional, or political—throughout Derrida's work, perhaps more directly in this quasi-Gödelian form
in his earlier texts. The result is an extraordinary achievement: a kind
of grand incompleteness and undecidability theorem concerning the system of philosophy, perhaps particularly, the Hegelian system—in a reso-
nant analogy to the theorem Gödel derived from the mathematical system that Russell and Whitehead assembled in *Principia Mathematica*. In
one of his key propositions, Derrida, as we have seen, says that "If there
were a definition of *différance*, it would be precisely the limit, the interruption, the destruction of the Hegelian *relève* [*Aufhebung*] *wherever* it
operates" (*Positions*, 40–41; *Positions*, 55). Undecidability is a crucial part
of this operation, although the results—deconstruction or even destruction [la destruction][12]—are far more radical than the effects of Gödel's
theorem on the practice of mathematics. In this sense, the analogy with
Gödel loses its force somewhat, although it retains its value with respect
to the metaphorical model of undecidability itself. Mathematics can, and
does, continue to operate under Gödelian conditions. Philosophy can no
longer quite function in the same way in view of deconstruction, even
given a more complex economy of the closure of philosophy. To be sure,
some philosophy or, rather, some philosophers continue to operate in the
classical regime. This possibility itself tells us something both about the
limits within which metaphorical analogies and transfers can be operative
and about the difference in the operation of different fields themselves.
But then, modern debates about the foundations of mathematics, too,
led some mathematicians (for example, those following intuitionism) to
question and even to abandon the standard forms of mathematics. These
differences are, as I have argued, never absolute or unconditional. Conditionally, however, they can be significant.

As I have stressed, we must respect conceptual, metaphoric, and institutional limits of this and other analogies at issue here. One may not be able to speak of a deconstruction of mathematical propositions, as opposed to the construction of undecidable propositions, at least not yet. This difference is due in part to the fact that the claims made by philosophy through its transcendental logic—and on the basis of its "undecidable propositions" and the consequences that are derived from them —are often unsustainable, even if, for various reasons, necessary for philosophy and beyond it. For these claims extend to politics, history, morality, and elsewhere. Mathematical logic, in contrast, does not entail such claims. In this sense, there is perhaps no transcendental logic, whereas there may as yet be formal, mathematical logic, although many things with which philosophy concerns itself in turn demand a different, nonstandard, logic—other "reasons than hitherto," as Nietzsche said. This is in part why the concept of undecidability can be applied only by analogy and metaphorically outside the field of mathematical logic. As the example of the natural sciences suggests, for philosophy or any theory to have undecidables in the rigorous sense could amount to their becoming mathematics. The case is not so simple in mathematics, either, partly because of undecidability. Mathematics "works" in part because of physics and technology. Complex complementarities are at stake. Spinoza, who sometimes modeled his discourse on mathematics, grasped that point when he said that "we must in no way despise technology," although he also had other things in mind. The specificity of mathematics as, *in a certain sense*, a universally communicable field remains its peculiar and, perhaps, unique feature. It must, however, be analyzed general economically.

Derrida's deconstruction leads to a kind of undecidability that, if not quite total, is everywhere operative, extending to all classical oppositions and propositions or theses across the text of philosophy. This undecidability is produced by exploring the athetic movement of *différance* or other Derridean structures, leading to a general economy and, often, a very different style of theoretical writing. Dissemination, "seminal *différance*" (*Positions*, 45; *Positions*, 61), enters this regime as much against Hegel and *Aufhebung* as against Lacan, two great cases of the controlled economy of plurality, or Heidegger. It leads to the undermining not only of the binary, but also of any contained multiplicity, such as Lacanian triangulations.[13] Dissemination thus also relates metaphorically and otherwise to the Gödelian problematic of numbers and to the question of continuum, which has profound connections to Hegel. Along with Plato, Hegel's is the central "propositional calculus" throughout *Dissemination,* from the "*Hors-Livre*" to Mallarmé and the undecidables of "The Double Session" to Sollers. Hegel, however, remains a crucial part of Derrida's undecidability theorem in the book.

Derrida constructs an extraordinarily effective matrix, along with deconstruction—and construction—of undecidables. This matrix makes deconstruction possible, with its production of undecidables through a repertoire of now standard techniques. As I have suggested, many Derridean configurations may be seen in terms of complementarity. The question of the intersections between undecidability and indeterminacy (or uncertainty) in Derrida is, however, more complex. In one of his later elaborations (1988) in the interview with Gerald Graff, which serves as an afterword to *Limited Inc,* Derrida differentiates indeterminacy and undecidability and dissociates, rather strongly, his analysis from the framework of indeterminacy:

> I do not believe I have ever spoken of "indeterminacy," whether in regard to "meaning" or anything else. Undecidability is something else again. While referring to what I have said above and elsewhere, I want to recall that undecidability is always a *determinate* oscillation between possibilities (for example, of meaning, but also of acts). These possibilities are themselves highly *determined* in strictly *defined* situations (for example, discursive—syntactical or rhetorical—but also political, ethical, etc.). They are *pragmatically* determined. The analyses that I have devoted to undecidability concerns just these determinations and these definitions, not at all some vague "indeterminacy." I say "undecidability" rather than "indeterminacy" because I am interested more in relations of force, in differences of force, in everything that allows, precisely, determinations in given situations to be stabilized through a decision of writing (in the broad sense I gave to this word, which also includes political action and experience in general). There would be no indecision or *double bind* were it not between *determined* (semantic, ethical, political) poles, which are upon occasion terribly necessary and always irreplaceably singular. Which is to say that from the point of view of semantics, but also of ethics and politics, "deconstruction" should never lead either to relativism or to any sort of indeterminism.
>
> To be sure, in order for structures of undecidability to be possible (and hence structures of decisions and of responsibilities as well),

there must be a certain play, *différance*, nonidentity. Not of indetermination, but of *différance* or of nonidentity with oneself in the very process of determination. *Différance* is not indeterminacy. It renders determinacy both possible and necessary. Someone might say: but if it renders determinacy possible, it is because it itself is "indeterminacy." Precisely not, since first of all it "is" in *itself* nothing outside of different determinations; second, and consequently, it never comes to a full stop anywhere, absolutely [*elle ne s'arrête nulle part*], and is neither negativity nor nothingness (as indeterminacy would be). Insofar as it is always determined, undecidability is also not negative in itself. (*Limited Inc*, 148–49)

This is an extremely interesting statement, and I shall consider it in some detail. First of all, by emphasizing the determinateness of undecidability and by contrasting it to indeterminacy, the statement clearly strengthens the main point suggested here: on the one hand, the proximity between Derridean and Gödelian matrices and, on the other, the juxtaposition between Derridean undecidability and Bohr's quantum mechanical—indeterminate and complementary—anti-epistemology and, by implication, to the matrix suggested by the present study. As we have seen, in his earlier *Introduction* to Husserl's "The Origin of Geometry," one of Derrida's key, and correct, points is that Gödel's undecidables are strictly determined. An analogous, although crucially not identical, determinability is stressed and perhaps overstressed here. This emphasis makes at least some of Derrida's claims and positions stated here finally excessive, even problematic, however necessary they may be in the context—a response to the claims of vagueness, indeterminacy, and negativity, allegedly advocated by Derrida and deconstruction.

Some of Derrida's points against indeterminacy here are well taken. These points would be equally pertinent in the case of indeterminacy in quantum mechanics and in Bohr's complementarity, and, by implication, in the complementary and indeterminate economy developed in this study. Certainly, in Bohr's matrix, quantum indeterminacy is theoretically determined, no less (although within a different framework) than mathematical undecidability is determined in Gödel or deconstructive undecidability in Derrida. Thus, the conditions under which one can observe, for example, the wave-like or, conversely, the particle-like effects are rigorously determinate. In general, even via uncertainty relations, quantum indeterminacy entails strict experimental and theoretical determinations and leads to highly determinate configurations of theory—for example, complementary ones, but also many others. By definition, however, one cannot suspend indeterminacy under these conditions. For, in contrast to classical physics, certain configurations, such as joint measurements or definitions of conjugate variables, can never be fully determined or be seen as determinate or determinable (rather than be subject to the undecidable determination Derrida invokes here), in part precisely because simultaneous joint determinations are at stake. This final impossibility of at least some joint determinations becomes equally crucial in the extrapolated framework at issue here. As I shall argue presently, however, Derrida in effect cannot and, I think, should not fully suspend indeterminacy either. Quantum indeterminacy is also determined similarly pragmatically, or programmatologically in Bohr. Bohr's matrix or the matrix of the present study, too, deals, at least in some situations, with "possibilities" that are "highly *determined* in strictly *defined* situations, . . . discursive-syntactical or rhetorical, . . . political, ethical," or "semantic," or still other. As the preceding analysis suggests, concerns with "relations of force, . . . differences of force, . . . everything that allows, precisely determinations in given situations to be stabilized through a decision of writing," would clearly apply to Bohr's analysis of experimental and theoretical determination (in given situations) in quantum mechanics or to the determinations at issue in the extrapolated matrix of this study. In the latter case, such determinations would, therefore, equally "include political action and experience in general," as both are refigured general economically, for example, via Derrida's *writing*.

These (complementary) determinations must, however, consider and take into account radical, irreducible indeterminacy, including the indeterminacy of meaning. I cannot quite see how indeterminacy, rather than only undecidability, can be avoided either at the level of meaning or context (as must in fact follow from Derrida's analysis in *Limited Inc*) but, as shall be seen below, at the level of theory as well. We certainly need to account for the indeterminacy—and in particular indeterminacy of meaning and context—and, in theoretical terms, for many a relativism and indeterminism. We do need to account for the possibility of their determination, as Derrida suggests, but we also need to account for the possibility of their indeterminacy or indetermination. Indeterminacy is in fact equally unavoidable in these accounts themselves, including Derrida's accounts, which, as undecidability oriented, may be more determinate, but which can never be fully determinate. One of the main reasons is that one must, as I said, confront the ineluctable necessity of multiple, rather than single, lines of determinations in many, and at a certain level all, interpretive and theoretical cases. Analogous to quantum mechanics, such determinations often mutually inhibit each other, and the increase in determinacy along some dimensions inhibits the degree of determinacy and the very possibility of determination along others. These determinations or determinations-indeterminations obey instead what may be called, by way of another recent mathematical theory, fuzzy logic. As in quantum mechanics, we must both analytically take this indeterminacy into account and, as in the case of uncertainty relations, use it as a constructive element of theory. For some interpretive, theoretical, and (perhaps particularly) political situations, determinations are in fact possible only by virtue of this indeterminacy. This indeterminacy need not lead to theoretical vagueness or prevent theoretical rigor, which are Derrida's obvious concerns in his statement. Actually, Derrida himself is here, uncharacteristically, vague on the concept of indeterminacy—or indeterminism and relativism. As throughout this study (and with the preceding analysis in mind), I refer here to indeterminacy conceived on the model of quantum mechanics as spelled out by the preceeding analysis, similarly to the way Derrida's undecidability is modeled on Gödelian mathematical logic. From Derrida's insistence on and his delineation of undecidability here, it appears that he would oppose this type of indeterminacy as well. I am not sure what, if any, indeterminacy would be more acceptable to him, as opposed to "some vague indeterminacy" he invokes.[14] A jointly more indeterminate and more complementary economy than that of undecidable determination suggested by Derrida here may finally be necessary, however.

The statement under discussion may even be read as, to a degree, a revision of Derrida's earlier understanding of *différance* and its theoretical economy. There would still remain the difference between the two models under discussion—complementarity (including indeterminacy) and Derrida's deconstructive undecidability, even as the latter is configured in Derrida's earlier writing. There is enough continuity between this 1988 statement and these writings, suggested in particular by Derrida's emphasis on *différance* as "the *systematic* [systématique] play of differences, of the traces of differences" (*Positions*, 27; *Positions*, 38; emphasis added). Beginning, as we have seen, with his earliest work on Husserl, Derrida's matrix has always been conceptually and metaphorically closer to Gödelian undecidability than to quantum-like indeterminacy, which is, of course, my main point here.[15] However, whether at the level of meaning and interpretation or at the level of theory or (which is in fact always the case) interactively both, Derrida's earlier economy appears to be closer to a more complementary and indeterminate economy than the statement at issue suggests. Without being accompanied by indeterminacy, or rather by the effects of indeterminacy—without some of its effects being determined as irreducibly undetermined—the play of *différance* inscribed "as nonidentity with oneself in the very process of determination" shifts closer to Heideggerian transformational play than to *différance* as inscribed in Derrida's earlier texts. One might argue that the economy thus suggested lacks a radical enough dissemination, which would imply a kind of indeterminacy or at least more than the undecidability defined by Derrida here.

One can, of course, also read Derrida's earlier texts differently, either in view of this elaboration or because of other forces—and differences of forces—that might be in play. Such different readings are possible, and they have been produced. At issue here is not a question of either some privileged "original" version or a fully *decidable* or fully *determined*—or even undecidably determinate—reading. It is rather the question of developing more (anti-epistemologically) effective theoretical possibilities and indeed determinations—*under the conditions of the irreducible indetermination and indeterminacy.* If the reading of Derrida's earlier texts offered here displaces them toward the anti-epistemological framework of the present study, I would stand by the framework itself, with or without Derrida—or Nietzsche, Bohr, or Bataille (for these figures, too, can be read differently). I cannot, however, think of propositions quite of that type in Derrida prior to the early 1980s. A similar revision appears to me to occur in a 1983 text, to which I have alluded earlier, where Derrida overtly claims a closer proximity to Heidegger, as against Nietzsche, for deconstruction (*Derrida and Différance*, 1–2). This understanding of deconstruction, too, appears to suggest a degree of displacement of the gradient of earlier works, which seem closer to Nietzsche.

It is, particularly, at the level of (determining) interpretation and meaning or context, that one would not be able to avoid indeterminacy, or at least an economy of indetermination more radical than the undecidability Derrida invokes here. As shall be seen, Derrida does in fact directly speak of indeterminacy or at least indetermination [indétermination] in the case of context in "Signature Event Context" and "Limited Inc," comprising *Limited Inc*. In particular, dissemination and its radical, irreducible more-

or-less-ness, cannot be subsumed—or would in present reading imply an economy that cannot be subsumed—by the conditions of undecidable determination suggested by Derrida here. The introduction of indeterminacy, for example, of the quantum mechanical type, would not suspend the situation, invoked by Derrida, of "indecision or *double bind* . . . between *determined* (semantic, ethical, political) poles, which are upon occasion terribly necessary and always irreducibly singular." It may not be possible, however, to reduce semantic, ethical, political, or theoretical fields to such situations and suspend more indeterminate situations in any of these fields.

It is possible that the statement only reflects Derrida's preference for certain—metaphorically, more Gödelian—analytic situations, as opposed to, for example, metaphorically, more quantum-mechanical situations, without arguing against more indeterministic forms of analysis themselves. This reading would remain in accord with my overall point concerning the difference between two models at issue—complementarity, including indeterminacy, and deconstructive undecidability. Even so, however, the statement would appear to displace or revise Derrida's earlier positions, which, I think, allow for more indeterminacy. Or, as I indicated, one would need a more radical economy of interpretation and theory—more complementary and indeterminate rather than (only) undecidable, or more effectively interlacing and complementarizing them than suspending either, as Derrida does in the case of indeterminacy here.

Some of Derrida's claims appear to be problematic under all conditions, including in the second paragraph of his statement, which offers key nuances and qualifications. Thus, it is obvious that, within—as *determined* by—Derrida's economy "undecidability is always determined" or that it "is also not negative in itself." It is equally clear that *différance* "is neither negativity nor nothingness." It is not clear, however, why, in contrast to *différance* as the efficacity of undecidability, the efficacities of some, or— as *efficacities*—even of any, forms of indeterminacy, or even indeterminacy itself, would necessarily always be either negativity or nothingness, as Derrida claims. Such is, *determinately*, not the case in Bohr's complementarity or, by extension, in this study. One can of course conceive of such usages of the term 'indeterminacy', uncharacteristically unspecified by Derrida and, it appears, here taken by him uncritically as a kind of general concept. This is the strategy he often justly criticizes elsewhere, as in his analysis of Foucault's usage of the concepts of "madness" in "Cogito and the History of Madness" (*Writing and Difference*).

The same appears to be the case in regard to "relativism" and "indeterminism." "*Any* sort of indeterminism"? Or any sort of relativism? Nietzsche's, for example? For Nietzsche's perspectivism can be seen as a form of relativism. It may be that Nietzsche's perspectivism is quite different from what Derrida opposes here, and Derrida, it is true, does not refer to Nietzsche's or any other perspectivism. One can, again, no doubt conceive of and find relativisms and determinisms—or again the concepts of indeterminacy—that are incompatible with Derrida's position here or in his earlier works (as read here), or of course with Nietzsche's perspectivism, or the economy developed in this study. Such relativisms or indeterminisms would, for example, uncritically suspend irreducible determinations and decisions, which (Derrida is correct here) we must always take into account—semantically, ethically, or politically. I would add, however, that such determinations and decisions must be taken into account, complementarily with indeterminacies and indecision, which appears to be more consistent with Derrida's positions and in accord with his statements elsewhere.

While Derrida is obviously correct to argue against the point that "if [*différance*] renders determinacy possible, it is because it itself is 'indeterminacy'," this objection itself is weak, even trivial, although I have very little doubt that Derrida had indeed encountered it more than once. *Différance* is, of course, not "indeterminacy." By the same token, however, it cannot, I think, be determinacy either; no more than it can, by itself, be either decidability or undecidability, whether determinate or indeterminate undecidability. As we have seen, it cannot be by itself or in itself either, or cannot "be" to begin with. *Différance* cannot be described in or mapped by any other terms, even though, and because, it cannot exist fully outside the processes of determination or indetermination, of decidability or undecidability. In this sense, it "is" indeed "in *itself* nothing outside of different determinations," as Derrida says, and one could add "different indeterminacies," which may irreducibly accompany such determinations under certain conditions. It must instead be seen as producing all these effects—determinacy and indeterminacy, decidability and undecidability, or in-itself-ness or by-itself-ness. By the same token, however, *différance* must also render (the effects of) indeterminacy, or various indeterminacies, or undecidability possible and, under certain conditions, necessary. In fact, under some conditions, it must also be seen as efficacity of a kind of indeterminacy Derrida argues against—or of whatever kind of indeterminacy he has in mind, whether one views it negatively, with Derrida, or positively, against Derrida. For this indeterminacy is operative as a perspective emerging in some discourses. It must, therefore, be produced within the play of certain forces and differences of forces and thus by some efficacity, which Derrida appears to approach through *différance* and his other structures. *Différance*, we recall, "produces what it forbids, makes possible the same thing [cela même] that it makes impossible" (*Of Grammatology*, 143; *De la grammatologie*, 206; translation modified). Even if unacceptable from a Derridean standpoint, a given theory or practice of indeterminacy must be seen as an effect of a semantic, ethical, or political *différance* of the Derridean type. It must, therefore, be reinscribed and be accounted for from within a Derridean perspective. Otherwise this perspective itself becomes theoretically insufficient.

I think that this position is consistent with or close to Derrida's analyses, at least in his earlier works, including both essays in *Limited Inc*, "Signature Event Context" and "Limited Inc," the reprinting of which occasioned the interview under discussion, or even in his elaborations on force immediately following the statement at issue (*Limited Inc*, 149–50). By the same token, however, such an efficacity would have to be more complementary or to imply more complementary effects—decidable and undecidable, determinate and indeterminate—than Derrida suggests in his statement. Or, if Derrida's propositions here are accepted so as to imply that the dynamics just described are in conflict with Derrida's matrix, *différance* can no longer be seen as sufficient in order to approach this efficacity. The complementary efficacity at issue must, then, at least to a degree and in some of its aspects, be juxtaposed to Derrida's economy, for example, via Nietzsche and Bohr and possibly Bataille or via more direct theoretical work as suggested here. It may be that one will have to abandon or extend and radicalize "deconstruction" if "deconstruction" is incompatible with some economies of indeterminacy. At the very least, we need a metaphorical and conceptual field that allows for more complementary engagements of undecidable and indeterminate configurations. The approaches based on complementarity may be more open to such possibilites than those based on undecidability. Perhaps, in the final account, even at their most anti-epistemological, *différance* and accompanying Derridean structures and efficacities remain too *determinate* and are, thus, not radical enough to account with sufficient effectiveness and richness for the practice of interpretation or theory.

Such possibilities are, however, suggested by Derrida's discourse, earlier and later, even if, to a degree, against some of his propositions or some strata of his text. Even at the level of theory, where determination may play a more significant role than in the case of broader interpretive meaning or context, many of Derrida's elaborations and his practice suggest more indeterminate landscapes—more "quantum mechanical" than "undecidable," or complementarizing undecidability and indeterminacy. These landscapes are unavoidable, whether they are deliberately (or unintentionally) practiced or thematized. One can only claim to practice theoretical determinacy, but never, in practice do so. This is why complementarity—and the radical indeterminacy it implies—can, and from the present perspective must, be metaphorically transferred at the level of theory and interactions between (or within) matrices, theories, and theoretical, or political, fields. Derrida's many elaborations on chance appear to suggest a similar attitude, for example, when he argues, in the passage considered earlier, that "in delineation of *différance* everything is strategic and adventurous. . . . The concept of *play* announc[es], on the eve of philosophy and beyond it, the unity of chance and necessity in calculations without end" (*Margins*, 7; *Marges*, 7). This point is expressed even more strongly in "My Chances," in the context of Lucretian *clinamen*, also understood at the level of theoretical or analytic practice (in either sense), which substitutes, rightly, play for unity: "The *clinamen* introduces the *play* of necessity and chance into what could be called, by anachronism, the *determinism* of the universe. Nonetheless, it does not imply a conscious freedom of the will, even if for some of us the principle of *indeterminism* is what makes the conscious freedom of man fathomable" (*Taking Chances*, 8; emphasis added).

Against his assertion or recollection in 1988, Derrida, thus, does speak of indeterminacy and indeterminism (be it of meaning, theory, or indeed of everything) and, as shall be seen presently, not only on this occasion. Much of the discussion of "Différance" appears to be not only against decidable determinations—interpretive, theoretical, or political—but also—via Freud, Bataille, and Nietzsche, via the unconscious—against determination without indetermination and indeterminacy. Let me qualify or rather reiterate, lest there be misunderstanding (by some *chance* or possibly necessity), that I am not attributing to the argument or style of "Différance," "My Chances," *Glas*, and other works that may be invoked here some absolute or unconditional—uncomplementarized—chance. Nor am I suggesting any such necessity, or indeed possibility, in the practice of theory in general. Throughout this study I have been concerned with a complementary interplay of chance and necessity, or indeterminacy and determination. This is the only indeterminacy there can be at issue in and engaged by the practice of general economy, whether in Nietzsche, Bohr, Bataille, Derrida, or here. For there can be no more absolute indeterminacy than absolute determination or anything absolute. Let me also reiterate that, again following, along with Derrida himself, Nietzsche, Bataille, and particularly Bohr, the *necessity*—the determinate (in either sense) necessity—of theoretical determination, including at times undecidable determination, and rigor remain key, defining features of a general economic and complementary approach. These features are not undermined but are reinforced by the fact that they are accompanied by their various complements—indeterminacy, play, forgetting, mistakes, and so forth. Even if finally against Derrida himself, however, his argument and practice suggest and enact a complementary interplay of chance and necessity, indeterminacy and determination, indeterminacy and undecidability, or of course decidability and undecidability.

Derrida, as I indicated, directly speaks of indeterminacy or at least of indetermination—*indétermination*—at some crucial junctures, which I shall briefly examine here. It is true, of course, that the occurrence of a given word or signifier—such as "indeterminacy"—is not the only or even the main indicator of whether one speaks of something so designated or not. Derrida, however, does use the term indeterminacy, and, again, at crucial junctures. Thus, indeterminacy appears in the very first phrase of "Economimesis" (1976), where Derrida speaks of "the cover of controlled indeterminacy" in Kant (3). A general economy, which is suggested by Derrida's essay in juxtaposition to and by way of a deconstruction of Kant's restricted economy, may, I think, be read as the economy of *indeterminacies* which cannot be *controlled* (that is, fully or unconditionally controlled). This indeterminacy also pertains to the relationships between the political and the aesthetic, such as mimetic, economies, which can thus be seen as complementary. Since, however, Derrida does not directly speak there of such uncontrolled indeterminacies, it is possible to read Derrida's economy of "economimesis" (which combines mimesis and economy) as undecidable and thus closer to the lines of the 1988 statement under discussion.

In one of his best known and most discussed earlier essays, "Structure, Sign and Play in the Discourse of the Human Sciences" (in *Writing and Difference*), Derrida speaks of *indétermination*—indeterminacy or indetermination (either translation is possible)—at a crucial juncture of Nietzschean affirmation and the inscription of trace: "In absolute chance, [Nietzschean] affirmation also surrenders itself to *genetic* indetermination, to the *seminal* adventure of trace" (*Writing and Différance*, 292; *L'écriture et la différance*, 427). Derrida complementarizes this indeterminacy in the essay, as one must under the conditions of Derridean trace. One might even argue that Derrida, on this occasion, misreads Nietzsche by attributing to him the concept of absolute chance. These qualifications, however, would not contradict the point at issue at the moment.

The analysis in "Signature Event Context" and "Limited Inc," key background texts for Derrida's statement under discussion, appears to lead (I think, uncircumventably) to the indeterminateness, rather than only undecidability of meaning and context. Again, contrary to his assertion or recollection, Derrida speaks of indeterminacy—or uncertainty (*Limited Inc*, 18)—directly and very much to the point in both texts. At the outset of "Signature Event Context," announcing his main goals, he says: "I shall try to demonstrate why a context is *never absolutely determinable*, or rather, why its *determination is never assured* or saturated." He also speaks of "the disqualification or the limiting of the concept of context, whether 'real' or 'linguistic,' inasmuch as its rigorous theoretical *determination* as well as its empirical saturation are *rendered impossible or insufficient by writing*" (*Limited Inc*, 3, 9; *Marges*, 368–69, 376; translation modified; emphasis added). At a key juncture of "Limited Inc." he says even more strongly: "What sets the times, the *vices*, is a strange law which prescribes that the simpler, poorer, and more univocal an utterance may seem, the more elusive the comprehension of its *meaningfulness* [English in the original] and greater its contextual *indeterminacy* [or *indetermination:* indétermination] will be (*Limited Inc*, 62; *Limited Inc A B C*, 34; translation modified). I do not think that this situation can be subsumed by the undecidable determination of Derrida's later statement.

Derrida's central example amply illustrates this point. He invokes Nietzsche's phrase "I forgot my umbrella," which is the subject of his extended analysis in *Spurs: Nietzsche's Styles:* "the phrase, 'I forgot my umbrella,' abandoned like an island among the unpublished writings of Nietzsche. A thousand possibilities will always remain open even if one understands something in this phrase that makes sense (as a citation? the beginning of a novel? a proverb? someone else's secretarial archives? an exercise in learning language? the narration of a dream? an alibi? a cryptic code—conscious or not? the example of a linguist or of a speech act theoretician letting his imagination wander for short distances, etc?)" (*Limited Inc, 63; Limited Inc A B C*, 34–35). Once we look, as we must, beyond Derrida's "even if," the economy transpiring here would complicate even further and finally limit and disable not only all possible decidable determinations, but also those defined by undecidable determinability or determinate undecidability. The description suggests something much closer to a multiple indeterminate play, similar to that of quantum field theory, rather than (only) Gödelian undecidability, although the latter can and must be engaged along the way. Derrida's analysis in *Spurs* would confirm and amplify this point. The radical dissemination suggested here and Derrida's dissemination in general make it very difficult to contain the economy of meaning and context, or perhaps any economy, by any form of determinate undecidability. As I have indicated, the relationship between dissemination and iterability emerge and play a key role from the onset of *Dissemination*. The radical—and, in my view, irreducible indeterminate—character of this economy is further suggested by Derrida's emphasis on the structural, irreducible unconscious, which he even, strategically, capitalizes here (*Limited Inc*, 73–74). Theoretically such a capitalization would, according to Derrida, be prohibited. The structural unconscious is, I would argue, even more an economy of indeterminacy than that of (determinate) undecidability, although, proceeding closer to (a certain) Freud and (a certain) Derrida, for example, the Derrida of the 1988 statement under discussion, it can be read in that way too.

One can perhaps, again closer to the 1988 statement, read the economy defined in these essays—"no meaning can be determined out of context, but no context permits saturation" ("Living On: Border Lines," *Deconstruction and Criticism*, 81)—as suggesting that "meaning" would still be *determined* within an economy of undecidability (as against a fixed or fully determined context) rather than ever remain indeterminate or retaining an indeterminate component or, to use Derrida own key term, an indeterminate remainder [réstance]. I do not think that this would be the most radical and effective reading, even assuming that Derrida himself *subscribed* to it, and the same would go for the very economy of signature brilliantly analyzed by Derrida there (*Limited Inc*, 19–21). Both essays do have many Gödelian echoes. At many key junctures they involve undecidability, set theory, and the structural lack of completeness—the lack of the completeness of a set (*Limited Inc*, 39). They also offer several propositions of a Gödelian type, such as: "The language of theory [here a theory of language—the theory of speech acts] always leaves a residue that is neither formalizable nor idealizable in terms of that theory of language" (69). At the theoretical level Derrida's emphasis, defining most of his theoretical practice, would remain on undecidability. A more radically indeterminate economy appears, however, to be addressed and enacted by both essays, particularly by Derrida's analysis of the conditions of his exchange with John Searle in *Limited Inc.*

Finally, although still other examples can be given, the economy of chance as explored by Derrida at both interpretive and theoretical, or biographical, levels in "My Chances" (1984) can be read as the economy of indeterminacy—more so, I think, than in terms of undecidability, specifically as defined by the statement under discussion. It is difficult to see how such an economy could conform to determinate undecidability of that type. It is interesting that the 1988 statement refers to "My Chances" in the context of pragmatic determination, or as it is called in "My Chances" a certain pragrammatology, introduced "at the intersection of a pragmatics and a grammatology" (*Taking Chances*, 27). Derrida's inscription of the economy of chance in "My Chances" does at times minimize the language of indeterminacy. His main concern appears to be the economy of determination by chance, which is, of course, a crucial factor. Moreover, as Derrida shows, what are conventionally seen as chance encounters must be configured and analyzed as the products of a complex interplay of chance and necessity. The latter terms and the economies they imply must, therefore, be understood as useful, and perhaps unavoidable, metaphorical models or, as Bohr would have it, idealizations. The analysis itself, however, and many *determinations*—or better, complementarily determinations-indeterminations—of chance, explored by Derrida there, would suggest that a certain indeterminacy is unavoidable, structural. Moreover, as we have seen, this (general-economic) indeterminacy is irreducible to classical statistical (or probabilistic) economies. It is analogous to the radical indeterminacy on which Bohr insists in the case of quantum mechanics, and as such it may be richer than Derrida would suggest by shifting this economy too much toward a certain (undecidable) determinacy.

In all the cases just considered, rather than only connecting undecidability and *determinability*, it would be more effective to speak of, complementarily, determinacy and indeterminacy of meaning or of "anything else," along with decidability and undecidability or undecidability and indeterminacy. Derrida's argument and, particularly, practice do enact this type of indeterminate complementary economy, even if to a degree against some of Derrida's overtly stated positions. In addition to "My Chances," such works as "Envois" (in *The Post Card*), "Ulysses Gramophone," and other texts offer examples of more indeterminate and complementary—"quantum"—processes at work, although their Gödelian components are irreducible and appear to remain the main focus of Derrida's own analysis.[16]

Thus, one can see the organization of *Glas* as the graphic complementarity of Hegel('s text) and Genet('s text), with many local complementary inclusions along the way.[17] Moreover, Hegel could be seen as the continuum part of this complementarity, and Genet as its quantum counterpart, with his emphasis on chance and on rupture as opposed to continuity. *Glas* thus exemplifies, *graphically* (in either sense), the relation of proximity and distance at once, even infinitesimal proximity and radical distance from Hegel. Both proximity and distance, however, are complementary in the present sense, as is the interpenetration of inclusions and the overall, Joycean—dadaist or Derridadaist—quantum landscape of the text, with its textual movement at once ruptured and continuous.[18] Genet's can already be seen as a complementary text, among other things, complementary with Hegel, although the vision of discontinuity—a radical rupture—is crucial in Genet, manifesting itself at many levels and in many economies, sexual, literary, theoretical, or political. The agenda of undecidability still dominates the theoretical field of *Glas*, even if its graphics or graphematics (*writing*) are given complementary and indeterminate play. Undecidability or indeterminacy of that type implies complementarity in action, as found in *Glas*. It cannot be played out without complementarity, whether the latter is articulated as such or not, just as complementarity in quantum physics underlies its entire practice. In this sense, complementarity comprehends indeterminacy and, by extension, undecidability. *Glas* enacts a kind of quantum landscape of complementarity and indeterminacy, ruptures and continuities, causalities and coordinations, constantly passing into each other, without final determination or synthesis.

In view of Derrida's position on undecidability and (and against) indeterminacy, as just considered, and his position on the question of closure, to be considered in the next chapter, one can argue that Derrida's *style* (at least in some of his works) enacts more radical anti-epistemological economies or possibilities than some of his *positions* suggest. One can, in addition to *Glas*, mention "Dissemination," "Living On: Border Lines," "Parergon" (in *The Truth of Painting*), "Envois" (in *The Post Card*), or nonclassical strategies, such as in particular the practice of athetic discourse in "To Speculate—on 'Freud'" or in "Différance," continuously engaged by Derrida in his more classically argued text. Naturally, one can speak of such juxtapositions only within certain limits. By the same token, however, such juxtapositions—and juxta-*positions*—are not only possible, but necessary. For we can no more fully unify style and argument (I am hesitant to use the word 'substance') than fully dissociate them. Certainly Derrida's *positions* and juxta-*positions*, such as those just discussed, must be considered, and his style elsewhere cannot cancel their impact. One can never contain or present a classical argument by classical means, or even possess, in practice or in principle, a fully classical argument. Conversely, the most classical, ontotheological positions can coexist with the most dadaistic styles. The athesis can be and has been practiced both via undecidability and deconstruction or within an indeterminate-complementary economy, although not by means of restricted economies.[19] The role and relative significance of this practice is different in different cases, such as in Nietzsche, Bataille, and Derrida or others whose work can be seen as deconstructive or related to deconstruction. Derrida's theoretical work itself proceeds by different means and in different styles, although, it appears, mostly, and perhaps in a certain sense always, on the margins of philosophy and by way of undecidability. It can proceed by more direct deconstructions that characterize most of Derrida's earlier works—such as his readings of Rousseau, Levinas, and Husserl; or primarily by following the flow of athesis, as in the case of Freud, particularly in *The Post Card;* or by exploring, through less deconstructive and more "cooperative" readings, the work of *différance*, dissemination, *writing*, and so forth in Mallarmé, Ponge, and other, mostly literary, figures. Conversely, complementarity can function both within deconstructive or undecidable and more overtly complementary frameworks; and it can lead to manifold, including deconstructive or postdeconstructive, forms of interaction with other texts. As Derrida argues, we cannot make a claim upon an underlying structure of reading, writing, theory, or history; which also means that we cannot claim any structure—undecidable, indeterminate, or complementary—as unconditionally underlying or controlling them. Hence we also cannot claim that any given mode or style is irreducible, be it deconstructive, complementarity, or both, or any other. One may, however, encounter local, which may also mean broadly ranged, and locally irreducible determinations—such as those necessitated by undecidability, indeterminacy, or complementarity.

CHAPTER 8

Closures

Transgressions

The closure [*clôture*] of philosophy in Derrida designates our continuing dependence on the language and concepts developed in philosophy, but operative elsewhere as well, compelling one to speak of the *closure* of philosophy as the metaphysics of presence and to pursue deconstruction in other fields. This dependence and this closure are, according to Derrida, fundamental and irreducible, even, and in particular, in the practice of deconstruction. The latter does not only engage metaphysics and philosophy, which is obviously necessary if one wants to deconstruct them, but must, according to Derrida, borrow from the resources of and, thus, depend on what it deconstructs. The metaphysics of presence operates outside the institutions and texts of philosophy, extending its closure and enabling deconstruction across a very large spectrum of texts in the human and social sciences, psychoanalysis, literature, and even the natural and exact sciences. Conversely, such exterior fields can be used to deconstruct philosophy, or each other. At issue in the question of grammatology as the (non)science of writing are also "the limits . . . of the classical notion of science, whose projects, concepts, and norms are fundamentally and systematically tied to metaphysics" (*Positions*, 13; *Positions*, 22). Derrida's deconstruction may thus also be seen as the investigation of the closure so conceived, which may well be an interminable project, as Derrida suggests on many occasions. On these grounds, from *Of Grammatology* on, "a distinction is proposed between *closure* [la *clôture*] and *end* [la *fin*]. What is held within the de-limited closure [la clôture dé-limitée] may continue indefinitely" (*Positions*, 13; *Positions*, 23; translation modified).

Thus, although the term 'closure' would suggest conclusion, end, or termination, and these connotations must be kept in mind, as understood by Derrida it implies instead, or simultaneously, a certain interminability—a certain inability to close or to leave behind—on the model of Freud's interminable analysis, which, as we have seen, plays a crucial role in Derrida. In French *clôture* also means enclosure; and one can, thus, also speak of the enclosure of metaphysics.

The closure philosophy or other theoretical closures may be related to, yet also differentiated from, a broader interpretive closure or closures, specifically the closure of presence itself. For compelling and perhaps irreducible reasons, 'presence' is a rubric of central significance for Derrida, and it is used by him with great effectiveness. Wherever it operates, inside or outside philosophy, metaphysics itself is, according to Derrida, always the metaphysics of presence, even if conceived by way of and in the name of difference, alterity, exteriority, becoming, transformation, or temporality. The (classical) concept of temporality in particular has, as Derrida demonstrates, always been grounded in the concept of presence. All these concepts, however, in turn affect the closure of metaphysics. Difference, exteriority, transformation, discontinuity (or of course continuity), and other rubrics of that type may variously overlap with configurations assembled under the rubric of presence. It is therefore more effective to complementarize such closures rather than to subsume them under any given rubric. One can suggest, however, a more general and stable, although complementarized, *interpretive* closure as opposed to more differentiated and more transformable *theoretical* closures.

While the question of the closure of metaphysics or philosophy may not be *Hegel's* question, it comes close enough to being a *Hegelian* question. In *Of Grammatology,* Derrida writes: "Hegel was already caught up in this game. . . . [H]e undoubtedly *summed up* the entire philosophy of the logos. He determined ontology as absolute logic; he assembled all the delimitations of being as presence" (*Of Grammatology,* 24; *De la grammatologie,* 39; translation modified). Hegel's discourse, thereby, may be seen as delimiting both philosophy and its closure. The economy of closure so conceived would, however, replace Hegel's conception of philosophy that gives philosophy the primary role in the history of consciousness and knowledge. *Glas* brilliantly mirrors and amplifies this transformation from philosophy to deconstruction and closure, introducing radical undecidability and, perhaps against Derrida, indeterminacy into philosophy, but also showing the overwhelming significance of Hegel for Derrida.[1]

In more general terms, what would be the relation of a general economic text to the *text* of philosophy and its margins? A necessary relation?
A unique relation? While the field of the metaphysics of presence or restricted economy is unified to a degree, it cannot be seen as fully unified,
and philosophy itself is not as unified as its own disciplinary (in either
sense) concept of itself would suggest. It is sufficiently unified, however,
to join the historico-theoretical forces of its many contingents.[2] What—
and in the name of what—would, then, relate and differentiate the different "margins" and "exteriors" of philosophy, or different general economies, such as Nietzsche's, Bataille's, and Derrida's, against the forces of
philosophy and restricted economies elsewhere? Is it possible for such
differences to introduce fields that may not be defined by their relations
to philosophy, for example, as the margins of philosophy in Derrida? "If
there are margins, is there still *a* philosophy, *the* philosophy? No answer,
then. Perhaps, in the long run, not even a question," Derrida asks ("Tympan," *Margin*, xvi; *Marges*, ix). No doubt for the questions just posed,
too, "the copulative correspondence, the opposition question/answer is
already lodged in a structure, enveloped in the hollow of an ear, which we
will go into to take a look" ("Tympan," *Margins*, xvi–xvii; *Marges*, ix). Still,
if there are margins, is there still *the* margin? Certainly there is no more
the margin than *the* center, although there are always, and everywhere,
margins and centers, boundaries within and without. "To philosophize
with a hammer. Zarathustra begins by asking himself if he will have to
puncture them, batter their ears (*Muss man ihnen erst die Ohren zerschla-
gen*), with the sound of cymbals or tympani, the instruments, always, of
some Dionysianism. In order to teach them 'to hear with their eyes' too.
But *we* [Derrida] will analyze the *metaphysical exchange*, the circular complicity of the metaphors of the eye and the ear" ("Tympan," *Margins*,
xii–xiii; *Marges*, iii–iv; emphasis added). This reading is no doubt both
possible and necessary. But is it the only possible or necessary analysis,
as against Nietzsche's, for example, in relation to philosophy? Perhaps we
are even no longer quite, or in quite the same way, "caught within the
metaphysical closure" that Derrida continuously invokes:

> I think that *all concepts hitherto proposed in order to think the articulation
> of a discourse and of an historical totality are caught within the meta-
> physical closure that I question here*, as we do not know of any other
> concepts and cannot produce any others, and indeed shall not pro-
> duce so long as this closure limits our discourse; as the primordial

and indispensable phase, in fact and in principle, of the development of this problematic, consists in questioning the internal structure of these texts as symptoms; as that is the only condition for determining these symptoms *themselves* in the totality of their metaphysical appurtenance. . . . (*Of Grammatology*, 99; *De la grammatologie*, 148)

The metaphysical closure that Derrida describes here refers more to the closure of philosophy as the metaphysics of presence, historically and theoretically demarcated through its institutional and cultural functioning and a certain field of texts. A more general representational or interpretive closure is also intimated, however, particularly as the closure of presence. The concept of closure is one of Derrida's most important theoretical contributions. I shall argue here, however, that there can be no untransformed or undifferentiated configuration of closure; and it may not be enough to insist, as Derrida does elsewhere, on the heterogeneity or transformability of closure within itself. There can be no totality of closure, whether it is conceived as the closure of metaphysics or otherwise. *The* closure is not possible. Nor can there be an absolute historical totality. Derrida's usage of the indefinite article—"*an* historical totality" (99)—is mandatory. A certain globalization of the closure of metaphysics—"*ALL concepts hitherto proposed* . . ."—could, however, be detected here and elsewhere in Derrida, even though he does offer important qualifications in this regard.[3] Derrida's proximities, however infinitesimal, even to the best metaphysics, such as Hegel or Heidegger, are always accompanied by differences, often radical. Such is in fact Derrida's own claim concerning his enterprise,[4] and the execution amply justifies it. As I indicated earlier, in Derrida's *case*, the closure of metaphysics, in the style of psychoanalysis, leads to the *interminable* "questioning [of] the *internal* structure of [the texts of philosophy as] these symptoms." Like all neuroses, philosophy itself must remain incurable, although some of its symptoms might be treated and controlled. We cannot produce new concepts "as long as this closure limits our discourse," Derrida says. This claim, however, may not be sustainable or must be further nuanced, in part because new concepts, or neither terms nor concepts, are produced in Derrida and elsewhere, as Derrida clearly recognizes. The main question is whether and to what extent this closure still limits our discourse, assuming that it has ever been one closure, which assumption, in my view, cannot be made. Derrida does not speak of the transformations of closure or of the plurality—or dissemination—of closures, although, as shall be seen, he does speak of the heterogeneity of (or within) the closure of metaphysics itself. This view positions him closer to Hegel and Heidegger than to Nietzsche, who is a more transgressive thinker.

The relationship between philosophy and its "others" defined by this Derridean economy are often those of undecidability—or determinate undecidability, as opposed to indeterminacy, as considered earlier. No such relationship can be determined once and for all, since all determinations, decidable or undecidable, are local. Nor can any text ever contain the heterogeneity of the field and the closure of philosophy. One of Derrida's main points is that philosophy is not a homogeneous—or complete or decidable—field that can be unconditionally defined or demarcated, even though the latter agenda has been persistent throughout the history of philosophy and may even be seen as defining it as a field. The *closure* of philosophy is distributed even more heterogeneously, and I shall comment on this heterogeneity presently. Philosophy is, however, a historically, institutionally, and politically established field and a relatively delineated ensemble of texts, fundamentally linked to the metaphysics of presence. Derrida's analysis proceeds, "living on: border lines," on the margins of this field. This analysis does generate complementary relations between the concepts and matrices generated in different fields and between these fields themselves, but, as a rule, via (complementarities with) philosophy and always within its closure. The "others" of philosophy in Derrida are many—literature, literary criticism and theory, linguistics, psychoanalysis, anthropology, or still other fields that may or may not be articulated in established terms. All such "others," however, are the others of *philosophy* and are within its closure, which relation may be seen as defining Derrida's project. Philosophy becomes a kind of everywhere irreducible complementary field of engagement there. Derrida himself often defines his project in this way, particularly in the earlier works. The economy itself, however, characterizes most of his later works as well, up to the most recent ones, and in some respects it may have become even more marked. The effects of Derrida's writing cannot, of course, be contained thereby, in part by virtue of his active engagement of different fields. Whatever Derrida's own aims and projects may be, his writing (in either sense) invades and transforms the exterior of philosophy, particularly the human sciences, literary criticism and theory, and psychoanalysis.[5]

As a practitioner of a plural style, and specifically of a plural style defining itself in relation to philosophy, Derrida has many predecessors,

perhaps particularly Bataille and Blanchot, although their textual practices are also different from Derrida's. A long list of other figures read
or analyzed by Derrida, from his earliest to his most recent works, could
further illustrate this point. All these readings, however, including those
of Bataille and Blanchot, are also "Derrida-based." Nietzsche in this
sense operates more radically, but not absolutely, outside and against philosophy. While he serves as a decisive frame of reference in Derrida,
Nietzsche may be seen as rather "less read" or less extensively textualized by Derrida than other figures, even taking *Spurs* into consideration.
The latter, however, is just as much a reading of Heidegger as of Nietzsche. Nietzsche, too, as Derrida points out, at certain points engages the
philosophical register for the purposes of the critique and deconstruction
of philosophy and, to a degree, remains within the closure of philosophy, or shares with philosophy a common closure or cluster of closures.[6]
These qualifications, however, do not erase the difference in balance and
attitude at issue. Derrida's text and style are determined by operating,
simultaneously, in the philosophical and nonphilosophical registers, both
in order to deconstruct philosophy, by way of undecidability and otherwise, and in order to investigate its conceptual and historical closure.
Derrida's many doubles—double gesture, double writing, double science
and double session [*double séance*], double strategy, even double deconstructions or two styles of deconstruction—complementarily employed
or played out, as in *Glas*, manifest this complementarity of philosophy and
its others. Along with and as a certain proximity-distance economy, this
complementarity also defines the economy of transformations of philosophy by "means of that circulation, simultaneously faithful and violent,
between the inside and outside of philosophy—that is of the Occident"
(*Positions*, 6; *Positions*, 15; translation modified). It is not altogether clear
whether and to what extent philosophy and its closure define (only) the
Occident.

On the one hand, this circulation offers a specific and important case
of a relation of continuity with philosophy, perhaps most specifically with
Hegel, although Heidegger's significance is, again, "uncircumventable"
in Derrida and on the French scene where this circulation takes place.
On the other hand, it enacts at certain points radical, "violent," transformations or at least deformations, mostly via "the unconscious," in proximity to Nietzsche, Freud, Bataille, Lacan, and several other figures. It
becomes, therefore, a (general) economy of transformations as the inter-

play or complementarity of continuities and breaks with philosophy and, one might suggest against Derrida, possibly even with its closure or its previous closure. New, even radically new, revolutionary concepts are produced—the " 'concept[s]' that could no longer, and never could be included in the previous regime" (*Positions*, 42; *Positions*, 57). According to Derrida, such transformations or deformations take place *within* the closure of philosophy as the metaphysics of presence (*Positions*, 6–7, 12–14, 24, 41–42; *Writing and Difference*, 280–81). For this reason "deformations" may be a more exact term here and a more graphic geometrical metaphor—an elliptical deformation of a circle—with a great history from Kepler on. The economy itself may be contrasted with Nietzschean transformations and what I called earlier, via Skolem, destandardization of classical models. Nonstandard models imply pluralizations and transformations of preceding theoretical closures, since preceding classical systems can be included in heterogeneous and thus at times incompatible regimes, along with more interactive ones. One might suggest, that while in Derrida, via Gödel, any given philosophical system is irreducibly undecidable and incomplete—uncontainable within itself—a certain *complete* or all-encompassing, if heterogeneous, theoretical closure becomes possible—the closure of philosophy as the metaphysics of presence. An analogous economy may actually be characterizing Gödel's own views. By contrast, the economy conceived or metaphorized via Skolem's theory may imply a more radical heterogeneity and multiplicity of closures.[7]

The circulation just described may also be seen as self-reflexive: the continuity is with continuum and the break is toward the discontinuous or complementary. For, as we have seen, the metaphysics of presence is also the metaphysics of continuity, even though the metaphysics of presence can also manifest itself, by virtue of unproblematized reversal or otherwise, as the metaphysics of absence, rupture, difference, exteriority. At the levels of interpretation and theory alike, there is, therefore, also the closure of discontinuity, along with and complementary to the closure of continuity, or the closure of difference or exteriority complementary to the closure of presence, proximity, similarity, or identity. The closure of classical theories may operate complementarily by way of continuities and discontinuities, or other complementary pairs of that type. From and before Parmenides and Plato, however, classical philosophy, as well as some modern and even some postmodern philosophy, has been the philosophy of presence or becoming-presence and continuum. Within Derrida's double or complementary economy, continuity or proximity within philosophy—as the metaphysics of presence, continuity, or proximity— proceeds especially via a proximity with Hegel and Heidegger.[8]

It is crucial that for both these great Heracliteans, "presence" is conceived within the economies of difference, exteriority, and transformation. These economies, however, are governed by a (broadly understood) continuous process—whether understood as mediation, becoming, time, history, or still otherwise—and "continuum" might be a better rubric than presence for such Heraclitean, but still restricted economies. The economy of continuum sustains and supports the continuity of philosophy itself and its history and their continuity with other classical fields. As Bohr's case would suggest, a break from philosophy can perhaps only be achieved by way of economies complementarizing continuities and discontinuous—or causality and indeterminacy, or chance and necessity— at various levels rather than unproblematized moves to absolute rupture, absolute difference or exteriority, absolute chance, and so forth. The absence of complementarity reinstates restricted economies.

"A radical trembling can only come from the *outside* [Un ébranlement radical ne peut venir que du *dehors*]," Derrida says ("The Ends of Man," *Margins*, 134; *Marges*, 163; Derrida's emphasis), even though he himself appears to favor a closer—an infinitesimal—proximity with philosophy, albeit accompanied by, at times, radical, distances. At issue in this statement is also the possibility, or necessity, to "change terrain [changer de terrain]" (*Margins*, 134; *Marges*, 162) away from philosophy. *Closing* (in either sense of the term) "The Ends of Man," Derrida speaks of two styles or strategies of deconstruction, one more continuous (Heideggerian) and the other more discontinuous (Nietzschean):

> a. To attempt an exit and a deconstruction without changing terrain, by repeating what is implicit in the founding concepts and the original problematic, by using against the edifice the instruments or stones available in the house, that is, equally, in language. Here, one risks ceaselessly confirming, consolidating, *relifting* (*relever*), at an always more certain depth, that which one allegedly deconstructs. The continuous process of making explicit, moving toward an opening, risks sinking into the autism of the closure.
>
> b. To decide to change terrain, in a discontinuous and irruptive fashion, by brutally placing oneself outside, and by affirming an absolute break and difference. Without mentioning all the other

forms of *trompe-l'oeil* perspective in which such a displacement can be caught, thereby inhabiting more naively and more strictly than ever the inside one declares one has deserted, the simple practice of language ceaselessly reinstates the new terrain on the oldest ground. The effects of such a reinstatement or of such a blindness could be shown in numerous precise instances.

Derrida adds: "It goes without saying that these effects do not suffice to annul the necessity of a 'change of terrain.' It also goes without saying that the choice between these two forms of deconstruction cannot be simple and unique" (*Margins*, 135; *Marges*, 162–63). Either of these strategies entails the considerable risk of confirming metaphysics, specifically in Heidegger, in the first case, and Lévi-Strauss or structuralism in general, in the second. Hence "a new writing *must* weave and interlace these two motifs of deconstruction. Which amounts to saying that one must speak several languages and produce several texts at once" (*Margins*, 135; *Marges*, 163; emphasis added). It is also quite clear, however, that here, in *Positions* and throughout his works, Derrida prefers to shift the balance toward the first (more Heideggerian) alternative, while portraying the second as being more likely to reinstate metaphysics.[9] It is correlative with the claim that "every transgressive gesture reencloses us—precisely by giving us a hold on the closure of metaphysics—*within this closure*" (*Positions*, 12; *Positions*, 21; emphasis added) and thus demands an interminable analysis.[10]

As I have stressed, Derrida's persistent warning against making too easy a break from philosophy is well justified, since such alleged breaks do often reinstate the metaphysics of presence in one form or another. Also, insofar as one's project is the investigation of the theoretical and historical, or political, closure of philosophy, Derrida's asymmetrical view is understandable, even necessary. In general, however, I would see the balance of such risks as more symmetrical, bound more closely to the circumstances of a given case. I am not sure, particularly given Nietzsche's case, that "*every* transgressive gesture necessarily reencloses us" within the same limits or, since there is a shift of theoretical limits in Derrida as well, within the same closure. I also think, in accord with Derrida's view in *Of Grammatology* (19–26), that in Heidegger's case the degree of reinstatement is much greater than in the case of Nietzsche, whose strategies are clearly closer to, but not confined within, Derrida's second possibility here. In emphasizing this more radically transgressive gesture in Nietzsche in "Tympan" and other later texts, Derrida also appears to suggest that it entails a greater risk of reinstating metaphysics. Although justified as a general warning, this implication does not appear to be valid in Nietzsche, who, as Derrida says in the same essay, "reminded us that [style] must be plural" (*Margins*, 135–36; *Marges*, 163).[11]

The two styles of deconstruction, which also imply a relation to and a transformation of a theory or field, do reflect a complementary economy of continuity and discontinuity—for Derrida, specifically with philosophy. By the same token, this Derridean economy still contains, en*closes*, the transformation itself within the closure of the previous field, carrying its shadow along, as it were. The economy of a break from a given field, which nontheless remains within its closure, is an important stratification. It is suggested more generally in Derrida's essay on the origin of two "Geneva linguistics"—Rousseau's and Saussure's—"The Lingustics Circle of Geneva," an important companion essay to *Of Grammatology*. With Rousseau and Saussure alike, linguistics is possible on two conditions: first, "the *opening of the field*," which is also "a *delimitation* of the field," the new field of linguistics—a "break"; and, second, a "continuity"—"the *closure of concepts*," which is in effect the closure of philosophy (*Margins*, 140). Throughout the essay, however, the possibility of break is seen as highly qualified, tentative and questionable, while closure appears to be maintained unequivocally. The very notion of "circle" is used to suggest the circulation within the closure of Western metaphysics and dependence on its "most ancient fund" (*Margins*, 140; *Marges*, 169), rather than transformations of this metaphysics or this closure. This point would be further supported by "The Pit and the Pyramid: Introduction to Hegel's Semiology" (in *Margins*) which shows that Saussurean linguistics is *enclosed* within the Hegelian economy, incorporating a Hegelian— or again, more generally metaphysical—closure.

Derrida's critique in these essays is extremely effective, and his numerous qualifications concerning breaks are well taken. His analysis of the extent and power of the operation of metaphysics and its closure in the human, social, or as we have seen, the natural and exact sciences, is indispensable. It also suggests a general economy (in either sense) of extending the field by way of closure and thereby affecting both the transformation of old fields and the opening and delimiting of new fields, as they are distinguished from previous ones. Nevertheless, the asymmetry of Derrida's claim is problematic, or at least too strong, even in the case of linguistics, which is the primary focus of these essays. But he continually advances similar claims concerning virtually all fields, even the natural and exact sciences and mathematics, in which his qualifications are stronger. We must carefully distinguish Derrida's positions on closure from Hegelian, Husserlian, or Heideggerian claims concerning the precomprehending of science by way of philosophy, in part by virtue of the—new—idea of closure used by Derrida. Since, however, the *closure* of philosophy is also the closure of *philosophy*, one cannot avoid relating these positions either.

An important, perhaps a decisive question becomes thus to what extent the production of new propositions and theoretical fields "outside" philosophy—such as linguistics and other human and social, or natural, sciences or literary criticism or theory—depends on the engagement with the text of philosophy. Let me stress that one cannot speak of any unconditional separation in this respect, for, under the conditions of general economy, one cannot speak of anything unconditional, to begin with. But, by the same token, one cannot speak of an unconditional inseparability from philosophy either. How interminable and how necessary is such an engagement, even under the conditions of the closure of metaphysics and philosophy? In many cases, such as in the case of Rousseau's and, to a lesser extent, Saussure's linguistics, this economy is clearly at work. Also, Derrida's textual practice, engaging the closure of philosophy and its concepts, has been extraordinarily productive with respect to *new* theoretical propositions and frameworks as well.[12] Derrida's strategies, however, might not be, indeed cannot always be the only successful strategies, however plural or heterogeneous they become. In contrast to Nietzsche, in Derrida their plurality always remains predicated upon, if not defined by, a necessary relation to and engagement with philosophy— a complementarity with philosophy within the closure of philosophy. Plural style, in Derrida, refers mainly to the double strategy of operating always, necessarily, simultaneously within philosophy and by exceeding philosophy. One cannot prohibit this strategy or deny its relative necessity. Nor would one want to, given how effective it is in Derrida and, conversely, how ineffective many declared breaks, reversals, attempts at overcoming, or radical disengagements have been—*a great many, but not all,* and *not always.* While one must, as I have said, adhere to Derrida's repeated warnings in this respect,[13] following Derrida's programs and practice as closely as possible, whether in the name of deconstruction or not, does not prevent reinstatements, at times most glaring, of metaphysics. Similarly, one would not object to many of Derrida's reservations about taking definite "positions" or about the very notion of definite position to begin with. A stronger position-taking is not without pitfalls, even in the almost "unerring" Nietzsche. Strong position-taking is more effective on some occasions and less so on others, more in one author, less in another. Derrida certainly takes what may be seen as strong theoretical or political positions. Nor is Nietzsche's text without errors and problems, or fully free of metaphysics. Nietzsche is only "almost" unerring, although he may make fewer errors than most other thinkers. He cannot fully control his own text, nor would he want to. He "knew" that some of the best insights are *unconscious,* although he may have been highly conscious which of his insights were his best.

Nietzsche often breaks radically from the previous, and particularly philosophical, registers and regimes, without reinstating anything, while maintaining the necessary theoretical rigor. Nietzsche's style is not usually associated with rigor. His theoretical work is, however, extraordinarily rigorous. This point is crucial; for without rigor, it is easy to apply strong terms to anything, for example, as has been done on many occasions, to Derrida or Nietzsche. One can, I think, claim a radical departure from philosophy in Nietzsche's case, even though he had moments of such engagement with philosophy. While also plural, Nietzsche's style is in this respect different from Derrida's, as, I think, is Bataille's. This style is defined by more active and more diverse complementary engagements of frameworks and theories—nonstandard models—fields and landscapes, without being based on a complementarity with philosophy, although without absolutely suspending philosophy either. An engagement with philosophy is necessary, for example, in view of Nietzsche's critical analyses of philosophy or because of various closures within which his analysis must operate at a given moment. Certainly, Nietzsche has a very different attitude to and relationship with philosophy than Derrida does. One can even suggest that Derrida's major critical target is a "naive"—uncritical—critique of philosophy (from within or from outside it) and a failure to see the same classical assumptions at work in other fields and defining positions from which philosophy is attacked. Fields and positions are always heterogeneous, with boundaries within and without, as well as multiply interactive—in short complementary in every respect. Thus, anticipating Derrida, Nietzsche profoundly understood the necessity of "presence" and thus of a certain closure. But he saw the foundations of philosophy and philosophy's handling of such concepts as presence, or difference, as making it just about impossible to salvage the whole enterprise in view of what it has become and what, in Nietzsche's view, it can possibly develop into.

As I have argued from the outset, any transformation is always a multiple complementarity of continuities and breaks, stratifying, extending, and multiplying fields and closures. In question is the extent to which a complementary field is or must be dominated by a given field, such as philosophy, or by a given closure; or to what extent the possibility of new—nonstandard—theories and models might extend and transform a given theoretical closure. Breaking away from philosophy and its closure is difficult, given their pervasiveness throughout history. In Derrida, philosophy functions as a kind of permanent component of complementarity, whatever its complements—its others—may be. Philosophy or at least the closure of philosophy emerges as an always irreducible complementary field, however heterogeneously distributed or hidden. Giving such a place to philosophy or other fields in a specific project cannot in itself be seen as problematic, especially given the significance of Derrida's project and the effectiveness with which he executes it. Seeing the closure of philosophy as irreducible and the implications of such a position may be more problematic.

Given the role of philosophy and its history, Derrida's project is of tremendous importance. Beyond the nature of Derrida's own major ideas, this project is, as I have indicated, equally significant for its engagement of multiple registers in the tradition of Valéry, Artaud, Bataille, Blanchot, and several others—all of them Derrida's subjects—as the outside of philosophy, often proceeding, as Bataille does, in "a nonphilosophical mode [un mode non philosophique]" (*Writing and Difference*, 253; *L'écriture and la différence*, 373). The value of Derrida's project or projects is not in question, only certain general theoretical possibilities and some of Derrida's claims. Nor can one discount the generative potential of philosophy, and not only in Derrida and related recent developments but also throughout its history, from (or before) Plato on.[14] From this perspective one can even see philosophy, throughout its history, concerned just as much with introducing and developing new conceptualities as with sustaining and reinforcing the power of the metaphysics of presence.

Not even Nietzsche discounts this potential, even though throughout his works he adopts a radically skeptical attitude toward philosophy, with the possible exception of Heraclitus, whom he regards "with the highest respect" as an extraordinary and special case (*Twilight of the Idols*, 480; *KSA* 6:75). As Derrida himself points out, in opposition to Heidegger's reading of Nietzsche, "radicalizing the concepts of *interpretation, perspective, evaluation, difference,* and all the 'empiricist' or nonphilosophical motifs that have constantly tormented philosophy throughout the history of the West, and besides, have had nothing but the *inevitable weakness of being produced in the field of philosophy*, Nietzsche, far from remaining *simply* (with Hegel and as Heidegger wished) *within* metaphysics, contributed a great deal to the liberation of the signifier from its dependence or derivation with respect to the logos and the related concept of truth or the primary signified, in whatever sense that is understood" (*Of Grammatology*, 19; *De la grammatologie*, 31–32; emphasis added). Nietzsche refigures the whole philosophical problematics through what I called earlier nonstandard models.

While not fully outside philosophy and its closure and while engaging both critically, Nietzsche was more radically outside philosophy than anyone before or perhaps after him. As we have seen, any form of absolute separation, difference, or exteriority is not possible. It is possible, however, to be sufficiently—and, at certain points, fully—separated from any given field, more precisely, from any given demarcation of a given field at a given moment: at other moments, separate configurations can be connected or reconnected and the fields and their boundaries, within and without, can be re-demarcated. Such connections and disconnections, demarcations and redemarcations cannot be determined once and for all. This is one of the reasons why one cannot speak of absolute exteriority, although this impossibility may affect interpretive closures more than theoretical ones, which appear to allow for more radical departures. By suspending the possibility of separation from a given field or closure altogether, one would reinstate a kind of Hegelian unified totality of knowledge and history, at least in principle. Under the conditions of general economy, this move is prohibited both in principle and in practice. It must, therefore, be also prohibited in the form of the total or unified, or untransformed, closure, whether of philosophy or of any other field. Otherwise, a kind of transcendental trace would be reinstated, along with a kind of Heideggerian, or Heideggerian-Hegelian, "closure," which Derrida's economy of the closure of philosophy may not entirely avoid. While in many cases absolute departures or transgressions are not radical enough and tend to reestablish a previous regime, at certain points the effects of absolute departure must be produced complementarily with the effects of continuity. Derridean underminings and deconstructions are radical, and one would not be able to identify the closure of *philosophy* in Derrida with Hegelian *Geist*, governed by the history of philosophy. The reinscription of the history of philosophy as the history of the closure or double closure—the closure of philosophy as the *metaphysics* of presence, or difference, and the closure of *presence,* or difference—is a brilliant and radical move. It may not, however, be able to escape at least the shadow— or the closure—of *Geist* and Hegel.

In contrast, the engagement with philosophy is only one moment in Nietzsche, and predominantly a critical or deconstructive one. Most of his theoretical work is multiply complementary and proceeds by engaging registers other than philosophy. As I suggested earlier, this type of complementarity is closer to Bohr's complementarity in quantum mechanics than to the exploration focused on undecidability or the interminable investigation of the closure of philosophy. Indeterminacy, or at certain points undecidability, and the impossibility of controlling interpretation, transformations, history, theory, or politics remain necessary conditions of theory for Nietzsche. Complementarity and nonstandard models play more active roles, however; and other complementarities than with philosophy are persistently engaged, both by using and transforming concepts borrowed elsewhere and by introducing new concepts.

One cannot claim that Nietzsche is fully disengaged from the field of philosophy or, especially, from what can be seen as post-philosophical philosophical thinking. Such a claim would be misleading, given both Nietzsche's critical engagement with—that is, against—philosophy and, more importantly, his reliance on the resources of philosophy, including its closure, for both his deconstructive and his constructive theoretical work. The difference is in the degree of engagement or disengagement— critical, theoretical, or positive—particularly with philosophy, coupled with the ensuing difference in the kinds of theoretical and critical projects that can be engaged. "I say it against Nietzsche perhaps: . . .," Derrida says in "Living On: Border Lines" (125), it is true, in the context of Nietzsche's claim that "triumph over oneself is also a pursuit of power (*Gewalt*)." The statement, however, may connote a more general difference in theoretical style and thus in the balance, or imbalance, of continuities and ruptures between the "old" and the "new."

Multi-Closures

Complementarity with *philosophy* in Derrida may in fact be seen as necessitated and determined by the *closure* of philosophy as the metaphysics of presence. This closure suggests, first, a form of correspondence principle—within certain limits, general economic and restricted economic theories coincide—and second, more problematically, an irreducible dependence on concepts developed within the field of philosophy. By complementarizing theoretical closure, however, one may bring together and mutually enrich both of Bohr's principles—the complementarity principle and the correspondence principle. In this plural economy, the closure of *presence*—or, more generally, the interpretive closure or closures accounting for the effects of presence and absence, identity and difference, interiority and exteriority, continuity and rupture, finitude and infinity, and so forth—may and perhaps must be differentiated from the closure of philosophy. This analytical and strategic discrimination need not imply absolute separation of such closures. These closures must instead be seen as complementary in the extended sense of this study. Such terms and concepts as presence, difference, alterity, and so forth themselves have genealogies in the history and text of philosophy and its closure. But they also have their genealogies elsewhere. The history of these concepts can be neither fully dissociated from the history and the text—and finally the closure—of philosophy nor fully contained there, which also entails a transformation of the concept of history, making it general economic and complementary. Instead the closure of philosophy itself emerges as an (acausal) effect of the closure of presence and related or complementary interpretive closures.

Operating jointly or complementarily, the interpretive closures of that type—the closures of presence, difference, exteriority, alterity, continuity, rupture, finitude, infinity, and so forth—can be understood as a kind of "psychologically" or even "biologically" induced conglomerate of constraints, always differentiated in practice, that affect all our interpretive processes. To a degree, it may be permissible to see this economy as one closure; but even in this case, a complementary economy of closures is more effective. For the sake of convenience, I shall use here mostly the rubrics of presence and difference (and in the next section alterity), although other forces and constraints just indicated will be implied throughout. Presence and difference may play a particularly, even uniquely important and pervasive role in most interpretive processes. They cannot, however, be seen as absolutely irreducible, always central, or fully determining any given interpretive or theoretical situation. Both are in turn always inhabited and inhibited, by each other or by other interpretive and theoretical forces. This differential-transformational and complementary play can always deviate from any given pattern or law—of presence, difference, transformation, inhibition, complementarity, law itself, or any other law. There may be more natural correspondences between such rubrics, such as presence and continuity, or difference and rupture; but they cannot be aligned in any unique or fixed manner, and they can intermix differently and themselves be governed by different patterns and laws.

Nietzsche was perhaps first to understand how such enclosures operates. One can encounter related ideas in many of his elaborations, most directly in his great statement on active forgetfulness opening "The Second Essay" of *On the Genealogy of Morals*. Many of Freud's ideas, which exhibit key proximities to Nietzsche in this respect, are equally important. As we have seen, Derrida suggests a closure of that type in *Of Grammatology* and elsewhere, perhaps most overtly in his essay on Artaud "The Theater of Cruelty and the Closure of Representation" (in *Writing and Difference*). This closure necessitates the repression of nonlinear (i.e., Derrida's) *writing:* "Writing in the narrow sense—and phonetic writing above all—is rooted in the past of non-linear writing. It had to be defeated, and here one can speak, if one wishes, of technical success; it assured a greater security and greater possibilities of capitalization in a dangerous and anguishing world. But that was not done *one single time*" (*Of Grammatology*, 85; *De la grammatologie*, 127). One can say that it happens all the time, as the forces of presence, difference, repression, and so forth interact and produce a closure or closures, interpretive and theoretical.

These closures must be seen as themselves produced by *différance* and other Derridean efficacities, including *writing*. The interpretive closure I am introducing here must also be seen as determined by the structures and efficacities of that type, which can themselves be approached only within such a closure or closures. The closure of *philosophy* is an effect of this closure or conglomerate of closures, producing philosophy *as* the metaphysics of presence, although there are many other factors shaping the emergence and history of philosophy. By the same token, this efficacity does not imply a strictly causal relation, historical or other, or an unconditional separation between both types of closure. As throughout the present study, one must think in terms of more remote efficacities. Such efficacities allow one to see interpretive closures as preceding the emergence of a given theoretical field, such as philosophy. This possibility, however, need not mean that one can speak of an absolutely original or primordial theoretical field, such as philosophy, as, for example, Husserl does in proposing his concept of the birth of geometry out of the spirit of philosophy. Instead, one must think in terms of more fluid and interactive or complementary processes in which theoretical fields and their closures interact and transform more readily, while the interpretive closure or closures may remain more stable.

In more Derridean terms, philosophical or otherwise theoretical writing is the effect of the closure of *writing* in Derrida's sense. "Our" discourse depends on this history, and one of Derrida's central points is that we can no more be only philosophical than only nonphilosophical. Often the first is the case particularly when we want to be philosophical, even as philosophical as possible; and the second, particularly when we want to be nonphilosophical, even as nonphilosophical as possible. Derrida's analysis of our dependence on such philosophical concepts is exquisite; but it equally shows the impossibility of fully containing any concept philosophically. As we have seen, Bohr suggests that an analogous economy is operative in physics or science in general. All such concepts are always complementary in this sense. At certain points, however, nonphilosophical conceptual complementarities can come into play.[15] There may therefore be effects of the closure of presence, difference, exteriority, or other such closures that cannot be contained by the closure of philosophy.

One could argue that by the closure of *philosophy*, as the metaphysics of *presence*, Derrida understands those interpretive and conceptual structures that share this differentiated efficacity and that manifest themselves as "effects" of that type.[16] In other words, such "effects" emerge in an analogous way in all theoretical structures, wherever *presence* enters—and, at one point or another, *presence*, or traces of presence, enters everywhere, as does difference, or do traces of difference. Thus the difference between the closure of *presence* and the closure of *philosophy* may appear reduced. But then one cannot, in all rigor, speak of the closure of metaphysics or philosophy nor of one closure of any type nor perhaps even of the closure of *presence* or *difference*, or *différance*, powerful and extensive as such closure may be. Some theoretical and, particularly, interpretive closures do extend very far. But they are also accompanied by other closures, which, particularly the closures of given theories or fields, no less transform and disappear at certain points than continue and extend at others. The closures are many, their behavior is diverse, and some theoretical closures may never enter certain fields. Interpretive closures may be more stable and pervasive, and they may even be seen as universal in some of their aspects. Theoretical closures appear to differentiate and transform themselves more readily and more radically. All closures, however, may be best seen as to one degree or another fluid—transforming—and complementary.

As I pointed out earlier, Derrida does not speak of the *transformation* of closure, by which—this is crucial—I refer here to transformations that cannot be re-enclosed within a single closure, but would enact instead a kind of *différance*-dissemination and complementarity at the level of closure. Such an economy would allow for relationships between successive or parallel closures, or closures related by still more complex—heterogeneously interactive and interactively heterogeneous, or complementary—economies. But it would disallow a re-enclosure within a single theoretical closure, however transformable within itself. Derrida does not appear to apply such a joint operator of *différance*-dissemination at the level of closure. Instead, to a degree, he re-encloses the functioning of both structures themselves within the closure of philosophy. Nor does the term 'closure' appear to occur in plural form in Derrida. He does, it is true, see closure as a heterogeneous structure:

> for me it was not a question of taking 'metaphysics' ("la" méta-physique) as the homogeneous unity of an ensemble. I have never believed in the existence or in the consistency of something like metaphysics *itself* (la *métaphysique*). . . . Keeping in account such and such a demonstrative sentence or such a contextual constraint, if I happened to say 'metaphysics' or 'the' closure of 'metaphysics' (an expression which is the target of [Paul Ricoeur's] *Live Meta-phor*), very often, elsewhere, but also in "White Mythology," I have put forward the proposition according to which there would never be 'metaphysics,' 'closure' not being here a circular limit border-ing a homogeneous field but a more twisted structure which today, according to another figure, I would be tempted to call: 'invagi-nated.' Representation of a linear and circular closure surrounding a homogeneous space is, precisely, the theme of my greatest empha-sis, an auto-representation of philosophy in its onto-encyclopedic logic. ("The *Retrait* of Metaphor," 14; "Le retrait de la métaphore," *Psyche*, 72) [17]

Derrida's difference, or *différance*, from ontotheology remains decisive, and Ricoeur clearly misses the point of Derrida's analysis. The closure of metaphysics cannot be seen as a fully homogeneous or decidable field or as a linear or circular closure. It does remain everywhere irreducible, however; and, while Derrida deconstructs philosophy's claim that it can be independent of its exterior or make decidable its own field, he in fact extends its closure. Whether on the philosophical or the nonphilosophical side, it is, according to Derrida, imperative to avoid assigning determinate or decidable boundaries within or without any given field. Yet, heterogeneous and undecidable as it is, Derrida's topology gives philosophy a position of unique density in this theoretical manifold, and no other field is assigned such a role in his work. Even though philosophy, according to Derrida, can never escape its many "others," no such "other" can invade philosophy in the way philosophy invades everything else. It is true, that, as in Blanchot, Bataille, and his other predecessors, or, differently, in de Man, literature plays a special role in Derrida. The special-ness and specificity of literature is defined, with some justification, by its relation to philosophy, as again *Glas* exemplifies perhaps most graphically.[18]

While, then, far from without historical and theoretical justification and carefully qualified, as in the passage just cited, Derrida's claims upon the closure of metaphysics can be sustained only up to a certain point. In fact, one might question whether and to what extent the very economy of presence and in particular the economy of *différance* and *writing*, as theorized by Derrida, belong to the (previous) closure of philosophy; or whether one can speak of the same *theoretical* closure *prior* to Derrida's and other contemporary texts, for example, in view of the undecidability and incompleteness economy introduced by Derrida and the nonstandard models that this economy may imply. One is compelled instead to consider the difference between the closure of philosophy and the closure of presence, or difference, and then the differentiation—dissemination— complementarization, and transformations of interpretive and theoretical closures, possibly even beyond the very idea of closure.

It is not immediately apparent whether a unitary closure—*one* closure—is "prohibited" by the (general) economy Derrida sets into operation, even given his heterogeneous inscription of the closure itself. For, as I just indicated, the Derridean "more twisted" or "invaginated"—noncircular—topology still appears to contain heterogeneity or transformability *within* the closure and by doing so to suggest the totality of this closure, albeit as a heterogeneous—twisted—totality. Instead of dissemination and transformations of closure, of which Derrida does not speak, this topology suggests . . . It is not easy to name this economy. Could one say the *presence* of closure? That would hardly be possible in Derrida. There appears to emerge, however, something like its irreducibility as *one* closure—*the* closure—Derrida's qualifications and quotation marks notwithstanding. Conceived as the closure of philosophy, this closure (re)introduces a perhaps excessive degree of both Hegelian and Heideggerian economy into Derrida's matrix. "The interruption, the destruction of the Hegelian [*Aufhebung*]" is, as we have seen, announced by the inscription of *différance*. It is announced unequivocally enough, insofar as anything can be unequivocal in Derrida. This announcement, however, is situated *within* the closure of philosophy and, it appears, as "the limit" that must be approached from its Hegelian (or Heideggerian) side. All circulations and transformations in Derridean economy must proceed, by means of interminable analysis, within this closure.

Replacing the *end* of philosophy with the *closure* of philosophy is a brilliant and necessary move, particularly in view of easily (pro)claimed but failed departures from metaphysics, within or outside philosophy, or from philosophy itself or other classical fields. To an extent, however, this move itself becomes a Hegelian or Heideggerian—and anti-Nietzschean—gesture, which returns to philosophy its primary, perhaps even unique significance. Since the power and impact of philosophy are undeniable, the question is, to what extent and in what measure can and should such a significance be claimed—let us say, historically. Derrida's analysis is just about unassailable within the limits at issue there—the limits of philosophy, its margins, and its closure or closures—and Derrida is right in claiming these limits to be very broad. One may, however, need a more complex economy of closure. First, beyond the exteriors or margins of philosophy functioning in Derrida's economy, more multiple stratifications and complementarities between different closures infringe upon and affect Derridean closure itself. Second, these exterior configurations need to be explored beyond their relations to philosophy and its closure.

One cannot claim that Derrida does not perceive the possibility or the necessity of "thinking"—*writing*—beyond the closure of metaphysics and philosophy, or beyond the closure of presence or difference, and of exploring textual styles, the styles of writing, whereby one can glimpse such a "beyond." On the contrary, in part again via analogy with Gödel, thinking beyond closure is crucial to Derrida, and statements to that effect recur throughout his works. The question is what are theoretical and interpretive economies that delimit or, conversely, exceed the (en)closure beyond which one can or must "glimpse." As we recall, "we can merely glimpse" even the *closure* itself, which is opposed to the *end*, of "the historico-metaphysical epoch" at issue (*Of Grammatology*, 4; *De la grammatologie*, 14). Thus, while again "within the closure," against "renouncing" classical concepts and urging the Derridean economy under discussion, Derrida invokes "the yet unnameable glimmer beyond the closure." Derrida's subject here is "the age of sign [which] is essentially theological. Perhaps it will never *end*. Its historical *closure*, however, is outlined." At issue in this statement are philosophy (as the metaphysics of presence) and its history, to which the concept and the history, or epoch, of the concept of sign belong and of which it is in fact "exemplary": "The concept of the sign—which has never existed or functioned outside the history of (the) philosophy (of presence)—remains systematically and genealogically determined by that history." The task, therefore, is the deconstruction of this history, as opposed to criticizing the concept of sign within the same regime and in the name "of the present truth, anterior, exterior or superior to the sign, or in terms of the place of the effaced difference" (*Of Grammatology*, 14; *De la grammatologie*, 25–26). The closure of the metaphysics of presence, within which such a deconstruction remains enclosed, must remain central to the problematics so announced, since, to begin with, the concept of the sign is indissociable from the concept of concept itself. This is the grounding concept of all philosophy, whose inability to sustain it rigorously on its own terms makes it deconstructable: "*From the inside the closure*, by an oblique and always perilous movement, incessantly risking falling back within what is being deconstructed, it is necessary to surround the critical concepts with a careful and thorough discourse—to mark the conditions, the medium, and the limits of their effectiveness and to designate rigorously their appurtenance to the machine whose deconstruction they permit; and, in the same movement [coup], designate the crevice through which the yet unnameable glimmer beyond the closure can be glimpsed" (*Of Grammatology*, 14; *De la grammatologie*, 25; emphasis added; translation modified).[19]

The reliance, here and throughout the opening part of the book, on classical philosophemes, from Plato's cave to Hegelian teleology, may be a bit excessive. This usage, however, is consistent with the point and most likely deliberately thematizes it. Moving beyond closure, theoretical or interpretive, may not be possible outside the closure or closures to which the notion of "moving beyond the closure"—or "moving beyond"—belongs. The present analysis does not deny this point or disregard Derrida's cautions. It confirms the irreducibility of such (en)closures. I shall consider this question of the "beyond" in the next section, together with the impossibility of there being a "beyond" of closure. "Beyond" will again imply, on the one hand, that there is no beyond of closure in the sense of absolute exteriority and, on the other, that one may need to introduce a more stable interpretive rather than theoretical enclosure. This interpretive closure may not be determined through the closure of philosophy alone, although it manifests itself in that closure, on which our analysis may still depend.

The historical dimensions of Derrida's economy of closure become particularly important at this juncture, although they are operative and irreducible throughout. History is always the history of many (en)closures —interpretive, theoretical, ideological, and political. As Derrida comments: "For a proper understanding of the gesture that we are sketching here, one must understand the expression 'epoch,' 'closure of the epoch,' 'historical genealogy' in a new way; and must first remove them from all relativism" (*Of Grammatology*, 14; *De la grammatologie*, 26). While many "relativisms" must no doubt be suspended and deconstructed, some of them, such as Nietzschean perspectivism—a radical heterogeneity of all perspectives and (en)closures—can, as I have indicated, be used against more Hegelian or otherwise epochal determinations, some of which Derrida's economy retains.[20] The historical economy Derrida suggests here is gradually transformed in the course of the book and in subsequent essays. It shifts away from more Hegelian or quasi-Hegelian epochal determinations. It does, however, retain a Hegelian trace at the level of Derrida's economy of closure, which governs both his theory and his practice. Derrida argues that what is "beyond the closure" of philosophy can be approached only from within this closure. The latter, we recall, is not identical, but extends the field of philosophy. In Derrida, new theoretical possibilities appear to remain contained within the closure of metaphysics and philosophy. It may, however, be necessary to extend this economy to complementary ensembles of closures, interpretive and theoretical, in order both to enhance new possibilities of theory and to account for the history of theoretical thinking, inside and outside philosophy, for example, in Nietzsche, Bohr, Bataille, or Derrida himself.

As I have emphasized throughout, Derrida's investigation of the closure of philosophy is an extraordinary achievement, and such a project may well be necessary, "uncircumventable," particularly as a deconstruction of philosophy—an exposure of its limits and the closure of its concepts. As a general claim, however, the significance Derrida assigns to philosophy and its closure is more problematic, implying globalizing possibilities that one might want to avoid. Whether by design or by chance, such possibilities establish an even closer proximity to Hegel or Heidegger, or in later works, Levinas and achieve a less radical difference from either than may be possible or necessary from the anti-epistemological perspective. One must, of course, be extremely careful in attributing to Derrida any globalizing possibilities. Propositions suggesting them do, however, occur throughout Derrida's texts, both early and later, specifically beginning with the opening of *Of Grammatology*, where Derrida speaks, in terms of the interesting conjunction of history and metaphysics, of "an historico-metaphysical epoch of which we merely glimpse the *closure*. I do not say the *end*" (*Of Grammatology*, 5; *De la grammatologie*, 14). Such propositions also punctuate *Positions;* and most of Derrida's positions presented there are defined by this economy of "the *closure* of an historico-metaphysical epoch." These are, it is true, Derrida's earlier texts (written between 1967 and 1972), and in more recent works the thematics of closure appears to recede, being taken over by other forces, some of which it may no longer control. The propositions and positions themselves, however, are reaffirmed by most of the later works, and the practice of complementarization with philosophy within the closure of philosophy continues throughout and even becomes enhanced and reinforced.

As Derrida remarked during the discussion after delivering "Différance" as a lecture (in 1968): "To ask about *différance* a question of origin or a question of essence, to ask oneself 'What is it?' is to return abruptly to the closure which I am attempting, with difficulty, laboriously and obliquely, to 'leave' [*faire sortir*]. Moreover, 'leave' is here a metaphor which does not satisfy me. It is less a question of jumping with both feet out of a circle than of scribing [*d'écrire*], of describing [*décrire*] the *elliptical* deformation by which perhaps a circle may repeat itself while referring to itself" (*Derrida and Différance*, 85). Such a question cannot of course be asked about *différance*, and Derrida clearly reinscribes philosophy, or the "preceding" configuration of philosophy, as the closure of philosophy. On this occasion—in an improvised response, it is true—Derrida does so in a particularly Hegelian self-reflexive fashion. The "*circle* [that] may repeat itself while referring to itself" reminds one of Hegel's spirals, here translated, via an "elliptical deformation," into the closure of philosophy. In "*Ousia* and *Grammē*" Derrida places "itself" under erasure (or in the erasure-like parenthesis). Deconstruction is always the deconstruction of self-reflexivity, prohibiting all absolute self-reflexivity.[21] Derrida does not perhaps avoid, however, a reinstatement of self-reflexivity at the level of closure, which repeats and refers to itself.

In effect, however, Derrida's elliptical deformation enacts a transformation, in fact quite radical, of our theoretical closure. As a result of this transformation, the very questions of philosophy and its closure and of the possibility of transgressing them acquire new limits, as Nietzsche or Bataille have already demonstrated in a rigorous but "nonphilosophical mode" or as Bohr's quantum anti-epistemology suggests. Demonstrating it in a philosophical mode, as Derrida does, may be equally important. Derrida sees these relations of transgression and nontransgression of philosophy as undecidable and as always remaining within the closure of philosophy. According to Derrida, "What is held within a de-limited closure may continue indefinitely." It may indeed, although it would depend on where and for whom. But must it? Or does it, except, of course, where it does?

Enclosures

Theoretical and more general interpretive (en)closures cannot be unconditionally or unequivocally dissociated. They can be sufficiently differentiated, however, and can never be fully united. They, and all closures, are complementary. To a degree, this economy remains within a Heraclitean closure, the closure of transformations, reshaped by Hegel and in many ways culminating in Nietzsche, even given Heidegger and Derrida after him. As we have seen, the "underlying" efficacious dynamics of the transformations of and interaction between closures—or other transformations and interactions, be they interpretive, theoretical, historical, or political—may not conform to any given form of transformation, difference, alterity, or dynamics; or to these or, possibly, any concepts or closures; or be "underlying." This "alterity" may in fact not conform to anything that can be approached through these or any terms—whether the terms of being or becoming, beginning or end, alterity or exteriority (or, of course, identity, sameness, or interiority) finitude or infinity, matter or spirit; or of *différance* and other Derridean operators or analogous efficacities in Nietzsche, Bohr, Freud, Bataille, and Lacan, which attempts to relate obliquely to this type of alterity and efficacious processes within our closure or closures. At issue is a "relation" of neither absolute (or potentially any) difference, exteriority, or disconnection—which, being absolute, is never radical enough—nor of absolute (or potentially any) connectability within or outside any form of closure, enclosure, or de-closure. The latter formulation, of course, also suggests a form or several forms of relationality and, as such, may be equally inapplicable here. Furthermore (and at this point placing one's terms under erasures or putting them in quotation marks becomes unavoidable) this "relation" "relates" to (or "disconnects" from) a "process" that may be neither being nor becoming, neither one nor many, neither finite nor infinite, has neither origins nor ends, nor middles, nor any other characterizations conceivable—whether in terms of general or restricted economy, by means of standard or non-standard models, or whatever—including any characterizations offered at the moment. Our "relation" to this alterity-efficacity is, of course, itself subject to the same economy. We may not be able to either dissociate or unite, either connect or disconnect ourselves with this alterity-efficacity through any interpretive, theoretical, or other technology (including more strictly technological ones) that is or ever will be available to us, if, like other terms used here, or again any terms, these terms are applicable here. The very conception of the impossibility of relating any interpretation, theory, or technology to this alterity-efficacity may itself be inapplicable.

Plato in *Parmenides* already sensed some of these complexities. In the dialogue, Parmenides shows how difficult, and finally impossible, it is to argue for the possibility of differing from the One. Conversely, one can argue in Heraclitean fashion that it would be equally impossible to sustain the logic of the One, as to some degree Plato does in *Theaetetus*, a companion—and in this sense complementary—dialogue to *Parmenides*, where he offers the following extraordinary elaboration:

> In my dream, I seem to hear some people saying that the primary elements, as it were, of which we and everything else are composed, are such that no account can be given of them. Each of them itself, by itself, can only be named, and one can't go on to say anything else, neither that it is nor that it isn't; because in that case, one would be attaching being or not being to it, whereas one ought not to add anything if one is going to express in an account that thing, itself, alone. In fact, one shouldn't even add itself, or that, or each, or alone, or this, or any of several other things of that kind; because those things run about and get added to everything, being different from the things they're attached to, whereas if the thing itself could be expressed in an account and had an account proper to itself, it would have to be expressed apart from everything else. As things are, it's impossible that any of the primary things should be expressed in an account; because the only thing that's possible for it is to be named, because a name is the only thing it has. But as for things composed of them, just as the things themselves are woven together, so their

names, woven together, come to be an account [*logos*]; because a weaving together of names is the being of an account. In that way, the [primary] elements have no account and are unknowable, but they're perceivable; and the complexes are knowable and expressible in an account and judgeable in a true judgement. Now when someone gets hold of the true judgement of something without an account, his soul [*psyche*] is in a state of truth about it but doesn't know it; because someone who can't give and receive an account of something isn't knowledgeable about that thing. But if he also gets hold of an account, then it's possible not only for all that to happen, but also for him to be in a perfect condition in respect to knowledge. (*Theaetetus*, 201e–202c) [22]

The doctrine is much closer to Kant (or, differently, to certain stages of Heidegger's thinking) than to the economy suggested here, and the calculus of the two dialogues anticipates and is a major source of the Hegelian and the Kantian calculus. In the (general) economy of "difference" and "alterity," or "efficacity," under consideration, one certainly cannot speak in terms of the primary elements (or elements, to begin with), or again any terms, names or unnameables. Socrates actually does not subscribe to the doctrine he discusses here; and the dialogue problematizes the possibility (or definition) of knowledge even further. Nowhere, however, whether in *Theaetetus*, arguably the most anti-epistemological (to the degree the term can apply to Plato) of Plato's dialogues, or elsewhere, does Plato approach the economy at issue at the moment. It took twenty-five centuries of history of the idea of difference—the history of Western philosophy—and, then, anti-epistemology, to arrive at the logic of the alterity and closure at issue here.

While this alterity-efficacity cannot be approached through classical (restricted-economic) terms or again "any" terms (including general economic ones), all the *effects* described via such terms, including the effects of various closures, are produced by this alterity-efficacity, making all our interpretation and theory, and all our approaches to this alterity itself, depend on these effects. This radical alterity of the efficacious process, on the one hand, and of the closure of its effects, on the other, necessitate the application of Derridean undecidable logic of "neither/nor, either/or" or complementary description and analysis, when one attempts to approach this "efficacity" and its "alterity." This point is important, both in relation to the various charges that radical anti-epistemology, such as Nietzsche's, Bohr's, Bataille's, or Derrida's, are negative, nihilistic, devoid of constructive potential, and so forth. All the thinkers just listed have much to respond—and do make a point of responding—to these charges. Nietzsche offers a massive critique of all nihilism hitherto, particularly nihilism as the will to nothingness.[23] 'Nothing,' of course, is just one term, if a very important one, among other terms within various closures, and the considerations just given by no means suggest that the process(es) and relation(s) at issue relate to nothingness. They may be no more 'nothing' than 'something,' or any other thing, while again generating a corresponding effect of nothingness or 'somethingness,' or 'thingness.' When Heidegger suggests that "nothing . . . is the veil of Being," he refers to a similar process.[24] In doing so, he follows Nietzsche and anticipates and influences Derrida, although within a restricted economy and, thus, reinstating metaphysics in the truth of Being (and displacing Nietzsche along the way). The recurrent propositions in Derrida—of the type that *différance* does not exist—or is nothing, means nothing, and so forth—do not identify *différance* with nothingness. They imply instead, *both* that *différance* cannot *be* (including in Heidegger's sense of Being, or conform to Heideggerian, rather than Derridean erasure of Being) and "is" *not* "nothing."

The moment, or the stage, of such an absolute negation—a radical supension of everything—or, conceived more generally, the stage of nihilism in Nietzsche, may well be an indispensable phase in a critical or deconstructive process. Nietzsche writes: "That it is the *measure of strength* to what extent we can admit to ourselves, without perishing, the merely *apparent* character [of things], the necessity of lies. To this extent, nihilism, as the denial of a truthful world, of being, might be *a divine way of thinking*" (*The Will to Power*, sec. 15, p. 15; *KSA* 12:354). This "phase of nihilism" is analogous to the phase of overturning in deconstruction that reverses such oppositions as signifier and signified, form and content, writing and speech, and so forth. This phase must be followed or accompanied by a phase of reinscription and recomprehension of all the concepts of the previous regime within refigured limits. It must thus be also accompanied by a radical suspension of nothingness, leading to a configuration of closure. One could even say that "a tragic flaw"—*hamartia*—of nihilism is that it forgets to negate 'nothing.' It may be more difficult to affirm life, as Nietzsche does, under these tragic conditions—to affirm life in even the greatest tragedy—than, nihilistically, to will nothingness.

Is it possible, is it conceivable, then? Is it possible to conceive of something that neither connects nor disconnects, is neither connected nor disconnected, that indeed is neither conceivable nor unconceivable, is never fully, or even in any way, inside or outside any closure, as this and all such questions themselves are the products of (en)closures, beyond some of which one must move and within others of which one must remain in approaching this radically, but never absolutely, unrepresentable process? Kantian things-in-themselves, while an important move in this respect, clearly fall far short of such a "difference," given their "thingness" or "themselves-ness," their absolute difference. Nietzsche immediately perceives that Kant has no right to speak about things-in-themselves and certainly not to distinguish them in the way he does from "appearances" (*The Will to Power*, sec. 553, p. 300). The radical "logic" at issue defines the general economic field in Nietzsche, Bohr, Bataille, and Derrida, who pursue it most relentlessly and laboriously. Freud's, Heidegger's, and Lacan's contributions have also been decisive, particularly Lacan's analysis of the Real in "The Eye and the Gaze," mentioned earlier. Nietzsche's understanding that one must simultaneously "abolish" [abschaffen] both the "true" and the "apparent" world [die wahre und die scheinbare Welt] (*Twilight of the Idols*, 486; *KSA* 6:81) necessitates or is necessitated by this radical alterity and this logic. His extraordinary elaboration "*against determinism and teleology*" is a condensed massive critique of virtually all prior metaphysics, of much preceding physics, and of much in physics and metaphysics yet to come. Nietzsche writes:

a. Necessity is not a fact but an interpretation.

b. When one has grasped that the "subject" is not something that creates effects, but only a fiction, much follows.

It is only after the model of the subject that we have invented the reality of things and projected them into the medley of sensations. If we no longer believe in the effective subject, then belief also disappears in effective things, in reciprocation, cause and effect between those phenomena that we call things.

There also disappears, of course, the world of effective atoms: the assumption of which always depended on the supposition that one needed subjects.

At last, the "thing-in-itself" also disappears, because this is fundamentally the conception of a "subject-in-itself." But we have grasped that the subject is a fiction. The antithesis "thing-in-itself" and "appearance" is untenable; with that, however, the concept "appearance" also disappears.

254   Complementarity and Deconstruction

c. If we give up the effective subject, we also give up the object upon which effects are produced. Duration, identity with itself,
being are inherent neither in that which is called subject nor in
that which is called object: they are complexes of events apparently
durable in comparison with other complexes—e.g., through the difference in tempo of the event (rest—motion, firm—loose: opposites
that do not exist in themselves and that actually express only variations in degree that from a certain perspective appear to be opposites. There are no opposites: only from those of logic do we derive
the concept of opposites—and falsely transfer it to things).

d. If we give up the concept "subject" and "object," then also the
concept "substance"—and as a consequence also the various modifications of it, e.g., "matter," "spirit," and other hypothetical entities,
"the eternity and immutability of matter," etc. We have got rid of
materiality. (*The Will to Power*, sec. 552, pp. 297–98; *KSA* 12:383–84)

At issue here is a theory that is, or is still best seen as, a materialist
one, *under the general economic conditions of the inscription of matter*, equally
implied by Bohr's complementarity and Bataille's and Derrida's general economies. As in the earlier *Philosophy in the Tragic Age of the Greeks*,
physics offers effective metaphors. But (classical) physics is as much of a
problem as metaphysics is and, as Nietzsche makes clear, both are complicit. His argument here is not only similar but is equivalent to Bohr's,
and Nietzsche's other commentaries on the concept of physical reality, to
which he applies his critique of causality, would reinforce these affinities.

In his equally extraordinary conclusion—the closure, in either sense—
of "*Ousia* and *Grammē*," Derrida follows Nietzsche's passage, which is
also cited in *Positions* at a crucial juncture of the question of matter discussed earlier (65, 105 n. 34).[25] Derrida's elaborations in the essay, particularly in its final section "The Closure of Grammē and Trace of Difference," and in the analysis, *closing* (again in either sense) "Différance,"
also translate Nietzsche into more Heideggerian terms, as Derrida simultaneously deconstruct Heidegger's ontic-ontological difference between
Being [*Sein*] and beings [*Seiende*], and different, but related, metaphysical
economies emerging in Heidegger's later writings, such as "The Anaximander Fragment."[26] Derrida uses Heidegger as his point of departure.
Derrida's argument at this juncture (*Margins*, 64–67) explores Heidegger's logic of presence, which finally leads to Derrida's conclusion. To
summarize, Heideggerian "presence, then, far from being, as is commonly thought, *what* the sign signifies, what a trace refers to, presence,

then, is the trace of the trace, the trace of the erasure of the trace" (*Margins*, 66; *Marges*, 76–77). It follows that the Heideggerian determination, or any determination, cannot be applied to such an efficacity, particularly any determination by way of presence, which is never abandoned but always reaffirmed by Heidegger, from *Being and Time* to *On Time and Being*.[27] One can see nearly the whole of Heidegger's analysis, in both its early and later stages, as being his own attempt to "think" the difference at issue interactively by way of both pre-Socratics and Nietzsche, whose thinking, as Derrida argues, becomes reappropriated accordingly. The double closure—the closure of presence or difference and the closure of philosophy as the metaphysics of presence—plays a crucial role in the process. Without realizing it, Heidegger inscribes the closure of metaphysics, specifically the metaphysics of temporality, rather than transcends it. Derrida then concludes:

> There may be a difference still more unthought than the difference between Being and beings. We certainly can go further toward naming it in our language. Beyond Being and beings, this difference, ceaselessly differing from and deferring (itself), would trace (itself) (by itself)—this *différance* would be the first or last trace if one still could speak, here, of origin and end.
>
> Such a *différance* would at once, again, give us to think a writing without presence and without absence, without history, without cause, without *archia*, without *telos*, a writing that absolutely upsets all dialectics, all theology, all teleology, all ontology. A writing exceeding everything that the history of metaphysics has comprehended in the form of the Aristotelian *grammē*, in its point, in its line, in its circle, in its time, and in its space. (*Margins*, 67; *Marges*, 77–78)[28]

This is a remarkable conception, which refigures the Heideggerian economy of difference, simultaneously showing its metaphysical appurtenance. In "*Ousia* and *Grammē*," "Différance," and throughout his writings, including very recent ones, the Heideggerian economy of difference and Being (whether the early or later concepts of difference and Being, even when Heidegger places Being under erasure) demands and becomes precomprehended by this *différance*. It is "older than Being itself" ("*Ousia* and *Grammē*," *Margins*, 67; *Marges*, 77)—in a prelogical, not an ontological sense, as it deconstructs all ontology.

Différance as structure or Derrida's multiple and disseminating ensembles are not reducible even to the complex differing-deferring suggested here, and certainly not to some simplified version of the claim that *différance* simultaneously differs and defers, suggested at the opening of "Différance." The joint difference-deferral at issue is, however, a *defining* aspect of it as the structure and economy. Beyond the Heideggerian process, both the Husserlian and the Saussurean, or the Hegelian, and many other economies of signification are fundamentally precomprehended by it. It "would give us to think"[29] and in fact demands Derrida's *writing*. While this economy is of tremendous significance, Derrida's claim here upon the structure of "difference" may need to be considered—and perhaps radicalized—still further, specifically in relation to "naming" or unnaming it, or the impossibility of doing so, "in our language."[30] If the extent to which "one could speak, here, of origin and end" is limited, the "difference" or "process" at issue may not be the difference and *différance* Derrida invokes, which "ceaselessly differing from and deferring (itself), would trace (itself) (by itself)."[31] It certainly would not be the first and the last, even if one places both concepts under erasure. The statement is in fact a somewhat metaphysical proposition on Derrida's part, even given its conditional nature and laborious surrounding qualifications here and in "Différance." If we want "to go further toward naming" or "unnaming" what is at stake here, we would have at certain points to suspend this Derridean process as well, particularly if understood only within the economy of determinate undecidability as considered earlier, important as this process is for the theory and practice of all interpretation.

Despite the immense precomprehending and deconstructive potential of this matrix, the "alterity-efficacy" I am attempting to approach here may finally not "be," and at certain points need not manifest itself as, "differing," "deferring," and "tracing" in this sense, or in any given sense—of itself, by itself, under erasure or not, within or without one closure or another, or of tracing something else. In this sense, all the precautions and dissemination of terms notwithstanding, *différance* may still not be an altogether precise name, first, by virtue of the multiplicity of effects at issue. Derrida amply qualifies this characteristic here and elsewhere, however, to prevent any misunderstanding: by definition, *différance* cannot be a unique or final name. Second, more interestingly, Derrida still names and wants to name it, even wants to name it multiply and to multiply names. This desire for naming may be seen as a Heideggerian gesture, even though it is also anti-Heideggerian in being a gesture against Heidegger's final word and unique name. In the context, it may be a necessary step, and, in one degree or another, it may be unavoidable in general. The impossibility of naming would, however, demand equal emphasis, which may be suggested more by Derrida's closing comments in "Différance."

The Derridean process, or any process, may be only an intermediate, and mediating, stage within a "process" considered here, which does not obey this structure or conform to any mediation or intermediation, and that neither "connects" nor "disconnects" anything. In this sense, one cannot say that the "difference" or alterity-efficacity at issue further differs from and defers (itself) or that is all it does; it cannot be iterated or reiterated, in Derrida's sense, although it does produce iterative effects of that type. But it may "produce" these effects differently from the way this production is inscribed by Derrida here or elsewhere, or even from whatever is offered by the present analysis. As a result, it may entail theoretical procedures "within a chain . . . that [*différance*] never will have governed" or in which it is not "enmeshing [enchaining, *enchaînement*]" itself at all (*Margins*, 7; *Marges*, 7). More generally, it would diminish a potential reach and significance of any given theoretical procedure and, closer to Nietzsche, imply a more radical form of multiplicity and perspectivism, along with a more radical form of alterity.

What are the traces of this alterity-efficacity, again if and to the degree that the term trace, whether classical or Derridean, can in turn apply? It may leave no trace or erase its trace entirely, as Derrida argues in relation to Heidegger's trace—a trace of the trace and a trace of the erasure of the trace of Being—and in general. Its "trace" may be left in the possibility of difference, which may not be *différance*, between Derrida's and Nietzsche's, or Bataille's, text and style, or in some aspects of Bohr's complementarity, as considered here. Or can one still argue that the effects or economies suggested here still be precomprehended by the Derridean economy? It would be tempting to repeat here Derrida's argument on the relationships between Heidegger's "uncircumventable" meditation on difference and the economy of *différance* (*Margins*, 22–27, 65–67; *Of Grammatology*, 134), and argue that the reverse may be the case. Derrida's argument reflects a relatively common theoretical strategy and a necessary critical procedure; and to a degree they are pursued by the present argument as well. The relationships between Derridean economy and the economy suggested here may, however, be more indeterminate or undecidable in this respect.[32] The propositions and qualifications offered here remain, nevertheless, necessary—perhaps all the more so.

It may, in particular, be pointed out that the process of difference or
différance described by Derrida in the passage just cited, mirrors, perhaps a bit too closely, Derrida's own project or process of interminable
analysis. Derrida's project proceeds by "ceaselessly deferring" and "differing." It certainly continuously "trace[s] (itself) by itself," in a simultaneous proximity to both Freud and Heidegger. That Derrida arrives at
this particular economy through Heidegger rather than through Nietzsche may be significant, although, as we have seen, a similar process is
attributed, perhaps questionably, to Nietzsche himself in "Différance"
(17–18).[33] Of course, one could argue that, conversely, Derrida's strategy
and process are determined by this structure and economy. Nor, as I have
said, can one, more generally, fully suspend or ignore the importance of
this and analogous theoretical processes. Yet in Nietzsche, or Bataille,
each of whom arrives at anti-epistemological results, the role of this type
of analysis and the overall balance of strategies is very different from
those in Derrida. This divergence itself may stem from a more radical and
simultaneously more diverse character of the alterity-efficacity at issue.

That is not to deny that, as Derrida shows, we can speak here only
within a certain closure or closures nor that at issue in Derrida is also
that which exceeds our closure or the possibility or impossibility of *tracing*
it. On the contrary, the present analysis explores both points simultaneously, suggesting, to use Lacan's term, a certain foreclosure, although,
by the same token, one cannot say that the alterity at issue is in fact (absolutely) foreclosed. It may be neither foreclosed nor opened; and the very
notion of closure or any of its complements, deformations, or suspensions, is again part of the same machinery. Instead the question is: Beyond
how many closures? It may be impossible to speak of any 'beyond' either,
whether in the metaphysical sense of absolute exteriority or even in any
articulable or conceivable sense. Nor, let me reiterate, conversely, can any
closure or enclosure, interpretive or theoretical, be self-contained, or all-
encompassing, even as we can extend indefinitely, interminably both the
inside and the outside of a given closure or cluster of closures. We may
be neither beyond nor within anything, while still en-closed or de-closed
enough to be able to suggest the possibility of such an alterity or difference. We are prevented from conceiving of it and yet are able to speak of
such a possibility or impossibility, although such an alterity may not be
approached even by the latter—or any—invocation.

To the extent that one can speak of closure here, however, this closure
may not be the closure of philosophy in Derrida's sense, which also ap-

pears to imply a certain ultimately totalizing economy (keeping in mind
all the necessary qualifications, Derrida's own and those given here).
Instead one can suggest, on the one hand, a more plural and complementary economy of theoretical closures, and on the other, a more general
economy (in either sense) of interpretive closure or closures, which in
a certain sense "precede" the closure of philosophy as the metaphysics
of presence. The radical nature of the alterity-efficacity considered here
need not globalize a theoretical or even an interpretive closure; on the
contrary, it would prohibit all such globalizations. Otherwise, it would be
metaphysically defined in relation to a globally demarcated field, whereas
we need much more complex, complementary topologies against Kant,
against Hegel, against Einstein, or against Heidegger.

As I said, we cannot dissociate the history of the concept of presence,
and all concepts at issue here, from the history of philosophy. But we cannot fully determine and connect them through this or any unified history
either. Derrida's economy may be seen as reintroducing an instance of
metaphysics into his matrix. It can be called the metaphysics of closure.
But then, perhaps the metaphysics of presence has always been or, rather,
can be reconceived in terms of the metaphysics of closure. Certainly, as
Derrida's own analysis intimates, such would be particularly the case in
both Heidegger and perhaps especially Hegel, whose philosophy would,
in this sense, extend to Derrida, although it will also be transformed by
him. It is quite clear, however, that in various forms the metaphysics of
closure has pervaded and perhaps defined the history of philosophy from
(or before) Plato on. In Derrida, this history—the history of the metaphysics of closure—reaches a stage without precedent, along with critical
resources and potential that are far from being exhausted yet.

Derrida's is an unprecedented step: before him, no other metaphysics,
no other thinker had taken it. Nietzsche, Bohr, and Bataille, in varying
measure, were exceptions and should in my view be placed outside this
tradition, even though they, too, share in it. While it follows that all other
metaphysics—the metaphysics of presence—can be reconceived as the
metaphysics of closure, the reverse, in view of Derrida's work, may not
be the case. Derrida's is a metaphysics of closure that cannot be thought
of by way of the metaphysics of presence, although it may remain within
the closure of the metaphysics of presence and the closure of presence,
or difference. Most of Derrida's points pertaining to the latter closure
will not be affected. Derrida's economy, however, retains the closure of
philosophy as the metaphysics of presence; in this sense it remains within

the limits of the metaphysics of closure. Derrida's economy of simultaneously infinitesimal proximity and radical difference leads to a closer
proximity to Hegel and Heidegger or Levinas than would be desirable or
permissible under the constraints emerging in the present analysis.

The preceding analysis cannot be seen as a deconstruction of Derrida,
unless the term is applied extremely generally. Deconstruction, at least
Derrida's deconstruction, is always a deconstruction of the metaphysics
of presence, from Plato to Heidegger, a project that Derrida accomplishes with great effectiveness. One cannot go any further along these
lines. Nor can Derrida's own text really be deconstructed by Derridean
means. Derrida's text is not deconstructable. "Derrida" cannot deconstruct himself. Of course, there will be points in his or any text where
deconstruction can apply, as Derrida argues, as part of the general deconstructive understanding of all textual practice. I am also not referring
to the self-deconstructive dimensions of deconstructive texts, which are
always and invariably self-deconstructive in various degrees. More generally, deconstructive texts are never in full control of themselves; and,
as opposed to classical or precritical texts, they "know" and play out this
impossibility. The latter has been a prominent topic in recent years, and,
as a recognized possibility and as a textual practice, it constitutes a crucial
difference from "the text of philosophy" before deconstruction. Unlike
classical texts, they also possess the means of self-correction. I am not,
however, concerned with these features at the moment, since such deconstructions and self-deconstructions remain within Derridean limits. The
process I describe cannot be comprehended under the Derridean rubrics
or under what Derrida himself deconstructs, even though there are moments of proximity and a certain closure here—a self-deconstruction of
deconstruction—and the suspension of the possibility of fully controlling one's text remains essential under all conditions. Here, however, one
is dealing with a kind of 'de-closing,' or in terms suggested earlier, destandardization of classical, and possible deconstructive, economies, and
stratifications and transformations of the closures that they may entail.

CHAPTER 9

Transformations
of Closure

In the wake of, if perhaps against, Derrida's analysis, the question of theoretical transformations acquires a new dimension; some, perhaps the most radical transformations can transform not only theories themselves or fields where such theories primarily operate, but also the closures of theories or fields as considered in the preceding chapter.[1] In the course of such a transformation, that is, a point may be reached when one no longer remains within the closure or configuration of closures dominating the field where the transformation has taken place, such as, and perhaps particularly, the closure of philosophy as the metaphysics of presence. The latter closure extends far and along a broad and varied historical and theoretical front, encompassing the field of this study, and it may not be possible as yet to claim that a transformation escaping this closure or altering it radically enough has taken place. As I have argued, however, one cannot maintain the possibility of a unitary—uncomplementarized—closure at any point. The economy developed in the preceding analysis allows for relationships between successive or parallel theoretical configurations or closures but disallows one to contain or reenclose them within any single closure, even if the latter is, within itself, transforming and heterogeneous. Moreover, the theoretical closure of the fields under consideration here must be seen as already transformed, given, among others', Nietzsche's and Derrida's analysis, even though it may continue to have a (complementary) philosophical closure-like componenent.

One can suggest, then, that a theoretical transformation of that type may, in the end, be so radical that no given form of philosophical discourse (demarcated here as the metaphysics of presence) and no extension of philosophy or its closure can produce or enter the resulting—new—configuration of theory, however crucial either philosophy itself or its analysis might have been during preceding stages of the process. Naturally, such new configurations may, then, be reabsorbed by or reconnected to philosophy, or whatever other "old" field may be in this position, and then transform or reconfigure that old field, or differently restratify it in relation to an "old" textual and institutional configuration.[2] In short, whether they have philosophical genealogies or not, such new configurations might be exterior enough to exceed philosophy itself and even its closure at some point, if not now, and leave them behind—assuming that one wishes to do so. Moreover, such genealogies, as we have seen, including the genealogy of philosophy itself, can never be purely philosophical. These new configurations fundamentally depend on and result from other developments, exterior to philosophy, understood, let me stress, as a sufficiently, if never unconditionally, demarcated institutional field and ensemble of texts. In fact one finds a considerable degree of transgression of philosophy—as well as, particularly in Derrida, reabsorption—already in the case of general economy and complementarity as considered here.

As I have stressed throughout, nothing in this process can be absolute. For nothing can be, in fact or in effect, absolutely exterior to anything. Thus nothing can exclude philosophy or anything else once and for all. Mixed as their genealogies are, many terms and concepts to which we must still relate and on which we might still depend—such as presence, difference, alterity, and most other concepts involved in the thematics of closure—have emerged primarily in the field of philosophy. Hence insofar as one wants to speak about and in such terms, a break may not be easy. This is one of the effects of the closure of metaphysics, as Derrida sees it. But then, at some point we might not want to speak in or about such terms any longer; and we can no longer (claim to) speak only in such terms, at least not as solely philosophical terms. Philosophy, as we have seen, can never own "its own" terms absolutely. So, while one might want to, or for now must, rely on these terms, a given matrix that uses them may be quite exterior to philosophy and may be accompanied by a different closure or an ensemble of closures. Nor can one claim that even these terms and concepts themselves cannot be radically or—*at certain points and under certain conditions*—even fully decoupled from philosophy. As I just indicated, one cannot claim that they can be decoupled from philosophy always or forever; for they or anything else can be joined or rejoined with philosophy at any point. To claim that they can never be so decoupled, however, would be equally impossible without reinstating a globalizing, transcendental presence or trace—Hegelian, Heideggerian, or other. For one would, then, (re)establish an absolute trace of a given term, concept or conceptual cluster—either in the form of an absolutely or uniquely privileged concept or in the form of an economy, such as Hegelian *Geist*, that would control the retention, or suspension, and, thus, the history of all possible concepts. Such an economy, by definition restricted, would— or should—be prohibited under the constraints of iterability of all terms and concepts implied by Derrida's analysis. If it is not, one would, as I said, have further to refigure the Derridean economy itself.

Heidegger, as we have seen, speaks of a presence everywhere of Being or (which in the ends amounts to the same) of a still higher transcendental to which one cannot relate by means of a name or a concept, as even Being itself is placed under erasure. Derrida deconstructs the Heideggerian economy or economies of the transcendental signified (*Of Grammatology*, 19–20). He speaks of "the Heideggerian hope," defined as "the quest for the proper word and unique name" (*Margins*, 27; *Marges*, 29). By contrast, *différance* cannot be seen as a "proper word" or "unique name." While it is never one thing, however, not even one *différance*, and while it endlessly disseminates itself and never has one, single position, *différance* cannot invade, whether in an open or hidden way, all positions or control the dissemination of Derridean concepts themselves.

It is sometimes possible to transform or depart from philosophy radically while still using similar or identical terms, or even *some* of the same concepts. The qualification "some" is crucial, for it is only through other, exterior concepts or, in particular, neither word nor concepts—that philosophy can be exceeded (leaving aside for the moment the general impossibility of anything being the same once inserted into a different configuration). For, as we have seen, "a radical trembling [énbranlement]" of any kind—Nietzschean, Bohrian, Derridean or other—"can only come from the *outside*" (*Margins*, 134, *Marges*, 162). "Names" may overlap to a greater extent, as some of the same names displace philosophical concepts most radically, as in Nietzsche, Bohr, or Bataille. But there are other names, too, that can be set against philosophy and that function as *new* names, such as some of Derrida's names. The language of Bataille and certainly of Nietzsche is, often on purpose, anything but what philosophy would associate with its own. The anti-epistemological transformations considered by the present study may not quite have left philosophy behind; and philosophy, at its best, remains far superior to many, but not all, proposed alternatives. But these transformations alter the relation of theory to philosophy, and they may even transform the closure, or closures, of theory. We may still need to use the terminology and economy of closure at least for now (which is not to say that it is absolutely indispensable), and this economy is itself a part of the transformed theoretical closure.

What is at stake in the question of general economy may, then, differ so radically from the metaphysics it dislocates that the closure of theory may no longer be seen as the closure of philosophy (as the metaphysics of presence). Many of its constraints and (en)closures become instead general economic. We do share and inherit from metaphysics some of our language, which, as Derrida points out, always makes a reinstatement of metaphysics possible which requires an extraordinary theoretical rigor and a different (from metaphysics), more plural style of discourse in order to avoid such a reinstatement. But our language may also be sufficiently different from that of metaphysics and philosophy. There is no special metaphysical or philosophical language that is unconditionally different from so-called ordinary, nonphilosophical language. The concept of "ordinary language" is one of the most problematic ever introduced. Nor is there such a thing as an unconditionally nonphilosophical language, either. Much of language may overlap, and general-economic, anti-epistemological theories have not removed or unbound all "old" closures. These theories, however, have created, for better or worse—better for some people in some aspects, worse for others and in other aspects— a different theoretical closure, in part by transforming the economy or the *closure* of the very concept(s) of transformation and of the accompanying concepts, such as difference, alterity, and exteriority, as considered earlier.

The fact that these concepts, to the degree that they may be seen as concepts, still belong—but only in part and no longer properly, authentically [eigentlich]—to some older theories and closures, such as that of metaphysics, would not undermine my point here. Such historico-theoretical connections necessitate and enable a partial continuity with classical theories and closures. The economy here suggested is that of complementarization and transformation of and not, or not yet, of a full, or even a radical enough, departure from a preceding configuration and its closure, for example, as delineated by Derrida. As a result of this transformation, however, philosophy will no longer be able to enact or claim a closure as irreducible as it may be or may appear at the present. Under all conditions, a more plural and complementary economy of closure is necessary in order to understand both modern theory and the history of theoretical developments in various fields, which cannot be contained within a single theoretical closure.

Transformations of the closure of theory as the closure of metaphysics or philosophy lead to a different closure or set of closures and constraints, beginning with those of general economy and complementarity. General economic closure or closures constitute a much larger configuration, of course, which includes classical theories, but is not restricted to them. These closures indicate the horizon, or rather, the spectrum of possibilities, a kind of complementary spectrum with continuous and discontinuous counterparts, similar to the quantum spectra of modern physics. The closure(s) of that type cannot conform to an economy of horizon, particularly not to the Heideggerian or post-Heideggerian hermeneutical restricted economies of horizon, such as in Hans-Georg Gadamer. One must engage, complementarily, continuities and breaks, whether one proceeds by extending preceding "new"—now "old"—conceptions and chains, such as those of deconstruction, or by radically breaking with them by entering other chains, or creating and pursuing "new" continuities. Such "new" continuities are still continuities, of course, the chains and networks of historical and other connections.[3] Nor need one claim that such different continuities—those exterior to a given configuration or field—are fully, absolutely separated from a given chain or a network of chains. They can be exterior or independent enough to merit the name "new," even radically new, once they lead to a transformation of a given—"old"—configuration, field, or closure. The economy emerging as a result may be more radically new than what appears to be suggested by Derrida's *approach* (in either sense of the term), for this approach may, finally, be shifted more toward continuity than "rupture," especially if compared to Nietzsche's practice.

A break, even a radical break, already characterizes this landscape. It is a landscape of both continuity and rupture, of many continuities and breaks—a multiple, "quantum," landscape, inhabited by Sibyline strangeness. It may be, however, that our landscape demands a still more radical break from philosophy, or rather from the closure of philosophy and its proper names—from (and before) Socrates to (and beyond) Heidegger and Derrida. It may even demand a break from the radical break being considered at the moment—a break from all these proper names, such as Derrida and deconstruction, which owe and want to owe much to philosophy and its names, or Nietzsche, who owes less to them and seems to want to owe still less, if anything. "Nietzsche" is perhaps still the name of the most radical break from philosophy and its names. Will a more radical break simultaneously, complementarily, demand a more radical continuity with these names as well? Possibly. But if so, it would have to be a *different* continuity. One would need complementarily both a different continuity and a different rupture—a different difference. Different *différance?* Different *from différance?*

Perhaps the closure of philosophy no longer is or will be as powerful and pervasive as it has been hitherto, assuming that this change is desirable. For one can, of course, move in the other direction—closer to philosophy and its closure. This closure cannot be seen at any moment of history as omnipotent or omnipresent (or present), even in fields such as the social and human sciences or literary criticism and theory, where the influence of philosophy has been felt most, or within philosophy itself, which is always invaded by other forces and closures. These fields are invaded, from within and without, and taken over by forces and fields, such as the natural sciences, that philosophy could not foresee or master. Or rather, such radical transformations emerge from an interplay of networks inside and outside philosophy. They emerge as philosophy is invaded by other fields or, conversely, as it invades other fields, particularly, but not exclusively, by way of the closure of philosophy, if again there could be only one such closure to begin with. As I have argued here, there can never be *one* closure of anything; moreover at certain moments one cannot effectively relate these transformations and mutual invasions of different fields to the fields of philosophy. Such a, to use Derrida's term, structural possibility of exclusion may, however, at some point lead to the death of philosophy or of any given field. Whether it does or will do so cannot be determined in advance. But, by the same token, neither can the possibility be excluded in advance or once and for all. Hence one can speak of the structural possibility of death or exclusion, even though, conversely, anything—dead or alive, or functioning elsewhere—always has the structural possibility of return.

Once a global closure is "prohibited," one must produce an economy of the complementarization and transformation of closure. "Prohibit" must likewise be put in quotation marks. Instead at work is a theoretical constraint: once a given theory is in operation, certain things become theoretically impossible. Otherwise, how can one prohibit anything?

Prohibit Hegel from speaking of Absolute Knowledge? Heidegger—of Being? Derrida—of closure, or even *the* closure, of whatever it may be the closure of? If, however, "the efficacity of the thematics of *différance* may very well, indeed must, one day be superseded, lending itself *if not to its own replacement,* at least to enmeshing [enchaînement] itself in a chain that in truth it never will have governed" (*Margins,* 7; *Marges,* 7, emphasis added), would such be the case for Derrida with the closure of metaphysics as well, or the economy so designated?

My argument here is that we must radically pluralize or complementarize and allow for transformations of theoretical and, perhaps even, interpretive closures—such as the closure of presence, difference, and so forth—however stable and general such interpretive closures may be in many of their aspects, lending themselves more to being seen as more permanent and more universal (en)closures. One may not be able to claim, however, that even such interpretive closures would operate in this form or under these names always and everywhere, however irreducible they may seem at a given moment and within certain fields. Derrida's economy of presence, let alone the (general) economy of *différance,* is in fact already a product of many closures and transforms many closures, just as Bataille's, Heidegger's, Freud's, and Nietzsche's terms and concepts did previously. Theory transforms interpretation; and the radical difference and alterity discussed earlier may, and indeed must, force us to transform again or to abandon any of these rubrics. One cannot transform without (using the concepts of) difference and transformation, or so it seems; and we may one day no longer speak in these terms, even if we continue to "transform," or to do what we see and call "transform," or "do"— for now. For, along with and as a part of the thematics of *différance,* such terms, too, "may very well, indeed must, one day be superseded, lending themselves, *if not to their own replacement,* at least to enmeshing themselves in chains that in truth they never will have governed"—subsumed and transformed by, relative to them, nonstandard models and regimes. Otherwise a certain absolute—and thus metaphysical—(en)closure of (the economy of) difference and of closure itself would be inscribed. In order to avoid such a reinstatement, we must *transform* the economy of closure so as to allow for plurality and transformations of closures. The exploration of transformations of closure or of the complementary interaction and multiple parallel processing of different closures in a given case is itself potentially an important historico-theoretical investigation. A theoretical closure or configuration of closures is perhaps, in any given case and at any given moment, the most stable aspect of a theory. Hence it tends to be the most resistant to transformation while being at times in need of the most extensive transformation.

The present study has been shaped by, in this sense, complementary historico-theoretical landscapes as it conjoins quantum mechanical—Bohr's—and general economic—Nietzsche's, Bataille's, and Derrida's—anti-epistemologies. Complementarity offers a break—a break that must itself be placed within a complementary economy of continuities and ruptures—from philosophy (as the metaphysics of presence) and its closure, from which we are compelled to break radically, but to which we are sometimes not close enough to be able to do so. Under many conditions one must engage restricted economic texts—such as the text of philosophy—and their closure in order to approach—historically and theoretically—the complementary general economy at issue in this study. But, even when one must do so, one can do so only by means of parallel, or again complementary, processing—that is, by reading the text(s) of philosophy along with other texts, some of them under more pronounced although never fully decidable signatures, such as Nietzsche, Bohr, Bataille, and Derrida, and others textualized more implicitly and indirectly. Philosophy and its closure may of course in turn inhabit and inhibit such parallel or complementary planes. The topology of such engagements, like all complementary topologies, is, as we have seen, inextricably tangled; and the closure of philosophy invades and inhibits both parts of the necessarily double economy of transformations: on the one hand, a necessary continuity with one history or ensemble of histories, and on the other, a necessary break from another history or ensemble of histories. Continuities with and continuations of philosophy invade transformations, even as transformations in turn invade these continuities. Philosophy is an extraordinarily, and historically perhaps uniquely, capacious and massive force, which has enabled the power and extension of its closure, again arguably a historically unique theoretical closure of that type. And as a field it is, of course, much more capacious than any single philosopher's contribution can be.

Within the closure of philosophy, Derrida conceives of this very continuity as the closure of philosophy and its terms, concepts, strategies, and many other things that philosophy offers to us and imposes upon us. All these terms—history, continuity, transformation, break, or closure itself—do belong to this closure. But philosophy cannot quite own them, either, and they have been *transformed* a great deal inside and, or, as . . . (many other conjunctions are possible) outside philosophy along with the boundaries between—and within—the fields where these concepts function. But, then, how far does the closure of philosophy extend? How far, even if admittedly it does extend very far? One may or may not agree with Bohr's claim that "no man who is called a philosopher really understands what is meant by complementary descriptions." This claim, however, will, I think, stand insofar as one understands it as the claim that complementarity, as a general-economic matrix, cannot be controlled by restricted-economic regimes—the regimes of philosophy; nor perhaps even by the far more complex and extended regime of the closure of philosophy. However irreducible and radical may be the ruptures it can and sometimes must effect, complementarity is also massive interconnectivity. As such it entails a multiple interplay—multiple parallel processing—of models and regimes, standard and nonstandard, or models and nonmodels, regimes and nonregimes, closures and unclosures; or still other economies, names, unnameables, or that which can be neither named nor claimed to be unnameable.

NOTES

1 General Economy 1: Bataille

1 Among the many works containing important direct references, one can mention Bataille's brilliant early essay, "Materialism"; "The Critique of the Foundations of the Hegelian Dialectic"; *Inner Experience; Guilty;* and *On Nietzsche.*

2 Other fields may be similarly engaged, notably biology, which played a significant role in Bataille's writing. It may be suggested that "life" is very likely much more complex than any general economy available thus far would allow, even though general economies at issue here are sufficiently capacious and open-ended to allow one to relate to such complexities.

3 Bataille pursued the thematics of general economy and employed general economic practices throughout his life. The main text is *La Part maudite* (in *La Part maudite précédé de Le notion de dépense* and *Oeuvres Complètes* 8); *The Accursed Share*, 3 vols. *The Accursed Share* offers a broad politico-economic theory, deconstructing classical—restricted—political economies and translating them into general economy. However, *L'Expérience intérieure, Sur Nietzsche,* and *Le Coupable,* comprising *La somme athéologique, L'Erotisme,* and other essays on Hegel, Nietzsche, Marxism, and expenditure pursue some of the most profound and radical implications of these ideas.

4 The term "vagueness" partly follows John Bell. In commenting on Bohr in *Speakable and Unspeakable in Quantum Mechanics* (hereinafter *SUQM*), Bell says with disappointment that if "Bohr's intuition [is] right . . . fundamental physical theory would remain fundamentally vague" (155). The term "more-or-less-ness" follows Derrida's elaborations, offered with a different attitude, on dissemination in *Dissemination,* although, as shall be seen elsewhere Derrida, too, expresses reservations concerning indeterminacy (*Limited Inc,* 148–49).

5 As I have indicated, Bataille's work was addressed in one way or another by nearly all major contemporary figures, and the French literature on Bataille is extensive. The relevant studies in English include Denis Hollier, *Against Architecture: The Writings of Georges Bataille;* Julian Pefanis, *Heterology and the Postmodern: Bataille, Baudrillard, and Lyotard;* Michèle Richman, *Reading Georges Bataille: Beyond the Gift;* and Allan Stoekl, *Politics, Writing, Mutilation,* and *Agonies of the Intellectual: Commitment, Subjectivity and the Performative in the Twentieth-Century French Tradition.*

6 I have explored some of these implications in *Reconfigurations: Critical Theory and General Economy,* where I specifically consider the question of complementary discursive

practice or style in Nietzsche, Bataille, and Derrida; and, in the context of the question of history, in *In the Shadow of Hegel: Complementarity, History, and the Unconscious.*

7   See his discussion of Hegel in *The Economic and Philosophic Manuscripts of 1844.*

8   See Derrida's analysis of this economy in Kant in "Economimesis." I consider this issue in the context of Bataille and Derrida in *Reconfigurations* (101–3).

9   Bataille introduces "heterology" in his earlier works, "The Use Value of D. A. F. de Sade" and "The Psychological Structure of Fascism" (both in *Visions of Excess*). Heterology deals with radical difference, exteriority, and multiplicity, correlative to the irreducible loss in representation defining the field of general economy. Heterology is opposed by Bataille to homology, which stands more or less for all classical (restricted-economic) theoretical knowledge and practice, whose possibilities heterology exceeds. Heterology is in effect correlative to general economy, which Bataille develops later, and other anti-epistemological forms of writing introduced by Bataille, as considered earlier.

10   Derrida connects the 'remainder' and 'dissemination' from the outset of *Dissemination.* The economy of 'remainder' and 'iterability' are further developed in "Signature Event Context," "Limited inc" (*Limited Inc*) and "Living On: Border Lines."

11   I have considered this issue in *Reconfigurations* (25–29). More problematic—utopian—dimensions appear at times in Bataille's vision of the possibilities offered by the "practice" of expenditure, as in his introductory remarks to the second volume of *The Accursed Share (The Accursed Share 2 & 3,* 16–17), or toward the end of *The Theory of Religion.*

2   General Economy 2: Derrida

1   Throughout the present study the word *writing* is italicized, when it refers to '*writing*' in Derrida's sense.

2   On the field of writing as a refiguration of the field of language, see specifically *Of Grammatology* (8–9), although one can refer to numerous passages in Derrida.

3   This formulation from the original version of "Différance" is omitted in the version published in *Margins.*

4   Throughout this study, the term structure, or "as structure," is used, following Heidegger and Derrida, mostly in the sense of "built-in" efficacious dynamics, such as the "as-structure [*Als-Struktur*]" operator used by Heidegger throughout *Being and Time, différance* as structure, structural—irreducible—loss defined by general economy, and the like.

5   See specifically Derrida's analysis in the chapter "Of Grammatology as a Positive Science" (*Of Grammatology,* 74–93).

6   See especially "Différance" (*Margins,* 14) and *Positions* (43–44), but in relation to Hegel and others, particularly Heidegger, this *position* is taken by Derrida throughout.

7   Derrida's taking concepts under erasure—crossing them out without fully erasing them, or taking them into quotation marks—connotes the absence of an original presence (or original absence), to which classical concepts would refer or from which they would be derived. Derrida's erasure does not imply dispensing with classical concepts, including the concept of presence. It entails their reinscription and re-delimitation in a general economy. Derrida's erasure of concepts is different from

Heidegger's erasure, insofar as the latter still refer to the original presence, if hidden and unrepresentable.

8   The Copenhagen school, here, is obviously not Bohr's quantum mechanics but glossematics, the post-Saussurean linguistics of Hjelmslev, who was a contemporary of Bohr and who might have had connections to Harald Høffding's philosophy.

9   From this perspective, as shall be seen in the next chapter, John Honner's choice of the term "transcendental philosophy" in *The Description of Nature: Niels Bohr and the Philosophy of Quantum Physics* in relation to Bohr is ineffective, although Bohr is indeed very much concerned with various "conditions of the possibility of knowledge" in the field of physics. Analogously, Rodolphe Gasché's introduction, in *The Tain of the Mirror*, of the economy of the quasitranscendental and of the term itself into his interpretation of Derrida displaces Derrida, if not quite into, then too close to a transcendental register. Derrida, it is true, does use the term quasitranscendental on occasion, but quite differently—far less transcendentally and far less centrally— than Gasché. As shall be seen, a certain reinstatement of the metaphysical register in Derrida takes place through the economy of the closure of metaphysics; or, rather, this economy leads to the emergence of a register that rejoins Derrida's economy and classical philosophy.

10 See "The Will to Power as Knowledge" (*The Will to Power*, 261–331), although many Nietzsche's works can be cited.

11 As shall be seen in chapter 7, Derrida juxtaposes the undecidable determinacy of his economy to indeterminacy.

12 See, for example, Derrida's formulation in *Dissemination* (26; *La Dissemination*, 33). See also Barbara Johnson's footnote (*Dissemination*, 26 n. 26).

13 John Archibald Wheeler, whose views are often close to Bohr's, sees quantum physics as undermining the primacy of "consciousness" ("Law without Law," *Quantum Theory of Measurement*, 207; "Information, Physics, Quantum: The Search for Links," *Complexity, Entropy, and Physics of Information*, 15).

14 See, for example, remarks in the later "An Outline of Psycho-Analysis," *The Standard Edition*, 23, 159.

15 This lack of a recomprehending economy is one of the reasons why Marx's reversal of the Hegelian dialectic remains within the limits of restricted economy. Marx's reversal of Hegel's dialectic gives the latter a materialist instead of an idealist base, but by bypassing, just as Hegel does, the economy of loss, this reversal produces, or reproduces, metaphysics and Hegelianism as the metaphysical materialism or, one could say, the "idealism" of matter and of materialist history.

16 *Writing*-criticism as *writing*-reading, interacting with or complementarizing *writing*-theory, was explored in and by the practice of de Man's writing (in either sense), at times with some important differences from Derrida, for whom *writing*-reading is likewise a crucial economy. Derrida's reading of Mallarmé in fact thematizes it ("The Double Session," *Dissemination*, 223).

17 Cited by Friedrich Waismann (*Introduction to Mathematical Thinking*, 107).

18 The economy of "scandal" plays a key role in Derrida's analyses of Rousseau and Lévi-Strauss in *Of Grammatology* and "Structure, Sign, and Play" (*Writing and Difference*), as well as in his reading of Bataille in "From Restricted to General Economy."

3   From the Quantum Postulate to Anti-Epistemology to Complementarity

1   It may be appropriate to offer here a general bibliographical remark concerning literature on quantum mechanics and complementarity and related areas. The relevant literature—popular, semipopular, and technical—is immense, even leaving aside the literature, in turn massive, on developments during the last two decades. Bohr's own major work on the philosophy of complementarity is assembled in three volumes of essays: *Atomic Physics and Human Knowledge*, and *Atomic Theory and the Description of Nature*, vols. 1 and 2. These writings are reprinted as *The Philosophical Writings of Niels Bohr*, vols. 1–3 (hereinafter *PWNB*). There are numerous relevant articles, archival sources, and extensive correspondence, to which I shall refer when appropriate. They include, in particular, materials from the Niels Bohr Archive: Bohr's Manuscripts (NBA: BMSS) and Bohr's Scientific Correspondence (NBA: BSC); *Archive for the History of Quantum* (hereinafter *AHQP*), T. S. Kuhn et al., *Sources for History of Quantum Mechanics*. Much of this material has been published in *Niels Bohr: Collected Works*, 6 vols., ed. Léon Rosenfeld and Erik Rüdinger. See also the bibliography in *Niels Bohr: A Centenary Volume* (385–91), edited by Anthony P. French and P. J. Kennedy. Beyond the works by the founders of quantum mechanics—Einstein, Bohr, Born, Heisenberg, Pauli, and Dirac—including their correspondence, and some classical works such as Max Jammer's *The Philosophy of Quantum Mechanics* and *The Conceptual Development of Quantum Mechanics* and Bernard d'Espagnat's *Conceptual Foundations of Quantum Mechanics*, several recent books may be mentioned here, most of which contain extensive bibliographies. The most comprehensive recent studies of Bohr are Jan Faye, *Niels Bohr: His Heritage and Legacy: An Anti-Realist View of Quantum Mechanics;* Henry J. Folse, *The Philosophy of Niels Bohr;* John Honner, *The Description of Nature: Niels Bohr and the Philosophy of Quantun Physics;* and Dugald Murdoch, *Niels Bohr's Philosophy of Physics*. Roger Penrose's *The Emperor's New Mind: Concerning Computers, Minds, and the Laws of Physics* contains an interesting and useful discussion of mathematical logic, including Gödel's theorem, special and general relativity, and quantum physics. I find some of the philosophical positions of the book untenable, however, as well as unnecessary for many of its arguments. Richard P. Feynman's *The Character of Physical Law* (1965) retains its value. One can also mention his more recent *QED: The Strange Theory of Light and Matter*. For a more technical discussion, see three excellent studies by Abraham Pais, *"Subtle is the Lord"; Inward Bound;* and *Niels Bohr's Times, in Physics, Philosophy, and Polity*. I have also used some more specialized literature. I am particularly indebted to three collections, *Quantum Theory and Measurement* (hereinafter *QTM*), ed. John Archibald Wheeler and Wojciech H. Zurek; *Three Hundred Years of Gravitation*, ed. Stephen Hawking and Werner Israel; and *Complexity, Entropy and The Physics of Information*, ed. Wojciech H. Zurek.

2   Two interpretations of quantum mechanics, Heisenberg's matrix mechanics and Schrödinger's wave mechanics, were quickly found to be mathematically equivalent. Uncertainty relations are the consequence of both models, as was first shown by Schrödinger himself, who resisted Bohr's interpretation.

3   Some recent experimental considerations (not available to Bohr) suggest that the wave and particle aspects may not be distinguished as sharply as Bohr's definition of complementarity suggests. These considerations appears to lead to a more com-

plex complementary model—a mutual inhibition and a complementary asynthesis of the wave and the particle aspects—rather than to a replacement of complementarity with a classical synthesis of the wave and the particle pictures. See, in particular, William K. Wootters and Wojciech H. Zurek, "Complementarity in the Double-Slit Experiments: Quantum Nonseparability and a Quantitative Statement of Bohr's Principle" and Lawrence S. Bartell, "Complementarity in the Double-Slit Experiment: On Simple Realizable Systems for Observing Intermediate Particle-Wave Behavior" (both in *Quantum Theory and Measurement*). These works appear to support the suggestion just made. While giving the situation further complexity, they suggest the complementarity rather than unity of the wave and the particle representations. They also support the general economic nature of quantum efficacities. Thus Bartell writes: "Expectation values of V (wave) and Pa (particle) [in a double-slit experiment with slits A and B] cannot both be unity simultaneously; the sacrifice of knowledge of one for another is plain" (*QTM*, 456). This picture is that of indeterminacy in distribution of the wave and the particle representations. Wootters and Zurek's article concludes with an information-theoretical rendition of complementarity. For other connections to the information theory, see *Complexity, Entropy and the Physics of Information*, edited by Zurek.

4   See Faye (*Niels Bohr*, 143–45), Honner (*The Description of Nature*, 50–52), and Murdoch (*Niels Bohr's Philosophy*, 66–71).

5   This interpretation has by no means been a universally accepted one. Interpretations insisting on the physical significance of quantum waves have continued to be advanced, particularly in the wake of the hidden-variables interpretation, to be considered in chapter 6. Nor can one say that one cannot encounter challenges to the complementarity of the wave-particle juncture itself. The wave aspect and the particle aspect have been simultaneously assigned to a quantum object at any point. Either approach, or frequently a combination of both—the suspension of the complementary and realism of interpretation—belong to what can be seen as the metaphysics or the restricted economy of quantum meta-physics. Among recent attempts of that type see, for example, Henry Krips's *The Metaphysics of Quantum Theory* (1987), according to whose anti-complementary interpretation a particle is always "guided by a [wavelike] probability field. Thus its wave and particles aspects are always co-present" (3). Krips's interpretation retains much of a customary, and, from the present perspective, problematic, metaphysical package. His critical claims concerning Bohr's interpretation are difficult to accept, particularly his association of Bohr with transcendental idealism (127). Franco Selleri's interpretation in *Quantum Paradoxes and Physical Reality* (73–180), arguing for the synthesis of the wave and particle aspects of quantum objects, appears to be even more problematic both in its metaphysics and in its claims concerning Bohr's interpretation. The results of Wootters and Zurek, and Bartell, certainly need a much more careful treatment than Selleri's comments allow for (102).

6   Different particles or wave-particles—such as the electron and the photon—do have different roles in physical theory. These roles determine the different relative significance of their wave and particle aspects, correspondingly reflected in their classical representations. Bohr's occasional emphasis on the more particle-like character of the electron, or the more radiation-like character of light, reflects this relative dif-

ference, rather than a fundamental preference, as Léon Rosenfeld appears to suggest ("The Wave-Particle Dilemma," *The Physicist's Conception of Nature*, 252).

7   I suggest here, first, that one should execute all aspects of the anti-epistemological protocol of Bohr's quantum mechanical complementarity in other fields. Second, I refer to Jacques Lacan's and, then, Derrida's deconstruction of classical philosophy and linguistics, which always privilege the signified over the signifier, particularly written signifier—the letter—and meaning or content over form.

8   Bohm's interpretation of complementarity is not sufficiently radical in this sense and is, in effect, Hegelian or Parmenidean, insofar as Bohm derives from quantum conditions "the indivisible unity of the world" (161–62). His hidden variables interpretation makes this metaphysics even more pronounced.

9   While the point is suggested or implied by most recent full-scale analyses of Bohr, Folse particularly stresses it (*The Philosophy of Niels Bohr*, 9–17).

10 I have considered this genealogy in *In the Shadow of Hegel* (54–93). Many studies cited here consider the philosophical connections just indicated and related links. While Hegel is conspicuous by his absence in most accounts of the philosophical genesis of quantum mechanics, he may also be seen as one of the sources of complementarity, particularly insofar as the interaction of continuity and discontinuity is concerned, which is a central issue for Høffding, whose philosophy Bohr perhaps knew best. See, however, Franco Selleri's comment, in the context of Kierkegaard and Høffding, on the anti-Hegelian—anti-synthesis—character of Bohr's complementarity (*Quantum Paradoxes and Quantum Reality*, 347–48). The interpretation itself of quantum mechanics advocated by Selleri is opposed to complementarity and Bohr, whom Selleri does not read carefully, however. John Honner points out that "complementarity is not to be confused with dialectic" (*The Description of Nature*, 60).

11 Bohr's assessment is supported by Einstein himself in his "Reply to Criticism" (*Albert Einstein: Philosopher-Scientist*, 674). Einstein's qualifications concerning the difference between his and Kant's attitude are important, but they do not substantially change either Bohr's assessment or my point here.

12 See "Verificationism and Transcendental Argument" and "Transcendental Argument, Self-Reference, and Pragmatism." For his most recent comments on the issue, see "Is Derrida a Transcendental Philosopher?" (in *Derrida: A Critical Reader*). I find more problematic Rorty's antitheoretical agenda in his more recent works, including the latter essay, which, however, offers some pertinent criticism of transcendental argument and of Rodolphe Gasché's reading of Derrida in *The Tain of the Mirror*.

13 Bohr's views undermine much in classical philosophy, history, and sociology of science. The power and potential of Bohr's ideas in this respect determine their value for the present analysis. Conversely, however, the same power and potential tend to provoke a search, in my view, mostly unsuccessful, for classical alternatives on the part of the philosophers and historians of science, or physicists themselves, beginning with Einstein. Paul Feyerabend and to a more limited extent Thomas S. Kuhn, for both of whom Bohr's works and thinking have particular importance, are exceptions, as are a number of other recent authors proceeding along these lines—among others, Barry Barnes, David Bloor, H. M. Collins, Ian Hacking, Bruno Latour, Gonzalo Munévar, and Andrew Pickering. The modern or postmodern history and sociology of science

has been a rich and fast-developing field since the nineteen sixties. It has generated many ideas, strategies, and projects relevant and often parallel to the main concerns of this study. For the current state of debate in the field, see *Science as Practice and Culture*, edited by Andrew Pickering.

14 Thus, for example, Richard Healey, in his *The Philosophy of Quantum Mechanics: An Interactive Interpretation*, in offering a critique and, in what he calls "interactive interpretation," an alternative to the Copenhagen interpretation, among others, treats a "weak" and a "strong" version of it. While both are defined in formal terms (13–14) and considered throughout the book in accordance with this definition, it is not clear who exactly, for example, among the founders of quantum mechanics, holds specifically either the weak or the strong version. With the exception of references to related mathematical considerations by John von Neumann, Henry Margenau, and Eugene P. Wigner, the book offers no real consideration of any of the specific texts or specific arguments advanced by Bohr or others who are usually associated with the Copenhagen interpretation. The latter is simply referred to as a prevalent interpretation. One can find various features of each version in different authors, specifically in Bohr, but neither version quite corresponds to Bohr's views or those of other major figures. Certainly, many of the claims Healey makes against the Copenhagen interpretation do not correspond to anything in Bohr's views (17–19). The technical discussion in the book would not affect my point here. Many of Healey's formal derivations are close to the major formal features of Bohr's interpretation, by virtue of their proximities to various shared features of the Copenhagen interpretation as defined by Healey (see in particular the discussion on pp. 184–205). Many extraphysical claims made by the book are not supported by its argument, whose metaphysical claims and agendas are problematic from the present position, specifically if compared with Bohr's (see pp. 17–19). Similar criticisms can be made concerning R. I. G. Hughes's *The Structure and Interpretation of Quantum Mechanics*. I cannot address here the question of the mathematical formalism of quantum mechanics, extensively considered by Hughes. Whatever are the relative merits or problems of this part of Hughes's analysis (and it has, I think, its share of both), it would not mitigate the problematic interpretive and philosophical claims of the book, particularly concerning the Copenhagen interpretation.

15 For James's significance in Bohr, see Folse (*The Philosophy of Niels Bohr*, 49–51, 180–81) and Faye (*Niels Bohr*, 32–35). Murdoch finds what he calls "Bohr's pragmatist theory of meaning . . . untenable" (*Niels Bohr's Philosophy*, 244), although on rather curious—and, I am tempted to say, untenable—grounds of "even better confirmed theories than those of physics, viz. our common-sense view of the world" (242).

16 Heisenberg commented extensively on them in his many philosophical and autobiographical writings, such as *Across the Frontiers, Physics and Philosophy; Physics and Beyond;* and *Philosophical Problems of Quantum Physics*.

17 The traffic and proximities at issue have generated multiple responses, including the field of literary and critical theory, and specifically in the context of Derrida's discourse. Thus, in her discussion of quantum mechanics and deconstruction in "Quantum Physics/Postmodern Metaphysics: The Nature of Jacques Derrida," Cristine Froula sees the proximity at issue as a part of the "crisis" of, jointly, representation and theoretical thinking. I find Froula's treatment of both quantum physics and

"postmodern metaphysics" problematic, missing or displacing most of their crucial proximities and their metaphorical and conceptual import. On many occasions Froula attributes to Derrida claims and positions that are explicitly argued against by Derrida; and Froula's rendition of Derrida's matrix is often, at best, a misunderstanding.

Another recent study, Alexander Argyros's *A Blessed Rage for Order: Deconstruction, Evolution, and Chaos* appears to be equally problematic with respect to both deconstruction and quantum physics. Argyros's discussion of many scientific theories he considers are often unrigorous and oversimplified, even within the limits of an account for nonspecialists. His argument concerning (actually against) Derrida is, again, at best a misunderstanding. It is, in my view, unsustainable on just about all counts, missing most of Derrida's key points, whether at issue are conceptual and political dimensions of his work (or the works of other poststructuralist authors) or the connections between this work and science, including chaos theory.

Nor are the anti-epistemological implications of quantum mechanics derived in Katherine N. Hayles's *The Cosmic Web: Scientific Models and Literary Strategies in the 20th Century*, where she discusses quantum mechanics, relativity, and modern mathematics; this study by Hayles, like her *Chaos Bound: Orderly Disorder in Contemporary Literature and Science*, is superior to either Froula's or Argyros's treatments. Hayles correctly stresses the difference between Bohr's and Heisenberg's interpretations and indicates some suggestive links in her summary of these developments (31–62). Throughout the book, however, her analysis remains within classical limits. As in *Chaos Bound*, this approach may be cogent for the literary works she considers, but it bypasses the more radical theoretical and metaphoric implications of modern science. *Chaos Bound* offers suggestive connections with and parallels to, specifically, deconstruction. As intimated by Hayles's title ("bound") and subtitle ("*orderly* disorder"), her position in *Chaos Bound* is shifted toward the metaphorics—and, I would argue, the metaphysics—of order. This shift is cogent insofar as one uses chaos theory or more recently complexity theory—both of which may in fact be seen as order theories or *order* in chaos theories—as metaphoric models, in contrast to what I assemble here under the rubric of anti-epistemology, more of a *chaos* in order theory.

18   In spite of some general problems, Heidegger offers an effective analysis of the issue. The major point is relating the *experimental* and *mathematical* character of modern science, rather than stressing only the mathematical one, decisive as the latter is. Husserl's analysis of Galileo and of the "mathematization of nature" in *The Crisis of European Sciences and Transcendental Phenomenology* is a crucial frame of reference in this context. The fundamental connections between mathematical and physical thinking have been stressed by Gaston Bachelard. See *The New Scientific Spirit*, 55–60. Bachelard effectively uses scientific and specifically quantum mechanical metaphors, such an Pauli's exclusion principle. See also Samuel Weber's engaging discussion in *Institution and Interpretation*, ix–xv. The question of experimental determination of physics and other exact sciences would require a separate study even in Bohr's case alone. In the wake of Kuhn and Feyerabend, this question has been a subject of many productive explorations in science studies. The works of, among other, Bruno Latour, Ian Hacking, and Andrew Pickering can be mentioned here. The question is addressed by most essays in *Science as Practice and Culture* (1992).

19   See Pais (*"Subtle is the Lord,"* 14).

20 Derrida comments on Galileo's passage just cited, by way of Ernst Robert Curtius, in *Of Grammatology* (16).
21 Heisenberg offers only general remarks here, rather than a full analysis. Heisenberg's essay was first given in 1964 in Athens. The essay has a Heideggerian ring to some of its elaborations and its references to the pre-Socratics and Plato, specifically in considering the question of language. Both Heisenberg here (119) and Heidegger in *What is a Thing?* (74), again in the context of mathematics, recount the *same* anecdote of a Sophist's encounter with Socrates always saying the same (thing) about the same (thing). Heisenberg, whose father was a Greek scholar, did study Plato's dialogues. Some of the references were prompted by the occasion: the essay was first delivered "on the hill of Pnyx, opposite the Acropolis in Athens" (*Across the Frontiers*, 104)—a very Heideggerian setting.
22 I allude to Husserl's title and analysis in *Formal and Transcendental Logic*. The formality of *formal* logic is a complex issue. As I have indicated, it is possible that only mathematical logic can be meaningfully seen as formal, even though in view of Gödel's theorem, it cannot be claimed to be complete, once it is rich enough to contain arithmetic.
    One could leave aside here, more or less, trivial claims to the effect that since, say, deconstruction uses logic—or produces true or meaningful statements, relies on classical modes of understanding in its functioning, and so forth—its arguments against logic or meaning must be seen as contradictory, were it not for the fact (and I do mean the *fact*, the *true* fact) that such attempts at refuting deconstruction or other anti-epistemological approaches at the level of disciplinary discourse continue to be made. These attempts ignore that at stake in anti-epistemological arguments are the limits of logic or other discursive and disciplinary boundaries. These argument are concerned with both a problematization of classical limits and the possibility and necessity of a redelimited functioning of classical structures of argument and discourse. One cannot therefore operate as if one were still within these limits without in any way problematizing them. For recent examples of that type in the field of critical theory, see, for example, John Ellis, *Against Deconstruction*, Joseph Claude Evans, *Strategies of Deconstruction: Derrida and the Myth of Voice*, or again Argyros's *A Blessed Rage for Order*. Along with the anti-epistemological redelimitations at issue here, such attempts also tend to forget some crucial classical or logical aspects of anti-epistemological arguments. The latter follow classical assumptions and arguments to their limits in order to derive their logical consequences, which lead to contradictions from within the classical theories themselves. See Feyerabend's witty discussion in "A Guide to the Perplexed" (*Science in a Free Society*, 156–63). In this respect, anti-epistemological arguments are no different from many classical arguments of that type, although—which is crucial—anti-epistemological theories themselves are not constrained (or are not constrained in the same way) by the *classical* principles and limits that they problematize. That is not to say that anti-epistemologies are not constrained by anything—quite the contrary; the very limitations upon the usage of classical theories is one class of such constraints. But there are many others. Multiplicity, too, may be constraining at times.

4 The Age of Quantum Mechanical Reproduction

1   See Wheeler's "Beyond the Black Hole" (*Some Strangeness in the Proportion*, 341).

2   These phenomena are far from accidental to the cultural or scientific framing of quantum theory, or postmodernism, richly supplemented (also in Derrida's sense) by photographs. Cf. Derrida's comments on photographs of Freud and Heidegger in *The Post Card*, 189–91.

3   This trace-supplementary economy—"photonomy"—becomes vastly more complicated in view of computerization and other modern and postmodern data production technologies. These complications and their implications for the practice of science have been explored in recent work in science studies. See specifically, Peter Galison, *How Experiments End*, and Ian Hacking, "The Self-Vindication of the Laboratory Science" (*Science as Practice and Culture*, 48–50). The general (in either sense) trace-supplementary economy and Derrida's *writing* offer an extremely effective "logic" for such an analysis, which can be productively utilized in science studies. Both studies just cited contain certain residual metaphysics, which could be avoided by exploring the strange structure and applying the strange logic of the supplement. Derrida's economy of *writing* must, let me note, be distinguished from that of inscription in Bruno Latour's works, for example, in chapter 6 of *Science in Action*. Latour's criticism of Derrida in "The Politics of Explanation: An Alternative" does not quite address key aspects of Derrida's thinking (*Knowledge and Reflexivity*, 166–69).

4   "The Work of Art in the Age of Mechanical Reproduction" (in *Illuminations*). Benjamin actually speaks of technical [technisch] reproduction.

5   "The question concerning technology" is featured prominently in recent discussion, often in the context of Heidegger and related poststructuralist developments, specifically Derrida and deconstruction. Relevant works would be too numerous to cite here. Derrida himself, as I said, addresses this thematics throughout his works.

6   For Bohr's description see *PWNB* 2:41–47. Feynman's *The Character of Physical Law* (127–48) and *QED* (76–83) and Penrose's *The Emperor's New Mind* (127–48) offer excellent discussions.

7   To simplify the reference, this and the following citations follow "Law without Law" published in *Quantum Theory and Measurement* (hereinafter *QTM*), the combined version of several articles and lectures by Wheeler (all written around 1980). For the references, see *Quantum Theory and Measurement*. See also his "World as System Self-Synthesized by Quantum Networking" and "Information, Physics, and Quantum: The Search for Links."

8   The nuances suggested by Wootters and Zurek and by Bartell in articles cited earlier, and more recent works, would give the situation further complexity, but will not change the main point.

9   See the articles assembled in *Quantum Theory and Measurement*. See also Bruce R. Wheaton, *The Tiger and the Shark: Experimental Roots of Wave Particle Dualism*.

10 The whole chapter (225–301) offers an excellent account in spite of its—in my view, unnecessary—metaphysical claims.

11 From that perspective, Murdoch's claim that for Bohr "successful observation or measurement reveals the objective, *pre-existing* value of an observable" (*Niels Bohr's*

Philosophy, 107), or a similar suggestion by d'Espagnat (*Conceptual Foundations*, 95), becomes particularly problematic.

12   For the discussion of actual experiments confirming the delayed choice data, see P. J. Kennedy's "Delayed-Choice Experiments" (in *Niels Bohr*, edited by A. P. French and P. J. Kennedy) and Abner Shimony's "The Reality of the Quantum World." Shimony's own views in this article and elsewhere, including his commentaries on the Bohr-Einstein debate, would have to be seen as metaphysical rather than anti-epistemological from the present perspective. Thus, Shimony's influential early article "Role of the Observer in Quantum Theory" suggests what may be seen as a deferred intrinsic properties interpretation or a deferred hidden variables interpretation—a subtle version of the Einsteinian or Bohmian position (772). It is, however, well short of Bohr's interpretation, which Shimony finds (given his views, predictably) philosophically deficient.

13   On some of these issues, in addition to Bataille's many passages and Derrida's discussion in "From Restricted to General Economy," see Derrida's "How to Avoid Speaking: Denials" (*Derrida and Negative Theology*). See also his comments on negative theology in "Différance" (*Margins*, 6–7).

14   On mysticism in Bohr, see Honner's discussion (*The Description of Nature*, 176–93). Honner rightly warns against confusing Bohr's view with naive forms of mysticism or, conversely, rationalism. He shows that, like many other polar opposites, both terms are used by Bohr in order to indicate the complexity of both quantum mechanics and theoretical thinking itself. Honner also suggests interesting connections to early Wittgenstein (189–90). His own analysis remains within the ontotheological and, at certain points, theological register.

15   Selleri's reading is particularly inattentive to Wheeler's qualifying formulations just discussed (*Quantum Paradoxes and Quantum Reality*, 114–18).

16   The reference is to Abner Shimony's article "Role of the Observer in Quantum Theory" cited earlier.

17   See also Murdoch (*Niels Bohr's Philosophy*, 96–97).

18   See Murdoch (*Niels Bohr's Philosophy*, 126–28). Von Neumann reaches his conclusion by analyzing the strict mathematical formalism of quantum mechanics. Brain or brain/mind itself may need to be considered as a quantum system, which is Penrose's main point in *The Emperor's New Mind*, made in the context of artificial intelligence (374–449).

19   Murdoch speaks at one point of Bohr's views as empirical realism, in opposition to radical empiricism (*Niels Bohr's Philosophy*, 210–13). While some of his qualifications presented under this rubric are well taken, I do not think that the rubric itself is effective; for it, too, prevents one from deriving the radical consequences of Bohr's ideas. If one wants to speak in terms of "isms," one might, as Pais does, speak of "complementarism," although one might be reluctant to speak in terms of any "ism." Feyerabend's "epistemological dadaism" is a fine description. Dada is an important historical connection to Bataille, or Derrida. One would have to radicalize further Feyerabend's framework. Feyerabend's views and agenda are not free from theoretical problems that complementarity and general economy address; these problems emerge, for example, in his utopian vision of the so-called "free society." In a way,

while influenced by Bohr's ideas and practice, Feyerabend has missed an opportunity to fully apply them to an analysis of the history, sociology, and politics of science, and its relation to society.

20   NBA: BSC, letter to Max Born, 2 March 1953, cited by Folse (*Philosophy of Niels Bohr*, 248). As we have seen, Folse himself claims, problematically, that Bohr's view entails the concept of the "*reality* of the system considered as an object existing independently of observational interactions" (151).

5   Complementarities, Correspondences, Asyntheses

1   Cited by Murdoch, who considered Bohr's sense of "the failure of spatio-temporal pictures" in detail (*Niels Bohr'r Philosophy*, 29–33).

2   Cited by Murdoch (*Niels Bohr's Philosophy*, 69). Bohr discusses these questions extensively in "The Quantum Postulate and the Recent Developments of Atomic Theory" (in *PWNB* 1). Bohr's point has a more general import against mathematical realism, or, which often amounts to the same, mathematical idealism.

3   Høffding placed the relationships between continuity and discontinuity at the centers of both his own philosophical system and his understanding of the history of philosophy. See his comment in *The Problems of Philosophy*, 8. See also Murdoch's comments (*Niels Bohr's Philosophy*, 72, 226) and Faye's discussion throughout Part I of his *Niels Bohr*. Høffding's view is understandable. The relationships between continuity and discontinuity has had a paramount significance in the history of philosophy, mathematics, and physics alike. In all of these aspects—philosophical, mathematical, and physical—this problematics is central for both Kant and Hegel (particularly in the first *Logic*), as it is for Husserl, Heidegger, and Derrida. It has been equally crucial for Bataille, particularly in *Erotism* and *The Theory of Religion*. This history is reflected in the mathematical and conceptual representations of Planck's law, dividing or complementarizing the black body radiation into its continuous and discontinuous parts, eventually leading to the wave-particle complementarity. It would not be possible here to explore the significance of this problematics in the history of mathematics and in the debate about the foundations of mathematics: the relationships between and the relative primacy of two respective idealizations—the concept of number and the continuous concepts of geometry, or (the conditions of) their possibility to begin with; the relative roles these idealizations play in different approaches to the foundation of mathematics—formalism, logicism, intuitionism, constructivism, or different forms of mathematical realism or platonism; the question of mathematical finitude and infinity; and so forth.

4   See Pais's discussion (*Inward Bound*, 195–96).

5   NBA: BSC, letter to C. G. Darwin, 24 November 1926. See the discussions in Folse (*The Philosophy of Niels Bohr*, 56–103) and Murdoch (*Niels Bohr's Philosophy*, 44–46).

6   Cited by Pais, who comments that Born thereby "beautifully expressed the essence of wave [quantum] mechanics" (*Inward Bound*, 258).

7   Nietzsche explores these themes throughout his writing. I have considered these issues in detail in *Reconfigurations*.

8   Beyond connections to Bataille and Hegel (who, according to Bataille, made himself blind to chance) in "From Restricted to General Economy" and *Glas*, perhaps the

most pertinent works are "My Chances" and *The Post Card,* particularly "To Speculate—On 'Freud'." These works also engage important Nietzschean and Lacanian trajectories. Derrida's critique of Lacan in "Le facteur de la vérité" is included in *The Post Card.* Lacan's discussions of chance in "The Eye and the Gaze" (in *Four Fundamental Concepts of Psycho-Analysis*) may be an important, if implicit, reference for Derrida and are pertinent in the present context. Lacan suggests a fundamentally complementary economy of chance and necessity. In "To Speculate—on 'Freud'," Derrida also mentions, very briefly, some connections to "a 'modern' problematic of biology, genetics, epistemology, or the history of life science (reading of Jacob, Canguilhem, etc.)," explored in his unpublished seminar on "life-death [la vie la mort]" (*The Post Card,* 259 n. 1). This is an extremely suggestive line of inquiry, whether in relation to the question of chance (where one can also mention Jacques Monod's *Chance and Necessity*), to Derrida and deconstruction, Nietzsche, Bataille (particularly in *Erotism*), or to anti-epistemological metaphorical and conceptual economies in general. One can also refer to the work of Humberto Maturana and Francisco J. Varela, which recently suggests some connection to Derridean problematics. See their *Autopoiesis and Cognition: The Realization of the Living; Understanding Origins: Contemporary Views in the Origin of Life, Mind, and Society,* edited by Varela and Jean-Pierre Dupuy; Francisco J. Varela, *Principles of Biological Autonomy* and *The Tree of Knowledge: The Biological Roots of Human Understanding;* and *The Embodied Mind: Cognitive Science and Human Experience,* ed. Francisco J. Varela, Evan Thompson, and Eleanor Rosch. For connections of their work to critical theory, see Barbara H. Smith, *Contingencies of Value* (95, 148) and "Belief and Resistance: A Symmetrical Account."

9   Thus, Lyotard in his analysis of "the postmodern condition" misses the complementarity of legitimation, which—whether it is modern, postmodern, premodern, or other—always proceeds by way of the interplay of chance and necessity, continuity and discontinuity, locality and globalization, logic and paralogy, and so forth. This lack of complementarization is a problem both of his own theoretical economy and his analysis of the legitimation of modern science which continues to depend as much on "logical" as on "paralogical" legitimation (*The Postmodern Condition,* 53–61). The complementary distributions may, of course, vary, establishing the differences among different theoretical, historical, and political conditions. The role of paralogical and other "extra-scientific" local determinations, or legitimations, is indeed irreducible. The very term "extra-scientific" is no longer applicable under these condition. What is classically perceived as exterior to science is irreducible in its practice, as has been shown by Feyerabend, who is one of Lyotard's principal references, and other recent authors. The power of nonparalogical, and specifically logical or methodological, determinations in the practice science is, however, equally irreducible, as Feyerabend also argues, specifically in countering his critics in *Science in a Free Society.*

10 While Dirac's preeminence in the development of these ideas is unquestionable, the preceding work on quantum statistics by Satendra Nath Bose and Einstein himself made a decisive contribution.

11 There are "less rich" systems to which Gödel's results do not apply. Gödel in fact demonstrated the completeness of some among such logical systems in his dissertation in 1929, before, or perhaps in the process of, his discovery of the incompleteness of arithmetic in 1930.

12 The question of the consistency of quantum mechanics and Bohr's interpretation is often discussed, for example, by both Murdoch (*Niels Bohr's Philosophy*, 61–66) and Folse (*The Philosophy of Niels Bohr*, 78–90). Neither relates the issue to the possible influence of Gödel's theorem. As I have indicated, it could have been important for Bohr in that it redefined the conditions of the possibility of the consistency and completeness of all mathematical knowledge. These questions, moreover, were a major part of the debate concerning the foundation of mathematics for about half a century before the discovery of quantum mechanics, beginning with the works of, among others, Frege, Dedekind, Georg Cantor, Russell, and David Hilbert. Bohr must have been familiar with these issues, given their prominence at the time. There are additional historical and biographical factors to support this claim. Bohr's brother, Harald, with whom Bohr had intense intellectual interactions throughout his life, was a very prominent mathematician. His dissertation was on Riemann, whose ideas influenced Bohr's early ideas in psychological epistemology, which anticipate complementarity. Harald Bohr spent some time at Göttingen, where he encountered David Hilbert. Hilbert, during his remarkable career, made momentous contributions in all three fields—general relativity (where he was a codiscoverer of Einstein's final equations), quantum mechanics (whose mathematical formalism is based on Hilbert spaces), and mathematical logic—along with other key areas of mathematics. Gödel's major findings were in response to the outstanding problems of mathematical logic as formulated by Hilbert in 1928. Gödel, astonishingly, answered all of them within two years, by the time he was twenty-four.

13 On the correspondence principle, see Faye (*Niels Bohr*, 113–19) and Honner (*The Description of Nature*, 27–28, 35, 60–65).

14 I refer to Lacan's seminar on Poe's "The Purloined Letter" and Derrida's reading of Lacan's analysis of the story in "Le facteur de la vérité" (in *The Post Card*).

15 See Pais, *Inward Bound*, 247–48.

16 It is a major point of *The New Scientific Spirit*.

17 The point has been discussed by most recent studies of Bohr cited here, although from a different perspective than the one developed here. Faye, in particular, stresses the significance of this problematic for Bohr (*Niels Bohr*, 132–46).

18 Jean-Baptiste Perrin, *Les Atomes (Atoms)*. Lyotard, who correctly perceives a broad significance of the point at issue here, cites Perrin's work (*The Postmodern Condition*, 55–57).

19 Otherwise, certain processes, such as the unification of weak and electromagnetic interactions in the so-called standard model (the currently accepted understanding of subnuclear physics), could not be explained. The literature on the last two decades of extraordinary developments in these areas needs a long bibliography in its own right. Several works cited earlier, such as Pais's *Inward Bound* and Penrose's *The Emperor's New Mind*, contain excellent accounts of these developments. For a popular account see, for example, Robert P. Crease and Charles C. Mann, *The Second Creation: Makers of the Revolution in Twentieth-Century Physics* (66–71). Dozens of new studies have appeared since; the update would have to be continuous.

20 One of the best-known manifestations of this double constraint is the paradox of Schrödinger's cat, described in most accounts of quantum mechanics. The following account follows, with minor modifications, Honner's description (*The Description of*

Nature, 152). According to Schrödinger's thought experiment, a cat is placed in a steel box containing a radioactive source, a counter, and a kind of electric chair arrangement for the cat. There is always a 50 percent chance that the radioactive source will disintegrate, allowing the counter to register an emission and trigger an electric signal that kills the cat. While the box remains closed, we do not know whether the cat is alive or dead, and the box can be kept closed for a while. According to the quantum formalism for this system, opening the box puts it into either "cat is alive" or "cat is dead" state. Yet, the cat is going to be dead or alive all this time, whether or not we open the box. One can argue, therefore, that there are real properties of the system independent of the observation. In Bohr's view, the cat itself is the macroscopic observer, and what is sometimes called the reduction of the wave packet—a shift from a quantum to a classical, observable, object—takes place the moment that the cat feels the electric jolt, assuming an emission occurs. The whole so-called paradox is based on a form of physical realism defined by a correspondence between theoretical formalism and physical object, which would be seen by Bohr as incompatible with quantum mechanical conditions. Bohr did not consider Schrödinger's paradox as significant. The paradox does appear to illustrate the fact, at issue here, that macroscopic systems may need to be treated classically, rather than quantum-mechanically.

21 Pais, in *"Subtle is the Lord,"* sees this shift, around the time of general relativity, as a major transformation of Einstein's philosophy of physics (460–69).

22 In his *Einstein versus Bohr,* Mendel Sachs characterizes Einstein's vision as abstract realism—a kind of fusion of Platonism and mathematical realism. Strangely, particularly given the book's subject (and its very title), Sachs barely addresses Bohr's overall views and, with few exceptions (141–43), even his arguments against Einstein. His treatment of complementarity is rather coarse, even in a popular exposition, as he often collates different positions without careful discrimination. Bohr's view would not survive the kind of gloss Sachs gives it. See, for example, his comments on p. 239.

23 Cited by Pais, *Inward Bound*, 244.

24 Conceptually, this is a well-known problem of Newtonian theory, from Berkeley on, as can be seen in Alexandre Koyré's "The Significance of the Newtonian Synthesis," in his *Newtonian Studies*. To a degree complementarity resolves it. In his essay on Newton, "Newton, Quantum Theory and Reality" (in *Three Hundred Years of Gravitation*), Penrose suggests that Newton's corpuscular theory of light is an intimation of complementarity. Penrose offers an intriguing analysis, and the issue certainly merits a separate study, extending Koyré's inquiry. His analysis serves Penrose to reaffirm his position concerning the objectivity of the state vector and thus of the mathematical representation of the quantum configuration. Penrose states explicitly: "I am expressing a point of view which, *for some reason,* is not often maintained" (29). The reasons are powerful. Certainly Bohr and others have offered their *reasons,* which Penrose does not consider here or in the subsequent *The Emperor's New Mind.*

25 In all of these cases, we deal with complex reasoning and positions that should not be oversimplified. It should also be stressed that in most cases the claims at issue proceed by way of expressing a hope that a physics eventually will be found that will justify a given metaphysics. Quantum physics is by no means a finished theory or one free of problems. The main issue here may well be to what extent future theories will retain the major constituents of quantum mechanics, such as uncertainty relations.

286 Notes to Chapter Five

26 See also his comments on pp. 118–26 and 144.

27 As I indicated earlier, the so-called mathematical realism is never purely mathematical. First, any mathematical realism is always grounded in metaphysics, by virtue of being realism. Second, Einstein, Heisenberg, and other major figures involved understood this relationship between mathematics and philosophy, although mostly within classical limits. Bohr is a unique case in this respect: he profoundly understood the constraints that quantum physics imposes not only on physics itself but also on interpretive and theoretical processes.

28 Heidegger's work and later that of post-Heideggerian Husserl, especially "The Origin of Geometry," remain key contributions, particularly relevant in the context of Einstein's geometrization of physics; and in both cases Hegel's influence was decisive. The question of Husserl's phenomenology and mathematical realism has a great historical relevance in this context, but it cannot be considered here.

29 See Honner's discussion (*The Description of Nature*, 161–65), although Honner again displaces Bohr toward the classical register.

30 *Hungarian Academy of Science, Report KFK-62, 1977*, quoted by Pais (*Inward Bound*, 255).

31 Cited in Pais, *Inward Bound*, 361.

32 That is not to dismiss logic, of course, specifically mathematical logic, all undecidables notwithstanding, since it works—finally, against the logic of philosophy. Nor, as I have pointed out, can the difference between mathematical and philosophical—formal or transcendental—logic be maintained in the way that philosophy wants and claims to maintain it.

33 See also his comments to that effect throughout *QED*.

34 Cited in Pais, *Inward Bound*, 256.

35 This is not meant, of course, fully to explain Einstein's resistance, or Bohr's or Born's acceptance of quantum mechanics, both of them being scientists of Einstein's generation as opposed to the younger creators of quantum mechanics, such as Heisenberg, Pauli, Dirac, or Schrödinger. The meta-configuration itself—continuum as continuity—is interesting, however, for one thing, because it connotes a history whose scope far exceeds Einstein's case. It implies the entire history of Western philosophy—"the continuum of continuum"—and its many interactions or complementarities: with science and mathematics, in the first place, or with moral and political, especially utopian thinking. I have discussed these issues, including the question of the continuum, in detail in *In the Shadow of Hegel*.

36 Cited by Folse (*The Philosophy of Niels Bohr*, 71).

37 I have discussed this issue in *In the Shadow of Hegel* (82–83). On "abyss" in Bohr, see the discussions in Folse (*The Philosophy of Niels Bohr*, 53–55), Faye (*Niels Bohr*, 153–54), and Heisenberg (*Physics and Beyond*, 209–10).

38 See both "Freud and the Scene of Writing" (*Writing and Difference*) and "To Speculate—on 'Freud' " (*The Post Card*).

39 Derrida invokes Nietzsche's as a key contrasting perspective here and in "Structure, Sign and Play in the Discourse of the Human Science" (*Writing and Difference*, 292).

40 "The old one" [der Alte] may be God, or Freud, to both of whom Einstein refers in this way, or it may even be Einstein himself. Einstein's comment on Freud is of some interest in this context (and Freud would in turn have much to comment on it): "The

old one [der Alte] [Freud] had . . . a sharp vision; no illusion lulled him asleep except for an often exaggerated faith in his own ideas" (Letter to A. Bachrach, July 25, 1949; cited by Pais in "*Subtle is the Lord*," 515).

41 See Folse's comment on Einstein's misunderstanding of complementarity as "a *principle* in the physical sense" (*The Philosophy of Niels Bohr*, 145).

6 Locality and Causality

1 Einstein's main target here is Henry Margenau's "Einstein's Concept of Reality" in the same volume (243–68).

2 Cf. Murdoch's comments (*Niels Bohr's Philosophy*, 194).

3 The questions of locality and action at a distance—and to what degree Bohr's views are permissive of such an influence—has been the subject of a long debate, complicated by differences in interpretations of the EPR argument, Bohr's reply, quantum mechanics, and the locality requirement itself. Some readings of Bohr's analysis see his treatment as incompatible with the locality requirement, in part in view of subsequent experiments of the EPR type, for example d'Espagnat's (*Conceptual Foundations*, 94–95, 255), Faye's (*Niels Bohr*, 181–82), and Honner's (*The Description of Nature*, 125–41), but not Murdoch's (*Niels Bohr's Philosophy*, 168–72, 179–95). Cf., also N. David Mermin, "A Bolt From the Blue: the E=P=R Paradox" (in *Niels Bohr*, edited by A. P. French and P. J. Kennedy). In view of the analysis given in this chapter, I do not think that Bohr's argument implies that locality needs to be abandoned, even given subsequent experimental findings and theoretical arguments. Bohr's interpretation remains consistent with all physics available so far, even if one agrees that some among the more recent hidden variable possibilities may not be discounted without further experimental evidence. Most of the debate at issue relates to subsequent developments and does not affect the logic of Bohr's reply to the EPR argument itself.

4 Hence it is crucial to Bohr's argument that an interaction with measuring instruments is itself quantum, even though the reading of the measuring data is classical.

5 Cited by Honner (*The Description of Nature*, 118–19).

6 Faye suggests that this aspect of the argument appears to have been developed by Bohr around 1938 (*Niels Bohr*, 182–83). Murdoch correctly argues that Bohr "uphold[s]" what he calls " 'the principle of local action' " (192–93), although he also ascribes to Bohr what he calls "the objective value theory" (192). The latter is, I think, unnecessary and finally untenable; and Murdoch's argument concerning locality need not depend on it.

7 See Fine's useful discussion (*The Shaky Game*, 59–63). Fine, conversely, undervalues the significance of the EPR reality criterion for Einstein. He is not wrong in suggesting that "that [EPR] reality criterion involves some ideas that Einstein toyed with but then thought better of following Bohr's critique of it" (62). The degree of difference, however, appears to be not all that significant, even within Fine's own, markedly realist, reading of Einstein. The concept of physical reality independent of observation is persistently invoked in Einstein's subsequent writings and remains central to his view of physics. The underlying metaphysics of this concept remains fundamentally the same as that of the EPR criteria of reality and completeness. Naturally, Einstein's philosophical view evolved and transformed throughout his life, for example (and in

particular), as he discovered his general, as opposed to special, theory of relativity. See Pais's account in *"Subtle is the Lord."* For an interesting account of his transition toward a more metaphysical view of physical reality, see Bruno Latour's "A Relativistic Account of Einstein's Relativity."

8   See Bell's comments where he cites the passage just cited (*SUQM*, 159), but the point is manifest throughout his work.

9   Other possible interpretations of all these concepts and theories would add important nuances, as for example does, in relation to Einstein's views, Fine's analysis in *The Shaky Game.* (On hidden variables see chapter 4 [40–63], but relevant discussions are found throughout the book.) These nuances would not change the main shape of the anti-epistemological argument offered here, whether in relation to Bell's views or in general.

10 Bohm's original articles, "A Suggested Interpretation of the Quantum Theory in Terms of 'Hidden' Variables," 1 and 2 (*QTM*, 369–96), appeared in 1952. Bohm's many philosophical works include *Causality and Change in Modern Physics, Fragmentation and Wholeness, Wholeness and the Implicate Order,* and (with F. David Peat), *Science, Order, and Creativity.* For a recent popular exposition of the EPR argument, Bohm's theory, and Bell's theorem, see F. David Peat, *Einstein's Moon: Bell's Theorem and the Curious Quest for Quantum Reality.*

11 See also Fine's discussion (*The Shaky Game,* 57–59).

12 Prior to new quantum theory, Bohr, along with Kramers and Slater, argued for abandoning the strict energy conservation law and replacing it with a statistical one. This attempt was prompted by the necessity of accounting for other data, unexplained at the time, rather than by meta-physical considerations. He had abandoned these ideas in view of experimental evidence even before Heisenberg's mechanics, which resolved the paradoxes that prompted them. See Honner (*The Description of Nature,* 36–40) and Pais (*Niels Bohr's Times,* 232–39). Bohr's preference for a statistical law may not have been accidental, of course, in view of the overall statistical character of quantum phenomena. One might argue that the law of energy conservation was derived in classical physics by causal considerations (which might have also been a factor in Bohr's thinking). It is an extraordinary example of a law arrived at within an old theory and retained by a new, when the old theory itself and the very principles responsible for the derivation of the law had to be abandoned.

13 See *SUQM,* 20 n. 2. I use here the (slightly modified) translation from Schilpp's revised edition (1979).

14 See also his related comments (*SUQM,* 150). Fine suggests that Einstein's locality (which he sees as different from Bell's locality) is compatible with Bell's theorem (*The Shaky Game,* 61).

15 For nuances concerning Einstein's view of locality and Bell's theorem, see Fine's discussion (*The Shaky Game,* 59–63).

16 Both Einstein and Gödel were at Princeton around 1933 and Gödel subsequently, in the late 1940s, did some work in general relativity. They developed close intellectual ties while in Princeton. While their philosophical views in general differ, Gödel appears to have shared Einstein's dissatisfaction with quantum theory. According to Hao Wang, Gödel found quantum theory—a "two [classical and quantum] level" theory—"very unsatisfactory" (*Reflections of Kurt Gödel,* 154). This position is close to both Einstein's and Bell's.

17 See Freeman Dyson's remarks on parallels between Gödel's findings and modern physics in his response to Wheeler (*Some Strangeness in the Proportion*, 379).

18 Several other interpretations are considered, critically, by Bell (*SUQM*, 181–95).

19 See also his elaborations in "Introduction to the Theory of Hidden Variables" (*SUQM*, 29).

20 The situation is, of course, more complex in view of the absence of a theory connecting—"unifying"—quantum physics and gravitation, but this problem does not appear to be Bell's concern here. Cf. Penrose's discussion (*The Emperor's New Mind*, 348–73). See also L. A. Khalfin and B. S. Tsirel'son, "A Quantitative Description of the Applicability of the Classical Description within the Quantum Theory."

7 Undecidability and Complementarity

1 The conjunction of Freud and Heidegger comes into the foreground in Derrida's later works on Freud, especially *The Post Card*, and on Heidegger. Nietzsche remains a major force, however, whether Freud or Heidegger is at issue, as again in *The Post Card*. More recent works, especially those on Heidegger, suggest an even closer proximity between Heidegger and Derrida.

2 Interestingly, Deleuze and Guattari relate Freudean Oedipal economy and undecidability (*Anti-Oedipus*, 81).

3 In these elaborations and elsewhere in the *Introduction*, Derrida refers to Jean Cavaillès (*Sur la Logique et la théorie de la science*), who was the author of an important study *Philosophie Mathématique* and other works in philosophy of mathematics. As Bennington reports, Derrida's study was awarded the Jean Cavaillès prize in modern epistemology (*Jacques Derrida*, 330). Derrida also refers, throughout the *Introduction*, to Bachelard, although mostly to his work on Husserl. These links further support the connections between Derrida and, on the one hand, mathematics and science and, on the other, the history and philosophy of science and recent anti-epistemological trends there.

4 Cf., however, Brian Rotman's discussion of these connections between philosophy and mathematics, at least the mathematics based on infinity (which is to say, just about all of mathematics, certainly that which is subject to Gödel's theorem) in *Ad Infinitum*. I am grateful to Rotman for suggesting this parallel between Gödel and Einstein, and for directing my attention towards Skolem's work.

5 These connections would require a separate analysis, as would Gödel's philosophy, which is, for good reason, usually seen, including by Gödel himself, in terms of objectivism and conceptual, or mathematical, realism. This analysis cannot be pursued here. For some of Gödel's views and positions see his "Russell's Mathematical Logic" and "What is Cantor's Continuum Problem?" in *Philosophy of Mathematics*, edited by Paul Benaceraff and Hillary Putnam. Hao Wang's *Reflections on Kurt Gödel* offers an extensive record, documentation, and relevant bibliography.

6 See also his "Quantum Mechanics and the Observer." Putnam's work on quantum mechanics and its connections to mathematical logic is extensive and it cannot be considered here. This work, however, appears to confirm the present assessment.

7 Skolem's mathematical results at issue are presented in "Über die Unmöglichkeit einer vollständigen Charakterisierung der Zahlenreihe mittels eines endlichen Axiomensystems." I cannot pursue here an analysis of Skolem's philosophical views. These views appear to be more flexible and less metaphysically committed than

Gödel's. In his address at the 1950 International Congress of Mathematicians, "Some Remarks on the Foundations of Set Theory," he speaks, albeit it with some reservations, of the possibility of "the opportunistic framework," which is somewhat similar to Bohr's: "One desires only to have a foundation which makes it possible to develop present day mathematics, and which is consistent so far as is known yet. Should any contradiction occur, we may try to make such restrictions in the underlying postulates that the deduction of the contradiction proves impossible.... But this standpoint has the unpleasant feature that we can never know when we have finished the foundation of mathematics. We are not only adding new floors at the top of our building, but from time to time it may be necessary to make changes in the basis" (700). Stewart Shapiro calls this "opportunistic" outlook "foundations without foundationalism." He comments: "Skolem was, of course, aware of the difficulties of the foundationalist [Hilbert] programme, but apparently he was reluctant to give up on foundationalism altogether. Today, some decades later, it is generally held that *nothing* can satisfy the requirement of foundationalism. That level of security cannot be attained. We are left with Skolem's 'opportunistic' option and anti-foundationalism" (*Foundations without Foundationalism*, 30). Skolem actually invokes another alternative toward the end of his address—the "finitistic" approach (702–3).

8 Hegel's first *Logic* (*The Science of Logic*) may be one of the intertexts of this reading. In fact, it never leaves the background of Derrida's book as a whole, beginning with Derrida's initial analysis of the preface/postface economy in Hegel.

9 See also his remarks in *Positions* (69–70, 79–80).

10 See, in particular, *The Post Card* (259–73).

11 The word "complement" is obviously not used by Derrida in the present sense. His point is that the supplement cannot be seen in absolute opposition to—as the full complement of—the inside. For, along with the undecidability of their relation and the deconstruction of all classical oppositions of that type, in practice neither "the outside" nor "the inside" is dispensable, either by way of absolute interiorization, as in Hegel, or by way of an uncritical, or insufficiently critical, exteriority, as in Kant or Levinas. Derrida's analysis of Levinas and closure in "Violence and Metaphysics" (in *Writing and Difference*) becomes extremely important at this particular juncture.

12 This usage is somewhat of an exception in Derrida, although its force is tempered by his accompanying remarks on Hegel. Derrida actually avoids this word, in contrast to Nietzsche and closer to Heidegger. Derrida, however, also distinguishes, particularly in his earlier works, the difference between deconstruction and the Heideggerian end or destruction [*Destruktion*] of metaphysics (via the ontology of Being). In his works after *The Post Card*, such as *Of Spirit*, Derrida speaks more often of Heideggerian *deconstruction*. See his remarks (in 1983) in *Derrida and Différance* (1–2), where he speaks of 'deconstruction' as a more Heideggerian term, in contrast to Nietzschean 'demolitions', which may be seen as a revision of his position in the essay itself. Compare, however, his remarks on postdeconstructive readings of Marx and Heidegger in *The Post Card* (276), although he refers there to Heidegger's other term *abbauen* (dismantle).

13 See Derrida's discussion in *Positions* and his reading of Lacan, "The Purveyor of Truth," in *The Post Card*.

14 French for indeterminacy is *indétermination*, as in "principe d'incertitude ou

d'indétermination de Heisenberg"—Heisenberg's uncertainty or indeterminacy principle. The English term 'indetermination' may suggest the absence of defined determination rather than the irreducible indeterminacy. Besides the fact that the English translation (by Samuel Weber) uses, with the same negative connotations, both "indeterminacy" and "indetermination," it appears that it is indeterminacy rather than indetermination (in the sense just indicated) that is at issue.

15 From this perspective, Rodolphe Gasché has a point by jointly stressing Derrida's proximity to Husserl and the role of undecidability in Derrida in *The Tain of the Mirror*.

16 In the wake of Derrida's writings and related anti-epistemological practices—for example, the writings of Luce Irigaray, Hélène Cixous, and Roland Barthes—such "quantum" theories have been interestingly pursued by others as well; recent examples include Gregory Ulmer's *Teletheory: Grammatology in the Age of Video* and Avital Ronell's *The Telephone Book: Technology—Schizophrenia—Electric Speech*, although the agenda and style of the latter book is closer to (determinate) undecidability than to "quantum" indeterminacy.

17 Both "Tympan" and "Living On: Border Lines," and most recently "Circumfession," coupled with Geoffrey Bennington's "Derridabase," in Geoffrey Bennington and Jacques Derrida's *Jacques Derrida*, play out similar, if less complex, structures. *Glas*, of course, involves many other models, such as modern newspapers with their structures of textual continuities and ruptures, although used (perhaps) for different reasons.

18 Hartman's reading of *Glas* in *Saving the Text* uses this parallel between Derridadaism and Joyce throughout.

19 It should be stressed that in Heidegger, Derrida, or de Man, the production of theses is never dismissed or simply suspended. Such an unequivocal suspension would in itself offer a thesis, or precisely *the* thesis. Hence, too, it is athesis, rather than (only) anti-thesis (or antithesis); or asynthesis and various forms of synthesis, necessarily accompanying antisynthesis. Similarly Feyerabend's "against-method" is in fact "a-method"; as "anything goes" (his famous but, as he points out, often misunderstood maxim), methods go, too. The problem is *the* thesis, the desire for *the* thesis, the thesis of thesis.

8 Closures

1 The pervasive influence of Heidegger complicates the genealogy of all Derridean concepts, including that of closure; and the question of the difference, or *différance*, between Heidegger's end and de(con)struction [Destruktion] of metaphysics and Derrida's deconstruction and the closure of metaphysics is crucial to the problematic of closure. The relationships between Heidegger and Derrida are complex, and they must be seen as a *différance*—the play of differences, proximities, and interactions. One can argue for a closer proximity of Derrida to Heidegger throughout, although this proximity is, I think, more pronounced in later Derrida. This proximity has been emphasized by Herman Rapaport's *Heidegger and Derrida: Reflections on Time and Language*. While the book considers the differences between Heidegger and Derrida and the dynamics of Derrida's thought in this respect, it suffers from a repression of the non-Heideggerian—such as the Nietzschean and the Freudian—aspects of Derrida's

text. Derrida never abandons such contra-Heideggerian dimensions of his discourse, even in his more recent work on Heidegger. Heidegger's thought, according to Derrida, never exceeds the metaphysics of presence, even though and because all such claims need to be qualified, with respect to both Heideggerian, or Derridean, economy itself and the possibility of such an excess. Rapaport's overall views appear to be much closer to Heidegger (and to Levinas) than to Derrida.

I would agree more with Gasché, who, in *The Tain of the Mirror* and his other writings, insists on differentiating the Heideggerian and the Derridean frameworks, even within the philosophical register. It may be that Gasché's analysis of Heidegger misses several points of closer proximity between Derrida and Heidegger. These omissions, however, would not eliminate the differences correctly pointed out by Gasché. As I have indicated, the problem in Gasché's analysis is in a too narrow, if deliberate and to a degree justified, confining of Derrida within the philosophical register. See also Derrida's comments on Gasché in *Acts of Literature* (70–72), where Derrida appears to dissociate himself from Gasché's analysis. Some of these problems could be avoided by engaging the thematics of closure. This approach would also allow for a more effective analysis of the relationships between Derrida and philosophy, including the philosophy of reflection. Gasché does mention the question of closure in Derrida in the context of the question of transgression—cogently and in accord with the analysis to be given here, but only marginally and reducing the complexity of the interactions between the inside and the outside of philosophy in Derrida (165–72). He does not consider the economy of closure *as* closure, whereby, as shall be seen, a very different form of proximity between Derrida and philosophy emerges. This proximity is further reinforced by Derrida's economy of determinate undecidability, as considered in the preceding chapter. As I have indicated, Gasché's analysis of undecidability in Derrida is in accord with this latter point, although this economy is differently evaluated by Gasché's than by the present analysis.

2   See Derrida's comments in "The Pit and the Pyramid" (*Margins*, 72) and his discussion of this issue throughout *Positions*, particularly the remarks on p. 51.

3   In her "Translator's Preface" to *Of Grammatology*, Gayatri C. Spivak detects "totalizations" in early Derrida that were replaced by more complex attitudes in his subsequent works. This assessment may be correct, but that is not what I am referring to at the moment. On closure ("*clôture*"), which does not seem to undergo such a transformation, Spivak comments, "We must know that we are *within* the 'clôture' of metaphysics, even as we attempt to undo it" (xx). This claim does correspond to Derrida's position and is consonant with the present reading. While, however, Derrida suspends the totalizing claims on which Spivak comments—largely even as the book proceeds—the globalizations determined by the economy of the closure of philosophy persist throughout Derrida's texts.

4   See in particular "Différance" (*Margins*, 14) and *Positions* (43–44).

5   I would claim less for literature, although Hartman's comparison in *Saving the Text* of *Glas* with Joyce remains useful and other aspects of the literary register may be invoked in relation to other texts. Within and between their texts, one could instead think of such "literary" figures as Mallarmé, Artaud, Valéry, Blanchot, Genet, or Bataille, who engage philosophical registers (from) within literary registers.

6   See in particular the opening discussion in "The Supplement of Copula" (*Margins*).

7   I use these ideas metaphorically here. It is possible, however, that questions of that type can be posed within the field of mathematics itself, specifically, to what extent the structure and functioning of the new system defined via a nonstandard model differs from the old system and how the functioning of the old system itself is transformed within a new, nonstandard model.

8   On the metaphysics of proximity and the metaphysics of presence, see Derrida's discussion of Heidegger's *Dasein* in "The Ends of Man."

9   Many passages in *Positions*, especially on or against transgression (12, 24), would further support this point.

10 See also elaborations in *Writing and Difference* (110–11, 280–81).

11 I have considered Nietzsche's strategies and style in detail throughout *Reconfigurations*, to which study I permit myself to refer on this point and in this chapter in general.

12 See again Derrida's remarks throughout *Positions*, particularly toward the end (90–91), but also on pp. 6, 12, 13–14, 17–18, 24, 41–42.

13 In addition to *Positions* and other texts, see in the opening of *Dissemination*, 3–7.

14 On the recent developments in France, see Jean-Luc Nancy's "Introduction" to *Who Comes After The Subject?*

15 Such complementarities may emerge in either direction—from philosophy to its exterior or from such an exterior toward philosophy. Derrida's analysis of the "metaphor in the text of philosophy" in "White Mythology" is especially important in this context. See also his analysis, especially his deconstruction of Benveniste's reading of Aristotle in "The Supplement of Copula."

16 Spivak suggests so ("Translator's Preface," *Of Grammatology*, xxi). Her point that "Derrida uses the word 'metaphysics' very simply as shorthand for any science of presence" is not wrong, but a degree of further discrimination is necessary. While, as we have seen, it is true that identical or analogous metaphysical economies operate across different fields inside and outside philosophy, the name "metaphysics" has its own historical and strategic appurtenances. These operational crossings of boundaries would prevent us from speaking, without further qualifications, about *the* closure of metaphysics.

17 See also his comments on the issue in *Positions*, in the context of Hegel and the question of history (56–57)—the topic that is of great significance in the question of closure, both in the historical dimensions of the economy of closure itself and in the effects this economy has on all historical considerations.

18 Most of Derrida's works on "literary" authors, and many elaborations in most of his other works, for example, *Positions*, *Disseminations*, and the introductory interview and essays in *The Acts of Literature*, can be cited here, however.

19 See also his remarks on the "circle" and the closure of metaphysics in "Structure, Sign and Play" (*Writing and Difference*, 280–81) and "The Linguistic Circle of Geneva" (*Margins*, 140).

20 I shall not consider the question of relativism at the moment. It has been the subject of much discussion during the last decade. As in his 1988 passage discussed in chapter 7, Derrida here uncharacteristically uses the term generally, rather than referring to a specific concept or a set of texts, as he usually does. These statements may have arisen partly out of his strong sense that one must rigorously explore Hegelian, Husserlian,

or Heideggerian problematics, rather than naively relativistically suspend them, and are understandable in view of the problematic character of many forms of relativism.

21 I have considered this issue in *In the Shadow of Hegel* (287–325).

22 John McDowell's translation is slightly modified here. My thanks to Ralph Rosen for his invaluable help.

23 See especially Nietzsche's notes on nihilism (*The Will to Power*, 7–81). The point, however, is developed and reiterated throughout Nietzsche's later works.

24 Heidegger's full sentence reads: "Nothing, conceived as the pure 'Other' than what-is, is the veil of Being [Das Nichts als das Andere zum Seienden ist der Schleier des Seins]" (*Existence and Being*, 360; *Wegmarken*, 107). This reflection suggests that at issue is precomprehending both beingness and nothingness by that which is neither. Also important in this context is his analysis in *The Question of Being* leading to placing Being under erasure.

25 In a certain way, "Différance" can be construed as continuously referring to the passage by Nietzsche just cited and to the analysis it metonymically represents. There are, of course, other key genealogical links in Hegel, Heidegger, Freud, Levinas, Blanchot, and Bataille. In the present context see in particular Bataille's extraordinary elaboration in *Inner Experience* (124–25).

26 See also his comment in *Of Grammatology* (143) and the concluding discussion in "Différance."

27 At this point and at a related juncture of his essay on Husserl "Form and Meaning: A Note on Phenomenology of Language," Derrida also refers to Plotinus on presence and form as the trace of nonpresence and of the formless, or of that which is neither one nor another (*Margins*, 66 n. 41; *Marges*, 172 n. 16). Cf. also Bataille's "Formless" (*Visions*, 31). Denis Hollier actually traces some of Bataille's pertinent ideas to Plato's *Parmenides* (*Against Architecture*, 99–102).

28 See also Derrida's comments on infinity and finitude and other oppositions in Hegel analogously demanding the closure of concepts (*Speech and Phenomena*, 101–2); and Wheeler's elaborations on "nothingness" in "Law without Law" (*QTM*, 205–9), although Wheeler does not quite reach the understanding suggested here. Bohr, it appears, does or comes very close to it.

29 Derrida's expression "would . . . give us to think . . . [nous donnerait . . . à penser . . .]" plays upon Heidegger's "es gibt denken," relating the thematics of thinking [*Denken*] and gift [*Gabe, Don*], which has been explored in Derrida's subsequent writings on Heidegger and his other later works.

30 Derrida alludes to Heidegger's notion of language as thinking, or thinking-poetizing, especially in "The Anaximander Fragment." French as the language of the difference and of the erasure of difference—*différance*—between "différence" and "*différance*" with an *a* could also be put into play here.

31 As I indicated earlier, placing "itself" in parenthesis or under erasure is crucial here, since a radical alterity at issue entails a deconstruction of all classical reflexivity.

32 One can, as we have seen, argue that the same may be said about Derrida and Heidegger, as is, to a degree, suggested by Derrida's own recent works on Heidegger.

33 Derrida's reading of Freud in "To Speculate—on 'Freud' " in *The Post Card*, which brings Nietzsche and Freud into closer proximity, is equally worth noting here.

9 Transformations of Closure

1 "The Linguistic Circle of Geneva" would be a natural place to suggest a transformation of the philosophical closure itself. Derrida does not do so, however, possibly because his emphasis is on closure itself and on the specific—a very Derridean—historico-theoretical configuration of the interaction between philosophy and (Saussure's and Rousseau's) linguistics which he positions within the closure of philosophy. It is possible, however, also to speak of a new, more linguistic, closure or of a transformed closure emerging as a result.

2 Cf. again Nancy's "Introduction" in *Who Comes After the Subject?*

3 This necessity need not imply that the emergence of "new" concepts must proceed according to textual practice or in a textual style of reading of "signed texts." On the contrary, transformations of theory need not and cannot always proceed by way of criticism or "reading," however effective such a textual style may be, as it has been in Derrida, de Man, and others, or however irreducible "reading" itself of one kind or another, or of one author or another, may be. "Nothing comes out of nothing." But no practice, whether "reading" or any other, can sustain the claim that it is always the most effective, let alone the only, practice—a claim that has been persistent, both inside and outside deconstruction. There are always other "texts" to "read," and these other texts are always read even in criticism and reading. There is no way to reduce or fully delimit a textual field by anything, including by a given field—such as that of literature, criticism, or philosophy—or a canon of any kind, even when, within such a field, such possibilities appear to be unlimited.

BIBLIOGRAPHY

Althusser, Louis, Étienne Balibar, and Roger Establet. *Lire le Capital.* Paris: François Maspero, 1965. Translated by Ben Brewster as *Reading Capital.* London: Verso, 1983.

Argyros, Alexander. *A Blessed Rage for Order: Deconstruction, Evolution, and Chaos.* Ann Arbor, Mich.: University of Michigan Press, 1991.

Bachelard, Gaston. *Le Nouvel esprit scientifique.* Paris: Presses Universitaires de France, 1934. Translated by Arthur Goldhammer as *The New Scientific Spirit.* Boston: Beacon Press, 1984.

——— . *La Poétique de l'Espace.* Paris: Presses Universitaires de France, 1957. Translated by Maria Jolas as *The Poetic of Space.* Boston: Beacon Press, 1969.

Bataille, Georges. *The Accursed Share,* 3 vols. Translated by Robert Hurley. New York: Zone, 1988–90.

——— . *Le Coupable.* Paris: Gallimard, 1961. Translated by Bruce Boon as *Guilty.* Venice, Calif.: Lapis Press, 1988.

——— . "The Critique of the Foundations of Hegelian Dialectics." In *Visions of Excess.* Edited by Alan Stoekl. Minneapolis: University of Minnesota Press, 1985.

——— . *L'Erotisme.* Paris: Éditions de Minuit, 1957. Translated by Mary Dalwood as *Erotism.* San Francisco: City Lights Books, 1986.

——— . *L'Expérience intérieure.* Paris: Gallimard, 1954. Translated by Leslie Anne Boldt as *Inner Experience.* Albany: State University of New York Press, 1980.

——— . "Hegel, la mort et le sacrifice," *Decaulion* 5 (1955):23–43.

——— . *Histoire de l'oeil.* Paris: Pauvert, 1967. Translated by Joachim Neugroschel as *Story of the Eye.* San Francisco: City Lights Books, 1987.

——— . "The Labyrinth." In *Visions of Excess.* Edited by Alan Stoekl. Minneapolis: University of Minnesota Press, 1985.

————. *Les Larmes d'Éros*. Paris: Pauvert, 1981. Translated by Peter Connor as *The Tears of Eros*. San Francisco: City Lights Books, 1989.

————. "Materialism." In *Visions of Excess*. Edited by Alan Stoekl. Minneapolis: University of Minnesota Press, 1985.

————. *Oeuvres complètes*. Paris: Gallimard, 1970–.

————. *"La Part maudite" précédé de "La Notion de dépense."* Paris: Éditions de Minuit, 1967. Translated by Robert Hurley as *The Accursed Share: An Essay on General Economy*. Vol. 1. New York: Zone, 1988.

————. *Sur Nietzsche*. Paris: Gallimard, 1945. Translated by Bruce Boon as *On Nietzsche*. New York: Paragon, 1990.

————. *Théorie de la Religion*. Paris: Gallimard, 1973. Translated by Robert Hurley as *Theory of Religion* New York: Zone Books, 1989.

————. *Visions of Excess: Selected Writings, 1927–1938*. Edited by Alan Stoekl. Minneapolis: University of Minnesota Press, 1985.

Bell, John S. *Speakable and Unspeakable in Quantum Mechanics*. Cambridge: Cambridge University Press, 1987.

Benacerraf, Paul, and Hilary Putnam, eds. *Philosophy of Mathematics*. Cambridge: Cambridge University Press, 1991.

Benjamin, Walter. *Illuminations*. Translated by Harry Zohn. New York: Schocken Books, 1969.

Bennington, Geoffrey. *Jacques Derrida*. Paris: Éditions du Seuil, 1991.

Bloom, Harold, et al. *Deconstruction and Criticism*. New York: Continuum, 1979.

Bohm, David. *Causality and Change in Modern Physics*. Philadelphia: University of Pennsylvania Press, 1971.

————. *Fragmentation and Wholeness*. Jerusalem: Van Leer Jerusalem Foundation, 1976.

————. *Quantum Theory*. 1951; rpt. New York: Dover, 1989.

————. *Wholeness and the Implicate Order*. London: Routledge, 1981.

Bohm, David, and F. David Peat. *Science, Order, and Creativity*. New York: Bantam, 1987.

Bohr, Niels. *Atomic Physics and Human Knowledge*. New York: Wiley, 1958.

————. *Atomic Theory and the Description of Nature*. Cambridge: Cambridge University Press, 1961.

————. "The Causality Problem in Atomic Physics." In *New Theories in Physics*. Paris: International Institute of Intellectual Collaboration, 1939.

————. Niels Bohr Archive, Copenhagen. Manuscripts and Scientific Correspondence.

————. *Niels Bohr: Collected Works*. Edited by Léon Rosenfeld and Erik Rüdinger. 6 vols. Amsterdam: North-Holland, 1972–85.

————. "Newton's Principle and Modern Atomic Mechanics." In *Royal Society Newton Tercentenary Celebration*. Cambridge: Cambridge University Press, 1946.

————. *The Philosophical Writings of Niels Bohr*. 3 vols. Woodbridge, Conn.: Ox Bow Press, 1987.

————. "The Quantum Postulate and the Recent Development of Atomic Theory." *Nature* 121 (1928).

————. "Quantum Physics and Philosophy: Causality and Complementarity." In *Philosophy in Mid Century: A Survey*. Edited by R. Klibansky. Florence: La Nuoava Italia Editrice, 1958.

————. "Über die Wirkung von Atomen bei Stossen." *Zeitschrift für Physik* 34 (1925):142–57.

Born, Max, and Albert Einstein. *The Born-Einstein Letters.* New York: Walker, 1971.

Cavaillès, Jean. *Philosophie Mathématique,* Paris: Hermann, 1962.

——— . *Méthode axiomatique et formalisme.* Paris: Hermann, 1938.

——— . *Sur la Logique et la théorie de la science.* Paris: Presses Universitaires de France, 1947.

Crease, Robert P., and Charles C. Mann. *The Second Creation: Makers of the Revolution in Twentieth-Century Physics.* New York: Macmillan, 1986.

Deleuze, Gilles. *Nietzsche et la philosophie.* Paris: Presses Universitaires de France, 1962. Translated by Hugh Tomlinson as *Nietzsche and Philosophy.* New York: Columbia University Press, 1983.

——— . *Le Pli: Leibniz et le baroque.* Paris: Les Edition de Minuit, 1988. Translated as *The Fold: Leibniz and the Baroque.* Minneapolis, Minn.: University of Minnesota Press, 1993.

Deleuze, Gilles, and Felix Guattari. *L'Anti-Oedipe: Capitalisme et schizophrénie.* Paris: Éditions de Minuit, 1972. Translated by Robert Hurley, Mark Seem, and Helen R. Lane as *Anti-Oedipus: Capitalism and Schizophrenia.* Minneapolis: University of Minnesota Press, 1983.

——— . *Mille Plateaux.* Paris: Éditions de Minuit, 1980. Translated by Brian Massumi as *A Thousand Plateaus.* Minneapolis: University of Minnesota Press, 1987.

Derrida, Jacques. *Acts of Literature.* Edited by Derek Attridge. New York: Routledge, 1992.

——— . *La Carte postale: De Socrate à Freud et au-delà.* Paris: Flammarion, 1980. Translated by Alan Bass as *The Post Card: From Socrates to Freud and Beyond.* Chicago: University of Chicago Press, 1987.

——— . "Comment ne pas parler: Dénégations." In *Psyché: Inventions de l'autre.* Paris: Galilée, 1987. Translated by Ken Frieden as "How to Avoid Speaking: Denials." In *Derrida and Negative Theology.* Edited by Harold Coward and Toby Foshay. Albany, N.Y.: State University of New York Press, 1992.

——— . *De la grammatologie.* Paris: Éditions de Minuit, 1967. Translated by Gayatri C. Spivak as *Of Grammatology.* Baltimore: Johns Hopkins University Press, 1976.

——— . *De l'esprit: Heidegger et la question.* Paris: Éditions Galilée, 1987. Translated by Geoffrey Bennington and Rachel Bowlby as *Of Spirit: Heidegger and the Question.* Chicago: University of Chicago Press, 1989.

——— . "La 'différance.' " *Bulletin de la Société Française de la Philosophie* 62, no. 3 (July–September 1968):73–101. Translated by David B. Allison as "Differance." In *Speech and Phenomena And Other Essays on Husserl's Theory of Science.* Translated by David B. Allison. Evanston, Ill.: Northwestern University Press, 1973.

——— . *La Dissémination.* Paris: Éditions du Seuil, 1972. Translated by Barbara Johnson as *Dissemination.* Chicago: University of Chicago Press, 1981.

——— . "Economimesis." In Sylviane Agacinski et al. *Mimesis des articulations.* Paris: Flammarion, 1975. Translated by Richard Klein as "Economimesis." *Diacritics* 11, no. 3 (1981):3–25.

——— . *L'Écriture et la différence.* Paris: Éditions du Seuil, 1967. Translated by Alan Bass as *Writing and Difference.* Chicago: University of Chicago Press, 1978.

——— . Trans. and intro. Edmund Husserl, *L'Origine de la géométrie.* Paris: Presses Universitaires de France, 1962. Translated by John P. Leavy, Jr., as *Edmund Husserl's Origin of Geometry: An Introduction.* Stony Brook, N.Y.: Nicolas Hays, 1978.

——— . *Éperons: Les Styles de Nietzsche.* Paris: Flammarion, 1976. Translated by Barbara

Harlow as *Spurs: Nietzsche's Styles*. Bilingual ed. Chicago: University of Chicago Press, 1979.

———. "How to Avoid Speaking: Denials." In *Derrida and Negative Theology*. Edited by Harold Coward and Toby Foshay. Albany, N.Y.: State University of New York Press, 1992.

———. *Glas*. Paris: Galilée, 1974. Translated by John P. Leavey, Jr., and Richard Rand as *Glas*. Lincoln: University of Nebraska Press, 1986.

———. *Limited Inc*. Evanston, Ill.: Northwestern University Press, 1988.

———. *Limit Inc A B C . . . .* Baltimore, Md.: Johns Hopkins University Press, 1977.

———. "Living On: Border Lines." Translated by James Hulbert. In Harold Bloom et al., *Deconstruction and Criticism*. New York: Seabury Press, 1979.

———. *Marges de la philosophie*. Paris: Éditions de Minuit, 1972. Translated by Alan Bass as *Margins of Philosophy*. Chicago: University of Chicago Press, 1982.

———. "My Chances/*Mes Chance:* A Rendezvous with Some Epicurean Stereophonies." In *Taking Chances: Derrida, Psychoanalysis, and Literature*. Edited by Joseph H. Smith and William Kerrigan. Baltimore: Johns Hopkins University Press, 1984.

———. *L'Oreille de l'autre*. Edited by Claude Lévesque and Cristie V. McDonald Montreal: VLB, 1982. Translated by Peggy Kamuf as *The Ear of the Other: Otobiography, Transference, Translation*. New York: Schocken, 1985.

———. *Parages*. Paris: Galilée, 1986.

———. *Positions*. Paris: Éditions de Minuit, 1972. Translated by Alan Bass as *Positions*. Chicago: University of Chicago Press, 1981.

———. *Le Problème de la genèse dans la philosophie de Husserl*. Paris: Presses Universitaires de France, 1990.

———. *Psyché: Inventions de l'autre*. Paris: Galilée, 1987.

———. "Le retrait de la métaphore." In *Psyché: Inventions de l'autre*. Paris: Éditions Galilée, 1987. Translated as "The *Retrait* of Metaphor." *Enclitic* 2 (Fall 1978):5–33.

———. "The Time of the Thesis: Punctuation." In *Philosophy in France Today*. Edited by Alan Montefiore. Cambridge: Cambridge University Press, 1983.

———. *Ulysse gramophone: Deux mots pour Joyce*. Paris: Galilée, 1987.

———. "Ulysses Gramophone." In *Acts of Literature*. Edited by Derek Attridge. New York: Routledge, 1992.

———. *La Vérité en peinture*. Paris: Flammarion, 1978. Translated by Geoffrey Bennington and Ian Mcleod as *The Truth in Painting*. Chicago: University of Chicago Press, 1987.

———. *La Voix et le phénomène*. Paris: Presses Universitaires de France, 1967. Translated by David B. Allison as *Speech and Phenomena*. In *Speech and Phenomena and Other Essays on Husserl's Theory of Science*. Translated by David B. Allison. Evanston, Ill.: Northwestern University Press, 1973.

D'Espagnat, Bernard. *Conceptual Foundations of Quantum Mechanics*. Redwood City, Calif.: Addison-Wesley, 1989.

Einstein, Albert. *Relativity: The Special and General Theory*. Translated by Robert W. Lawson. New York: Crown, 1961.

———. "Reply to Criticisms." In *Albert Einstein: Philosopher-Scientist*. Edited by Paul Arthur Schilpp. New York: Tudor, 1949.

———. *Out of My Later Years*. New York: Philosophical Library, 1950.

Evans, Joseph Claude. *Strategies of Deconstruction: Derrida and the Myth of Voice*. Minneapolis: University of Minnesota Press, 1991.

Faye, Jan. *Niels Bohr: His Heritage and Legacy. An Anti-Realist View of Quantum Mechanics.* Dordrecht: Kluwer, 1991.

Feyerabend, Paul. *Against Method: Outline of an Anarchistic Theory of Knowledge.* London: Verso, 1975.

———. "Problem of Microphysics." In *Frontiers of Science and Philosophy.* Edited by R. G. Colodny. London: Allen & Unwin, 1962.

———. *Science in a Free Society.* London: Verso, 1978.

Feynman, Richard. *The Character of Physical Law.* Cambridge, Mass.: MIT Press, 1965.

———. *QED: The Strange Theory of Light and Matter.* Princeton, N.J.: Princeton University Press, 1985.

Fine, Arthur. *The Shaky Game: Einstein, Realism and the Quantum Theory.* Chicago: University of Chicago Press, 1986.

Folse, Henry J. *The Philosophy of Niels Bohr: The Framework of Complementarity.* Amsterdam: North-Holland, 1985.

French, Anthony P., and P. J. Kennedy, eds. *Niels Bohr: A Centenary Volume.* Cambridge, Mass.: Harvard University Press, 1985.

Freud, Sigmund. *The Standard Edition of the Complete Psychological Works of Sigmund Freud.* Edited and translated by James Strachey. London: Hogarth Press, 1953–66.

Froula, Cristine. "Quantum Physics/Postmodern Metaphysics: The Nature of Jacques Derrida," *Western Humanities Review* 39 (1985): 287–311.

Galilei, Galileo. *Assayer.* In *The Controversy on the Comets of 1618.* Translated by Stillman Drake and C. D. O'Malley (Philadelphia: University of Pennsylvania Press, 1966).

Galison, Peter. *How Experiments End.* Chicago: University of Chicago Press, 1987.

Gasché, Rodolphe. "Deconstruction as Criticism." In *Glyph 6,* 177–215. Baltimore: Johns Hopkins University Press, 1979.

———. "Joining the Text: From Heidegger to Derrida." In *The Yale Critics: Deconstruction in America.* Edited by Jonathan Arac, Wlad Godzich, and Wallace Martin. Minneapolis: University of Minnesota Press, 1983.

———. *System und Metaphorik in der Philosophie von Georges Bataille.* Bern: Peter Lang, 1978.

———. *The Tain of The Mirror: Derrida and the Philosophy of Reflection.* Cambridge, Mass.: Harvard University Press, 1986.

Gödel, Kurt. "Russell's Mathematical Logic." In *Philosophy of Mathematics.* Edited by Paul Benaceraff and Hillary Putnam. Cambridge: Cambridge University Press, 1991.

———. "What is Cantor's Continuum Problem?" In *Philosophy of Mathematics.* Edited by Paul Benaceraff and Hillary Putnam. Cambridge: Cambridge University Press, 1991.

Hacking, Ian. *Representing and Intervening.* Cambridge: Cambridge University Press, 1983.

———. "The Self-Vindication of the Laboratory Science." In *Science as Practice and Culture.* Edited by Andrew Pickering. Chicago: University of Chicago Press, 1992.

Hartman, Geoffrey. *Saving the Text.* Baltimore: Johns Hopkins University Press, 1981.

Hawking, Stephen. "Quantum Cosmology." In *Three Hundred Years of Gravitation.* Edited by Stephen Hawking and Werner Israel. Cambridge: Cambridge University Press, 1987.

———. *A Brief History of Time: From the Big Bang to Black Holes.* New York: Bantam, 1988.

Hawking, Stephen, and Werner Israel, eds. *Three Hundred Years of Gravitation.* Cambridge: Cambridge University Press, 1987.

Hayles, N. Katherine. *Chaos Bound: Orderly Disorder in Contemporary Literature and Science.* Ithaca, N.Y.: Cornell University Press, 1990.

———. *The Cosmic Web: Scientific Field Models and Literary Strategies in the Twentieth Century.* Ithaca, N.Y.: Cornell University Press, 1984.

Healey, Richard. *The Philosophy of Quantum Mechanics: An Interactive Interpretation.* Cambridge: Cambridge University Press, 1989.

Hegel, Georg Wilhelm Friedrich. *Gesammelte Werke.* Hamburg: Felix Meiner, 1968.

———. *Hegel's Science of Logic.* Translated by A. V. Miller. Atlantic Highlands, N.J.: Humanities Press International, 1990.

———. *Werke in 20 Bänden.* Edited by Eva Moldenhauer and Karl Markus Michel. Frankfurt am Main: Suhrkamp, 1970–71.

———. *Werke in 20 Bänden.* Vol. 3, *Phänomenologie des Geistes.* Frankfurt am Main: Suhrkamp, 1970. Translated by A. V. Miller as *Phenomenology of Spirit.* Oxford: Oxford University Press, 1977.

———. "Who Thinks Abstractly?" In *Hegel: Texts and Commentary,* trans. and ed. Walter Kaufmann. Garden City, N.Y., 1965, 114–18.

Heidegger, Martin. *Early Greek Thinking.* Translated by David Farrell Krell and Frank A. Capuzzi. San Francisco: Harper & Row, 1984.

———. *Die Frage nach dem Ding.* Tübingen: Max Niemeyer Verlag, 1962. Translated by W. B. Barton, Jr., and Vera Deutsch as *What is a Thing?* South Bend, Ind.: Gateway, 1967.

———. *Existence and Being.* Chicago: Gateway, 1949.

———. *Gesamtaufgabe.* Frankfurt am Main: Klostermann, 1975–.

———. *Gesamtausgabe.* Vol. 40, pt. 2, *Einführung in die Metaphysik.* Translated by Ralph Manheim as *An Introduction to Metaphysics.* New Haven: Yale University Press, 1979.

———. *Hegels Phänomenologie des Geistes.* Frankfurt am Main: Klostermann, 1980. Translated by Parvis Emad and Kenneth Maly as *Hegel's Phenomenology of Spirit.* Bloomington: Indiana University Press, 1988.

———. *Holzwege.* Frankfurt am Mein: Klostermann, 1975.

———. *Identity and Difference.* Bilingual edition. Translated by Joan Stambaugh. New York: Doubleday, 1961.

———. *Nietzsche.* 2 vols. Pfullingen: Günter Neske, 1961. Translated by Donald Farrell Krell as *Nietzsche.* 4 volumes in 2. Vol. 1, *The Will to Power as Art.* Vol. 2, *The Eternal Recurrence of the Same.* Vol. 3, *The Will to Power as Knowledge and Metaphysics.* Vol. 4, *Nihilism.* New York: Harper & Row, 1979.

———. *The Question Concerning Technology and Other Essays.* Translated by William Lovitt. New York: Harper & Row, 1977.

———. *The Question of Being.* Bilinguial edition. Translated by J. Wilde and W. Kluback. New York: College and University Press, 1958.

———. *Sein und Zeit.* Tübingen: Niemeyer, 1979. Translated by John Macquarrie and Edward Robinson as *Being and Time.* New York: Harper & Row, 1962.

———. *Wegmarken.* Frankfurt am Main: Vittorio Klosterman, 1967.

———. *Zur Sache des Denkens.* Tübingen: Niemeyer, 1969. Translated by Joan Stambaugh as *On Time and Being.* New York: Harper & Row, 1972.

———. *Zur Seinfrage.* Frankfurt am Main: Klostermann, 1956. Translated by J. Wilde and W. Kluback as *The Question of Being.* New York: College and University Press, 1958.

Heisenberg, Werner. *Across the Frontiers.* Translated by Peter Heath. Woodbridge, Conn.: Ox Bow Press, 1990.

———. *Encounters with Einstein.* Princeton, N.J.: Princeton University Press, 1983.

———. *Philosophical Problems of Quantum Physics.* Translated by F. C. Hayes. Woodbridge, Conn.: Ox Bow Press, 1979.

———. *Physics and Beyond.* New York: Harper & Row, 1971.

———. *Physics and Philosophy.* New York: Harper & Row, 1962.

———. "Quantum Theory and its Interpretation." In *Niels Bohr: His Life and Work as Seen by his Friends and Colleagues.* Edited by Stefan S. Rozental. Amsterdam: North-Holand Publishing Company, 1967.

———. "Remarks on the Origin of the Relations of Uncertainty." In *The Uncertainty Principle and the Foundation of Quantum Mechanics.* Edited by William C. Price and Seymour S. Chissick. London: Wiley, 1977.

Hilbert, David. *Grundlagen der Geometrie.* Leipzig and Berlin: B. G. Teubner, 1899.

Høffding, Harald. *The Problems of Philosophy.* Translated by G. M. Fisher. London: Macmillan, 1906.

Hollier, Denis. *Against Architecture: The Writings of Georges Bataille.* Translated by Betsy Wing. Cambridge, Mass.: MIT Press, 1989. Originally published as *La Prise de la Concorde.* Paris: Éditions Gallimard, 1974.

Honner, John. *The Description of Nature: Niels Bohr and the Philosophy of Quantum Physics.* Oxford: Clarendon, 1987.

Hughes, R. I. G. *The Structure and Interpretation of Quantum Mechanics.* Cambridge, Mass.: Harvard University Press, 1989.

Husserl, Edmund. *Ideen zu einer reinen Phänomenologie und phänomenologischen Philosophie.* Vol. 3 of *Gesammelte Werke (Husserliana).* Edited by Walter Biemel. The Hague: Nijhof, 1950. Translated by W. R. Boyce Gibson as *Ideas: General Introduction to Pure Phenomenology.* 1931; rpt. New York: Collier Books, 1972.

———. *Die Krisis der europäischen Wissenschaften und die transzendentale Phänomenologie: Einer Einleitung in die phänomenologische Philosophie.* Vol. 6 of *Gesammelte Werke (Husserliana).* Edited by Walter Biemel. The Hague: Nijhof, 1950. Translated by David Carr as *The Crisis of European Sciences and Transcendental Phenomenology: An Introduction to Phenomenological Philosophy.* Evanston, Ill.: Northwestern University Press, 1970.

James, William. *The Principles of Psychology.* 2 vols. 1918; rpt. New York: Dover, 1950.

Jammer, Max. *The Philosophy of Quantum Mechanics: The Interpretation of Quantum Mechanics in Historical Perspective.* New York: Wiley, 1974.

———. *The Conceptual Development of Quantum Mechanics.* New York: McGraw Hill, 1966.

Jung, Carl Gustaf. *Gesammelte Werke,* 20 vols. Olten: Walter, 1966–83.

Kant, Immanuel. *Critique of Pure Reason.* Translated by Norman Kemp Smith. New York: St. Martin's Press, 1965.

———. *Kritik der Urteilskraft.* Vol. 10 of *Werkausgabe in 12 Bänden.* Frankfurt am Main: Suhrkamp, 1974. Translated by J. H. Bernard as *The Critique of Judgement.* New York: Hafner Press, 1951.

———. *Werkausgabe in 12 Bänden.* Frankfurt am Main: Suhrkamp, 1974.

Kayser, Rudolf. *Spinoza, Portrait of a Spiritual Hero.* New York: Philosophical Library, 1946.

Khalfin, L. A., and B. S. Tsirel'son. "A Quantitative Description of the Applicability of the Classical Description within the Quantum Theory." In *The Copenhagen Interpreta-*

tion Sixty Years After the Como Lecture. Edited by P. Lahti and P. Mittelstaedt. Teaneck, N.J.: World Sci. Publ., 1987, 369–401.

Kierkegaard, Søren. *Kierkegaard's Concluding Unscientific Postscript.* Translated by David F. Swenson. Princeton, N.J.: Princeton University Press, 1968.

Koyré, Alexandre. *Newtonian Studies.* Chicago: University of Chicago Press, 1965.

Krips, Henry. *The Metaphysics of Quantum Theory.* Oxford: Clarendon, 1987.

Kuhn, Thomas S., et al. *Sources for the History of Quantum Mechanics.* Philadelphia: American Philosophical Society, 1967.

———. *The Structure of Scientific Revolutions.* Chicago: University of Chicago Press, 1965.

Lacan, Jacques. *Le Seminaire de Jacques Lacan XI: Les Quatre concepts fondamentaux de la psychoanalyse.* Edited by Jacques-Alain Miller. Paris: Éditions du Seuil, 1973. Translated by Alan Sheridan as *The Four Fundamental Concepts of Psycho-Analysis.* New York: Norton, 1978.

Lacoue-Labarthe, Philippe. *La Fiction du politique: Heidegger, l'art et la politique.* Paris: Christian Bourgois Editeur, 1987. Translated by Chris Turner as *Heidegger, Art and Politics: The Fiction of the Political.* Oxford: Basil Blackwell, 1990.

Latour, Bruno. "The Politics of Explanation: An Alternative." In *Knowledge and Reflexivity.* Edited by Steve Woolgar. London: Newbury Park. Calif.: Sage, 1988.

———. "A Relativistic Account of Einstein's Relativity," *Social Studies of Science* 18 (1988): 3–44.

———. *Science in Action: How to Follow Scientists and Engineers through Society.* Cambridge, Mass.: Harvard, 1987.

Lyotard, Jean-François. *La Condition postmoderne: Rapport sur le savoir.* Paris: Éditions de Minuit, 1979. Translated by Geoffrey Bennington and Brian Massumi as *The Postmodern Condition: A Report on Knowledge.* Minneapolis: University of Minnesota Press, 1984.

Marx, Karl, and Friedrich Engels. *The Marx-Engels Reader.* Edited by Robert C. Tucker. New York: Norton, 1978.

———. "*Ökonomisch-philosophische Manuskripte (1844).*" In Vol. 2, *Marx/Engels Gesamtausgabe, Erste Abteilung.* Berlin: Dietz, 1982–. Translated as "Economic and Philosophical Manuscripts of 1844." In *The Marx-Engels Reader.* Edited by Robert C. Tucker. New York: Norton, 1978.

Maturana, Humberto R., and Francisco J. Varela. *Autopoiesis and Cognition: The Realization of the Living.* Dordrecht: Reidel, 1980.

———. *The Tree of Knowledge: The Biological Roots of Human Understanding.* Boston: Shambala, 1987.

Monod, Jacques. *Chance and Necessity.* Trans. Austryn Wianhouse. New York: Vintage, 1971.

Murdoch, Dugald. *Niels Bohr's Philosophy of Physics.* Cambridge: Cambridge University Press, 1987.

Nancy, Jean-Luc. Introduction. *Who Comes After The Subject?* Edited by Eduardo Cadava, Peter Connor, and Jean-Luc Nancy. New York: Routledge, 1991.

Newton, Isaac, Sir. *Optics.* New York: McGraw Hill, 1931.

Nietzsche, Friedrich. *The Birth of Tragedy and the Case of Wagner.* Translated by Walter Kaufmann. New York: Vintage, 1966.

——. *The Complete Works of Friedrich Nietzsche.* 18 vols. Translated by Oscar Levy. New York: Russell & Russell, 1964.

——. *Daybreak.* Translated by R. J. Hollingdale. Cambridge: Cambridge University Press, 1982.

——. *The Gay Science.* Translated by Walter Kaufmann. New York: Vintage, 1974.

——. *On the Genealogy of Morals and Ecce Homo.* Translated by Walter Kaufmann. New York: Vintage, 1969.

——. *Philosophy in the Tragic Age of the Greeks.* Translated by Marianne Cowan. Chicago: Gateway, 1962.

——. *The Portable Nietzsche.* Translated by Walter Kaufmann. New York: Viking, 1954.

——. *Sämtliche Werke: Kritische Studienausgabe.* 2nd ed. Edited by Giorgio Colli and Mazzino Montinari. 15 vols. Munich: Deutscher Taschenbuch Verlag; Berlin and New York: Walter de Gruyter, 1988.

——. *Twilight of the Idols.* In *The Portable Nietzsche.* Translated by Walter Kaufmann. New York: Viking, 1954.

——. *The Will to Power.* Translated by Walter Kaufmann and R. J. Hollingdale. New York: Vintage, 1968.

Pais, Abraham. *Inward Bound: Of Matter and Forces in the Physical World.* Oxford: Oxford University Press, 1986.

——. *Niels Bohr's Times, in Physics, Philosophy, and Polity.* New York: Oxford University Press, 1991.

——. *"Subtle is the Lord . . .": The Science and the Life of Albert Einstein.* Oxford: Oxford University Press, 1982.

Peat, F. David. *Einstein's Moon: Bell's Theorem and the Curious Quest for Quantum Reality.* Chicago: Contemporary Books, 1990.

——. *Superstrings and the Search for the Theory of Everything.* Chicago: Contemporary Books, 1988.

Pefanis, Julian. *Heterology and the Postmodern: Bataille, Baudrillard, and Lyotard.* Durham, N.C.: Duke University Press, 1991.

Penrose, Roger. *The Emperor's New Mind: Concerning Computers, Minds, and the Laws of Physics.* Oxford: Oxford University Press, 1989.

——. "Newton, Quantum Theory, and Reality." In *Three Hundred Years of Gravitation.* Edited by Stephen Hawking and Werner Israel. Cambridge: Cambridge University Press, 1987.

——. "On the Origins of Twistor Theory." In *Gravitation and Geometry.* Edited by W. Rindler and A. Trautman. Naples: Bibliopolis, 1987.

Perrin, Jean-Baptiste. *Les Atomes.* 1913; rpt. Paris: Press Universitaires de France, 1970. Translated. D. Ll. Hammick as *Atoms.* Woodbridge, Conn.: Ox Bow, 1990.

Pickering, Andrew. *Constructing the Quarks: A Sociological History of Particle Physics.* Edinburgh: Edinburgh University Press, 1983.

——. "Knowledge, Practice, and Mere Construction," *Social Studies of Science* 20:652–729.

——, ed. *Science as Practice and Culture.* Chicago: University of Chicago Press, 1992.

Pinkard, Thomas. "Hegel's Philosophy of Mathematics." *Philosophy and Phenomenological Research* 41 (June 1981):452–64.

Plato. *Theaetetus.* Translated by John McDowell. Oxford: Clarendon: 1973.

Plotnitsky, Arkady. *Reconfigurations: Critical Theory and General Economy.* Gainesville: University Press of Florida, 1993.

——. *In the Shadow of Hegel: Complementarity, History and the Unconscious.* Gainesville: University Press of Florida, 1993.

Powers, Jonathan. *Philosophy and the New Physics.* London: Methuen, 1982.

Prigogine, Ilya, and Isabelle Stengers. *Order out of Chaos: Man's New Dialogue with Nature.* New York: Bantam, 1984.

Putnam, Hilary. "Models and Reality." In *Philosophy of Mathematics.* Edited by Paul Benacerraf and Hilary Putnam. Cambridge: Cambridge University Press, 1991.

——. "Quantum Mechanics and the Observer." *Erkenntnis* 16:193–220.

Rapaport, Herman. *Heidegger and Derrida: Reflections on Time and Language.* Lincoln: University of Nebraska Press, 1989.

Readhead, Michael. "A Philosopher Looks at Quantum Field Theory," in *Philosophical Foundations of Quantum Field Theory.* Edited by Harvey R. Brown and Rom Harré. Oxford: Clarendon, 1988.

Richman, Michèle. *Reading Georges Bataille: Beyond the Gift.* Baltimore: Johns Hopkins University Press, 1982.

Riemann, Bernhard. *Gesammelte Mathematische Werke und Wissenschaftliche Nachlass. The Collected Works of Bernhard Riemann.* Edited by Heinrich Weber. New York: Dover, 1953.

Ronell, Avital. *The Telephone Book: Technology—Schizophrenia—Electric Speech.* Lincoln: University of Nebraska Press, 1989.

Rorty, Richard. *The Consequences of Pragmatism: Essays, 1972–1980.* Minneapolis: University of Minnesota Press, 1982.

——. "Is Derrida a Transcendental Philosopher?" In *Derrida: A Critical Reader.* In *Derrida: A Critical Reader.* Edited by David Wood. Oxford: Basil Blackwell, 1992.

——. *Objectivity, Relativism, and Truth.* Cambridge: Cambridge University Press, 1991.

——. "Transcendental Argument, Self-Reference, and Pragmatism," *Transcendental Argument and Science,* ed. Peter Bieri, Rolf-P. Horstman, and Lorenz Kruger (Dordrecht: Reidel, 1979), 77–103.

——. "Verificationism and Transcendental Argument," *Nous* 5 (1971), 3–14.

Rosenfeld, Léon. "The Wave Particle Dilemma." In *The Physicist's Conception of Nature.* Edited by Jagdish Mehra. Dordrecht: Reidel, 1973.

Rotman, Brian. *Ad infinitum: The Ghost in Turing's Machine.* Stanford, Calif.: Stanford University Press, 1993.

Russell, Bertrand. *The Principles of Mathematics.* New York: Norton, 1903.

Sachs, Mendel. *Einstein versus Bohr.* La Salle, Ill.: Open Court, 1988.

Schilpp, Paul Arthur, ed. *Albert Einstein: Philosopher-Scientist.* New York: Tudor, 1949.

Selleri, Franco. *Quantum Physics and Physical Reality.* Dordrecht: Kluwer, 1990.

Shapiro, Stewart. *Foundations without Foundationalism: A Case for Second-Order Logic.* Oxford: Clarendon Press, 1991.

Shimony, Abner. "The Reality of the Quantum World," *Scientific American* 251 (1): 46–53.

——. "Role of the Observer in Quantum Theory." *The American Journal of Physics* 31 (1963): 755–73.

Skolem, Thoralf. "Some Remarks on the Foundations of Set Theory," *Proceedings of the*

International Congress of Mathematicians. Providence, R. I.: American Mathematical Society, 1952, 695–704.

——. *"Über die Unmöglichkeit einer vollständigen Charakterisierung der Zahlenreihe mittels eines endlichen Axiomensystems."* Norsk Matematisk Forenings Skrifter, series 2, no. 10 (1933):73–82.

Smith, Barbara Herrnstein. *Contingencies of Value: Alternative Perspectives for Critical Theory.* Cambridge, Mass.: Harvard University Press, 1988.

——. "Belief and Resistance: A Symmetrical Account." *Critical Inquiry* 18 (1991):125– 39.

Smith, Joseph H., and William Kerrigan, eds. *Taking Chances: Derrida, Psychoanalysis, and Literature.* Baltimore: Johns Hopkins University Press, 1984.

Spivak, Gayatri C. Translator's preface. *Of Grammatology.* Translated by Gayatri C. Spivak. Baltimore: Johns Hopkins University Press, 1975.

Stoekl, Alan. *Agonies of the Intellectual: Commitment, Subjectivity, and the Performative in the Twentieth-Century French Tradition.* Lincoln, Nebraska: University of Nebraska Press, 1992.

——. *Politics, Writing, Mutilation: The Cases of Bataille, Blanchot, Roussel, Leiris, and Ponge.* Minneapolis: University of Minnesota Press, 1985.

Thomson, Sir J. J., ed. *James Clerk Maxwell: A Commemoration Volume.* Cambridge: Cambridge University Press, 1931.

Tucker, Robert C., ed. *The Marx-Engels Reader.* New York: Norton, 1978.

Ulmer, Gregory. *Teletheory: Grammatology in the Age of Video.* New York: Routledge, 1989.

Varela, Francisco J. *Principles of Biological Autonomy.* New York: North Holland, 1979.

Varela, Francisco J., and Jean-Pierre Dupuy, eds. *Understanding Origins: Contemporary Views in the Origin of Life, Mind, and Society.* Dordrecht: Kluwer, 1992.

Varela, Francisco J., Evan Thompson, and Eleanor Rosch, eds. *The Embodied Mind: Cognitive Science and Human Experience.* Cambridge, Mass.: MIT Press, 1991.

Waismann, Friedrich. *Einführung in das mathematische Denken.* Wien: Gerold, 1936. Translated by Theodore J. Benac as *Introduction to Mathematical Thinking: The Formation of Concepts in Modern Mathematics.* New York: Frederick Ungar, 1951.

Wang, Hao. *Reflection of Kurt Gödel.* Cambridge, Mass: MIT Press, 1987.

Weber, Samuel. "The Debts of Deconstruction and Other, Related Assumptions." In *Taking Chances: Derrida, Psychoanalysis, and Literature.* Edited by Joseph H. Smith and William Kerrigan. Baltimore: Johns Hopkins University Press, 1984.

——. *Institution and Interpretation.* Minneapolis: University of Minnesota Press, 1987.

——. *The Legend of Freud.* Minneapolis: University of Minnesota Press, 1982.

Weyl, Herman. *Space—Time—Matter.* Translated by Henry L. Brose. New York: Dover, 1950.

Wheaton, Bruce R. *The Tiger and the Shark: Experimental Roots of Wave-Particle Dualism.* Cambridge: Cambridge University Press, 1983.

Wheeler, John Archibald. "Beyond the Black Hole." In *Some Strangeness in the Proportion.* Edited by Harry Woolf. Reading, Mass: Addison-Wesley, 1980.

——. "Information, Physics, Quantum: The Search for Links." In *Complexity, Entropy, and the Physics of Information.* Edited by Wojciech H. Zurek. Redwood City, Calif.: Addison-Wesley, 1991, 3–28.

——. "Law without Law." In *Quantum Theory and Measurement.* Edited by John

Archibald Wheeler and Wojciech H. Zurek. Princeton, N.J.: Princeton University Press, 1983.
———. "World as System Self-Synthesized by Quantum Networking." *IBM Journal of Research and Development* 32 (1): 4–15.
Wheeler, John Archibald, and Wojciech H. Zurek, eds. *Quantum Theory and Measurement.* Princeton, N.J.: Princeton University Press, 1983.
Wittgenstein, Ludwig. *Tractatus Logico-Philosophicus.* Trans. C. K. Ogden. London: Routledge, 1985.
Wood, David., ed. *Derrida: A Critical Reader.* Oxford: Basil Blackwell, 1992.
Wood, David, and Robert Bernasconi, eds. *Derrida and Différance.* Evanston, Ill.: Northwestern University Press, 1988.
Woolf, Harry, ed. *Some Strangeness in the Proportion.* Reading, Mass: Addison-Wesley, 1980.
Woolgar, Steve, ed. *Knowledge and Reflexivity: New Frontiers in the Sociology of Knowledge.* London: Newbury Park. Calif.: Sage, 1988.
Zurek, Wojciech H., ed. *Complexity, Entropy, and the Physics of Information.* Redwood City, Calif.: Addison-Wesley, 1991.

INDEX

Absolute past, 45, 105, 108–9; and presence, 105, 108
Abyss, 147, 286n.37
Action at a distance (also propagation of signals faster than light), 165–66, 168, 171, 177, 185, 189, 287n.3
Adorno, Theodor W. 18; force field, 18
Alembert, Jean Le Rond d', 92
Alterity (*see also* Exteriority, Difference): *key discussions, 249–60 (Ch. 8)*; 35, 45–46, 53, 57–58, 81–82, 102, 107–11, 116, 118–19, 249–60 (passim), 264, 267, 294n.31; absolute, 46, 53, 57–58, 119, 249; and closure(s), 249–60 (passim); as efficacity (and alterity-efficacity), 109, 111, 116, 118, 249–60 (passim); matter (*see* Matter); and the oppositions of philosophy, 118; as presence, 226; radical (as opposed to absolute): *key discussions, 249–60 (Ch. 8)*; 35, 46, 53, 57–58, 81–82, 102, 108–9, 111, 118, 249–60 (passim), 267, 294n.31; and reality, 102, 108, 118; reciprocal, 108; and text, 53; and the unconscious, 45, 57
Ambrosino, Georges, 18

Anaxagoras, 125
Anthropology, 17, 38, 229
Anti-epistemology: *key discussions, 10 (Introduction)*; as general economy, 2, 11
Aporia, 205
Argyros, Alexander, 278n.17
Aristotle, 9, 66, 144, 146, 204, 255, 293n.15
Artaud, Antonin, 205, 292n.5
Artificial intelligence, 281n.18
Asynthesis. *See* Synthesis.
A-thesis, 205, 223, 291n.19; and thesis, 205, 291n.19
Aufhebung. See Hegel.

Bachelard, Gaston, 278n.18, 289n.3
Barnes, Barry, 276n.13
Bartell, Lawrence S., 275nn.3, 5, 280n.8
Barthes, Roland, 291n.16
Bataille, Georges: *key discussions, 17–36 (Ch. 1)*; 1–2, 4, 12-13, 38, 41–43, 54, 57–58, 74, 78, 83, 105, 116–17, 125–26, 128, 194, 207, 213, 217–18, 227, 229–30, 235–37, 244, 247, 249, 251, 253, 257–59, 263, 267–68, 271–73nn.1–

Bataille, Georges (*continued*)
3, 6, 8–9, 18, 281nn.13, 19, 282nn.3,
8, 292n.5, 294nn.25, 27; and Blake,
28–29; on chance, 125, 282n.8; communication, 22; and Derrida (*see* Derrida);
on economics, 32–33; eroticism, 28;
excess of theory, 25; expenditure, loss,
waste (*see also* Expenditure; Loss); general economy (*see* General economy);
on global and local sciences, 32–33;
and Hegel, 21, 25, 43; on Hegel, 21,
282n.8; Hegelian mastery [Herrschaft]
and sovereignty, 25, 26; heterogeneity,
29; heterology, 29, 272n.9; interior
(or inner) experience, 22, 24–26; loss
of meaning, 25; and mathematics and
science, 17–18; on mathematics and science, 17–18; on matter and materialism,
57; on meaning and non-meaning, 23;
on Nietzsche, 27; and physics, quantum
physics, 17–18; on physics, quantum
physics, 32–33; poetic discourse (or "literature"), 24–25; political economy and
sovereignty, 27; project and counter-
project, 24; sacrifice, 22; sovereignty,
21–27, 37, 43; sovereignity and general economy (interactions), 21–23,
26; subjectivity, 24; unknowledge (also
nonknowledge), 22–23, 25; writing (of
sovereignity), 24–25
Baudrillard, Jean, 19
Beam-splitter experiment, 96–97
Becoming, 46, 226; as presence, 226
Being, 46, 226; and presence, 226
Bell, J. S.: *key discussions, 172–190 (Ch. 6)*;
4, 149, 152–53, 169, 171–90 (passim),
271n.4, 288–89nn.8, 9, 10, 14, 15, 16,
18; on Bohm, 173–75; on Bohr, 173,
176, 183–84, 186–90; on causality, 182;
on complementarity, 183; on determinism, 182; and Einstein, 185; and Gödel's
theorem, 179; on hidden variables, 173–
77, 181; on objectivity, 182; on quantum
mechanics, 176; theorem: *key discussions,
176–90 (Ch. 6)*; 4, 149, 152–53, 169,
172, 174–90 (passim), 288nn.10, 14, 15
Bell's theorem. *See* Bell, theorem.
Benjamin, Walter, 95, 280n.4
Bennington Geoffrey, 291n.17

Benveniste, Emile, 293n.15
Berkeley, George, 285n.24
Big Bang, The, 107, 137
Biology, 271n.2
Black body radiation, 282n.3
Blake, William, 28–29
Blanchot, Maurice, 17, 205, 229–30, 244,
292n.5, 294n.25
Bloor, David, 276n.13
Bohm, David, 74, 152–53, 169–78, 180,
182, 276n.8, 288n.10; interpretation of
quantum mechanics (hidden variables),
170–71, 178, 276n.8
Bohr, Harald, 284n.12
Bohr, Niels Henrik David: *key discussions,
65–168 (Chs. 3, 4, 5, 6)*; on classical
concepts and terms, 130; displacement
of concepts, 101, 117, 130; and Einstein, *key discussions, 133–48 (Ch. 5),
149–68 (Ch. 6)*; 1, 3, 8, 75–76, 79–80,
92–93, 128, 132–168 (passim), 200,
281n.12, 285n.22; and Einstein (as
parallel to Gödel and Derrida), 3–4,
200; and the Einstein-Podolsky-Rosen
(EPR) argument, *key discussions, 149–68
(Ch. 6)*; 149–68 (passim), 183, 186–
90; on the epistemological lesson of
quantum mechanics, 72; and Gödel,
128; and Heisenberg, 278n.17; on hidden variables, 176; and Høffding, 81;
holism, 79; and James, 277n.15; and
Kant, 79; on locality, 167; on matter, 58;
on measurement and observation, 109;
and metaphor, 59–60; on orienting in
a dark room, 113; phenomenon (Bohr's
concept of), 82, 101–7, 109, 117; and
Picasso, 91; and positivism, 84; and
pragmatism, 84–85, 182–83, 277n.15;
on reality, 82, 100, 117, 134, 151; on
relativity, 134; on self-consciousness,
55; on statistics, 126, 288n.12; on visualization and pictorial representation,
122–27
Born, Max, 69, 83–84, 124, 133, 146–47,
172–73, 282n.20, 282n.6, 286n.35
Bose, Satendra Nath, 283n.10
Brouwer, Luitzen Egbertus Jan, 201

Cantor, Georg, 3, 284n.12

Carnap, Rudolf, 201
Catachresis, 58–60; and metaphor (*See*
Metaphor)
Cavaillès, Jean, 289n.3
Causality (a-causality, anti-causality) (*see
also* Complementarity, of coordination
and causality): *key discussions, 149–90
(Ch. 6)*; 4, 6, 20, 38–39, 41, 46, 65,
67–69, 72, 78–79, 115, 124–28, 134,
144–46, 148–90 (passim), 253–54,
288n.12; a-causality, anti-causality, 7,
65, 124–27, 149; and complementarity
(*see* Complementarity); and continuity,
123–5, 144–46, 172; and *différance* (*see
Différance*); and determinism, 169; and
locality, 149–90 (passim); and the quantum postulate, 65; and randomness,
46, 124–27; and supplementarity (*see*
Supplement)
Chance (*see also* Indeterminacy; Randomness; Uncertainty), 39, 110, 124–27,
217, 219, 221, 232, 282–83nn.8–9;
absolute, 126, 219, 232; and necessity
(*see also* Causality), 39, 110, 124–27, 217,
283nn.8, 9
Chaos theory, 18, 278n.17
Choice, 110; and necessity, 110
Chromodynamics, 173
Cixous, Hélène, 19, 291n.16
Classical theories, 2, 46, 53; as restricted
economies, 2
Closure: *key discussions, 225–69 (Ch. 8 and
Ch. 9)*; 11, 30, 38, 53, 109–10, 118–19,
129, 131–33, 136–37, 181, 191, 203,
225–69 (passim), 291–93nn.1, 3, 16, 17,
19; absolute, 267; beyond closure (in
Derrida), 245–47; of classical physics,
133; of classical theories, 46, 53; and
complementarity, 191, 239–49; of concepts, 119, 234; conceptual, 136–37; of
continuity and discontinuity, 231; and
the correspondence principle, 129, 132;
and deconstruction, 225; in Derrida, 38;
of difference, 238–49 (passim); different
interpretive closures, 240; dissemination (or *différance*-dissemination) of,
243–44; and "end" (in Derrida), 225,
245; and foreclosure, 258; the globalization or totalization of (in Derrida),

228, 292n.3; heterogeneity of, 228–
29; and history, 247; interpretive: *key
discussions, 225–49 (Ch. 8)*; 109, 136–
37, 225–49 (passim), 267; interpretive
and theoretical: *key discussions, 225–
49 (Ch. 8)*; 225–49 (passim), 259, 267;
mathematical, 136; of metaphysics (or
the metaphysics of presence, or philosophy): *key discussions, 225–49 (Ch. 8),
261–69 (Ch. 9)*; 11, 35, 38, 109, 129, 132,
225–49 (passim), 259, 273n.9, 292–
93nn.3, 16, 19, 295n.1; the metaphysics
of, 259–60; multiplicity (or plurality)
of: *key discussions, 239–49 (Ch. 8)*; 231,
236, 239–49 (passim), 266–67; non-
Derridean, 258–60; of phenomenology,
119–20; of philosophy (*see* of metaphysics); plurality of (*see* multiplicity
of); the presence of, 244; of presence:
key discussions, 225–49 (Ch. 8); 225–
49 (passim), 259; of presence and the
metaphysics of presence (juxtaposed),
225–49 (passim); psychological, 137;
in quantum mechanics, 181; of realism, 119; of representation, 30, 110,
181; stratification of, 119, 132–33, 228,
225–49, 260; theoretical (of theory),
109, 131, 225–49 (passim), 261–69
(passim); theoretical closure and the
closure of philosophy, 225–49 (passim),
261–69 (passim); the totality of, 228,
238, 259, 292n.3; transformations of
(*see* Transformations, of closure); and
transformations of theory, 131; and undecidability (in Derrida), 244; of *writing*,
242
Collins, Harry M., 276n.13
Complementarism, 281n.19
Complementarity: *key discussions, 1 (Introduction), 65–76 (Ch. 3)*; and Bell's
theorem, 177; and causality, 39; of
chance and necessity (randomness and
causality), 44, 126, 218, 283n.8; of clo-
sure(s): *key discussions, 239–49 (Ch. 8)*;
30, 239–49, 259, 264–67; of complementarities, 75; of complementarity
and undecidability, 206–7; completeness and incompleteness, 5, 128, 148;
of concept and intuition, 40; of con-

Complementarity (*continued*)
sciousness and the unconscious, 57,
198; constraints of, 74, 77; of consumption (conservation, production) and
expenditure, 36; of continuity and discontinuity, 6, 67–68, 111, 124, 147, 198,
231–32, 236, 268, 276n.10, 282n.3; of
coordination and causality, 6–8, 40, 67,
69, 124, 198; of decidability and undecidability, 218; and deconstruction, 3,
5, 12, 193–269 (passim); of description
and event (in quantum mechanics), 72;
of determinacy, determinability, 210–11;
of determinacy and indeterminacy, 218;
and dialectic, 276n.10; and *différance*,
40, 46; extension of the concept, 73–
76; the exterior and the interior (the
inside and the outside), 22, 40, 112,
180; of fields of discourse or inquiry,
32; as framework (or matrix), 9, 40, 72,
75–76, 148; of frameworks (or matrices), 73–76; of gain and loss, 36; and
general economy, 2, 7–8, 11, 18, 75–
76, 85; and Hegel, 11; of the immediate
and the mediated, 198; and indeterminacy, uncertainty, 191–223 (passim); of
indeterminacy and undecidability, 217–
18; and interconnectivity, 75, 269; the
kinematic-dynamic (*see* of position and
momentum); of literature and philosophy, 244; of literature and theory, 204;
of local and global (part and whole),
31; and materiality, matter, 115; as matrix (*see* as framework or matrix); as
metaphor, metaphoric model, 74, 77; of
models, 32; multiple (as against paired)
complementary relations, 75; and nonstandard models, 204; of object and
subject, 40, 112; and objectivity, 116;
of the outside and the inside (*see* of exteriority and interiority); and parallel
processing, 73–74; of philosophy and its
exterior (in Derrida), 230; of *physis* and
mimesis, 40; of position and momentum
(or kinematic-dynamic), 6–8, 40, 69–
70; of randomness and causality (*see* of
chance and necessity); of representable
and unrepresentable, 30; of signifier
and signified, 198; and subjectivity,
115; and supplementarity, 51; and syn-

thesis (a-synthesis, anti-synthesis), 74;
and uncertainty relations, 69; and the
unconscious, 55; and undecidability, 4,
191–223 (passim); the wave-particle,
6–7, 40, 68–69, 97, 124, 275n.5, 282n.3
Completeness and incompleteness, 127–
29, 134; in mathematics (*see also* Undecidability); in quantum mechanics (*see*
Quantum mechanics); and synthesis,
127
Complexity, 32; and simplicity, 32
Complexity theory, 18
Conceptual homogeneity and unity, 144–
145
Conjugate variables (in quantum mechanics), 8, 70
Consciousness (*see also* Self-consciousness), 37, 55–57, 226, 273n.13; and the
unconscious (*see also* Complementarity,
of consciousness and the unconscious),
55–57;
Conservation, 33; and presence, 33
Constraints, 77, 205, 279n.22; of multiplicity, 279n.22; productive, 77, 205
Consumption, 33–34; and expenditure,
34; and production, 33
Context, 211, 213, 220
Continuity, continuum (*see also* Complementarity, of continuity and discontinuity), 20, 65, 123–25, 134, 141–42,
144–48, 172, 200, 231–32, 240–41, 268,
286n.35; and causality (*see* Causality);
and discontinuity (*see also* Complementarity, of continuity and discontinuity),
65, 123–25, 144, 231, 282–83nn.3, 9;
and synthesis, 145; and temporality, 148
Copenhagen Interpretation of quantum
mechanics, the. *See* Quantum mechanics.
Copenhagen School of linguistics, the, 47,
273n.8
Correspondence principle, the, 11, 35,
119, 129, 131–32, 240, 284n.13; and the
closure of metaphysics, 35, 240
Crease, Robert P., 284n.19
Cubism, 17, 91
Curtius, Ernst Robert, 279n.20

D'Alembert, Jean Le Rond. *See* Alembert,
Jean Le Rond, d'.

Dadaism, 222, 281n.19
Darwin, C. G, 282n.5
De Broglie, Louis, 68, 170–74, 178, 180
De-closing, 260
Deconstruction, *key discussions, 37–64*
(Ch. 2), 193–269 (Chs. 7, 8, 9); 1, 3, 5,
12, 37–64, 77, 110–11, 114–15, 120, 122,
193–269 (passim), 276–79nn.7, 17, 22,
280n.5, 290nn.11, 12, 291n.1, 294n.31,
295n.3; and closure (*see* Closure); and
complementarity (*see* Complementarity);
of consciousness, 55; and desedimentation, 199; and destruction, 207; and
distortion, 115; of Heidegger, 254,
290n.12; the incompleteness theorem,
205; and logic, 279n.22; and mathematics, 208; and nonstandard models, 204;
of origin (*see* Origin); of presence, 54–
55; of the primary, 114–15; and reflexivity, 248, 294n.31; self-deconstruction,
260; strategies or styles (different), 232;
and undecidability, 191–223 (passim),
290n.11
Dedekind, Richard, 284n.12
Definition, 43; deconstruction of the
concept of, 43
Delayed choice experiment, the, 97, 104–
11, 281n.12; on cosmological scale,
106–7
Deleuze, Gilles (also with Guattari,
Félix), 2, 18–19, 29, 195, 289n.2; and
Bataille, 19; capitalism and schizophrenia, 19; and Einstein, 19; on Foucault,
19; mathematical models, 19; and restricted economy, 19; Riemann spaces
(or manifolds), 19; schizophrenia, 19; on
undecidability, 289n.2
De Man, Paul, 204–5, 244, 273n.16,
291n.19; and Derrida, 273n.16
Democritus, 125
Derrida, Jacques: *key discussions, 37–*
64 (Ch. 2), 193–269 (Ch. 7, 8, 9); on
Artaud, 241; on Bataille, 21, 23, 42;
on Bataille and Hegel, 21; on chance,
125–26, 217, 283n.8; and closure (*see*
Closure, in Derrida); on closure, 243;
on context, 219; deconstruction (*see*
Deconstruction); deformations of
philosophy or theory, 231, 248–49; *dif-*
férance (*see Différance*); difference (*see*

Différance); dissemination (*see* Dissemination); double economies, 230; erasure
(*see* Erasure); and Freud, 194–95, 258;
on Freud, 147, 294n.33; on Freud and
Heidegger, 195, 289n.1; general economy (*see* General economy); and Gödel,
3, 194, 196–200, 207, 210, 212, 214;
gram, 206; grammatology, 38, 41, 84,
221, 225; and Hegel, 21, 43, 245, 248;
on Hegel, 11, 42–43, 290n.8; and Heidegger, 43, 194, 213, 245, 248, 258,
291–92n.1, 294n.32; on Heidegger,
48, 193, 195, 230, 254–55, 290n.12,
294n.30, 32; on Heidegger and Nietzsche, 193; on history and metaphysics,
248; on Husserl, 32, 44, 47, 62, 198–
201, 210; hymen, 206; incision, 206; on
indeterminacy, 95, 126; interminability
and interminable analysis, 194–195,
225; invagination, 243; iterability,
remainder, remnant (*see* Iterability);
on Kant, 218; and Lacan, 283n.8; on
Leibniz, 62; on Levinas, 290n.11; on
mathematics, 62; on mathematical logic,
205; and matter, materialism, 57; on
metaphor, 58–60; on metaphysics, 243;
and Nietzsche: *key discussions, 235–39*
(Ch. 8); 194–95, 213, 230–31, 233, 235–
39, 258, 265; on Nietzsche, 55, 193, 219,
230, 237; on Peirce, 49; and philosophy (*see also* Closure, in Derrida): *key*
discussions, 225–49 (Ch. 8); 38, 225–49
(passim), 292n.1; pharmakon, 206; philosophy and its exterior, 229–30; "postal
economy," 130; pragrammatology, 84,
221; production of new concepts, 231;
on Rousseau, 44; on sign, 246; spacing,
206; on supplement (*see* Supplement);
trace (*see* Trace); on truth, 193; on
undecidability, 126, 204; *writing* (*see*
Writing)
Descartes, René, 9, 145–46
Desedimentation, 199
D'Espagnat, Bernhard, 112, 274n.1,
281n.11, 287n.3
Destandardization (*see also* Nonstandard
models), 204
Determinability, determinacy, determination, 209–23; in Derrida, 209–23;
and indeterminability, indeterminacy,

Determinability (*continued*)
  indetermination, 209–23; in quantum
  mechanics, 211; and undecidability, 210
Determinism, 170, 174, 180, 182, 253
Dialectic, 20, 25, 32, 42–43, 55, 62, 206,
  255, 273n.15, 276n.10
Différance: key discussions, *37–44, 46*
  (Ch. 2); 29, 32, 45–64 (passim), 74–
  76, 87, 95, 104–5, 108–9, 111, 114–15,
  118, 136, 140, 193–95, 205, 207–8, 210–
  17, 219, 223, 241–44, 248–49, 252,
  255–57, 263, 266–67, 272n.4, 291n.1,
  294n.30; as alterity, 53; and *Aufhebung*,
  42, 55, 207; and causality, 39, 46; and
  consciousness, 56; and determinacy
  (determination), 210, 215; and dialectic, 42–43, 55; and difference, 40, 50,
  110, 211–12, 254–58, 294n.30; and
  difference-deferral, 39–40, 108–9, 195,
  255–56; and dissemination, 29, 32, 54,
  110, 208, 243; and distortion-repetition,
  111; and energy-entropy, 41; and finitude, 53; and force, play of forces, 55,
  216; and general economy (*see* General
  economy); and indeterminacy, 210, 215;
  and infinity, 53; and life, 53; and loss,
  41; and matter, 115, 118; and the middle
  voice, 39; naming and unnaming of,
  256; and Nietzsche, 193; and presence,
  41, 46; in quantum mechanics, 95, 108–
  9, 136; replacement of, 267; and the
  same, the economy of the same, 54, 75,
  194, 196; and sovereignty, 37; strategy
  of, 38–39; and supplementarity, 51; and
  trace, 45; and the unconscious, 54–57;
  and *writing*, 25, 38, 42
Difference, 40, 50, 55, 109–10, 212, 226,
  232, 239–49 (passim), 253–58, 264,
  267, 272n.9, 294n.30; absolute, 22, 36,
  46, 57, 109, 119, 232, 253; in Derrida
  (*see also Différance*), 254–58; and *différance* (*see Différance*); and force, 55;
  general economy of (*see* General economy); Heideggerian (ontic-ontological),
  254–55; and presence, 226; radical (as
  opposed to absolute), 22, 109, 267,
  272n.9
Dirac, Paul Adrien Maurice, 9, 83, 126–
  27, 133, 141, 145–47, 173, 283n.10,
  286n.35; equation, 145, 173

Discontinuity (break, rupture), 65–66,
  232, 241, 268; quantum (also individuality), 65–66; absolute, 232; and
  continuity (*see* Continuity); and complementarity (*see* Complementarity)
Dissemination: *key discussions, 53–54*
  (Ch. 1); 29, 32, 37–38, 44, 53–54, 56,
  110, 205, 208, 213, 220, 223, 243–44,
  271–72nn.4, 10; and the *Aufhebung*, 53;
  of closure, 228; of Derrida's terms, 54;
  and *différance* (*see Différance*); general
  economy of (*see* General economy); and
  indeterminacy, 54; and iterability (or
  remainder), 220, 272n.10; and polysemy (as controlled plurality), 53; and
  undecidability, 54, 208–9; and *writing*,
  61
Distortion, 111, 114–15
Disturbance, 111, 161
Double bind, 209, 214
Durkheim, Emil, 17
Dyson, Freeman, 289n.17

Economics, 17
Economy: metaphors of, 21
Efficacity, 4, 38, 69, 72, 94, 109–11, 116–
  17, 124, 194, 214, 216, 241, 249–60
  (passim); and alterity (*see* Alterity); causality, 4, 38, 69, 72; Derridean, 216; and
  efficacy, 4, 38; general economic, 37;
  quantum, 94, 110, 117; supplementary,
  51, 94, 110
Ehrenfest, Paul, 92–93, 166
Einstein, Albert *key discussions, 133–48*
  (Ch. 5), *149–168* (Ch. 6); 1–4, 9, 13,
  19, 58, 65–66, 76, 79, 82–83, 86–87,
  91–93, 98–100, 102, 108, 111, 114, 116,
  118–19, 122–23, 125–26, 128, 133–90
  (passim), 200–1, 259, 276n.11, 281n.12,
  283–87nn.10–12, 22, 27, 35, 40, 287–
  88nn.1, 7, 9, 14, 15, 16, 289n.4; on
  Bohm and hidden variables, 152, 171–
  72; and Bohr (*see* Bohr); and causality,
  134, 138–39; and/or complementarity,
  and quantum mechanics, 3–4; on continuity and continuum, 134, 138–39,
  141–42, 145; and Dirac, 145; equations
  (of general relativity), 3; on Freud, 286–
  87n.40; and Gödel, 3–4, 200, 288n.16,
  289n.4; and Hegel, 143; on locality,

168; on Maxwell, 141–42; and the metaphysics of presence, 143; on Newton, 141–42, 147; philosophical views, 134, 138–39, 153, 172, 182, 185, 287–88n.7; on reality, 134, 138–39, 141, 287–88n.7; relativity (*see* Relativity theory); and Riemann, 140

Einstein, Margot, 91

Einstein-Podolsky-Rosen (EPR) argument, the: *key discussions, 149–90 (Ch. 6)*; 3, 71, 128, 135, 149–90 (passim), 287–88nn.3, 7, 10; criteria of reality and completeness, 154, 156, 163–64, 189, 287n.7

Ellis, John, 279n.22

Empiricism, 39, 59, 81, 84, 118; logical, 84; and metaphysics, 59; and philosophy, 39

Enclosure (*see also* Closure), 226

Energy, 20, 34–35, 41; energy conservation law, 288n.12; and entropy, 34, 41

Entropy (*see also* Thermodynamic; Machine), 34, 41; and energy (*see* Energy)

Epistemology, 10, 77–80, 82, 200; and anti-epistemology, 77–80

Erasure: in Derrida, 250, 272–73n.7, 294n.31; in Heidegger, 252, 272–73n.7, 294n.24

Evans, Joseph Claude, 279n.22

Excess, 2, 20, 22, 35, 116

Exclusion principle (Pauli's), 127, 278n.18

Expenditure (*see also* Loss; Waste), 20–21, 28, 34–36, 271n.3

Experiment, 60, 69, 84–85, 99–101, 109, 114–15, 134–35, 278n.18; creation (of quantum object) by experiment, 109, 115; distortion (of quantum object) by experiment, 109, 114–15, 136;

Exteriority, otherness (*see also* Alterity; Difference), 232, 242, 258, 262, 264, 272n.9; absolute, 28, 46, 232, 247, 258, 262; and interiority, the outside and the inside (*see also* Complementarity; the exterior and the interior), 290n.11; and presence, 226; radical (as opposed to absolute), 272n.9

Faye, Jan, 78–79, 81–82, 103, 160, 274–75nn.1, 4, 284nn.13, 17, 286n.37, 287n.6

Feyerabend, Paul K., 2, 278–79nn.18, 22, 281–82n.19, 283n.9, 291n.19; "against method," 291n.19

Feynman, Richard, 146, 274n.1, 280n.6

Fine, Arthur, 131, 139, 287–88nn.7, 9, 11, 14

Finitude, 282n.3, 294n.28; and infinity, 282n.3, 294n.28

Folse, Henry J., 78, 80–81, 103, 132, 136, 141, 147, 274n.1, 282n.20, 286–87nn.36–37, 41

Force, differences of forces, play of forces, 55, 209, 211, 213, 216

Foucault, Michel, 2, 18–19, 29, 214

Frank, Philipp, 9–10, 84

Frege, Gottlob, 3, 63–64, 87, 284n.12

French, Anthony P., 274n.1, 281n.12

Freud, Sigmund, 2, 13, 38, 41, 45, 55–57, 76, 95, 130, 147, 194–95, 217, 222–23, 230, 249, 258, 267, 286–87nn.38, 40, 289n.1, 291n.1, 294nn.25, 33; Nachträglichkeit, 45

Froula, Cristine, 277–78n.17

Gadamer, Hans Georg, 265

Galileo, 87, 278–79nn.18, 20

Game. *See* Play

Gasché, Rodolphe, 273n.9, 276n.12, 291n.15, 292n.1

Geist. See Hegel

General economy, *key definitions and discussions: 1–2 (Introduction), 17–36 (Ch. 1)*; and the *Aufhebung*, 42; in Bataille: *key discussions, 17–36 (Ch. 1)*; 2, 17–36, 218; Bataille's definition of, 19–20; in Bohr, 2, 5, 218; and chaos theory (*see* Chaos theory); and complementarity (*see* Complementarity); in Derrida: *key discussions, 37–64 (Ch. 2)*; 2, 37–64 (passim), 218; of *différance*, 37, 39, 41; different forms of, 227; expansion of, 26–29; gain and loss (production and expenditure, conservation and waste), 34–35; as global economy, 31–33; and grammatology, 38; the interactive character of, 32; and interior experience (in Bataille), 25; and knowledge, 25; as materialist theory, 116; of matter, 22, 57–58, 254; in Nietzsche, 2, 218; and nonstandard models, 203; and philosophy, 227; and physics,

General economy (*continued*)
10, 73; and political economy, 19–20, 28; and production, 34–36; and quantum physics, 18, 20, 72; and restricted economy, 2, 9, 18–20, 28, 34–35, 37, 41, 57, 77, 79, 127, 200, 239, 269; as rigorous theory (or "science"), 21, 25; and statistics, 18; of the unconscious, 55; of *writing* (*see also* Derrida, grammatology), 38

Genet, Jean, 205, 222, 292n.5

Geometry (*see also* Riemann; Einstein; Physics; Husserl); and philosophy, 241

Gleason, Andrew M., 172

Globalization, 33–34

Gödel, Kurt (*see also* Undecidability; Incompleteness): *key discussions, 196–202 (Ch. 7)*; 3–4, 63, 128, 179, 191, 193, 196–202, 204, 207, 210, 212, 214, 220, 231, 245, 274n.1, 279n.22, 283–84nn.11–12, 288–89nn.16, 17, 289–90nn.4–5, 7; and Derrida (*see* Derrida); and Einstein (*see* Einstein); and Husserl, 199–200; and Leibniz, 201; philosophical views, 197, 200–1, 289–90nn.5, 7; on quantum mechanics, 288n.16; on relativity, 3; theorem (also the incompleteness theorem), 4, 63, 128, 179, 196, 199, 204–5, 274n.1, 279n.22, 284n.12, 289n.4

Graff, Gerald, 209

Grammatology. *See* Derrida.

Gravitation, 289n.20

Guattari, Félix. *See* Deleuze.

Habermas, Jürgen, 80

Hacking, Ian, 276n.13, 278n.18, 280n.3

Hartman, Geoffrey, 291n.18, 292n.5

Hawking, Stephen W., 274n.1

Hayles, Katherine N., 278n.17

Healy, Richard, 277n.14

Hegel, Georg Wilhelm Friedrich, 2, 5, 9–11, 17, 20–22, 24–27, 30-31, 32, 36, 38, 41–44, 46, 49, 53, 55–56, 62, 73–74, 76, 79, 88, 100, 122, 125, 133, 138–39, 143–46, 148, 191, 196, 207–9, 222, 226, 228–31, 234, 238–39, 245–48, 251, 256, 259–60, 263, 267, 271–72nn.3, 7, 272–73nn.6, 15, 276nn.8, 10, 282nn.3, 8, 290nn.8, 12, 293–94nn.17, 20, 25, 28; Absolute Knowledge, 267; and Aris-

totle, 146; *Aufhebung*, 36, 42–43, 53, 55, 122, 207; dialectic, 20, 25, 32, 42, 55; Geist, 21, 238–39, 263; history, 238; knowledge and history, 238; master and slave, 20; mastery [Herrschaft], 21; spirit (*see* Geist); synthesis, 5, 26, 32

Heidegger, Martin, 2, 9, 13, 34, 38, 41–43, 46, 48, 79, 83, 86-88, 88, 94, 139, 143, 191, 193–95, 208, 212–13, 228–33, 235, 238, 245, 248, 252, 254–60, 263, 265, 267, 272–73nn.4, 6–7, 278–79nn.18, 21, 280n.5, 282n.3, 286n.28, 289–91nn.1, 12, 19, 291–92n.1, 294nn.20, 24–25, 29, 30, 32; Being, 252, 254–55, 263, 267, 294n.24; on modern science, 278n.18; nothingness, 252; presence, 263; thinking (as poetizing), 294n.30

Heisenberg, Werner (*see also* Uncertainty relations), 5, 7, 9, 68-69, 83–84, 86–87, 93, 94, 99, 142, 147, 170, 173, 274n.2, 277–79nn.16, 17, 21, 286nn.27, 37, 288n.12, 291n.14

Heraclitus, Heraclitean, 125, 127, 130, 171, 232, 237; the Many, 127

Heterogeneity, heterogeneous, 10–11, 22, 24, 29–30; and expenditure, 29; and incompleteness, 29; and interactiveness, 10–11, 22, 24; and loss, 29; and multiplicity, 29; radical, 30

Hidden variables: *key discussions, 168–90 (Ch. 6)*; 31–32, 71, 152–53, 168–90 (passim), 275–76nn.5, 8, 281n.12, 287–88nn.3, 9; and intrinsic properties, 153; metaphysical features, 175; the non-local character, 153, 170–71, 174, 177

Hilbert, David, 3, 70, 284n.12

Hilbert space, 70

History, 238, 240, 248, 268, 293n.17; and knowledge, 238; and metaphysics, 248

Hjelmslev, Louis, 47, 273n.8

Høffding, Harald, 76, 81, 103, 123, 145, 273n.8, 276n.10, 282n.3; on complementarity, 81; on continuity and discontinuity, 282n.3

Hollier, Denis, 271n.5, 294n.27

Honner, John, 78–79, 91–93, 273n.9, 274–76nn.1, 4, 10, 281n.14, 284nn.13, 20, 286n.29, 287nn.3, 5, 288n.12

Horizon, 265

Hughes, R. I. G., 277n.14
Human sciences, 225, 229
Hume, David, 78
Husserl, Edmund, 9, 32, 38, 41, 44, 46–
    47, 62, 79, 82, 88, 101, 139, 143, 148,
    198–201, 210, 223, 235, 241, 256, 278–
    79nn.18, 22, 282n.3, 286n.28, 289n.3,
    291n.15, 293–94nn.20, 27; on geome-
    try ("The Origin of Geometry"), 62,
    198–99, 241; phenomenology, transcen-
    dental phenomenology, 47, 82, 286n.28;
    "the principle of all principles," 148

Idealism, 84–85, 110, 115, 120, 282n.2; and
    realism, 282n.2 transcendental, 275n.5
Idealization, 66, 121–23, 135, 198, 282n.3;
    continuous and discontinuous, 282n.3; in
    mathematics, 282n.3
Identity, 46; and difference (see Difference)
Incompleteness (See also Completeness
    and incompleteness), 3–5, 29, 128, 196–
    97, 201, 231, 244, 283–84nn.11, 12;
    of knowledge, 4; in mathematical logic
    (Gödel's theorem), 3, 196–97, 284n.12;
    and philosophy, 231
Indeterminacy (also indetermination):
    key discussions, 193–223 (Ch. 7); 3–4, 7,
    10, 20, 29, 31, 46, 54, 71–72, 77, 95,
    108, 124–27, 135–36, 138, 170, 190,
    191–223 (passim), 226, 229, 271n.4,
    273n.11, 275n.3, 290–291n.14, 16; and
    completeness, or incompleteness (see
    Incompleteness); controlled (restricted
    economic), 218; of the exterior and the
    interior (or the outside and inside),
    112; and loss, 20; radical, 31; and un-
    certainty, 7, 71; and undecidability:
    key discussions, 193–223 (Ch. 7); 3, 126,
    193–223 (passim), 229, 273n.11; and
    unknowability, 7
Infinity, infinitude, 282n.3, 294n.28; and
    finitude (see Finitude)
Information theory, 275n.3
Interactiveness, 10–11, 22, 24, 32
Interconnectivity, 75, 269
Interminability and interminable analy-
    sis, 194–95, 225–26, 228, 245, 258; of
    closure, 245
Intuitionism, 207
Irigaray, Luce, 19, 291n.16

Israel, Werner, 274n.1
Iterability (also remainder, remnant), 29–
    30, 220, 263, 272n.10; remainder and
    the cut, 115

Jabès, Edmond, 205
James, William, 76, 84, 145, 277n.15; and
    Bohr (see Bohr)
Jammer, Max, 169–70, 274n.1
Jauch, Joseph M., 172
Johnson, Barbara, 273n.12
Jordan, Pascual, 84
Joyce, James, 17, 26, 222, 291n.18, 292n.5

Kafka, Franz, 58
Kant, Immanuel, 9, 22, 36, 46, 48, 76,
    78–79, 88, 101, 115, 133, 138–40, 143–
    46, 195, 218, 251, 253, 259, 272n.8,
    276n.11, 282n.3, 290n.11; absolute
    exteriority, difference, 36; things-in-
    themselves, 22–23, 253
Kennedy, P. J., 274n.1, 281n.12
Kepler, Johannes, 2, 66, 87, 231
Kertész, André, 111
Khalfin, L. A., 289n.20
Kierkegaard, Søren, 76, 145
Klee, Paul, 94
Klein, Oscar, 147
Knowledge, 37, 226, 238; and history,
    238; unity of, 37; and un-knowledge (see
    Bataille, un-knowledge)
Kojève, Alexandre, 21, 43
Koyré, Alexandre, 285n.24
Kramers, Hendrik Anton, 288n.12
Krips, Henry, 275n.5
Kuhn, Thomas S., 274n.1, 278n.18

Lacan, Jacques, 2, 19, 38, 208, 230, 249,
    253, 258, 276n.7, 283-84nn.8, 14,
    290n.13; on chance, 283n.8
Language(s): mathematical, 132; ordinary
    language (and concepts), 38, 87–88, 98,
    119, 130–132, 264; philosophical, 88,
    132, 263–64; scientific, 132; theoretical,
    38, 132; theory of, 220; and writing,
    272n.2
Latour, Bruno, 276n.13, 278n.18, 280n.3,
    288n.7
Leibniz, Gottfried Wilhelm, 9, 62, 146,
    201

Levinas, Emmanuel, 39, 41, 46, 95, 223, 260, 290n.11, 292n.1, 294n.25
Lévi-Strauss, Claude, 17, 233, 273n.18
Linguistics, 38, 47, 60, 229, 234–35, 273n.8, 276n.7, 295n.1, 3; and philosophy, 235, 276n.7, 295n.1, 3
Literature, 204–5, 244, 292–93nn.5, 18; and philosophy, 205, 244, 292n.5; and science, 225; and theory, 204
Literary criticism and theory, 38, 229
Locality (in quantum mechanics): *key discussions, 149–90 (Ch. 6)*; 33–34, 149–190 (passim), 287–88nn.3, 6, 14, 15; and globality, 33–34
Logic: *key discussions*, 3, 53, 63, 88, 146, 194, 203–6, 208, 226, 243, 251, 254, 279n.22, 283–84nn.9, 12, 286n.32; absolute (in Hegel), 226; classical, 53; and complementarity (*see* Complementarity); the excess of, 88; formal, 63, 88, 143, 208, 279n.22; fuzzy, 212; limits of, 279n.22; mathematical, 3, 63, 194, 203–5, 208, 284n.12, 286n.32; "neither nor, either or" logic, 206, 251; onto-encyclopedic (in Derrida), 243; and philosophy, 286n.32; transcendental, 63, 88, 143, 208, 279n.22; and *writing*, 63
Logocentrism (*see also* Metaphysics of presence; Ontotheology), 10, 41, 62; phonocentrism, 62
Logos, 48, 226
Lorentz, Hendrik Antoon, 185; invariance, 185
Loss (*see also* Expenditure; Waste), 1–2, 20–23, 26, 28–30, 33–36, 41, 100, 105, 118, 272n.9; and conservation (*see* Conservation); and consumption (*see* Consumption); and globalization, 33; and knowledge, 34; and multiplicity 30; in quantum mechanics, 30, 100, 105; in representation, 34
Lucretius, 217; *clinamen*, 217
Lyotard, Jean-François, 19, 29, 283–84nn.9, 18; on logic and paralogy, 283n.9

McDowell, John, 294n.22
Mallarmé, Stéphane, 53, 62, 204–6, 209, 223, 273n.16, 292n.5

Mann, Charles C., 284n.19
Margenau, Henry, 277n.14, 287n.1
Marx, Karl, Marxism, 2, 17, 19–20, 27, 83, 271n.3, 273n.15, 290n.12; political economy (*see* Political economy); restricted economy (*see* Restricted economy); reversal of dialectic and Hegel, 273n.15
Materialism, 110, 273n.15; metaphysical ("idealism of matter"), 273n.15
Mathematics, 17, 62–64, 207–8, 282n.3, 284n.12, 286n.27, 289n.4, 293n.7; completeness, 284n.12; consistency, 284n.12; continuity and discontinuity, 282n.3; foundations of, 3, 282n.3, 284n.12; infinity and finitude, 282n.3; and philosophy, 207, 286n.27, 289n.4; and physics, 208; and technology, 208; and *writing*, 62–64
Matter, materiality: *key discussions, 57–58 (Ch. 1)*; 46–47, 52-53, 57–58, 83, 94, 110, 115, 118, 143, 254; and alterity or exteriority, radical alterity, 52–53, 57–58, 110; and dialectic (*see* Dialectic); and *différance* (*see* Différance); as efficacity, 94; and representation, 143; and the unconscious, 57
Maturana, Humberto, 283n.8
Mauss, Marcel, 17
Maxwell, James Clerk, 141, 144–46
Meaning, 20–21, 23, 50, 209, 211, 220–21; indeterminacy of, 211, 220–21; and non-meaning, 23
Measurement (*see also* Observation): *key discussions, 149–68 (Ch. 6)*; 58, 68, 70–72, 80, 94–95, 100–2, 106, 108–9, 114–15, 118, 135, 149–68 (passim), 186–90, 211, 280n.11, 287n.4; and the Einstein-Podolsky-Rosen (EPR) argument, 149–68 (passim), 186–90; measurement (or observation) and object interactions: *key discussions 149–68, (Ch. 6)*; 95, 97–98, 101–3, 108, 113–14, 132–33, 149–68 (passim), 186–90, 287n.4; simultaneous measurement and definition of conjugate variables: *key discussions, 149–68 (Ch. 6)*; 70, 136, 149–68 (passim), 186–90, 211; simultaneous measurement and prediction (of conjugate variables), 165
Mermin, N. David, 287n.3

Metamathematics, 3–4, 10
Metaphor, metaphoricity, metaphorical
  models: *key discussions, 58–60 (Ch. 1)*;
  58–60, 86–88, 104; and catachresis,
  58–59; and philosophy, 293n.15; photography metaphor, 92–93; theater
  metaphor, 92; transfer of metaphors and
  metaphorical models, 86–88; as writing,
  58–60, 104
Metaphysics (*see also* Closure, Metaphysics
  of presence, Meta-physics, Philosophy, Restricted economy), 1, 10, 35,
  46, 53, 58–59, 61, 66, 83, 85, 87, 172–
  74, 179, 200, 225–28, 233, 243, 248,
  253–55, 259, 273n.9, 275–76nn.5, 8,
  278n.17, 285n.25, 287n.7, 293n.16; of
  closure (in Derrida), 259–60; language
  of, 53; and mathematics, 200; and the
  metaphysics of presence, 226, 228; and
  meta-physics (*see* Meta-physics); and
  philosophy, 293n.16; and physics, 6, 58,
  87, 172, 200, 254, 275n.5, 285n.25; of
  temporality, 255
Meta-physics, 1, 9–10, 77, 83, 85, 87,
  190; and metaphysics, 1, 9–10, 87; and
  physics, 83, 85, 87, 190
Metaphysics of presence (*see also* Clo-
  sure(s); Logocentrism; Philosophy;
  Ontotheology), 4, 9–10, 37, 41, 43,
  53, 77, 81–82, 117–18, 120, 143, 200,
  225–27, 231, 233, 238–39, 242, 246,
  259–61, 292–93nn.1, 8, 16; and closure
  (in Derrida), 259; and continuity (or
  continuum), 200, 231; and philosophy,
  293n.16; and proximity, 231, 293n.8;
  restricted economy (*see* Restricted
  economy); and rupture, 231
Metzinger, Jean, 91
Minkowski, Hermann, 122
Momentum conservation law, 155–56, 159,
  166
Monod, Jacques, 283n.8
Multiplicity (or plurality), 9, 29–31, 53–54,
  208, 272n.9, 279n.22; absolute, 53–54;
  controlled, 53, 208; and loss (*see* Loss);
  in quantum mechanics, 9; radical (*see
  also* Dissemination), 30, 208, 272n.9;
  uncontrolled (dissemination), 53, 208
Munévar, Gonzalo, 276n.13
Murdoch, Dugald, 78, 80–81, 84–85, 128,

138, 140, 144, 160, 162, 167–68, 177,
  275n.4, 277n.15, 280–81nn.11, 17–19,
  282nn.1, 2, 5, 287nn.2, 3, 6
Mysticism, mystical discourse, 105,
  281n.14

Nancy, Jean-Luc, 293n.14, 295n.2
Negativity, 210, 214
Newton, Sir Isaac, 6, 18, 87, 133, 141–47,
  181–82, 285n.24; theory of light, 147,
  285n.24
Nietzsche, Friedrich: *key discussions, 235–
  39 (Ch. 8)*; 1–2, 4–5, 12–13, 17, 26–27,
  31, 35, 38, 41, 48, 50–51, 54–55, 74, 76,
  78, 82–83, 95, 115, 125–26, 193–95, 200,
  202–4, 207–8, 213, 215, 217–19, 227,
  229–39, 241, 245, 247, 249, 251–55,
  257–59, 261, 263, 265–68, 271–73nn.3,
  6, 10, 282–83nn.7, 8, 286n.39, 290n.12,
  291n.1, 292–93n.11, 294nn.23, 25,
  33; active forgetting (*aktive Vergesslich-
  keit*), 241; active interpretation, 193–94;
  Apollinian and Dionysian, 203–4; on
  appearance, 253; asceticism, 204; on
  causality, 51, 78, 253–54; on chance,
  125, 219, 283n.8; on determinism, 253;
  Dionysian, Dionysus, 203–4, 227; eternal recurrence, return, 193–94; and
  Freud, 194–5; general economy (*see*
  General economy, in Nietzsche); on
  Heraclitus, 237; on Kant, 78, 195; on
  Kant and causality, 78; on logic, 254;
  matter, materiality, 254; nihilism, 252;
  and nonstandard models, 203–4; perspectivism, 215, 247; and philosophy,
  230, 237–39; on philosophy, 204; rigor,
  236; on spirit, 254; style, 236; on subjectivity (subject-object opposition),
  253–54; on substance, 253; on things-
  in-themselves, 253; tragic, 252; in the
  true and apparent world, 253; on truth,
  193, 195, 253; the unconscious, 54–55;
  on Wagner, 195; Zarathustra, 227
Nihilism (*see also* Nothingess), 252,
  294n.23
Nonstandard models, 4, 191, 194, 202–4,
  237, 239, 244, 267, 269, 293n.7
Nothing, nothingness, 210, 214, 252,
  294nn.24, 28

Object, objectivity, 22, 182, 253–54; and subject, 22, 112, 117, 253–54
Objectivism, 47, 81, 110, 116, 118; scientific, 47
Observation (*see also* Measurement), 66–68, 80, 98, 102, 109, 114, 118, 280n.11, 282n.20
Occam's Razor, 85
Ontology, 10, 34, 226, 255
Ontotheology (*see also* Logocentrism; Metaphysics of presence), 4, 9–10, 41, 43, 82, 118, 223, 243, 281n.14; negative, 118
Oppositions, 82, 118
Origin, 40, 44, 110; deconstruction of (*see* Deconstruction), 40, 44, 109–10; deferral of, 44

Pais, Abraham, 73, 91, 141–42, 145, 155, 165, 274n.1, 278n. 19, 282nn.4, 6, 284–87nn.15, 19, 21, 23, 31, 34, 40, 288n.7
Parallel processing, 73–74, 76, 267–69; of closures, 267–69; and complementarity (*see* Complementarity)
Parmenides, 127, 130, 231, 276n.8; the One, 127
Pauli, Wolfgang, 83–84, 133, 146, 173, 286n.35
Peat, F. David, 288n.10
Pefanis, Julian, 271n.5
Peirce, Charles Sanders, 49–50
Penrose, Roger, 99, 124, 142, 179, 196, 274n.1, 280–81nn.6, 18, 284–85nn.19, 24, 289n.20
Perrin, Jean-Baptiste, 136, 284n.18
Phenomenality, 110
Phenomenology, 10, 45, 47, 56, 81–82, 111, 116–17, 286n.28; in Hegel (*see* Hegel); in Husserl (*see* Husserl); transcendental, 47
Phenomenon, Bohr's concept of. *See* Bohr.
Philosophy (*see also* Closure, of metaphysics): *key discussions 225–49, (Ch. 8), 261–69 (Ch. 9)*; 38–39, 42, 60, 82, 124, 185, 188, 193, 204–5, 207–8, 218, 225–49 (passim), 261–69 (passim), 273n.9, 276n.7, 286nn.27, 32, 289n.4, 292–93nn.1, 5, 15, 295nn.1, 3; and closure (*see* Closure); and complementarity (*see* Complementarity); and deconstruction (*see* Deconstruction); and Derrida (*see* Derrida, philosophy; Closure, in Derrida); exterior of, 235, 247, 266, 293n.15; and general economy (*see* General economy); and linguistics (*see* Linguistics); and logic (*see* Logic); margins of (*see* Margins); and mathematics (*see* Mathematics); and physics, 124, 185, 188, 208; as restricted economy, 117; transformations of, 230; and transformations of theory, 230, 261–69; and *writing*, 60
Physics, 124, 185, 188, 208
Picasso, Pablo, 91, 184
Pickering, Andrew, 276–78nn.13, 18
Pilot-wave (de Broglie-Bohm's), 171
Piron, C., 172
Planck, Max, 1, 3, 65, 282n.3; law, 3, 282n.3
Plato, 9, 22, 50, 53, 145, 191, 208, 231, 237, 246, 250–51, 259–60, 279n.21, 294n.27; *Parmenides*, 22, 250, 294n.27; *Theaethetus*, 22, 250–51
Platonism, 140–42, 200
Play, 50, 59, 212, 217; as the absence of transcendental signified, 50; of chance and necessity, 39, 125, 217; in Derrida, 39, 43; of determinacy and indeterminacy, 217; of differences, 212, 217; of forces and differences and forces (*see* Force); in Heidegger, 43; as metaphor and catachresis, 59; and supplementarity, 50; transformational, controlled (restricted economic), 43, 212; transformational, radical (general economic), 43; and *writing*, 50
Plotinus, 294n.27
Plurality. *See* Multiplicity
Poe, Edgar Allan, 284n.14
Political economy, 19–20, 27–28, 271n.3; in Marx, 27; in Smith, Adam, 27; and restricted economy (*see* Restricted economy)
Ponge, Francis, 205, 223
Positivism, 4, 84–85, 102, 110, 115–16
Postmodernism, 278n.17, 280n.3, 283n.9
Poststructuralism, 278n.17, 280n.5
Pragmatism, 84–85
Presence (*see also* Closure; Metaphysics

of presence): *key discussions, 225–49*
(Ch. 8); 33, 37, 40–41, 45–46, 51–52,
55–56, 94, 105, 108, 225–49 (passim),
254, 259, 263, 267, 272–73nn.7, 293–
94nn.16, 27; the closure of (*see* Closure,
of presence); and difference, 232; and
exteriority, 232; living presence, 45; and
loss (*see* Loss); the metaphysics of (*see*
Metaphysics of presence); original, 51;
and past, 46; and supplement, 52; and
transformations, 232
Pre-Socratic philosophy, 22, 279n.21
Probability. *See* Statistics.
Production, 34–36; and expenditure, 36
Properties of quantum objects (*see also*
States); independent, 98, 114; intrinsic,
153, 169, 178
Proust, Marcel, 17, 26
Proximity-distance (the economy of), 222,
232–34, 260
Psychoanalysis, 17, 38, 204, 225, 228–29
Putnam, Hilary, 202–3, 289n.6

Quantum of action, 66, 130
Quantum electrodynamics, 9, 127, 141,
173
Quantum field theory, 127; gauge theories,
173
Quantum mechanics (also quantum
physics and quantum theory); and classical physics, 136, 180–82, 288nn.12;
the completeness (and incompleteness)
of; *key discussions, 149–90 (Ch. 6)*; 3,
5, 8–9, 99, 127–29, 149–90 (passim);
consistency, 3, 284n.12; the Copenhagen interpretation of, 83, 277n.14;
the cut (and the arbitrariness of the
cut), 111–15, 180–81; the cut and (Derrida's) trace, 114; and discontinuity (or
individuality) of quantum events, 65;
and gravitation, 289n.20; idealization,
66; and information theory, 275n.3;
mathematical formalism, 69–71, 83,
85–87, 99, 104, 156, 281n.18; matrix
(Heisenberg) mechanics, 170, 274n.2;
"old quantum theory," 65; the orthodox
interpretation (standard model), 71;
and relativity, 146, 178–79; standard
model, 284n.19; statistical character of,
168–69, 180; symbolization, 66; wave

(Schrödinger) mechanics, 170, 274n.2;
wave theory, 122
Quantum postulate, 7, 65–66, 68, 122–23,
141, 164
Quarks, 173

Randomness (*see also* Chance), 46, 124–27
Rapaport, Herman, 291–92n.1
Readhead, Michael, 127
Reading, 189–90, 273n.16, 295n.3; and
physics, 190; and writing, 273n.16
Realism, 81, 84–85, 120, 140, 142, 282n.2,
286nn.27, 28, 289n.5; anti-realism, 81;
and idealism (*see* Idealism); mathematical, 140, 142;, 282nn.2, 3, 286nn.27, 28,
289n.5; scientific, 81
Reality, 66–67, 72, 80–82, 85, 100, 102,
108–10, 112, 114, 116-19, 134, 138–48,
151, 149–68 (passim), 186–90, 282n.20,
287–88n.7; independent, 66–67, 72,
80–81, 100, 109, 114, 118–19, 134, 138–
43, 153–68 (passim), 186–90, 282n.20,
287n.7; material, 110; mathematical
representation, 142; metaphysical,
110; objective, 81; and presence, 110;
simultaneous, of quantum variables, 151
Recomprehension (precomprehension,
redelimitation, reinscription) of classical
theories and concepts, 61–62, 119, 133,
272n.7
Reflexivity, 248, 294n.31
Reinscription. *See* Recomprehension.
Relativism, 209, 211–12, 215, 247,
294n.20
Relativity theory, 9, 19, 91, 98, 122, 134,
140–41, 144–47, 157, 165, 171, 173, 181,
184, 200–1, 274n.1, 288n.7; and deconstruction of simultaneity, 122; relativity
theory, general, 9, 19, 91, 122, 141, 145,
147, 157, 201, 274n.1, 284n.12, 288n.7;
relativity theory, special, 9, 122, 145,
274n.1, 287n.7
Remainder. *See* Iterability.
Remnant. *See* Iterability.
Restricted economy: *key definitions and
discussions, 2 (Introduction)*; 9, 18–20,
24, 27, 28, 30, 32, 34–35, 37, 41–42,
44, 52–54, 57, 59, 60, 62, 77, 79, 81,
83, 85, 88, 94, 101, 117, 127, 137, 197,
200, 218, 223, 227, 232, 239, 251, 263,

Restricted economy (*continued*)
269, 271–72nn.3, 9, 275n.5; of absolute exteriority, 28; of absolute multiplicity, 53; and complementarity (*see* Complementarity); of consciousness, 57; and dialectic, 62; in Hegel, 20–21, 32; Hegelian, 21–22, 30; in Kant, 218; Kantian, 22; of matter, 57; of meaning, 20–21; as the metaphysics of presence, 41, 227; and political economy, 19–20, 27; and quantum physics, 19; and scientific theories (as metaphors), 18; of signification, 24; of transformations, 43
Reversal (unproblematized reversal), 35–36, 61, 81, 231, 273n.15
Richman, Michèle, 271n.5
Ricoeur, Paul, 243
Riemann, Georg Friedrich Bernhard, 19, 76, 111, 122–23, 140, 142, 144, 284n.12; geometry, 140, 142; spaces (or manifolds), 19
Rigor, 236
Ronell, Avital, 291n.16
Rorty, Richard, 79, 276n.12
Rosen, Ralph, 294n.22
Rosenfeld, Léon, 173, 274n.1, 276n.6
Rotman, Brian, 289n.4
Rousseau, Jean-Jacques, 41, 44, 49, 52, 92, 223, 234–35, 273n.18
Rüdinger, Erik, 274n.1
Russell, Bertrand, 207, 284n.12

Sachs, Mendel, 285n.22
Saussure, Ferdinand de, 41, 47, 49–50, 60, 74, 234–35, 256
Scandal, 63–64, 87, 273n.18
Schilpp, Paul Arthur, 170, 189
Schrödinger, Erwin (*see also* Wave function), 68–69, 83, 124, 133, 147, 170–71, 180, 274n.2, 284–86nn.20, 35; Schrödinger's cat, 284–85n.20
Science, natural and exact, 86–87; and the human sciences, 86–87; the mathematical character of, 86–87, 132
Science studies, 276–77n.13, 280n.3
Searle, John, 221
Self-consciousness (*see also* Reflexivity), 37, 55
Selleri, Franco, 275–76nn.5, 10, 281n.15
Serres, Michel, 18

Shakespeare, William, 92
Shapiro, Stuart, 290n.7
Shimony, Abner, 112, 281nn.12, 16
Sign, 48–51, 238, 246; in Hegel, 49; in Peirce, 49–50; in Saussure, 49–50; signifier and signified, 48–51, 238, 276n.7
Skolem, Thoralf (*see also* Nonstandard models), 4, 191, 194, 199, 202–3, 231, 289–90nn.4, 7; Löwenheim-Skolem theorem, 203; philosophical views, 289–90n.7
Slater, John Clarke, 288n.12
Smith, Adam, 20, 27
Smith, Barbara Herrnstein, 283n.8
Socrates, 130, 193, 251, 265
Sollers, Philippe, 54, 204, 209
Sovereignty. *See* Bataille; sovereignty.
Space, spatiality, 67, 255; space-time, 121–22
Spinoza, Benedict, 9, 144–46
Spivak, Gayatri Chakravorty, 292–93nn.3, 16
States (quantum), 114, 135, 142, 160, 163; independent, 114, 135, 160–61; real, 160–61; the state-vector, 142, 285n.24
Statistical physics, 8, 18
Statistics (and probability), 8, 18, 30–31, 33, 69, 124–27, 145, 168, 171, 221, 275n.5, 288n.12; classical 8, 18; classical and quantum (compared), 8, 18, 31, 126; quantum, 8, 18, 31, 127, 168; and wave function, 124
Stoekl, Allan, 271n.5
Structuralism, structuralist, 233
Structure, 272n.4
Style, 32, 222–23, 229–30, 234–36, 239; plural, 32, 229–30, 234–36, 239; in Bataille, 229; in Blanchot, 229; in Derrida, 222–23, 229, 235, 239; in Nietzsche, 229–30, 236, 239; theoretical, 222–23, 239
Subject, subjectivity, 22, 115–16, 173, 253–54; and object (*see* Object); and *writing*, 116
Subjectivism, 110, 115, 172; and writing, 115
Supplement, supplementarity: *key discussions, 51–53 (Ch. 2)*; 37–38, 44, 46, 50–53, 94–95, 110, 137, 193, 206,

280n.3; and causality, 46, 51; and complementarity (*see* Complementarity); in quantum mechanics, 94–95, 110, 137; in Rousseau, 52; and sign, 51; and writing, 51

Surrealism, 17

Suspension: radical (as opposed to absolute), 11, 117; rigorous, 11, 117

Synthesis: *key discussions, 133–48 (Ch. 5)*; 6, 11, 29, 32, 36, 44, 74, 103, 122, 127, 133–48, 196, 223, 275–76nn.3, 5, 10, 291n.19; asynthesis (or anti-synthesis), 133–48 (passim), 275n.3, 276n.10, 291n.19; and complementarity (*see* Complementarity); of the macroscopic and the microscopic, 137

Technology, 60, 95, 208, 280n.5; and writing, 60

Teleology, 255

Temporality. *See* Time

Text, textuality, 47, 51; classical, 49; critical or ultratranscendental, 47, 49; in Derrida, 52; precritical or metaphysical (or transcendental), 47, 49; and signification, 52; and supplement, 52; as *writing* (in Derrida's sense), 51–52

Theology, 105, 255, 281n.14; negative, 105, 281n.13

Thermodynamics, 18

Time, temporality, 45, 67, 148, 226, 255; and presence, 45, 226

Totality, wholeness, 29–31, 34, 128, 227–28, 292n.3; of closure (*see* Closure); hidden, 29–31; historical, 227–28; of knowledge and history (in Hegel), 238

Trace: *key discussions, 44–50 (Ch. 2)*; 29, 37–38, 63–64, 87, 91, 93–95, 101, 104–5, 109–11, 114, 137, 212, 219, 255–57, 263, 280n.3, 294n.27; absolute, 263; arbitrariness, 114; arche-trace, 47; and consciousness, 45; in Heidegger, 47, 257; and origin, 47; and presence, 45, 47; and quantum mechanics, 49, 91, 93–95, 101, 104–5, 109–11, 137; the scandal of trace, 63–64, 104, 110–11; and the unconscious, 56

Trakl, Georg, 94

Transcendental, transcendentality, transcendentalism, 47–48, 78-80, 110,

276n.12; and "the conditions of possibility," 48, 78–79; idealism, 275n.5; in Kant, 48, 78–79; philosophy, 78–79, 273n.9; quasitranscendental, 273n.9; and transcendent, 48

Transcendental signified, 48, 263

Transformations: *key discussions, 261–69 (Ch. 9)*; 46, 212, 226, 230, 232, 236, 260–69, 295nn.1, 3; of closure: *key discussions, 261–69 (Ch. 9)*; 119, 133, 191, 228, 230, 242–44, 260–69, 295n.1; and complementarity (*see* Complementarity); continuity and discontinuity, 230, 236–37, 265, 268; controlled, metaphysical, restricted economic, 43, 212; deformations, elliptical deformations, 231; general economy of (*see* General economy); general and restricted economy of, 43; and presence, 226; restricted economy of (*see* Restricted economy); of theory: *key discussions, 261–69 (Ch. 9)*; 131, 147, 230, 234, 261–69, 295n.3

Transgression, 233; absolute and radical, 36

Truth, 37, 81, 193–94; truth and error, 193–94

Tsirel'son, B. S., 289n.20

Ulmer, Gregory, 291n.16

Uncertainty (*See also* Indeterminacy), 7, 71, 136; and indeterminacy, 206

Uncertainty relations, 5, 7–8, 68–71, 77, 114, 135–37, 148–50, 158, 162, 166, 274n.2, 285n.25, 291n.14; and noncommutativity of quantum variables, 70; and simultaneous definition of quantum variables, 70–71, 135, 158–59

Unconscious: *key discussions, 54–57 (Ch. 1)*; 45, 47, 54–57, 217, 220, 230; and consciousness (*see* Consciousness); and *différance* (*see* Différance); general economy of (*see* General economy); and general economy (*see* General economy); and matter (*see* Matter); structural, irreducible, 55, 220

Undecidability (*see also* Gödel): *key discussions, 193–223 (Ch. 7)*; 3–4, 12, 54, 126, 138, 191–223 (passim), 226, 229–31, 244, 251, 273n.11, 286n.32, 289–91nn.2, 11, 15, 16, 292n.1; and

Undecidability (*continued*)
   complementarity (*see* Complementarity);
   and deconstruction (*see* Deconstruction); and Derrida (*see* Derrida); and
   différance (*see Différance*); and dissemination (*see* Dissemination); of the exterior
   and the interior (or the outside and
   inside), 112; and indeterminacy (*see* Indeterminacy); metaphysics of, 179; and
   philosophy, 231

Vagueness, 20, 173, 179, 186, 271n.4
Valery, Paul, 292n.5
Varela, Francisco J., 283n.8
Vigies, Jean-Pierre, 178
Visualization and pictorial (spatio-
   temporal) representation in quantum
   mechanics, 97, 121–22, 127, 282n.1
Von Neumann, John C., 113, 172–73,
   277n.14, 281n.18

Wagner, Richard, 195
Wang, Hao, 200–1, 288n.16, 289n.5
Waste (*see also* Loss; Expenditure), 36
Wave-function (Schrödinger's), 69, 124,
   168, 171; and statistical interpretation of
   quantum mechanics, 69

Weber, Samuel, 278n.18, 291n.14
Wheeler, John Archibald, 91, 100–1, 104–
   8, 273n.13, 274n.1, 280-81nn.1, 7, 15,
   289n.17, 294n.28
Whitehead, Alfred North, 207
Wholeness. *See* Totality
Wigner, Eugene Paul, 83–84, 277n.14
Wittgenstein, Ludwig, 201, 281n.14
Wootters, William, K., 275nn.3, 5, 280n.8
Writing (in Derrida's sense): *key discussions,*
   60–64 (Ch. 1); 25, 37–38, 41–42, 44,
   49–52, 59–64, 87, 93, 104, 111, 116, 139,
   147, 205, 211, 223, 241–42, 244, 255,
   272–73nn.1, 2, 16, 280n.3; and complementarity (*see* Complementarity, and
   writing); and *différance* (*see Différance*);
   general economy of (*see* General economy); and mathematics and science,
   62; as metaphor, 59; nonlinear, 241; in
   quantum mechanics, 93–94, 139; repression of, 241; and speech (or voice),
   38, 50–51, 60–64; and technology (*see*
   Technology)

Zurek, Wojciech H., 274n.1, 275nn.3, 5,
   280n.8

Arkady Plotnitsky is Assistant Professor in the Department of
English at the University of Pennsylvania. He is the author of
Reconfigurations: Critical Theory and General Economy and *In the
Shadow of Hegel: Complementarity, History and the Unconscious.*

Library of Congress Cataloging-in-Publication Data
Plotnitsky, Arkady.
Complementarity : anti-epistemology after Bohr and Derrida /
Arkady Plotnitsky.
Includes bibliographical references and index.
ISBN 0-8223-1433-9. — ISBN 0-8223-1437-1 (pbk.)
1. Complementarity (Physics) 2. Bohr, Niels Henrik David,
1885–1962. 3. Derrida, Jacques. I. Title.
QC174.17.C63P55 1994
149—dc20 93-29583CIP